CliffsTestPrep®

CompTIA A+®

CliffsTestPrep®
CompTIA A+®

By
Toby Skandier

Wiley Publishing, Inc.

Publisher's Acknowledgments

Editorial

Acquisitions Editors: Maureen Adams and Jeff Kellum

Production Editor: Rachel Meyers

Copy Editor: Tiffany Taylor

Technical Editor: Neil Hester

Production

Proofreader: Nancy Riddiough

CliffsTestPrep® CompTIA A+

Published by:

Wiley Publishing, Inc.

111 River Street

Hoboken, NJ 07030-5774

www.wiley.com

Copyright © 2007 Wiley, Hoboken, NJ

Published by Wiley, Hoboken, NJ

Published simultaneously in Canada

ISBN-13: 978-0-470-11751-4

Printed in the United States of America

10 9 8 7 6 5 4 3 2 1

WILEY

PART I: INTRODUCTION TO THE COMPTIA A+ EXAMS

PART II: FULL-LENGTH PRACTICE TESTS

CliffsTestPrep®
CompTIA A+®

INTRODUCTION TO THE COMPTIA A+ EXAMS

CompTIA A+ certification confirms the candidate's ability to demonstrate the skills needed by today's computer support professionals. It is an international, vendor-neutral certification recognized by major players in the computing and networking industries. The exams test the technician's ability to install, configure, diagnose, and perform preventive maintenance on desktop and laptop computer systems as well as perform tasks related to basic networking. Security, safety, environmental issues, and communication and professionalism are also broad objectives assessed by CompTIA across the four exams.

Required Experience

CompTIA suggests the A+ certification is ideal for those with entry-level knowledge, but those with six months of hands-on experience will fare better. Of course, it is possible to study the objectives of an exam and pass it, but such certification is less useful to employers and is often discovered when the certified individual begins their new job.

How to Become Certified

To become certified, you must pass the A+ Essentials exam, 220-601, and one of the other three elective exams: IT Technician, Remote Support Technician, or Depot Technician (all are discussed shortly). The elective exam that you choose should be related to your area of expertise or to the sector of the market with which you intend to become involved. CompTIA does not discourage a candidate from taking all four exams and will certify you in all three specialties if you are successful at passing all four exams. The exams can be taken in any order, but the Essentials exam must be passed before you will receive your certificates, even if you pass the other three exams first.

> CompTIA also offers those who are already A+ certified the opportunity to upgrade their certification. If you are A+ certified, you only need to take the Essentials exam to upgrade your certification.

The A+ IT Technician designation, exam 220-602, is appropriate for candidates in or aspiring to roles such as enterprise technician, PC technician, desktop support technician, field technician, and PC support specialist. It's also the suggested path for students and those in roles such as sales or office manager of a small to midsize business.

The A+ Remote Support Technician designation, exam 220-603, is designed for candidates in or aspiring to roles such as remote support technician, helpdesk technician, or call center technician.

The A+ Depot Technician designation, exam 220-604, is geared toward candidates in or aspiring to roles such as depot technician or bench technician and concentrates less on operating systems and customer interaction than the other certifications and the Essentials exam.

Pearson VUE/Thomson Prometric

When ready to sit for one of the four exams, the candidate can choose to test with a Pearson VUE or Thomson Prometric authorized testing center. Generally, the decision is made based on which group offers a testing facility closest to the candidate or which one has a center with available testing slots that match the schedule of the candidate. CompTIA standardizes the exams so that the candidate's experience with either type of facility is roughly the same as with the other. Visit VUE at www.vue.com and Prometric at www.prometric.com to sign up for an exam and explore testing center locations, test scheduling and cancellation policies, the procedure to obtain a testing ID, and more.

Format of the Examination	
A+ Essentials	Approximately 100 Questions
A+ IT Technician	Approximately 80 Questions
A+ Remote Support Technician	Approximately 90 Questions
A+ Depot Technician	Approximately 90 Questions

Passing Scores	
A+ Essentials	675
A+ IT Technician	700
A+ Remote Support Technician	700
A+ Depot Technician	700

Each exam is a computer-based, proctored exam and is scored out of a maximum of 900 points. The exams are not adaptive, which means that the content and length of your exam will not change dynamically based on how well you are doing. You have 90 minutes to complete each exam. You will receive a score report at the end of the exam indicating whether you were successful and in which objectives you missed questions, if any.

Q. How can I guarantee my success when taking a certification exam?

A. There's no guarantee that anyone will pass any exam that they take. This uncertainty helps make each industry certification valuable. If there were any way to guarantee success, the certification wouldn't be worth anything to employers and clients.

Q. Can I take notes or books into the exam?

A. Absolutely not. One of the ways high-stakes, proctored exams level the playing field is to standardize the materials with which everyone enters the examination room. These include only what the proctor gives you, which are generally scratch paper or an erasable board and something to write with, all of which you must return to the proctor after your exam. These materials do not include your own study materials or notes, watches with calculators, or cell phones. You will be able to check your prohibited items with the proctor before the exam and pick them up afterward.

Q. What if I am unable to keep my scheduled exam appointment?

A. Both VUE and Prometric have liberal policies concerning canceling and postponing exams. Check their websites or call for more information, but expect quite a bit of leeway up to and including the day before your scheduled exam.

Q. What if I need a break during my exam?

A. Generally, you are permitted to leave the exam room to go to the restroom or get a drink. However, individual testing centers may differ in the way they exercise these liberties. Your exam clock continues to run while you are away, so it is in your best interest to take care of everything before sitting down to your exam.

Q. What if my exam terminal malfunctions or I have other technical difficulties during my exam?

A. You must notify your proctor immediately about any issues you have with the functionality of your exam station, such as loss of power, lockups, or input-device inoperability, all of which are very rare. Your proctor is not allowed to answer any questions about the exam itself.

Q. What if I forget all the stuff I have to memorize for the exam?

A. It's legal to perform a complete brain dump onto your scratch material of all the things you are afraid you will forget as soon as you sit down for your exam. That way, you don't have to concentrate as much on retaining everything you struggled to store away in your brain before the exam.

Q. What do I need to have with me when I arrive at the testing center?

A. Generally, you must have two picture IDs with you. These can include a driver's license, a military ID, a credit card with your picture, and a number of other official forms of picture identification. You should have any testing confirmations you received by e-mail with you as well, but feel free to leave these in your vehicle until you find them necessary to clear up any discrepancies. Normally, you will not need them.

Q. What happens if I am caught violating any of the policies governing my sitting for a certification exam?

A. Penalties are harsh for anyone caught in violation of official exam policy. You will fail the current exam regardless of your score and forfeit any examination fees paid. You will likely be subject to an extended delay before you will be eligible to sit for that exam again and possibly for any exam by the same exam sponsor, which will also delay your certification. If your certification is required for employment or advancement, you can imagine the extent of the ramifications.

Introduction

The following section lists the objectives found on CompTIA's website for each of the four exams. You will notice areas of overlap among all four exams. You should use this Cliffs TestPrep in its entirety because of the overlap but concentrate on the exam for which you are currently preparing.

Ability Tested

Essentials Exam, 220-601

1.0 Personal Computer Components (21%)

  1.1 Identify the fundamental principles of using personal computers

- Identify the names, purposes and characteristics of storage devices
  - FDD
  - HDD
  - CD / DVD / RW (e.g. drive speeds, media types)
  - Removable storage (e.g. tape drive, solid state such as thumb drive, flash and SD cards, USB, external CD-RW and hard drive)
- Identify the names, purposes and characteristics of motherboards
  - Form Factor (e.g. ATX / BTX, micro ATX / NLX)
  - Components
    - Integrated I/Os (e.g. sound, video, USB, serial, IEEE 1394 / firewire, parallel, NIC, modem)
    - Memory slots (e.g. RIMM, DIMM)
    - Processor sockets
    - External cache memory
    - Bus architecture
    - Bus slots (e.g. PCI, AGP, PCIe, AMR, CNR)
    - EIDE / PATA
    - SATA
    - SCSI Technology
  - Chipsets
  - BIOS / CMOS / Firmware
  - Riser card / daughter board
- Identify the names, purposes and characteristics of power supplies, for example: AC adapter, ATX, proprietary, voltage
- Identify the names purposes and characteristics of processor / CPUs
  - CPU chips (e.g. AMD, Intel)
  - CPU technologies
    - Hyperthreading
    - Dual core

- o Throttling
- o Micro code (MMX)
- o Overclocking
- o Cache
- o VRM
- o Speed (real vs. actual)
- o 32 vs. 64 bit
- Identify the names, purposes and characteristics of memory
  - o Types of memory (e.g. DRAM, SRAM, SDRAM, DDR / DDR2, RAMBUS)
  - o Operational characteristics
    - o Memory chips (8, 16, 32)
    - o Parity versus non-parity
    - o ECC vs. non-ECC
    - o Single-sided vs. double-sided
- Identify the names, purposes and characteristics of display devices, for example: projectors, CRT and LCD
  - o Connector types (e.g. VGA, DVI / HDMi, S-Video, Component / RGB)
  - o Settings (e.g. V-hold, refresh rate, resolution)
- Identify the names, purposes and characteristics of input devices for example: mouse, keyboard, bar code reader, multimedia (e.g. web and digital cameras, MIDI, microphones), biometric devices, touch screen.
- Identify the names, purposes and characteristics of adapter cards
  - o Video including PCI / PCIe and AGP
  - o Multimedia
  - o I / O (SCSI, serial, USB, Parallel)
  - o Communications including network and modem
- Identify the names, purposes and characteristics of ports and cables for example: USB 1.1 and 2.0, parallel, serial, IEEE 1394 / firewire, RJ45 and RJ11, PS2 / Mini-DIN, centronics (e.g. mini, 36) multimedia (e.g. 1 / 8 connector, MIDI Coaxial, SPDIF)
- Identify the names, purposes and characteristics of cooling systems for example heat sinks, CPU and case fans, liquid cooling systems, thermal compound

1.2 Install, configure, optimize and upgrade personal computer components
- Add, remove and configure internal and external storage devices
  - o Drive preparation of internal storage devices including format / file systems and imaging technology
- Install display devices
- Add, remove and configure basic input and multimedia devices

1.3 Identify tools, diagnostic procedures and troubleshooting techniques for personal computer components
- Recognize the basic aspects of troubleshooting theory for example:
  - o Perform backups before making changes
  - o Assess a problem systematically and divide large problems into smaller components to be analyzed individually
  - o Verify even the obvious, determine whether the problem is something simple and make no assumptions
  - o Research ideas and establish priorities
  - o Document findings, actions and outcomes
- Identify and apply basic diagnostic procedures and troubleshooting techniques for example:
  - o Identify the problem including questioning user and identifying user changes to computer
  - o Analyze the problem including potential causes and make an initial determination of software and / or hardware problems

- o Test related components including inspection, connections, hardware / software configurations, device manager and consult vendor documentation
- o Evaluate results and take additional steps if needed such as consultation, use of alternate resources, manuals
- o Document activities and outcomes
- Recognize and isolate issues with display, power, basic input devices, storage, memory, thermal, POST errors (e.g. BIOS, hardware)
- Apply basic troubleshooting techniques to check for problems (e.g. thermal issues, error codes, power, connections including cables and / or pins, compatibility, functionality, software / drivers) with components for example:
  - o Motherboards
  - o Power supply
  - o Processor / CPUs
  - o Memory
  - o Display devices
  - o Input devices
  - o Adapter cards
- Recognize the names, purposes, characteristics and appropriate application of tools for example: BIOS, self-test, hard drive self-test and software diagnostics test

1.4 Perform preventive maintenance on personal computer components

- Identify and apply basic aspects of preventive maintenance theory for example:
  - o Visual / audio inspection
  - o Driver / firmware updates
  - o Scheduling preventive maintenance
  - o Use of appropriate repair tools and cleaning materials
  - o Ensuring proper environment
- Identify and apply common preventive maintenance techniques for devices such as input devices and batteries

2.0 Laptops and Portable Devices (11%)

2.1 Identify the fundamental principles of using laptops and portable devices

- Identify names, purposes and characteristics of laptop-specific:
  - o Form factors such as memory and hard drives
  - o Peripherals (e.g. docking station, port replicator and media / accessory bay)
  - o Expansion slots (e.g. PCMCIA I, II and III, card and express bus)
  - o Ports (e.g. mini PCI slot)
  - o Communication connections (e.g. Bluetooth, infrared, cellular WAN, Ethernet)
  - o Power and electrical input devices (e.g. auto-switching and fixed-input power supplies, batteries)
  - o LCD technologies (e.g. active and passive matrix, resolution such as XGA, SXGA+, UXGA, WUXGA, contrast ratio, native resolution)
  - o Input devices (e.g. stylus / digitizer, function (Fn) keys and pointing devices such as touch pad, point stick / track point)
- Identify and distinguish between mobile and desktop motherboards and processors including throttling, power management and WiFi

2.2 Install, configure, optimize and upgrade laptops and portable devices

- Configure power management
  - o Identify the features of BIOS-ACPI
  - o Identify the difference between suspend, hibernate and standby

9

- Demonstrate safe removal of laptop-specific hardware such as peripherals, hot-swappable devices and non-hot-swappable devices

2.3 Identify tools, basic diagnostic procedures and troubleshooting techniques for laptops and portable devices

- Use procedures and techniques to diagnose power conditions, video, keyboard, pointer and wireless card issues, for example:
  - Verify AC power (e.g. LEDs, swap AC adapter)
  - Verify DC power
  - Remove unneeded peripherals
  - Plug in external monitor
  - Toggle Fn keys
  - Check LCD cutoff switch
  - Verify backlight functionality and pixilation
  - Stylus issues (e.g. digitizer problems)
  - Unique laptop keypad issues
  - Antenna wires

2.4 Perform preventive maintenance on laptops and portable devices

- Identify and apply common preventive maintenance techniques for laptops and portable devices, for example: cooling devices, hardware and video cleaning materials, operating environments including temperature and air quality, storage, transportation and shipping.

3.0 Operating Systems—unless otherwise noted, operating systems referred to within include Microsoft Windows 2000, XP Professional, XP Home and Media Center. (21%)

3.1 Identify the fundamentals of using operating systems

- Identify differences between operating systems (e.g. Mac, Windows, Linux) and describe operating system revision levels including GUI, system requirements, application and hardware compatibility
- Identify names, purposes and characteristics of the primary operating system components including registry, virtual memory and file system
- Describe features of operating system interfaces, for example:
  - Windows Explorer
  - My Computer
  - Control Panel
  - Command Prompt
  - My Network Places
  - Task bar / systray
  - Start Menu
- Identify the names, locations, purposes and characteristics of operating system files for example:
  - BOOT.INI
  - NTLDR
  - NTDETECT.COM
  - NTBOOTDD.SYS
  - Registry data files
- Identify concepts and procedures for creating, viewing, managing disks, directories and files in operating systems for example:
  - Disks (e.g. active, primary, extended and logical partitions)
  - File systems (e.g. FAT 32, NTFS)
  - Directory structures (e.g. create folders, navigate directory structures)
  - Files (e.g. creation, extensions, attributes, permissions)

3.2 Install, configure, optimize and upgrade operating systems—references to upgrading from Windows 95 and NT may be made

- Identify procedures for installing operating systems including:
  - o Verification of hardware compatibility and minimum requirements
  - o Installation methods (e.g. boot media such as CD, floppy or USB, network installation, drive imaging)
  - o Operating system installation options (e.g. attended / unattended, file system type, network configuration)
  - o Disk preparation order (e.g. start installation, partition and format drive)
  - o Device driver configuration (e.g. install and upload device drivers)
  - o Verification of installation
- Identify procedures for upgrading operating systems including:
  - o Upgrade considerations (e.g. hardware, application and / or network compatibility)
  - o Implementation (e.g. backup data, install additional Windows components)
- Install / add a device including loading, adding device drivers and required software including:
  - o Determine whether permissions are adequate for performing the task
  - o Device driver installation (e.g. automated and / or manual search and installation of device drivers)
  - o Using unsigned drivers (e.g. driver signing)
  - o Verify installation of the driver (e.g. device manager and functionality)
- Identify procedures and utilities used to optimize operating systems for example, virtual memory, hard drives, temporary files, service, startup and applications

3.3 Identify tools, diagnostic procedures and troubleshooting techniques for operating systems

- Identify basic boot sequences, methods and utilities for recovering operating systems
  - o Boot methods (e.g. safe mode, recovery console, boot to restore point)
  - o Automated System Recovery (ASR) (e.g. Emergency Repair Disk (ERD)
- Identify and apply diagnostic procedures and troubleshooting techniques for example:
  - o Identify the problem by questioning the user and identifying user changes to the computer
  - o Analyze problem including potential causes and initial determination of software and / or hardware problem
  - o Test related components including connections, hardware / software configurations, device manager and consulting vendor documentation
  - o Evaluate results and take additional steps if needed such as consultation, alternate resources and manuals
  - o Document activities and outcomes
- Recognize and resolve common operational issues such as bluescreen, system lock-up, input / output device, application install, start or load and Windows-specific printing problems (e.g. print spool stalled, incorrect / incompatible driver for print)
- Explain common error messages and codes for example:
  - o Boot (e.g. invalid boot disk, inaccessible boot drive, missing NTLDR)
  - o Startup (e.g. device / service failed to start, device / program in registry not found)
  - o Event Viewer
  - o Registry
  - o Windows reporting
- Identify the names, locations, purposes and characteristics of operating system utilities for example:
  - o Disk management tools (e.g. DEFRAG, NTBACKUP, CHKDSK, Format)
  - o System management tools (e.g. device and task manager, MSCONFIG.EXE)
  - o File management tools (e.g. Windows Explorer, ATTRIB.EXE)

3.4 Perform preventive maintenance on operating systems

- Describe common utilities for performing preventive maintenance on operating systems for example, software and Windows updates (e.g. service packs), scheduled backups / restore, restore points

4.0 Printers and Scanners (9%)

4.1 Identify the fundamental principles of using printers and scanners

- Identify differences between types of printer and scanner technologies (e.g. laser, inkjet, thermal, solid ink, impact)
- Identify names, purposes and characteristics of printer and scanner components (e.g. memory, driver, firmware) and consumables (e.g. toner, ink cartridge, paper)
- Identify the names, purposes and characteristics of interfaces used by printers and scanners including port and cable types for example:
  - Parallel
  - Network (e.g. NIC, print servers)
  - USB
  - Serial
  - IEEE 1394 / firewire
  - Wireless (e.g. Bluetooth, 802.11, infrared
  - SCSI

4.2 Identify basic concepts of installing, configuring, optimizing and upgrading printers and scanners

- Install and configure printers / scanners
  - Power and connect the device using local or network port
  - Install and update device driver and calibrate the device
  - Configure options and default settings
  - Print a test page
- Optimize printer performance for example, printer settings such as tray switching, print spool settings, device calibration, media types and paper orientation

4.3 Identify tools, basic diagnostic procedures and troubleshooting techniques for printers and scanners

- Gather information about printer / scanner problems
  - Identify symptom
  - Review device error codes, computer error messages and history (e.g. event log, user reports)
  - Print or scan test page
  - Use appropriate generic or vendor-specific diagnostic tools including web-based utilities
- Review and analyze collected data
  - Establish probable causes
  - Review service documentation
  - Review knowledge base and define and isolate the problem (e.g. software vs. hardware, driver, connectivity, printer)
- Identify solutions to identified printer / scanner problems
  - Define specific cause and apply fix
  - Replace consumables as needed
  - Verify functionality and get user acceptance of problem fix

5.0 Networks (12%)

5.1 Identify the fundamental principles of networks

- Describe basic networking concepts
  - Addressing

- o Bandwidth
- o Status indicators
- o Protocols (e.g. TCP / IP including IP, classful subnet, IPX / SPX including NWLINK, NETBEUI / NETBIOS)
- o Full-duplex, half-duplex
- o Cabling (e.g. twisted pair, coaxial cable, fiber optic, RS-232, USB, IEEE 1394 / Firewire)
- o Networking models including peer-to-peer and client / server
- Identify names, purposes and characteristics of the common network cables
- o Plenum / PVC
- o UTP (e.g. CAT3, CAT5 / 5e, CAT6)
- o STP
- o Fiber (e.g. single-mode and multi-mode)
- Identify names, purposes and characteristics of network connectors (e.g. RJ45 and RJ11, ST / SC / LC, MT-RJ)
- Identify names, purposes and characteristics (e.g. definition, speed and connections) of technologies for establishing connectivity for example:
- o LAN / WAN
- o ISDN
- o Broadband (e.g. DSL, cable, satellite)
  - o Dial-up
  - o Wireless (all 802.11)
  - o Infrared
  - o Bluetooth
  - o Cellular
  - o VoIP

5.2 Install, configure, optimize and upgrade networks
- Install and configure network cards (physical address)
- Install, identify and obtain wired and wireless connection

5.3 Identify tools, diagnostic procedures and troubleshooting techniques for networks
- Explain status indicators, for example speed, connection and activity lights and wireless signal strength

6.0 Security (11%)
6.1 Identify the fundamental principles of security
- Identify names, purposes and characteristics of hardware and software security for example:
- o Hardware deconstruction / recycling
- o Smart cards / biometrics (e.g. key fobs, cards, chips and scans)
- o Authentication technologies (e.g. user name, password, biometrics, smart cards)
- o Malicious software protection (e.g. viruses, Trojans, worms, spam, spyware, adware, grayware)
- o Software firewalls
- o File system security (e.g. FAT32 and NTFS)
- Identify names, purposes and characteristics of wireless security for example:
- o Wireless encryption (e.g. WEP.x and WPA.x) and client configuration
- o Access points (e.g. disable DHCP / use static IP, change SSID from default, disable SSID broadcast, MAC filtering, change default username and password, update firmware, firewall)
- Identify names, purposes and characteristics of data and physical security
- o Data access (basic local security policy)

       o Encryption technologies

       o Backups

       o Data migration

       o Data / remnant removal

       o Password management

       o Locking workstation (e.g. hardware, operating system)

- Describe importance and process of incidence reporting
- Recognize and respond appropriately to social engineering situations

6.2 Install, configure, upgrade and optimize security

- Install, configure, upgrade and optimize hardware, software and data security for example:

       o BIOS

       o Smart cards

       o Authentication technologies

       o Malicious software protection

       o Data access (basic local security policy)

       o Backup procedures and access to backups

       o Data migration

       o Data / remnant removal

6.3 Identify tool, diagnostic procedures and troubleshooting techniques for security

- Diagnose and troubleshoot hardware, software and data security issues for example:

       o BIOS

       o Smart cards, biometrics

       o Authentication technologies

       o Malicious software

       o File system (e.g. FAT32, NTFS)

       o Data access (e.g. basic local security policy)

       o Backup

       o Data migration

6.4 Perform preventive maintenance for computer security

- Implement software security preventive maintenance techniques such as installing service packs and patches and training users about malicious software prevention technologies

7.0 Safety and Environmental Issues (10%)

7.1 Describe the aspects and importance of safety and environmental issues

- Identify potential safety hazards and take preventive action
- Use Material Safety Data Sheets (MSDS) or equivalent documentation and appropriate equipment documentation
- Use appropriate repair tools
- Describe methods to handle environmental and human (e.g. electrical, chemical, physical) accidents including incident reporting

7.2 Identify potential hazards and implement proper safety procedures including ESD precautions and procedures, safe work environment and equipment handling

7.3 Identify proper disposal procedures for batteries, display devices and chemical solvents and cans

8.0 Communication and Professionalism (5%)

8.1 Use good communication skills including listening and tact / discretion, when communicating with customers and colleagues

- Use clear, concise and direct statements
- Allow the customer to complete statements—avoid interrupting
- Clarify customer statements—ask pertinent questions
- Avoid using jargon, abbreviations and acronyms
- Listen to customers

8.2 Use job-related professional behavior including notation of privacy, confidentiality and respect for the customer and customers' property

- Behavior
  - o Maintain a positive attitude and tone of voice
  - o Avoid arguing with customers and / or becoming defensive
  - o Do not minimize customers' problems
  - o Avoid being judgmental and / or insulting or calling the customer names
  - o Avoid distractions and / or interruptions when talking with customers
- Property
  - o Telephone, laptop, desktop computer, printer, monitor, etc.

IT Technician Exam, 220-602

1.0 Personal Computer Components (18%)

1.1 Install, configure, optimize and upgrade personal computer components

- Add, remove and configure personal computer components including selection and installation of appropriate components for example:
  - o Storage devices
  - o Motherboards
  - o Power supplies
  - o Processors / CPUs
  - o Memory
  - o Display devices
  - o Input devices (e.g. basic, specialty and multimedia)
  - o Adapter cards
  - o Cooling systems

1.2 Identify tools, diagnostic procedures and troubleshooting techniques for personal computer components

- Identify and apply basic diagnostic procedures and troubleshooting techniques
  - o Isolate and identify the problem using visual and audible inspection of components and minimum configuration
- Recognize and isolate issues with peripherals, multimedia, specialty input devices, internal and external storage and CPUs
- Identify the steps used to troubleshoot components (e.g. check proper seating, installation, appropriate components, settings and current driver) for example:
  - o Power supply
  - o Processor / CPUs and motherboards
  - o Memory
  - o Adapter cards
  - o Display and input devices
- Recognize names, purposes, characteristics and appropriate application of tools for example:
  - o Multimeter

      o Anti-static pad and wrist strap

      o Specialty hardware / tools

      o Loop back plugs

      o Cleaning products (e.g. vacuum, cleaning pads)

1.3 Perform preventive maintenance of personal computer components

- Identify and apply common preventive maintenance techniques for personal computer components for example:

      o Display devices (e.g. cleaning, ventilation)

      o Power devices (e.g. appropriate source such as power strip, surge protector, ventilation and cooling)

      o Input devices (e.g. covers)

      o Storage devices (e.g. software tools such as Disk Defragmenter and cleaning of optics and tape heads)

      o Thermally sensitive devices such as motherboards, CPU, adapter cards memory (e.g. cleaning, air flow)

2.0 Laptops and Portable Devices (9%)

2.1 Identify fundamental principles of using laptops and portable devices

- Identify appropriate applications for laptop-specific communication connections such as Bluetooth, infrared, cellular WAN and Ethernet

- Identify appropriate laptop-specific power and electrical input devices and determine how amperage and voltage can affect performance

- Identify the major components of the LCD including inverter, screen and video card

2.2 Install, configure, optimize and upgrade laptops and portable devices

- Removal of laptop-specific hardware such as peripherals, hot-swappable and non-hot-swappable devices

- Describe how video sharing affects memory upgrades

2.3 Use tools, diagnostic procedures and troubleshooting techniques for laptops and portable devices

- Use procedures and techniques to diagnose power conditions, video, keyboard, pointer and wireless card issues for example:

      o Verify AC power (e.g. LEDs, swap AC adapter)

      o Verify DC power

      o Remove unneeded peripherals

      o Plug in external monitor

      o Toggle Fn keys

      o Check LCD cutoff switch

      o Verify backlight functionality and pixilation

      o Stylus issues (e.g. digitizer problems)

      o Unique laptop keypad issues

      o Antenna wires

3.0 Operating Systems—unless otherwise noted, operating systems referred with within include Microsoft Windows 2000, XP Professional, XP Home and Media Center. (20%)

3.1 Identify the fundamental principles of operating systems

- Use command-line functions and utilities to manage operating systems, including proper syntax and switches for example:

      o CMD

      o HELP

      o DIR

      o ATTRIB

      o EDIT

- COPY
- XCOPY
- FORMAT
- IPCONFIG
- PING
- MD / CD / RD
- Identify concepts and procedures for creating, viewing and managing disks, directories and files on operating systems
  - Disks (e.g. active, primary, extended and logical partitions and file systems including FAT32 and NTFS)
  - Directory structures (e.g. create folders, navigate directory structures)
  - Files (e.g. creation, attributes, permissions)
- Locate and use operating system utilities and available switches for example:
  - Disk management tools (e.g. DEFRAG, NTBACKUP, CHKDSK, Format)
  - System management tools
    - Device and Task Manager
    - MSCONFIG.EXE
    - REGEDIT.EXE
    - REGEDT32.EXE
    - CMD
    - Event Viewer
    - System Restore
    - Remote Desktop
  - File management tools (e.g. Windows EXPLORER, ATTRIB.EXE)

3.2 Install, configure, optimize and upgrade operating systems—references to upgrading from Windows 95 and NT may be made
- Identify procedures and utilities used to optimize operating systems for example:
  - Virtual memory
  - Hard drives (e.g. disk defragmentation)
  - Temporary files
  - Services
  - Startup
  - Application

3.3 Identify tools, diagnostic procedures and troubleshooting techniques for operating systems
- Demonstrate the ability to recover operating systems (e.g. boot methods, recovery console, ASR, ERD)
- Recognize and resolve common operational problems for example:
  - Windows specific printing problems (e.g. print spool stalled, incorrect / incompatible driver form print)
  - Auto-restart errors
  - Bluescreen error
  - System lock-up
  - Device drivers failure (input / output devices)
  - Application install, start or load failure
- Recognize and resolve common error messages and codes for example:
  - Boot (e.g. invalid boot disk, inaccessible boot drive, missing NTLDR)
  - Startup (e.g. device / service failed to start, device / program in registry not found)
  - Event Viewer

- o Registry
- o Windows reporting
- Use diagnostic utilities and tools to resolve operational problems for example:
  - o Bootable media
  - o Startup modes (e.g. safe mode, safe mode with command prompt or networking, step-by-step / single step mode)
  - o Documentation resources (e.g. user / installation manuals, internet / web based, training materials)
  - o Task and Device Manager
  - o Event Viewer
  - o MSCONFIG command
  - o Recover CD / recovery partition
  - o Remote Desktop Connection and Assistance
  - o System File Checker (SFC)

3.4 Perform preventive maintenance for operating systems

- Demonstrate the ability to perform preventive maintenance on operating systems including software and Windows updates (e.g. service packs), scheduled backups / restore, restore points

4.0 Printers and Scanners (14%)

4.1 Identify the fundamental principles of using printers and scanners

- Describe processes used by printers and scanners including laser, ink dispersion, thermal, solid ink and impact printers and scanners

4.2 Install, configure, optimize and upgrade printers and scanners

- Install and configure printers / scanners
  - o Power and connect the device using local or network port
  - o Install and update device driver and calibrate the device
  - o Configure options and default settings
  - o Install and configure print drivers (e.g. PCL™, Postscript™, GDI)
  - o Validate compatibility with operating system and applications
  - o Educate user about basic functionality
- Install and configure printer upgrades including memory and firmware
- Optimize scanner performance including resolution, file format and default settings

4.3 Identify tools and diagnostic procedures to troubleshooting printers and scanners

- Gather information about printer / scanner problems
- Review and analyze collected data
- Isolate and resolve identified printer / scanner problem including defining the cause, applying the fix and verifying functionality
- Identify appropriate tools used for troubleshooting and repairing printer / scanner problems
  - o Multimeter
  - o Screwdrivers
  - o Cleaning solutions
  - o Extension magnet
  - o Test patterns

4.4 Perform preventive maintenance of printers and scanners

- Perform scheduled maintenance according to vendor guidelines (e.g. install maintenance kits, reset page counts)
- Ensure a suitable environment
- Use recommended supplies

5.0 Networks (11%)

  5.1 Identify the fundamental principles or networks

   • Identify names, purposes and characteristics of basic network protocols and terminologies for example:
     o ISP
     o TCP / IP (e.g. gateway, subnet mask, DNS, WINS, static and automatic address assignment)
     o IPX / SPX (NWLink)
     o NETBEUI / NETBIOS
     o SMTP
     o IMAP
     o HTML
     o HTTP
     o HTTPS
     o SSL
     o Telnet
     o FTP
     o DNS

   • Identify names, purposes and characteristics of technologies for establishing connectivity for example:
     o Dial-up networking
     o Broadband (e.g. DSL, cable, satellite)
     o ISDN networking
     o Wireless (all 802.11)
     o LAN / WAN
     o Infrared
     o Bluetooth
     o Cellular
     o VoIP

  5.2 Install, configure, optimize and upgrade networks

   • Install and configure browsers
     o Enable / disable script support
     o Configure proxy and security settings

   • Establish network connectivity
     o Install and configure network cards
     o Obtain a connection
     o Configure client options (e.g. Microsoft, Novell) and network options (e.g. domain, workgroup, tree)
     o Configure network options

   • Demonstrate the ability to share network resources
     o Models
     o Configure permissions
     o Capacities / limitations for sharing for each operating system

  5.3 Use tools and diagnostic procedures to troubleshoot network problems

   • Identify names, purposes and characteristics of tools for example:
     o Command line tools (e.g. IPCONFIG.EXE, PING.EXE, TRACERT.EXE, NSLOOKUP.EXE)
     o Cable testing device

- Diagnose and troubleshoot basic network issue for example:
  - o Driver / network interface
  - o Protocol configuration
    - TCP / IP (e.g. gateway, subnet mask, DNS, WINS, static and automatic address assignment)
    - IPX / SPX (NWLink)
  - o Permissions
  - o Firewall configuration
  - o Electrical interference
  5.4 Perform preventive maintenance of networks including securing and protecting network cabling
6.0 Security (8%)
  6.1 Identify the fundamentals and principles of security
  - Identify the purposes and characteristics of access control for example:
    - o Access to operating system (e.g. accounts such as user, admin and guest. Groups, permission actions, types and levels), components, restricted spaces
  - Identify the purposes and characteristics of auditing and event logging
  6.2 Install, configure, upgrade and optimize security
  - Install and configure software, wireless and data security for example:
    - o Authentication technologies
    - o Software firewalls
    - o Auditing and event logging (enable / disable only)
    - o Wireless client configuration
    - o Unused wireless connections
    - o Data access (e.g. permissions, basic local security policy)
    - o File systems (converting from FAT32 to NTFS only)
  6.3 Identify tool, diagnostic procedures and troubleshooting techniques for security
  - Diagnose and troubleshoot software and data security issues for example:
    - o Software firewall issues
    - o Wireless client configuration issues
    - o Data access issues (e.g. permissions, security policies)
    - o Encryption and encryption technology issues
  6.4 Perform preventive maintenance for security
  - Recognize social engineering and address social engineering situations
7.0 Safety and Environmental Issues (5%)
  7.1 Identify potential hazards and proper safety procedures including power supply, display devices and environment (e.g. trip, liquid, situational, atmospheric hazards and high-voltage and moving equipment)
8.0 Communication and Professionalism (15%)
  8.1 Use good communication skills including listening and tact / discretion, when communicating with customers and colleagues
  - Use clear, concise and direct statements
  - Allow the customer to complete statements—avoid interrupting
  - Clarify customer statements—ask pertinent questions
  - Avoid using jargon, abbreviations and acronyms
  - Listen to customers
  8.2 Use job-related professional behavior including notation of privacy, confidentiality and respect for the customer and customers' property

- Behavior
  - Maintain a positive attitude and tone of voice
  - Avoid arguing with customers and / or becoming defensive
  - Do not minimize customers' problems
  - Avoid being judgmental and / or insulting or calling the customer names
  - Avoid distractions and / or interruptions when talking with customers
- Property
  - Telephone, laptop, desktop computer, printer, monitor, etc.

Remote Support Technician Exam, 220-603

1.0 Personal Computer Components (15%)

  1.1 Install, configure, optimize, and upgrade personal computer components

  - Add, remove, and configure display devices, input devices and adapter cards including basic input and multimedia devices.

  1.2 Identify tools, diagnostic procedures, and troubleshooting techniques for personal computer components

  - Identify and apply basic diagnostic procedures and troubleshooting techniques, for example:
    - Identify and analyze the problem/potential problem
    - Test related components and evaluate results
    - Identify additional steps to be taken if/when necessary
    - Document activities and outcomes

  - Recognize and isolate issues with display, peripheral, multimedia, specialty input device and storage.

  - Apply steps in troubleshooting techniques to identify problems (e.g. physical environment, functionality and software/driver settings) with components including display, input devices and adapter cards

  1.3 Perform preventive maintenance on personal computer components

  - Identify and apply common preventive maintenance techniques for storage devices, for example:
    - Software tools (e.g., Disk Defragmenter, Check Disk)
    - Cleaning (e.g., optics, tape heads)

2.0 Operating Systems—unless otherwise noted, operating systems referred to within include Microsoft Windows 2000, XP Professional, XP Home and Media Center. (29%)

  2.1 Identify the fundamental principles of using operating systems

  - Use command-line functions and utilities to manage Windows 2000, XP Professional and XP Home, including proper syntax and switches, for example:
    - CMD
    - HELP
    - DIR
    - ATTRIB
    - EDIT
    - COPY
    - XCOPY
    - FORMAT
    - IPCONFIG
    - PING
    - MD / CD/ RD

- Identify concepts and procedures for creating, viewing, managing disks, directories and files in Windows 2000, XP Professional and XP Home, for example:
  - Disks (e.g. active, primary, extended and logical partitions)
  - File systems (e.g. FAT 32, NTFS)
  - Directory structures (e.g. create folders, navigate directory structures)
  - Files (e.g. creation, extensions, attributes, permissions)
- Locate and use Windows 2000, XP Professional and XP Home utilities and available switches
  - Disk Management Tools (e.g. DEFRAG, NTBACKUP, CHKDSK, Format)
  - System Management Tools
    - Device and Task Manager
    - MSCONFIG.EXE
    - REGEDIT.EXE
    - REGEDIT32.EXE
    - CMD
    - Event Viewer
    - System Restore
    - Remote Desktop
  - File Management Tool (e.g. Windows Explorer, ATTRIB.EXE)

2.2 Install, configure, optimize and upgrade operating systems

- Identify procedures and utilities used to optimize the performance of Windows 2000, XP Professional and XP Home, for example:
  - Virtual memory
  - Hard drives (e.g. disk defragmentation)
  - Temporary files
  - Services
  - Startup
  - Applications

2.3 Identify tools, diagnostic procedures and troubleshooting techniques for operating systems.

- Recognize and resolve common operational problems, for example:
  - Windows-specific printing problems (e.g. print spooler stalled, incorrect/incompatible driver form print)
  - Auto-restart errors
  - Bluescreen error
  - System lock-up
  - Device drivers failure (input/output devices)
  - Application install, start or load failure
- Recognize and resolve common error messages and codes, for example:
  - Boot (e.g. invalid boot disk, inaccessible boot device, missing NTLDR)
  - Startup (e.g. device/service has failed to start, device/program references in registry not found)
  - Event viewer
  - Registry
  - Windows
- Use diagnostic utilities and tools to resolve operational problems, for example:
  - Bootable media
  - Startup Modes (e.g. safe mode, safe mode with command prompt or networking, step-by-step/single step mode)

- o Documentation resources (e.g. user/installation manuals, internet/web-based, training materials)
- o Task and Device Manager
- o Event Viewer
- o MSCONFIG command
- o Recovery CD / Recovery partition
- o Remote Desktop Connection and Assistance
- o System File Checker (SFC)

2.4 Perform preventive maintenance for operating systems

- Perform preventive maintenance on Windows 2000, XP Professional and XP Home including software and Windows updates (e.g. service packs)

3.0 Printers and Scanners (10%)

3.1 Identify the fundamental principles of using printers and scanners

- Describe processes used by printers and scanners including laser, ink dispersion, impact, solid ink and thermal printers.

3.2 Install, configure, optimize and upgrade printers and scanners

- Install and configure printers and scanners
  - o Power and connect the device using network or local port
  - o Install/update the device driver and calibrate the device
  - o Configure options and default settings
  - o Install and configure print drivers (e.g. PCL™, Postscript™ and GDI)
  - o Validate compatibility with OS and applications
  - o Educate user about basic functionality
- Optimize scanner performance for example: resolution, file format and default settings

3.3 Identify tools, diagnostic procedures and troubleshooting techniques for printers and scanners

- Gather information required to troubleshoot printer/scanner problems
- Troubleshoot a print failure (e.g. lack of paper, clear queue, restart print spooler, recycle power on printer, inspect for jams, check for visual indicators)

4.0 Networks (11%)

4.1 Identify the fundamental principles of networks

- Identify names, purposes, and characteristics of the basic network protocols and terminologies, for example:
  - o ISP
  - o TCP/IP (e.g. Gateway, Subnet mask, DNS, WINS, Static and automatic address assignment)
  - o IPX/SPX (NWLink)
  - o NETBEUI/NETBIOS
  - o SMTP
  - o IMAP
  - o HTML
  - o HTTP
  - o HTTPS
  - o SSL
  - o Telnet
  - o FTP
  - o DNS

- Identify names, purposes, and characteristics of technologies for establishing connectivity, for example:
  - Dial-up networking
  - Broadband (e.g. DSL, cable, satellite)
  - ISDN Networking
  - Wireless
  - LAN/WAN

4.2 Install, configure, optimize and upgrade networks

- Establish network connectivity and share network resources

4.3 Identify tools, diagnostic procedures and troubleshooting techniques for networks

- Identify the names, purposes, and characteristics of command line tools, for example:
  - IPCONFIG.EXE
  - PING.EXE
  - TRACERT.EXE
  - NSLOOKUP.EXE
- Diagnose and troubleshoot basic network issues, for example:
  - Driver/network interface
  - Protocol configuration
    - TCP/IP (e.g. Gatway, Subnet mask, DNS, WINS, static and automatic address assignment)
    - IPX/SPX (NWLink)
  - Permissions
  - Firewall configuration
  - Electrical interference

5.0 Security (15%)

5.1 Identify the fundamental principles of security

- Identify the names, purposes, and characteristics of access control and permissions
  - Accounts including user, admin and guest
  - Groups
  - Permission levels, types (e.g. file systems and shared) and actions (e.g. read, write, change and execute)

5.2 Install, configure, optimizing and upgrade security

- Install and configure hardware, software, wireless and data security, for example:
  - Smart card readers
  - Key fobs
  - Biometric devices
  - Authentication technologies
  - Software firewalls
  - Auditing and event logging (enable/disable only)
  - Wireless client configuration
  - Unused wireless connections
  - Data access (e.g. permissions, security policies)
  - Encryption and encryption technologies

5.3 Identify tools, diagnostic procedures and troubleshooting techniques for security issues

- Diagnose and troubleshoot software and data security issues, for example:
  - Software firewall issues
  - Wireless client configuration issues

o Data access issues (e.g. permissions, security policies)

o Encryption and encryption technology issues

5.4 Perform preventive maintenance for security

- Recognize social engineering and address social engineering situations

6.0 Communication and Professionalism (20%)

6.1 Use good communication skills, including listening and tact / discretion, when communicating with customers and colleagues

- Use clear, concise and direct statements
- Allow the customer to complete statements—avoid interrupting
- Clarify customer statements—ask pertinent questions
- Avoid using jargon, abbreviations and acronyms
- Listen to customers

6.2 Use job-related professional behavior including notation of privacy, confidentiality and respect for the customer and customers' property

- Behavior
  o Maintain a positive attitude and tone of voice
  o Avoid arguing with customers and / or becoming defensive
  o Do not minimize customers' problems
  o Avoid being judgmental and / or insulting or calling the customer names
  o Avoid distractions and / or interruptions when talking with customers
- Property
  o Telephone, laptop, desktop computer, printer, monitor, etc.

Depot Technician Exam, 220-604

1.0 Personal Computer Components (45%)

1.1 Install, configure, optimize and upgrade personal computer components

- Add, remove and configure internal storage devices, motherboards, power supplies, processor/CPU's, memory and adapter cards, including:
  o Drive preparation
  o Jumper configuration
  o Storage device power and cabling
  o Selection and installation of appropriate motherboard
  o BIOS set-up and configuration
  o Selection and installation of appropriate CPU
  o Selection and installation of appropriate memory
  o Installation of adapter cards including hardware and software/drivers
  o Configuration and optimization of adapter cards including adjusting hardware settings and obtaining network card connection
- Add, remove and configure systems

1.2 Identify tools, diagnostic procedures and troubleshooting techniques for personal computer components

- Identify and apply diagnostic procedures and troubleshooting techniques, for example:
  o Identify and isolate the problem using visual and audible inspection of components and minimum configuration

- Identify the steps used to troubleshoot components (e.g. check proper seating, installation, appropriate component, settings, current driver), for example:
  - Power supply
  - Processor/CPU's and motherboards
  - Memory
  - Adapter cards
- Recognize names, purposes, characteristics and appropriate application of tools, for example:
  - Multimeter
  - Anti-static pad and wrist strap
  - Specialty hardware/tools
  - Loop back plugs
  - Cleaning products (e.g. vacuum, cleaning pads)

1.3 Perform preventive maintenance of personal computer components

- Identify and apply common preventive maintenance techniques, for example:
  - Thermally sensitive devices (e.g. motherboards, CPU's, adapter cards, memory)
    - Cleaning
    - Air flow (e.g. slot covers, cable routing)
  - Adapter cards (e.g. driver/firmware updates)

2.0 Laptop and Portable Devices (20%)

2.1 Identify the fundamental principles of using laptops and portable devices

- Identify appropriate applications for laptop-specific communication connections, for example:
  - Bluetooth
  - Infrared devices
  - Cellular WAN
  - Ethernet
- Identify appropriate laptop-specific power and electrical input devices, for example:
  - Output performance requirements for amperage and voltage
  - Identify the major components of the LCD (e.g. inverter, screen, video card)

2.2 Install, configure, optimize and upgrade laptops and portable devices

- Demonstrate the safe removal of laptop-specific hardware including peripherals, hot-swappable and non hot-swappable devices
- Identify the affect of video sharing on memory upgrades

2.3 Identify tools, diagnostic procedures and troubleshooting techniques for laptops and portable devices.

- Use procedures and techniques to diagnose power conditions, video issues, keyboard and pointer issues and wireless card issues, for example:
  - Verify AC power (e.g. LED's, swap AC adapter)
  - Verify DC power
  - Remove unneeded peripherals
  - Plug in external monitor
  - Toggle Fn keys
  - Check LCD cutoff switch
  - Verify backlight functionality and pixilation
  - Stylus issues (e.g. digitizer problems)
  - Unique laptop keypad issues
  - Antenna wires

3.0 Printers and Scanners (20%)

    3.1 Identify the fundamental principles of using printers and scanners

- Describe the processes used by printers and scanners including laser, inkjet, thermal, solid ink, and impact printers

    3.2 Install, configure, optimize and upgrade printers and scanners

- Identify the steps used in the installation and configuration processes for printers and scanners, for example:
  - Power and connect the device using network or local port
  - Install and update the device driver
  - Calibrate the device
  - Configure options and default settings
  - Print test page
- Install and configure printer/scanner upgrades including memory and firmware

    3.3 Identify tools, diagnostic methods and troubleshooting procedures for printers and scanners

- Gather data about printer/scanner problem
- Review and analyze data collected about printer/scanner problems
- Implement solutions to solve identified printer/scanner problems
- Identify appropriate tools used for troubleshooting and repairing printer/scanner problems
  - Multimeter
  - Screw drivers
  - Cleaning solutions
  - Extension magnet
  - Test patterns

    3.4 Perform preventive maintenance of printer and scanner problems

- Perform scheduled maintenance according to vendor guidelines (e.g. install maintenance kits, reset page counts)
- Ensure a suitable environment
- Use recommended supplies

4.0 Security (5%)

    4.1 Identify the names, purposes and characteristics of physical security devices and processes

- Control access to PCs, servers, laptops and restricted spaces
  - Hardware
  - Operating systems

    4.2 Install hardware security

- Smart card readers
- Key fobs
- Biometric devices

5.0 Safety and Environmental Issues (10%)

    5.1 Identify potential hazards & proper safety procedures including power supply, display devices and environment (e.g. trip, liquid, situational, atmospheric hazards, high-voltage and moving equipment)

Basic Skills Necessary

In order to pass the A+ exams, you must be able to reason quickly and weed out superfluous information that can lead you down the wrong track or waste your time. You have roughly a minute per question, which should be plenty if you do not dwell on each question. Know the material coming and going so you are not blindsided when a familiar topic makes it into a question that puts a spin on the subject. Really understand the subject matter related to the objectives for the exam you are taking.

Types of Questions You Will Find on the A+ Exam

CompTIA tests your knowledge of material based on the published objectives for each exam with multiple-choice questions, some of which contain exhibits for you to study before answering the question. By default, each question has one and only one answer. The question will state when two or more options are required to answer the question, and you will not be permitted to answer more than the number of options that the question expects. Occasionally, you can advance to the next question without selecting the required number of options, so be careful before advancing. Fortunately, CompTIA allows you to go back to previous questions and mark questions for later review before ending your exam.

The Multiple-Choice Format

Multiple-choice questions are characterized by a question, sometimes written as a scenario, sometimes simple and straightforward, followed by four or more options.

Sample

> **1.** The main board in a computer is known as which of the following?
>
>   **A.**   Hard drive
>
>   **B.**   Expansion card
>
>   **C.**   Motherboard
>
>   **D.**   Power supply

The correct answer is C because the motherboard contains the CPU, memory, chipset, and expansion slots for expansion cards. The other devices are peripheral to the motherboard, which alone can be considered to be the computer. All other options connect into the motherboard.

Exhibits

The exhibits on the A+ exams are most often diagrams of motherboard landmarks with a question that asks you to identify which of the various items in the exhibit is a given type.

Sample

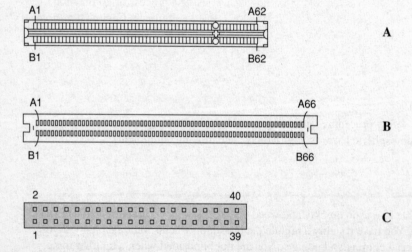

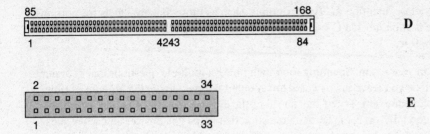

2. Which item in the diagram is a memory slot?

    A. B

    B. D

    C. A

    D. C

    E. E

The correct answer is B because the image of the DIMM slots has the letter D next to them. Don't be confused that the correct answer is B, even though the memory slots are represented with a D. You need to look for the D in the options, not the option labels.

Test-Taking Tips

As with all certification exams, there is a right way and a wrong way to prepare for and take the A+ exams. Although not preparing is indeed one wrong way to go about things, the way you prepare is of utmost importance.

Suggested Approaches

Pay attention to the objectives as published by CompTIA. Practice getting to and using the utilities and features mentioned. Read between the lines, and know all things surrounding an objective. If the objective mentions the PING utility, know every way to conduct a ping and any switches or options available for each method.

Study guides and textbooks are excellent, but without the confidence that comes from hands-on experience and practice, any certification candidate can be easily distracted by options that sound feasible. The problem is, most incorrect options sound feasible. You have to know the right answer. Finding the right answer using a process of elimination should be reserved only for emergencies. At least two options are routinely impossible to eliminate. Enough questions like that, and you're going to need to take the exam again—and the second time will be no easier than the first because you don't have the luxury of knowing which questions you answered wrong. As a result, you have to study for subsequent attempts just like you did for the first—or maybe even harder, because you have nagging notions in the back of your mind spawned by things you remember from the exam. Furthermore, your certification exam is put together from a pool of possible questions many times larger than the number of questions that appear on your personal exam. Although they all draw from the same objectives, and certain questions are staples for almost every instance of the exam, the vast majority of the questions will appear new and unfamiliar. Know your stuff before your first attempt.

It sounds like preparation is the key. It is, but over-preparation is not good. You have to memorize quite a few things that many people can figure out while in front of a live system but can't rattle off in conversation. Doing so leaves little room in most minds for ancillary information that is not tested.

During the exam, don't overanalyze. Every question has an answer; You just have to spot it. As mentioned earlier, most options of most questions will appear feasible at first blush. Therefore, you must read the entire question and *all* of the options, even if you are certain you understand the question or have found the correct answer. The old adage that you should go with your first answer on multiple-choice questions holds true only if you read the entire thing. Otherwise, you're making an uninformed decision. Pay close attention to cryptic options, such as those that are labels for portions of an exhibit. Although you believe that the portion labeled C is correct, the correct choice might not be C. It depends on which option letter the label C appears beside.

Always keep an eye on the time remaining in your exam. Spending too much time on multiple questions can guarantee you will not complete the exam. Any questions you leave unanswered are counted wrong. Divide the amount of time you are given by the number of questions on your exam. Try to stay ahead of the average, but avoid reducing your effectiveness to the point that it does you no good. If you come across a question that helps you answer an earlier question, take advantage of the Back button if you think you may have answered it incorrectly, but only if you feel you have the time. You can always play it safe and find the earlier question during your review if you have time left at the end of your exam.

Best Practices for Prep

The following list contains some of the more important things to consider when preparing for your A+ exams:

- It can't be overemphasized: Pay close attention to the objectives, but read between the lines. The objectives are written in a concise fashion. A simple one-word objective can translate into a plethora of subject matter.

- Use whatever combination of self-study, web learning, and instructor-led training is right for you. Everyone has a mix of learning that works best for them. If self-study is your thing, this book goes well with Sybex's CompTIA A+ Complete Study Guide (ISBN: 0470048301) or the CompTIA A+ Complete Study Guide, Deluxe Edition (ISBN: 047004831X). Consult CompTIA's website and Internet search engines for training options.

- There is a difference between the operating systems covered on the exams, and CompTIA will make sure you are familiar with the one that will make the biggest difference in the job roles to which their certifications apply, such as Windows 2000 and Windows XP. Furthermore, you need to know the more prominent differences between XP Professional and XP Home. Make sure you are familiar with all covered operating systems, which are listed in the objectives of each exam. If you need to borrow time on one or more computers to become familiar with one or more operating systems that you do not own, in order to learn names and paths to different utilities and other applications and command-line processes, do so. Make sure getting around in each operating system is second nature.

- Chat with professionals in the industry and related educational programs to get an idea of real-world troubleshooting scenarios and techniques where possible. Some of the questions CompTIA writes test your experience as much as your technical prowess. If your experience is minimal, listen to some war stories for the vicarious benefit. Use the objectives to steer the conversation to your advantage. The good news is that, time permitting, professionals in this field enjoy chatting about such things.

- Join an online study group or forum to learn more about the topics covered by the exams you are taking. Never doubt the power of two or more heads to figure out even the trickiest of paradoxes.

- Include vendor websites in your studies. Sometimes the best way to learn about a technology is to study a component of that technology. For example, if you have a tough time understanding what a router does, it can't hurt to visit the sites of vendors such as Cisco, Nortel Networks, Juniper, and a host of others. Don't be afraid to fire off an e-mail to vendors with questions that are still out of your reach after investigating a bit. Some vendors consider it good customer development to give out free technical support. You may even get one of your questions answered by a live, knowledgeable individual if you call or request a chat session online.

- Use your favorite Internet search engine to locate more information on tough topics. If you do not have a favorite, Google, among others, does a nice job of bringing pertinent results to the top of the list for highly technical topics.

PART II

FULL-LENGTH PRACTICE TESTS

Answer Sheets for Practice Test 1

(Remove This Sheet and Use It to Mark Your Answers)

Section 1
Multiple Choice Questions

1 Ⓐ Ⓑ Ⓒ Ⓓ Ⓔ	51 Ⓐ Ⓑ Ⓒ Ⓓ Ⓔ
2 Ⓐ Ⓑ Ⓒ Ⓓ Ⓔ	52 Ⓐ Ⓑ Ⓒ Ⓓ Ⓔ
3 Ⓐ Ⓑ Ⓒ Ⓓ Ⓔ	53 Ⓐ Ⓑ Ⓒ Ⓓ Ⓔ
4 Ⓐ Ⓑ Ⓒ Ⓓ Ⓔ	54 Ⓐ Ⓑ Ⓒ Ⓓ Ⓔ
5 Ⓐ Ⓑ Ⓒ Ⓓ Ⓔ	55 Ⓐ Ⓑ Ⓒ Ⓓ Ⓔ
6 Ⓐ Ⓑ Ⓒ Ⓓ Ⓔ	56 Ⓐ Ⓑ Ⓒ Ⓓ Ⓔ
7 Ⓐ Ⓑ Ⓒ Ⓓ Ⓔ	57 Ⓐ Ⓑ Ⓒ Ⓓ Ⓔ
8 Ⓐ Ⓑ Ⓒ Ⓓ Ⓔ	58 Ⓐ Ⓑ Ⓒ Ⓓ Ⓔ
9 Ⓐ Ⓑ Ⓒ Ⓓ Ⓔ	59 Ⓐ Ⓑ Ⓒ Ⓓ Ⓔ
10 Ⓐ Ⓑ Ⓒ Ⓓ Ⓔ	60 Ⓐ Ⓑ Ⓒ Ⓓ Ⓔ
11 Ⓐ Ⓑ Ⓒ Ⓓ Ⓔ	61 Ⓐ Ⓑ Ⓒ Ⓓ Ⓔ
12 Ⓐ Ⓑ Ⓒ Ⓓ Ⓔ	62 Ⓐ Ⓑ Ⓒ Ⓓ Ⓔ
13 Ⓐ Ⓑ Ⓒ Ⓓ Ⓔ	63 Ⓐ Ⓑ Ⓒ Ⓓ Ⓔ
14 Ⓐ Ⓑ Ⓒ Ⓓ Ⓔ	64 Ⓐ Ⓑ Ⓒ Ⓓ Ⓔ
15 Ⓐ Ⓑ Ⓒ Ⓓ Ⓔ	65 Ⓐ Ⓑ Ⓒ Ⓓ Ⓔ
16 Ⓐ Ⓑ Ⓒ Ⓓ Ⓔ	66 Ⓐ Ⓑ Ⓒ Ⓓ Ⓔ
17 Ⓐ Ⓑ Ⓒ Ⓓ Ⓔ	67 Ⓐ Ⓑ Ⓒ Ⓓ Ⓔ
18 Ⓐ Ⓑ Ⓒ Ⓓ Ⓔ	68 Ⓐ Ⓑ Ⓒ Ⓓ Ⓔ
19 Ⓐ Ⓑ Ⓒ Ⓓ Ⓔ	69 Ⓐ Ⓑ Ⓒ Ⓓ Ⓔ
20 Ⓐ Ⓑ Ⓒ Ⓓ Ⓔ	70 Ⓐ Ⓑ Ⓒ Ⓓ Ⓔ
21 Ⓐ Ⓑ Ⓒ Ⓓ Ⓔ	71 Ⓐ Ⓑ Ⓒ Ⓓ Ⓔ
22 Ⓐ Ⓑ Ⓒ Ⓓ Ⓔ	72 Ⓐ Ⓑ Ⓒ Ⓓ Ⓔ
23 Ⓐ Ⓑ Ⓒ Ⓓ Ⓔ	73 Ⓐ Ⓑ Ⓒ Ⓓ Ⓔ
24 Ⓐ Ⓑ Ⓒ Ⓓ Ⓔ	74 Ⓐ Ⓑ Ⓒ Ⓓ Ⓔ
25 Ⓐ Ⓑ Ⓒ Ⓓ Ⓔ	75 Ⓐ Ⓑ Ⓒ Ⓓ Ⓔ
26 Ⓐ Ⓑ Ⓒ Ⓓ Ⓔ	76 Ⓐ Ⓑ Ⓒ Ⓓ Ⓔ
27 Ⓐ Ⓑ Ⓒ Ⓓ Ⓔ	77 Ⓐ Ⓑ Ⓒ Ⓓ Ⓔ
28 Ⓐ Ⓑ Ⓒ Ⓓ Ⓔ	78 Ⓐ Ⓑ Ⓒ Ⓓ Ⓔ
29 Ⓐ Ⓑ Ⓒ Ⓓ Ⓔ	79 Ⓐ Ⓑ Ⓒ Ⓓ Ⓔ
30 Ⓐ Ⓑ Ⓒ Ⓓ Ⓔ	80 Ⓐ Ⓑ Ⓒ Ⓓ Ⓔ
31 Ⓐ Ⓑ Ⓒ Ⓓ Ⓔ	81 Ⓐ Ⓑ Ⓒ Ⓓ Ⓔ
32 Ⓐ Ⓑ Ⓒ Ⓓ Ⓔ	82 Ⓐ Ⓑ Ⓒ Ⓓ Ⓔ
33 Ⓐ Ⓑ Ⓒ Ⓓ Ⓔ	83 Ⓐ Ⓑ Ⓒ Ⓓ Ⓔ
34 Ⓐ Ⓑ Ⓒ Ⓓ Ⓔ	84 Ⓐ Ⓑ Ⓒ Ⓓ Ⓔ
35 Ⓐ Ⓑ Ⓒ Ⓓ Ⓔ	85 Ⓐ Ⓑ Ⓒ Ⓓ Ⓔ
36 Ⓐ Ⓑ Ⓒ Ⓓ Ⓔ	86 Ⓐ Ⓑ Ⓒ Ⓓ Ⓔ
37 Ⓐ Ⓑ Ⓒ Ⓓ Ⓔ	87 Ⓐ Ⓑ Ⓒ Ⓓ Ⓔ
38 Ⓐ Ⓑ Ⓒ Ⓓ Ⓔ	88 Ⓐ Ⓑ Ⓒ Ⓓ Ⓔ
39 Ⓐ Ⓑ Ⓒ Ⓓ Ⓔ	89 Ⓐ Ⓑ Ⓒ Ⓓ Ⓔ
40 Ⓐ Ⓑ Ⓒ Ⓓ Ⓔ	90 Ⓐ Ⓑ Ⓒ Ⓓ Ⓔ
41 Ⓐ Ⓑ Ⓒ Ⓓ Ⓔ	91 Ⓐ Ⓑ Ⓒ Ⓓ Ⓔ
42 Ⓐ Ⓑ Ⓒ Ⓓ Ⓔ	92 Ⓐ Ⓑ Ⓒ Ⓓ Ⓔ
43 Ⓐ Ⓑ Ⓒ Ⓓ Ⓔ	93 Ⓐ Ⓑ Ⓒ Ⓓ Ⓔ
44 Ⓐ Ⓑ Ⓒ Ⓓ Ⓔ	94 Ⓐ Ⓑ Ⓒ Ⓓ Ⓔ
45 Ⓐ Ⓑ Ⓒ Ⓓ Ⓔ	95 Ⓐ Ⓑ Ⓒ Ⓓ Ⓔ
46 Ⓐ Ⓑ Ⓒ Ⓓ Ⓔ	96 Ⓐ Ⓑ Ⓒ Ⓓ Ⓔ
47 Ⓐ Ⓑ Ⓒ Ⓓ Ⓔ	97 Ⓐ Ⓑ Ⓒ Ⓓ Ⓔ
48 Ⓐ Ⓑ Ⓒ Ⓓ Ⓔ	98 Ⓐ Ⓑ Ⓒ Ⓓ Ⓔ
49 Ⓐ Ⓑ Ⓒ Ⓓ Ⓔ	99 Ⓐ Ⓑ Ⓒ Ⓓ Ⓔ
50 Ⓐ Ⓑ Ⓒ Ⓓ Ⓔ	100 Ⓐ Ⓑ Ⓒ Ⓓ Ⓔ

CUT HERE

Directions: For each of the following questions, select the choice that best answers the question or completes the statement.

1. Which of the following choices is part of the definition of a personal computer?

   A. A device that is not usable by itself
   B. A device whose only function is to access a group computer
   C. A device made up of distinct components that all function together
   D. A device that can be carried in a pocket for mobile use

2. Which of the following is not a common component found on a motherboard?

   A. CPU
   B. HDD
   C. RAM
   D. BIOS

3. Which of the following motherboard form factors is not a standard?

   A. ATX
   B. microATX
   C. BTX
   D. LPX

4. Which of the following motherboard form factors uses a riser card?

   A. BTX
   B. ATX
   C. LPX
   D. microATX

5. All of the following statements about chipsets are true *except*:

   A. By definition, a chipset is always made up of two or more chips and related circuitry.
   B. Chipset functionality is divided into Northbridge and Southbridge.
   C. The same manufacturer creates all chips in a chipset.
   D. A chipset assists the CPU in its interface and peripheral functions.

6. Which of the following is the pathway over which communication between the processor and memory occurs?

   A. Northbridge
   B. Southbridge
   C. Frontside bus
   D. Backside bus

7. All of the following are expansion slots *except*:

   A. ISA
   B. PCI
   C. AGP
   D. IDE

8. What is the primary function of an expansion card inserted in an AGP slot?

   A. NIC
   B. FireWire
   C. Video
   D. Audio

9. Which of the following slots is the longest?

   A. 1X PCIe
   B. AGP
   C. CNR
   D. PCI

10. Memory slots on a motherboard are for

    A. Memory modules
    B. Memory chips
    C. Insertion of the CPU to gain access to the system memory
    D. Cables that connect from the memory to the CPU

GO ON TO THE NEXT PAGE

11. Which of the following is *not* a common pin count for DIMMs?

A. 168
B. 184
C. 196
D. 240

12. Which of the following statements regarding cache memory is true?

A. Because cache stores what the CPU uses, there must be at least 10 times more cache than RAM.
B. Because cache is placed closer to the CPU than RAM is, cache can be made slower than RAM.
C. SDRAM is used for cache because of its speed.
D. Cache is used to store what the CPU has needed from RAM most recently and what the cache controller predicts is needed next.

13. Which of the following CPU/socket pairings is incorrect?

A. Pentium 200MHz: Socket 7
B. Pentium II: Socket 1
C. Pentium 4: Socket 478
D. Itanium: PAC418

14. Which of the following statements about onboard drive interfaces is true?

A. *Onboard* refers to the fact that the controller electronics are built into the hard drive.
B. Black 40-pin connectors are for PATA, and blue 40-pin connectors are for SATA.
C. SATA connectors have more pins than FDD connectors.
D. The technology behind the interface could be ATA or SCSI.

15. When you remove the cover of your computer's case, you find that your video interface is attached to the motherboard without a cable. What is this method of attachment called?

A. Header connection
B. Perma-mount
C. Direct-solder
D. Fixed attachment

16. All of the following statements about the BIOS are true *except*:

A. If the BIOS does not know about a piece of hardware, the operating system will likely require a device driver for the hardware.
B. The BIOS is generally implemented as a removable chip or a flashable component.
C. The BIOS is responsible for the primary POST process.
D. Once the BIOS passes control to the operating system, it essentially goes to sleep until the next boot.

17. What is the term for Intel's technology that allows a single processor to appear to be two processors to the operating system?

A. Hyperthreading
B. Symmetric multiprocessing
C. Split microcode
D. Dual processing

18. Which of the following is an accurate representation of microcode?

A. A microcode instruction is an application instruction that is half the length of a normal application instruction.
B. Programmers can write applications with smaller file sizes by using microcode.
C. Microcode is the trade name for all instructions in software written by Microsoft.
D. One instruction in the code of an application may result in multiple microcode instructions.

19. Which of the following best describes parity checking?

A. An error-checking scheme for RAM
B. An error-checking and -correction scheme for RAM
C. Matching colors between the monitor and the printer
D. Matching the configured borders to those of the printed page

20. All of the following are differences between DRAM and SRAM *except*:

A. SRAM is generally more expensive per quantity than DRAM.

B. SRAM is generally faster and more responsive than DRAM.

C. SRAM requires periodic refreshing, and DRAM does not.

D. SRAM is generally used for cache, whereas DRAM is used for standard RAM.

21. All of the following statements about DDR2 SDRAM are accurate *except*:

A. DDR2 suffers from more latency than does DDR.

B. The chips on the DDR2 module are named based on the perceived clock rate.

C. DDR2 generates more heat than DDR because it is twice as fast and uses the same voltage.

D. The throughput of DDR is four times that of SDR SDRAM at the same clock rate.

22. Which of the following statements about primary memory modules is *not* true?

A. If you use memory rated at a frequency that is lower than that of the FSB, performance will be suboptimal.

B. Double-sided memory modules are required to satisfy two banks at a time.

C. A SIMM and a DIMM are not interchangeable.

D. When upgrading memory, you must satisfy entire banks at a time.

23. Which of the following statements about SoDIMMs and MicroDIMMs is *not* true?

A. MicroDIMMs are smaller but plug into the same slots.

B. They are used in small-scale applications, such as for laptops.

C. Both come in a 144-pin version.

D. Both come in a 64-bit version.

24. Which of the following statements about CD-ROM drives and discs is true?

A. A standard CD-ROM disc can hold up to 4.7GB of data.

B. The original CD-ROM drives transferred data at a rate of 150KBps.

C. A 52X CD-ROM drive spins the disc 52 times faster than the original drives.

D. With the proper software, you can burn data to a CD-ROM disc.

25. Which of the following is *not* a memory card format?

A. MicroCard

B. SD

C. SmartMedia

D. Memory Stick

26. Which of the following items is *not* commonly found on an external USB-attached hard disk drive?

A. A place to insert disks

B. A Type-B USB interface

C. A DC power input

D. A power switch

27. How are power supplies rated for comparison of load capacity?

A. Ohms

B. Amps

C. Watts

D. Volts

28. All of the following apply to AT system connectors, *except*:

A. There are two connectors with five pins each.

B. The connectors are known as P8 and P9.

C. When inserting the connectors into the motherboard, you must take care to place grounds adjacent to each other.

D. The connectors are keyed to prevent flipping them 180 degrees.

29. Which of the following is the least amount of video memory listed that is capable of supporting 1024×768 resolution using 32-bit color?

A. 1MB

B. 2MB

C. 4MB

D. 16MB

GO ON TO THE NEXT PAGE

30. Which of the following video technologies offers the highest quality?

   A. S-video
   B. Composite video
   C. Component video
   D. EGA

31. Which adapter card is most likely to have an empty ROM socket and a modular connector?

   A. Video
   B. Sound
   C. NIC
   D. Super I/O

32. All of the following statements about USB are true *except*:

   A. USB 1.1 supports data rates of up to 12MBps.
   B. USB 2.0 supports data rates of up to 60MBps.
   C. USB 2.0 requires better shielding for its cables.
   D. USB 1.1 and 2.0 connectors are identical.

33. What is historically the most common use for a Centronics connector?

   A. Networking
   B. Video
   C. Sound
   D. Printer

34. With USB cabling, all of the following statements help you to know the type of connector a device is likely to require *except*:

   A. Type B connectors face the component.
   B. For ease of connectivity, as well as plug-and-play support, USB cables have the same type of connector on each end of the cable.
   C. USB hubs appear to be the system to the component and appear to be the component to the system.
   D. Type A connectors face the system.

35. What normally happens when the lower temperature threshold set in the BIOS routine for the CPU is reached?

   A. The system shuts down to prevent damage to components.
   B. The operating system goes into standby mode to avoid damage to components.
   C. An alarm sounds, indicating that the CPU and surrounding components are in imminent danger.
   D. The system administrator is paged, and an e-mail is sent.

36. Which of the following is true regarding modern UltraDMA drives?

   A. Due to interference caused by the additional 40 wires of an 80-wire cable, performance is increased by using a standard 40-wire cable.
   B. These drives do not require master/slave designations.
   C. They cannot be used when standard IDE devices are installed.
   D. The BIOS should not be configured for DMA or PIO when using these drives.

37. All of the following are considerations with SCSI *except*:

   A. One device must be set as master. All others must be set as slaves.
   B. Each device on the bus must have a unique configurable address.
   C. Two devices must be terminated.
   D. In certain cases, active termination is preferred or required over passive termination.

38. Which of the following statements about SCSI is *not* true?

   A. The lower the address, the higher the device's priority on the bus.
   B. If you have a bus with 8 addresses, you can chain a maximum of 4 such buses to obtain 32 addresses.
   C. It is common practice that the primary hard disk be set to address 0.
   D. A SCSI hard drive's onboard BIOS is required for booting to the disk.

39. In attempting to take the front faceplate off of a computer, you meet with considerable resistance. What should you do?

    A. Using a flat-blade screwdriver, gently pry the faceplate from the chassis.

    B. Turn off the computer's power, and the faceplate latch will release automatically.

    C. Faceplates cannot be removed from the chassis.

    D. Remove the case cover, and look for one or more screws in the chassis that are holding the faceplate in place.

40. When using compressed air, all of the following are considerations *except*:

    A. Compressed air is usually impure and can leave heavy deposits on electronic components.

    B. Inverting the can may blow refrigerant onto the components.

    C. Canned compressed air can be expensive.

    D. When used in the wrong environment, compressed air can cause dust to enter ventilation systems and contaminate other computers.

41. What is one of the primary differences between measuring current and voltage with a multimeter?

    A. The positive and negative probes must be reversed with respect to one another.

    B. You cannot measure both with the same type of multimeter.

    C. To measure voltage, you must place the multimeter in series with the circuit. Current is measured in parallel.

    D. To measure current, you must place the multimeter in series with the circuit. Voltage is measured in parallel.

42. When troubleshooting, which of the following statements best describes how to handle testing multiple solutions?

    A. Because there may be multiple issues causing the problem, try all combinations of potential solutions simultaneously until the problem is resolved.

    B. If an attempt at a remedy does not resolve the problem, revert to the previous state before trying anything else.

    C. Because the customer is most familiar with the symptoms of the problem, present options and their expected outcomes so that the customer can suggest where to start.

    D. Implement all possible solutions to the particular problem and then back them out, one by one, until the problem reoccurs. Add the solution back, and remove all other attempted fixes.

43. All of the following are examples of common causes of motherboard damage *except*:

    A. Physical trauma

    B. Short circuiting

    C. ESD

    D. Overheating

44. Which of the following options results in the most cost-effective solution for a standard keyboard with sticking keys?

    A. Purchase the most inexpensive keyboard cleaning solvent, and meticulously clean the component.

    B. Submerge the entire keyboard in clean water for 30 minutes, scrub the crevices, submerge it again, and then let it air dry.

    C. Remove the keys and soak them in water, and use an alcohol-dipped swab to clean all other areas.

    D. Purchase a new keyboard.

GO ON TO THE NEXT PAGE

45. What is the term that refers to the repeated heating and cooling of internal components, causing them to become unseated over time and lead to intermittent failures?

    A. Convection reaction

    B. Card wander

    C. Chip creep

    D. Heat cycling

46. Which of the following is one of the biggest differences between laptop and desktop computers?

    A. Similar internal components function differently.

    B. Laptops have increased heat production.

    C. External components connect differently.

    D. Laptops are considerably less expensive to produce.

47. What is a micro-FCBGA?

    A. A miniaturized video standard

    B. A motherboard form factor

    C. A processor form factor and attachment standard

    D. A laptop computer model

48. Which of the following statements is true?

    A. All laptops have an internal floppy drive.

    B. Some laptops have a universal drive bay that accepts a floppy drive or a CD/DVD drive.

    C. All laptops have an internal CD or DVD drive.

    D. All laptops have a connector for external floppy attachment.

49. With respect to the keyboard on a laptop, which of the following statements is most likely true?

    A. The key layout and size of the keys and keyboard are similar to those of a standard keyboard.

    B. A special key needs to be held down while another key is pressed to access certain functions that have their own key on a standard keyboard.

    C. Because the keys on a laptop keyboard are smaller, all the standard keys are present, in addition to special keys.

    D. The functionality of a laptop keyboard is highly inferior to that of a standard keyboard.

50. Which PC Card type is most commonly used for modems and LAN adapters?

    A. Type I.

    B. Type II.

    C. Type III.

    D. These devices cannot be implemented on PC Cards.

51. Which of the following is *not* a form of communication connectivity commonly found on laptops?

    A. Cellular

    B. Microwave

    C. Infrared

    D. Bluetooth

52. What is the name of the specification that hands control over power management to the operating system?

    A. SoftPower

    B. APC

    C. WinPower

    D. ACPI

53. Which of the following is likely to be the most commonly removed or inserted internal laptop component, often involving removing one or more screws?

    A. Hard drive

    B. Memory

    C. Sound card

    D. CD/DVD drive

54. All of the following statements about video troubleshooting on laptops are legitimate *except*:

    A. Check the brightness level on the internal display, just as you would on an external monitor.

    B. Make sure to check all three modes: LCD only, external only, and both, before assuming the internal display is bad.

    C. If the laptop has a backlight feature, try to turn it on, especially in dim environments.

    D. If neither the internal display nor an external monitor works, replacing the internal display should fix both problems.

55. Which of the following is the fundamentally most important type of software on a computer?

A. Word processor
B. E-mail and messaging
C. Payroll and financial
D. Operating system

56. What is the meaning of the term *shell* with respect to operating systems?

A. A front for an application to distract hackers and make it harder to gain access.
B. A program that runs on top of the operating system to provide a custom or friendlier interface that the operating system does not provide.
C. A fragile application that collapses frequently, leaving a mess for the operating system to clean up.
D. A portal from one application, through the operating system, to another application.

57. All of the following are operating systems in a rivalry with Windows *except*:

A. Mac OS X
B. Unix
C. Datacenter
D. Linux

58. Which of the following represent the recommended RAM and available hard disk space, respectively, to run Red Hat Linux 8.0 Professional?

A. 192MB; 4.5GB
B. 256MB; 4GB
C. 128MB; 3.5GB
D. 384MB; 5.25GB

59. What does an arrow to the right of an item in the Start menu represent?

A. Clicking the item launches a separate application.
B. Double-clicking the item attempts to link to a related web page.
C. The item has a submenu that is displayed by hovering over the item.
D. Help for the item is launched.

60. Looking through the items in the All Programs list in XP, you notice that a couple of them appear to be highlighted. What does this mean?

A. They are newly installed.
B. Windows will archive these items in less than 24 hours.
C. The items are not fully Windows-compatible. You should use caution when executing these items.
D. The software publishers paid advertising dollars to Microsoft to have their products highlighted in Windows.

61. You delete an icon with an arrow in the bottom-left corner from your Desktop. Which of the following statements is most accurate?

A. The icon was a shortcut to the actual program, which is untouched and remains executable.
B. The icon was a shortcut to the actual program, which is deleted as well.
C. The icon was the actual executable, which is now completely removed from the hard drive.
D. Deleting the icon partially removed the related application from the hard drive, making it difficult to properly remove the remainder.

62. All of the following statements about the Recycle Bin are true *except*:

A. The icon of an empty Recycle Bin differs from that of a Recycle Bin with something in it.
B. Any file or folder deleted from any location is sent to the Recycle Bin.
C. The Recycle Bin holds deleted files from the hard disk so they can be restored if necessary.
D. Items in the Recycle Bin can be restored until the Recycle Bin is emptied.

63. Which one of the following methods does *not* close an open window?

A. Double-click the Control box in the upper-left corner of the window.
B. Click the X button in the upper-right corner of the window.
C. Double-click the title bar.
D. Press Alt-F4 while the window is active.

GO ON TO THE NEXT PAGE

64. Double-clicking which of the following icons in Control Panel has the same effect as right-clicking My Computer and then clicking Properties?

   A. System
   B. Network Connections
   C. Display
   D. Taskbar and Start Menu

65. Which of the following methods leads to being able to change the name by which a computer is known on the network?

   A. Click the Change button in the Computer Name page of System Properties.
   B. Right-click My Computer, and click Rename.
   C. Click My Computer, wait a couple of seconds, click My Computer again, enter the new name, and press Enter.
   D. In Device Manager, right-click the computer name at the top of the tree, and click Rename.

66. Under which tab in System Properties do you change virtual memory settings, adjust how resources are allocated to the processor, configure user profiles, and adjust startup and recovery settings?

   A. System Restore
   B. General
   C. Hardware
   D. Advanced

67. When a user attempts to invite you to provide remote assistance, the following message pops up: "Your current system settings prevent you from sending an invitation." What should you have the user do to enable this capability?

   A. Use the original XP distribution disc to install this feature.
   B. Download this feature for free from Microsoft's website.
   C. This is a third-party utility that must be purchased from the publisher.
   D. Check the box in the Remote Assistance section under the Remote page in System Properties.

68. Which pair of terms is used most often when discussing the Registry?

   A. Tree; branch
   B. Hive; key
   C. Record; field
   D. Parent; child

69. Which of the following best describes virtual memory?

   A. Using an Internet service as a network share to augment local disk storage
   B. Using RAM to create a RAM drive
   C. The operating system's technique of stacking two bits in locations that normally store only one
   D. The use of the hard drive to supplement RAM

70. Which of the following describes the NTLDR system file?

   A. Starts the loading of the operating system
   B. A text file that points to the partitions where one or more operating systems are installed
   C. The core of the operating system that must remain loaded at all times, never being paged to disk
   D. Parses the system for current configuration information as the operating system starts, and creates the dynamic portion of the Registry

71. Which of the following describes the NTDETECT.COM system file?

   A. Starts the loading of the operating system
   B. A text file that points to the partitions where one or more operating systems are installed
   C. The core of the operating system that must remain loaded at all times, never being paged to disk
   D. Parses the system for current configuration information as the operating system starts and creates the dynamic portion of the Registry

72. What can be found on a memory module?

   A. Other memory modules
   B. Cable headers
   C. Memory chips
   D. Firmware

73. Which one of the following is *not* a difference between primary and extended partitions?

   A. You can assign multiple drive letters to an extended partition but only one to a primary partition.

   B. Only primary partitions can be made active and used for booting.

   C. Generally speaking, a single physical drive can have more primary partitions than extended partitions.

   D. You can assign a single drive letter to a primary partition, but an extended partition requires multiple drive letters.

74. Which of the following is the primary method for a Microsoft operating system to track the purpose of a file?

   A. A specific extension is added to the file's name.

   B. The icon assigned to the file denotes its purpose.

   C. All files of a specific purpose are grouped together in the same folder.

   D. Windows writes a header to the beginning of each file, tracking its purpose and other variable information.

75. Which of the following is recommended by Microsoft to be higher for the installation of Windows 2000 Professional than for the installation of Windows XP Professional?

   A. Memory

   B. Free hard disk space

   C. Processor model

   D. Video standard

76. What is an unattended installation?

   A. An installation where a Windows expert talks a novice through the installation process remotely

   B. An installation that is pushed to the computer from an SMS server

   C. An installation that uses an answer file so that no human intervention is required

   D. A direct image copy using only Sysprep

77. After you install Windows XP, what must be done within 30 days in order to continue using it?

   A. You must fill out the warranty registration card and send it in to Microsoft with the original UPC symbol.

   B. You must install SP2 and all patches up to a minimum level to avoid contamination from the Internet, or your system will disable itself for protection.

   C. XP must be activated online or by phone with Microsoft.

   D. You must reboot the system at least once.

78. From which of the following operating systems must you run `WINNT.EXE` and not `WINNT32.EXE` to perform a clean Windows XP installation?

   A. Windows 3.1

   B. Windows 98

   C. Windows 95

   D. Windows Me

79. All of the following are reasons to use Task Manager *except*:

   A. Stopping an unresponsive application

   B. Finding out how much your hard drives are fragmented

   C. Finding out which processes are using the CPU the most

   D. Finding out how much memory and virtual memory is being used

80. Which function key, when pressed at the appropriate time during boot-up, presents you with advanced startup options?

   A. F1

   B. F5

   C. F8

   D. F12

81. What is the term that refers to the frequent disk access, which is accompanied by degraded system performance and that is caused by a full or corrupt swap file?

   A. Foundering

   B. Thunking

   C. Thrashing

   D. Battering

GO ON TO THE NEXT PAGE

82. All of the following are functions of a printer driver *except*:

- **A.** Uses a page-description language to convert print jobs into a format for the printer
- **B.** Ensures that the printer is ready to print
- **C.** Changes the way on-screen documents appear once the output device is selected
- **D.** Sends information to the printer

83. How does the writing step in the EP print process place the image on the photosensitive drum?

- **A.** Light reflects off of the original image in varying intensities onto the drum.
- **B.** A corona wire scribes the image onto the drum.
- **C.** Electrodes inside the drum create the image through the wall of the drum.
- **D.** The uniform −600VDC charge is reduced to −100VDC wherever the image lies.

84. All of the following are printer communication methods *except*:

- **A.** IEEE 1284
- **B.** IEEE 802.11
- **C.** IEEE 1394
- **D.** IEEE 802.1D

85. All of the following components are part of the scanning head of a scanner *except*:

- **A.** CCD or CIS
- **B.** Light source
- **C.** Stepper motor
- **D.** Mirrors

86. When working with printers and scanners, what term refers to synchronizing the device's perception with its results?

- **A.** Regulation
- **B.** Adjustment
- **C.** Tuning
- **D.** Calibration

87. While troubleshooting a paper-feed jam problem with a page printer, you confirm that the drive gear is operating smoothly, but jams still occur regularly. Which of the following is another possible problem that can cause paper-feed jams?

- **A.** Worn feed rollers
- **B.** Worn exit rollers
- **C.** Damaged drum
- **D.** Dry paper

88. All of the following are possible solutions when a scanner fails to scan *except*:

- **A.** Reposition the object being scanned.
- **B.** Check the scanning-head lock.
- **C.** Check the power.
- **D.** Do nothing, and try again.

89. In which type of network do devices request and offer services simultaneously, with no devices defined for specialized access from others?

- **A.** Nondedicated network
- **B.** Peer-to-peer network
- **C.** Client-server network
- **D.** Local area network

90. Which IEEE working group specifies the media access method for Ethernet, and what is the media access method called?

- **A.** 802.3; CSMA/CD
- **B.** 802.5; token-passing ring
- **C.** 802.1; CSMA/CA
- **D.** 802.11; wireless networks

91. Which of the following protocols is *not* routable?

- **A.** IP
- **B.** IPX
- **C.** AppleTalk (DDP)
- **D.** NetBEUI

92. How many bits make up a complete IPX address?

- **A.** 32
- **B.** 48
- **C.** 64
- **D.** 80

93. Which class of IP addresses can be identified by a first-octet value ranging from 192 to 223?

    A. Class A
    B. Class B
    C. Class C
    D. Class D

94. Cat-*x* is a common reference used for what type of transmission medium?

    A. Coaxial
    B. Twisted pair
    C. Fiber
    D. Wireless

95. Among the following, which is the slowest Internet connection?

    A. POTS
    B. ISDN
    C. DSL
    D. DOCSIS (cable)

96. How does full-duplex transmission differ from half-duplex?

    A. Full-duplex requires more cabling than half-duplex.
    B. With full-duplex, transmission can occur in only one direction for full use of the bandwidth by one device.
    C. With full-duplex, transmission can occur in both directions, but in only one direction at a time.
    D. With full-duplex, transmission can occur in both directions simultaneously.

97. How does a worm differ from a virus?

    A. A worm is self-contained and can reproduce itself. A virus relies on a host application and spreads through human interaction.
    B. A virus is harmless, and a worm is destructive.
    C. A worm burrows deeper into an application than a virus does.
    D. Only viruses affect personal computer workstations. Worms affect larger systems, including some personal computer–based servers.

98. Which of the following terms is *not* directly related to wireless security?

    A. WTLS
    B. WLAN
    C. WEP
    D. WPA

99. All of the following are sound environmental considerations for a computer *except*:

    A. Cover open slots in the back of the chassis with blank brackets.
    B. Do not expose the computer to harmful fumes or substances, especially anything airborne that can leave a residue.
    C. In less acceptable environments, place the computer in an airtight enclosure to avoid contaminants.
    D. Use your own tolerance to temperature extremes to gauge if the computer should be exposed to a given temperature or climate.

100. If a customer accuses you of being the source of the problem, which of the following is the best course of action?

    A. Protect your company at all costs. The company is your bread and butter and must not come into question.
    B. Without actually accusing the customer of any wrongdoing before it is proven, attempt to equalize the situation by getting the customer to take some of the blame as well.
    C. Keep your cool and do not take things personally. The customer is reacting to a stressful situation.
    D. Escalate the incident to someone that can handle the abuse.

Answer Key for Practice Test 1

1. C	26. A	51. B	76. C
2. B	27. C	52. D	77. C
3. D	28. A	53. B	78. A
4. C	29. C	54. D	79. B
5. A	30. C	55. D	80. C
6. C	31. C	56. B	81. C
7. D	32. A	57. C	82. C
8. C	33. D	58. A	83. D
9. D	34. B	59. C	84. D
10. A	35. C	60. A	85. C
11. C	36. D	61. A	86. D
12. D	37. A	62. B	87. A
13. B	38. B	63. C	88. A
14. D	39. D	64. A	89. B
15. C	40. A	65. A	90. A
16. D	41. D	66. D	91. D
17. A	42. B	67. D	92. D
18. D	43. D	68. B	93. C
19. A	44. D	69. D	94. B
20. C	45. C	70. A	95. A
21. C	46. B	71. D	96. D
22. B	47. C	72. C	97. A
23. A	48. B	73. D	98. B
24. B	49. B	74. A	99. C
25. A	50. B	75. B	100. C

Answer Explanations for Practice Test 1

1. **C.** A personal computer is a self-contained stand-alone device that can be connected to others but promotes productivity on its own as well. Some mobile devices can be classified as personal computers, but this group is too narrow to define all personal computers.

2. **B.** The hard disk drive is not attached to the motherboard but is mounted in a drive bay and cabled to most motherboards.

3. **D.** The LPX form factor was popular in its day but was never standardized, leading to compatibility issues.

4. **C.** The low-profile form factors, LPX and NLX, use risers so that their expansion cards can be mounted parallel with the motherboard, allowing for a case of more diminutive height.

5. **A.** A chipset, despite the implication, could be a single chip.

6. **C.** The frontside bus is the data pathway that joins the CPU, the Northbridge, and SDRAM, if used.

7. **D.** IDE is the popular term for ATA, a drive interface that often appears on the motherboard for cabling to off-board drives but is not used for the connection of expansion cards.

8. **C.** Accelerated Graphics Port was created primarily for use with video adapters to answer the need for high-speed video to keep up with faster computers and more demanding software.

9. **D.** PCI slots are the longest of those listed. Although PCIe slots can be longer, the 1X slot is very short.

10. **A.** Slots receive modules. Chips mount in sockets. Today's motherboards have abandoned memory sockets in favor of slots for modules of primary RAM.

11. **C.** SDRAM DIMMs have 168 pins. DDR DIMMs have 184 pins, and DDR2 DIMMs have 240 pins.

12. **D.** The cache controller pre-fetches data and instructions that it predicts the CPU will need. For this reason, a very small amount of cache is required for proper performance and extremely high hit rates. Cache is usually forged from SRAM, not slower SDRAM. Regardless of proximity to the CPU, slower memory would not be an improvement over standard RAM alone.

13. **B.** The Pentium II uses Slot 1, not Socket 1.

14. **D.** Onboard drive interfaces are ATA or SCSI interfaces built right the motherboard. Integrated Drive Electronics (IDE) places controller electronics on the drive. SATA has its own small connectors with fewer pins than a 34-pin floppy connector, 7 pins for the data connector and 15 pins for the power connector. Forty-pin connectors are for PATA only.

15. **C.** The direct-solder method attaches interfaces to the motherboard, along with supporting circuitry, so that fewer expansion cards and less cabling are necessary.

16. **D.** The BIOS is active as long as the machine is running. It must be able to accept interrupts from the operating system and communicate with hardware as a liaison for the operating system. Today's BIOS also handles power management, hot swapping, and thermal management after boot. This is so important that part of the BIOS is often loaded into RAM to speed up access to BIOS routines throughout your session.

17. **A.** Hyperthreading-capable processors appear to the operating system to be two processors. The operating system can schedule two processes at the same time, as in the case of symmetric multiprocessing (SMP), where two or more processors use the same system resources. The operating system must support SMP in order to take advantage of hyperthreading.

18. **D.** Microcode is the programming language that the CPU understands and operates on. All high-level application and operating-system instructions must eventually be broken down into microcode for the CPU to process. A single high-level instruction is typically broken down into several microcode instructions.

19. **A.** Parity is an error checking scheme only. The memory subsystem uses parity in some computers to make sure that data and instructions are not compromised as they travel along the frontside bus. There is not enough error information included in parity checking to allow even one-bit error correction.

20. C. Quite the opposite. DRAM requires frequent refreshing, or it loses its contents, much like a battery eventually loses its ability to power devices. SRAM is built in such a way that the presence of power allows it to keep its own contents fresh without a refresh cycle.

21. C. In order to reduce the heat output of DDR2, a lower voltage is used compared to that of DDR.

22. B. Double-sided modules have chips on both sides to offer more RAM per module, but the module satisfies the same bit width as a single-sided module.

23. A. The edge form-factors are different between SoDIMMs and MicroDIMMs and are not interchangeable.

24. B. A standard CD-ROM holds upwards of 640MB of data, nowhere near the 4.7GB of DVD-ROM. Although 52X denotes that these drives have a transfer rate 52 times that of the original 1X CD-ROM drives, techniques other than spin speed have had to be employed after a certain point. Only CD-R and CD-RW discs can be burned, not CD-ROM discs.

25. A. MicroCard is not an actual memory card format, although there is a new version of MMC known as MMCmicro Card as well as other "micro" formats.

26. A. Just like standard internal hard drives, no disk insertion is necessary or possible. External drive enclosures contain a standard internal hard disk drive.

27. C. Power supplies are rated by watts, the unit of measure for power. Power supplies are commonly in the 250W to 500W range, denoting how much the computer and its internal peripherals (and external peripherals, if devices such as a monitor are connected directly to the power supply externally) can draw from the power supply before issues arise.

28. A. The P8 and P9 connectors each have 6 pins and must be inserted with black ground wires together in the middle. Although P8 and P9 can be swapped, resulting in black not being together in the middle, these connectors are keyed so that you cannot turn them around on the same connector.

29. C. There are $1024 \times 768 = 786{,}432$ pixels at this resolution. Each pixel requires 32 bits, so $786{,}432 \times 32 = 25{,}165{,}824$ bits are required for 32-bit color, which provides a palette of over 4 billion colors per pixel. Dividing the number of bits by 8 reveals the number of bytes required for such color at this resolution: $25{,}165{,}824 \div 8 = 3{,}145{,}728$ bytes. 1MB is equivalent to 1,048,576 bytes, so there are $3{,}145{,}728 \div 1{,}048{,}576 = 3$MB of required video memory, making 1MB and 2MB insufficient for displaying this resolution. Of the choices offered, 4MB is the least amount of video memory that meets the stated requirements.

30. C. EGA is an older lower-resolution digital technology with a resolution of 640×350. The other three options are all analog NTSC baseband signal interfaces with resolutions as high as 650×480. Given that all three analog technologies are operating at this resolution, they have the potential to produce higher-quality output than does EGA. Composite, S-video, and component use different encoding techniques, using 1, 2, and 3 wires with increasing quality, respectively, meaning component video delivers the highest resolution at the highest quality.

31. C. Ethernet NICs can use 8-pin modular connectors for twisted-pair cabling, and they have a socket that can accept a boot-ROM to allow booting from the network.

32. A. USB 1.1 supports data rates of only 1.5MBps, which equates to 12Mbps, not 12MBps. USB 2.0 cables have far more shielding than those used with 1.1 but are backward compatible. The standard connectors have not changed across the versions of the specification.

33. D. Among these items, only printers ever used Centronics connectors.

34. B. Only extension cables have the same type of connector at both ends. Standard USB cables have a Type A connector at one end and a Type B connector at the other end.

35. C. When the first temperature threshold is reached, generally, the computer continues to operate but alerts you to the event. When the next threshold is reached, the computer shuts itself down to avoid damage.

36. D. UDMA drives operate in a similar fashion to standard ATA hard drives, but they benefit from the grounding of the 80-wire cables, which allow these drives to operate at their full potential. The BIOS should not be configured for DMA or PIO when using UDMA drives, however.

37. **A.** SCSI does not use master/slave for multiple drives on the same controller. It uses a series of 8 or 16 addresses. Devices at the physical ends of the chain must be terminated. Active termination uses voltage regulators inside the terminator. Use active termination whenever you have fast, wide, or Ultra SCSI devices on the chain and/or more than two SCSI devices on the chain.

38. **B.** Every SCSI chain is independent and unable to be expanded.

39. **D.** Most faceplates are removable for access to wiring, LEDs, and other components built into the faceplate. Never pry a faceplate from the chassis.

40. **A.** Canned compressed air is quite pure but not cheap when compared with air from a mechanical compressor. The can should not be inverted during use, and care should be taken to avoid spreading dust indoors and onto other components.

41. **D.** With a multimeter, by definition, you can measure voltage, current, and resistance. When dealing with alternating current, the positive and negative probes are always oriented the same, regardless of what you are measuring. Voltage is measured with the circuitry intact, whereas current must be measured inline with the circuitry; you must often detach components to do so.

42. **B.** The rule of thumb here is to change one thing at a time. If it doesn't work, you may have inadvertently created a new problem that will mask your solving the original problem. Put things back the way they were before you try anything else. Although it's true that more than one thing can be wrong, generally, multiple problems cause different symptoms. It is rare to find two problems manifesting the same symptom. Operate on one symptom at a time.

43. **D.** Although overheating causes damage to the CPU, which resides on the motherboard, damage to the motherboard itself from overheating is not common.

44. **D.** Keyboards are cheap. Replace a keyboard before spending valuable hours trying to repair one. Even a partial hour's worth of repair time can cost more than the price of a new keyboard. The customer will likely be happier with the new keyboard as well. Keyboards take a lot of abuse, and replacing them from time to time is part of the cost of computer ownership.

45. **C.** As campy as it sounds, *chip creep* is a longstanding industry term that refers to the gradual ejection of a chip from its socket due to frequent cycles of alternating heating and cooling.

46. **B.** Heat production is one of the biggest challenges facing laptop manufacturers, keeping performance of laptops slightly behind that of desktop computers and contributing to the higher cost of producing laptops. Standard external device connectivity is no different between laptops and desktops, nor is the functionality of internal components designed for the same purpose. Everything is a bit smaller and closer together, another factor contributing to increased cost of laptop production.

47. **C.** The Flip Chip Ball Grid Array (FCBGA) standard uses balls instead of pins for attachment to the motherboard, resulting in less area required over CPUs that employ pins for attachment. The FCBGA form factor is ideal for use in laptops.

48. **B.** Blanket statements can often be ruled out. Many laptops offer a universal bay for attachment of various drives and extra batteries.

49. **B.** It is true that the keys on a laptop keyboard are usually smaller than those on a full-size keyboard, but they must fit in a smaller space, so there is rarely room to reproduce the full-size keyboard on the laptop. However, key functions that are not represented directly are often reproduced as alternative functions on other keys. To access these alternative functions, you most often need to hold down a complementary key, such as Ctrl, Space, or a special function key (sometimes labeled *Fn*) while pressing the key on which the alternative function is labeled.

50. **B.** The Type II PC Card is by far the most popular implementation overall and the one used for these expansion cards.

51. B. Microwave is not a small-scale communications medium. Large antennae and repeaters must be set up to produce a highly dedicated communications network. Little difference exists with cellular technology, except for the size of the end devices and the commercial popularity of the network infrastructure. More and more cellular attachments and built-in components are making their way to laptops. Infrared and Bluetooth are two technologies designed for very short-range cord and cable replacement and thus are popular in the laptop arena.

52. D. Advanced Configuration and Power Interface (ACPI) defines common interfaces for hardware recognition and configuration and power management. APC is a manufacturer of power conditioning equipment. The other two terms are not standard.

53. B. Possibly owing to the fact that memory upgrades give you the most for your upgrade dollar, and because, unlike sound cards, memory can be upgraded incrementally, this type of upgrade is the most common. Laptops often have a small access panel on the bottom that secures with one or more screws. Removing the panel gives you access to the memory slots. Hard-drive access can be similar, but upgrading hard drives is less common. CD and DVD drives are more often slid into a multiuse bay, which does not require the removal of screws.

54. D. The interface for the external monitor is not related to the internal display. Changing the internal display does nothing for external monitor issues, as a general rule. However, it is possible that the key sequence that switches between external monitor, internal display, and both is set for only the external monitor, so there may be nothing wrong with the LCD.

55. D. Without the operating system, there is no need for the other types of software listed.

56. B. The command.com and cmd.exe applications are examples of shells that run on top of Windows to provide an interface similar to the original DOS command-line interface.

57. C. Datacenter is a highly advanced Windows server platform.

58. A. Red Hat recommends 192MB of memory and 4.5GB of free hard drive space to install their version of Linux. Other Linux distributions may have different recommended minimums.

59. C. When an item in the Start menu has a right-arrow next to it, you can hover over the item to expand a hidden submenu.

60. A. Provided the Windows XP setting is enabled, newly installed programs are temporarily highlighted on the Start menu.

61. A. Such icons are known as shortcuts and are links to the actual executable application. Deleting a shortcut removes only that icon, not the application it links to. One caveat: Deleting applications outside of Add or Remove Programs is more harmful than deleting shortcuts. Although you think you have found and eradicated the entire application, you are most likely leaving rubbish in the Registry as well as ancillary files and folders elsewhere on the hard drive, gradually reducing the performance of your system.

62. B. Each hard drive volume contains a folder named Recycled; these are represented as the collective Recycle Bin on the Desktop. CD drives, DVD drive, floppy drives, and certain other removable media do not have a Recycled folder, meaning that objects deleted from such a drive are permanently deleted, at least from the file system's perspective.

63. C. Double-clicking the title bar of a window alternates between maximizing the window and restoring it. It does not serve to close the window.

64. A. The System applet in Control Panel is another way to access the System Properties pages that are accessible by right-clicking My Computer and then clicking Properties.

65. A. To change the name of your computer, enter System Properties (for example, by double-clicking the System icon in Control Panel), and then click the tab labeled Computer Name. Finally, click the Change button on this page. In the resulting Computer Name Changes dialog, you can change the value in the Computer Name field, which may require domain-administrator credentials.

66. D. The Advanced tab of System Properties has Performance, User Profiles, and Startup and Recovery sections wherein these functions can be performed.

67. **D.** The Remote page in System Properties has a check box labeled Allow Remote Assistance Invitations to Be Sent from This Computer. This box must be checked in order to request remote assistance.

68. **B.** The main categories in the Registry are known as hives, and Registry keys are the subcategories beneath hives where values and their data are stored.

69. **D.** Virtual memory creates a hidden system file, called a page file or a swap file, in a nonfragmented area of the hard drive. The file is used to swap the contents of RAM in pages out to the hard drive when RAM is needed for other instructions and data. The use of virtual memory gives the impression of more RAM than is physically present.

70. **A.** NTLDR bootstraps the system by beginning the loading of the operating system. The other options describe, in order, BOOT.INI, NTOSKRNL.EXE, and NTDETECT.COM.

71. **D.** The NTDETECT.COM file configures the dynamic portion of the Registry with the current configuration information of the system as it starts up.

72. **C.** Memory chips only a few generations removed from those found on the original motherboards are mounted on memory modules to save space on motherboards and other circuit boards. Memory chips had to be spread out flat across the motherboard, whereas memory modules insert perpendicular to the motherboard, taking far less room.

73. **D.** Although extended partitions can accommodate multiple drive letters, there is no requirement for any partition to have more than one drive letter.

74. **A.** Microsoft operating systems, as well as most others, use an extension to the filename to signify the file's type. Furthermore, these extensions can be associated with an application, which can be used to launch the application automatically when the file is opened.

75. **B.** Microsoft's recommended free hard-disk space for Windows 2000 (2GB) was higher than that for Windows XP (1.5GB).

76. **C.** An unattended installation is not the use of an image file to make an exact duplicate of an original installation of the operating system, but instead uses an answer file to supply variable input to the installation process. Even using Sysprep to create an image for use with an operating-system installation requires the use of a third-party package to copy the image.

77. **C.** In order to reduce the instances of piracy, Microsoft has initiated the policy that their operating systems must be registered online or by phone before they are completely unlocked and legitimate. If the product is not activated with Microsoft, it will stop working when it reaches the activation deadline.

78. **A.** While running a 16-bit operating system, in this case DOS with a Windows 3.1 shell on top, you must run the 16-bit version of the 32-bit operating system's installation program: WINNT.EXE. For 32-bit operating systems (Windows 9*x* and later, that is), WINNT32.EXE is the necessary program.

79. **B.** Analyzing the fragmentation of your hard drive is done with a separate application known as Disk Defragmenter. Task Manager is not capable of revealing such information.

80. **C.** The F8 key, when pressed at the appropriate time early in the boot-up process, generates a menu of boot-up options that you can use to control how the operating system starts for diagnostic and troubleshooting purposes.

81. **C.** *Thrashing* is the correct term here. None of the others are valid terms for this phenomenon.

82. **C.** If anything, a printer driver is designed to make the printed output more closely resemble on-screen text and graphics.

83. **D.** Although scribing the image onto the drum might sound like the job of the transfer corona wire, there is no scribing or etching on the drum, which would limit its life and cause it to play out after only a few printings. The negative charge on the drum is selectively reduced so that the more negatively charged toner is attracted to the less negative, almost positive, charge of the areas on the drum that represent the image to be printed.

84. **D.** IEEE 802.1D is also known as Spanning Tree, which is completely unrelated to the topic at hand. The other three standards (parallel, FireWire, and wireless) provide for methods of communication between the printer and one or more computers.

85. **C.** The stepper motor moves the scanning head but is not part of it.

86. **D.** Although all the terms mean roughly the same thing, the industry term for aligning the print and scanning heads is *calibration*.

87. **A.** High humidity levels in the paper can cause such a problem, but dry paper does not. The drum and exit rollers are too far along in the paper path to cause jams at the point where the paper is first fed into the printer.

88. **A.** A working scanner will scan with no object present, so repositioning the object has nothing to do with such a problem.

89. **B.** Peer-to-peer networks are characterized by devices offering and requesting services on the network. In a true peer-to-peer network, no one device stands out as a server among the others. LANs can be made up of peer-to-peer, client-server, or both models in a hybrid arrangement.

90. **A.** IEEE 802.3 specifies the CSMA/CD media access method that Ethernet uses.

91. **D.** Of the protocols listed, only NetBEUI lacks the address structure to differentiate networks from the devices on those networks, making NetBEUI-based networks completely flat and unroutable.

92. **D.** The IPX address is made up of a 32-bit network ID for all devices behind the same router and a particular device's 48-bit MAC address, which serves as a unique host ID for that particular node to differentiate it from others on the same network.

93. **C.** Class C addresses start with a first-octet decimal value ranging from 192 to 223, inclusive. Class A is identified by values in the range 1 to 127, with 127 being reserved for software loopbacks. Class B ranges from 128 to 191, and Class D uses the range 224 to 239.

94. **B.** Twisted-pair cabling is manufactured to ANSI/TIA/EIA-568-B standards, which specify electrical performance limits for classifications known as *categories*. Categories are numbered starting at 1, with each higher number representing more stringent requirements to allow increasing frequencies to transmit data with an acceptable and predictable loss of quality.

95. **A.** POTS is limited by the FCC to a bit rate of 53Kbps. The other standards have upper limits starting at over twice this rate, some of them increasing on a somewhat regular basis.

96. **D.** Full-duplex (FD) communication allows bidirectional (duplex) communication simultaneously (full, as in full use of the bandwidth per link). Half-duplex (HD) communication allows bidirectional (duplex) communication, but only one direction at a time (half, as in half of the link's bandwidth at any one time). Simplex communication allows unidirectional communication only, as with public-address systems.

97. **A.** Viruses and worms affect the same systems and rival one another in their destructive ability. Worms do not burrow into applications but instead are self-contained and promote their own spreading and infection.

98. **B.** A wireless LAN (WLAN) can be secured, but it does not have to be. The other terms are all wireless security terms.

99. **C.** The flow of fresh, cooler air across the warmer internal components of a computer is vital to its health. If you contain the computer in an airtight enclosure, the computer will overheat and cease to work or will self-destruct, neither of which is generally desirable.

100. **C.** It is never in your best interest or the best interest of your employer for you to turn tail and run or transfer blame or responsibility to others. Identify with the pain and frustration of the customer, and work through the issue using your expertise and standard troubleshooting methods. Stay calm and in control.

Answer Sheets for Practice Test 2

(Remove This Sheet and Use It to Mark Your Answers)

Section 1
Multiple Choice Questions

1 Ⓐ Ⓑ Ⓒ Ⓓ Ⓔ	51 Ⓐ Ⓑ Ⓒ Ⓓ Ⓔ
2 Ⓐ Ⓑ Ⓒ Ⓓ Ⓔ	52 Ⓐ Ⓑ Ⓒ Ⓓ Ⓔ
3 Ⓐ Ⓑ Ⓒ Ⓓ Ⓔ	53 Ⓐ Ⓑ Ⓒ Ⓓ Ⓔ
4 Ⓐ Ⓑ Ⓒ Ⓓ Ⓔ	54 Ⓐ Ⓑ Ⓒ Ⓓ Ⓔ
5 Ⓐ Ⓑ Ⓒ Ⓓ Ⓔ	55 Ⓐ Ⓑ Ⓒ Ⓓ Ⓔ
6 Ⓐ Ⓑ Ⓒ Ⓓ Ⓔ	56 Ⓐ Ⓑ Ⓒ Ⓓ Ⓔ
7 Ⓐ Ⓑ Ⓒ Ⓓ Ⓔ	57 Ⓐ Ⓑ Ⓒ Ⓓ Ⓔ
8 Ⓐ Ⓑ Ⓒ Ⓓ Ⓔ	58 Ⓐ Ⓑ Ⓒ Ⓓ Ⓔ
9 Ⓐ Ⓑ Ⓒ Ⓓ Ⓔ	59 Ⓐ Ⓑ Ⓒ Ⓓ Ⓔ
10 Ⓐ Ⓑ Ⓒ Ⓓ Ⓔ	60 Ⓐ Ⓑ Ⓒ Ⓓ Ⓔ
11 Ⓐ Ⓑ Ⓒ Ⓓ Ⓔ	61 Ⓐ Ⓑ Ⓒ Ⓓ Ⓔ
12 Ⓐ Ⓑ Ⓒ Ⓓ Ⓔ	62 Ⓐ Ⓑ Ⓒ Ⓓ Ⓔ
13 Ⓐ Ⓑ Ⓒ Ⓓ Ⓔ	63 Ⓐ Ⓑ Ⓒ Ⓓ Ⓔ
14 Ⓐ Ⓑ Ⓒ Ⓓ Ⓔ	64 Ⓐ Ⓑ Ⓒ Ⓓ Ⓔ
15 Ⓐ Ⓑ Ⓒ Ⓓ Ⓔ	65 Ⓐ Ⓑ Ⓒ Ⓓ Ⓔ
16 Ⓐ Ⓑ Ⓒ Ⓓ Ⓔ	66 Ⓐ Ⓑ Ⓒ Ⓓ Ⓔ
17 Ⓐ Ⓑ Ⓒ Ⓓ Ⓔ	67 Ⓐ Ⓑ Ⓒ Ⓓ Ⓔ
18 Ⓐ Ⓑ Ⓒ Ⓓ Ⓔ	68 Ⓐ Ⓑ Ⓒ Ⓓ Ⓔ
19 Ⓐ Ⓑ Ⓒ Ⓓ Ⓔ	69 Ⓐ Ⓑ Ⓒ Ⓓ Ⓔ
20 Ⓐ Ⓑ Ⓒ Ⓓ Ⓔ	70 Ⓐ Ⓑ Ⓒ Ⓓ Ⓔ
21 Ⓐ Ⓑ Ⓒ Ⓓ Ⓔ	71 Ⓐ Ⓑ Ⓒ Ⓓ Ⓔ
22 Ⓐ Ⓑ Ⓒ Ⓓ Ⓔ	72 Ⓐ Ⓑ Ⓒ Ⓓ Ⓔ
23 Ⓐ Ⓑ Ⓒ Ⓓ Ⓔ	73 Ⓐ Ⓑ Ⓒ Ⓓ Ⓔ
24 Ⓐ Ⓑ Ⓒ Ⓓ Ⓔ	74 Ⓐ Ⓑ Ⓒ Ⓓ Ⓔ
25 Ⓐ Ⓑ Ⓒ Ⓓ Ⓔ	75 Ⓐ Ⓑ Ⓒ Ⓓ Ⓔ
26 Ⓐ Ⓑ Ⓒ Ⓓ Ⓔ	76 Ⓐ Ⓑ Ⓒ Ⓓ Ⓔ
27 Ⓐ Ⓑ Ⓒ Ⓓ Ⓔ	77 Ⓐ Ⓑ Ⓒ Ⓓ Ⓔ
28 Ⓐ Ⓑ Ⓒ Ⓓ Ⓔ	78 Ⓐ Ⓑ Ⓒ Ⓓ Ⓔ
29 Ⓐ Ⓑ Ⓒ Ⓓ Ⓔ	79 Ⓐ Ⓑ Ⓒ Ⓓ Ⓔ
30 Ⓐ Ⓑ Ⓒ Ⓓ Ⓔ	80 Ⓐ Ⓑ Ⓒ Ⓓ Ⓔ
31 Ⓐ Ⓑ Ⓒ Ⓓ Ⓔ	81 Ⓐ Ⓑ Ⓒ Ⓓ Ⓔ
32 Ⓐ Ⓑ Ⓒ Ⓓ Ⓔ	82 Ⓐ Ⓑ Ⓒ Ⓓ Ⓔ
33 Ⓐ Ⓑ Ⓒ Ⓓ Ⓔ	83 Ⓐ Ⓑ Ⓒ Ⓓ Ⓔ
34 Ⓐ Ⓑ Ⓒ Ⓓ Ⓔ	84 Ⓐ Ⓑ Ⓒ Ⓓ Ⓔ
35 Ⓐ Ⓑ Ⓒ Ⓓ Ⓔ	85 Ⓐ Ⓑ Ⓒ Ⓓ Ⓔ
36 Ⓐ Ⓑ Ⓒ Ⓓ Ⓔ	86 Ⓐ Ⓑ Ⓒ Ⓓ Ⓔ
37 Ⓐ Ⓑ Ⓒ Ⓓ Ⓔ	87 Ⓐ Ⓑ Ⓒ Ⓓ Ⓔ
38 Ⓐ Ⓑ Ⓒ Ⓓ Ⓔ	88 Ⓐ Ⓑ Ⓒ Ⓓ Ⓔ
39 Ⓐ Ⓑ Ⓒ Ⓓ Ⓔ	89 Ⓐ Ⓑ Ⓒ Ⓓ Ⓔ
40 Ⓐ Ⓑ Ⓒ Ⓓ Ⓔ	90 Ⓐ Ⓑ Ⓒ Ⓓ Ⓔ
41 Ⓐ Ⓑ Ⓒ Ⓓ Ⓔ	91 Ⓐ Ⓑ Ⓒ Ⓓ Ⓔ
42 Ⓐ Ⓑ Ⓒ Ⓓ Ⓔ	92 Ⓐ Ⓑ Ⓒ Ⓓ Ⓔ
43 Ⓐ Ⓑ Ⓒ Ⓓ Ⓔ	93 Ⓐ Ⓑ Ⓒ Ⓓ Ⓔ
44 Ⓐ Ⓑ Ⓒ Ⓓ Ⓔ	94 Ⓐ Ⓑ Ⓒ Ⓓ Ⓔ
45 Ⓐ Ⓑ Ⓒ Ⓓ Ⓔ	95 Ⓐ Ⓑ Ⓒ Ⓓ Ⓔ
46 Ⓐ Ⓑ Ⓒ Ⓓ Ⓔ	96 Ⓐ Ⓑ Ⓒ Ⓓ Ⓔ
47 Ⓐ Ⓑ Ⓒ Ⓓ Ⓔ	97 Ⓐ Ⓑ Ⓒ Ⓓ Ⓔ
48 Ⓐ Ⓑ Ⓒ Ⓓ Ⓔ	98 Ⓐ Ⓑ Ⓒ Ⓓ Ⓔ
49 Ⓐ Ⓑ Ⓒ Ⓓ Ⓔ	99 Ⓐ Ⓑ Ⓒ Ⓓ Ⓔ
50 Ⓐ Ⓑ Ⓒ Ⓓ Ⓔ	100 Ⓐ Ⓑ Ⓒ Ⓓ Ⓔ

Directions: For each of the following questions, select the choice that best answers the question or completes the statement.

1. Which of the following statements about a personal computer is not accurate?

   A. Most computers today are modular.
   B. Each component in a computer has a specific function.
   C. The primary circuit board in a personal computer is known as a motherboard.
   D. There is only one device on the market for each specific function within a personal computer.

2. Which of the following integrated motherboard components is not generally found on a non-integrated motherboard?

   A. NIC
   B. CMOS
   C. HDD header
   D. PCI slot

3. Which motherboard form factor dissipates heat best?

   A. ATX
   B. BTX
   C. LPX
   D. NLX

4. Which of the following best describes a chipset?

   A. The collection of all chips and circuits on the motherboard
   B. The CPU and RAM
   C. The collection of all chips and circuits in a computer that are not on the motherboard
   D. A collection of chips or circuits that performs functions for the CPU

5. Which of the following components is responsible for facilitating communications between the CPU and memory?

   A. BIOS
   B. Memory controller
   C. Northbridge
   D. Interrupt controller

6. Which of the following depends on the Northbridge for communication with the rest of the computer?

   A. Southbridge
   B. PCI
   C. IEEE 1284
   D. USB

7. Which of the following existed in the original personal computers?

   A. ISA
   B. PCI
   C. AGP
   D. DDR

8. Which of the following statements about PCIe is *not* true?

   A. A PCIe slot will not accommodate a PCI card.
   B. PCIe is capable of being faster than AGP.
   C. PCIe uses one or more lanes to communicate along the bus.
   D. Each PCIe slot is the same length.

9. Which of the following is *not* a speed level for PCIe?

   A. 1X
   B. 2X
   C. 3X
   D. 4X

10. Which of the following statements about memory is true?

    A. Today's motherboards take memory in the form of individual chips.
    B. Today's processors have memory on board, obviating the need for memory on the motherboard.
    C. Memory for today's computers is most often installed on a riser card.
    D. A variety of module types are in use today.

GO ON TO THE NEXT PAGE

11. Which *two* of the following pin counts can be found on SoDIMMs?

    A. 30
    B. 72
    C. 144
    D. 168

12. All of the following are accurate statements about the CPU *except*:

    A. For each generation of personal computer CPUs, there is only a single type of CPU.
    B. The CPU performs the majority of all computer functions.
    C. Modern CPUs generally require a fan, a heat sink, or both.
    D. Pentium is the trade name for the fifth major Intel CPU family.

13. Which of the following CPU/socket pairings is incorrect?

    A. Athlon: Socket A
    B. Celeron: Socket C
    C. Xeon: Socket 603
    D. Athlon 64: Socket 754

14. All of the following statements about the 80-wire UDMA cable are true *except*:

    A. Half the wires serve as ground wires.
    B. The cables are capable of higher transfer rates that 40-wire cables.
    C. The connectors attached to the cable have 80 contacts.
    D. There is less crosstalk among the 40 signal wires than with 40-wire cables.

15. Which of the following is the best description of firmware?

    A. A 3.5″ microfloppy, because its casing is more solid than that of a 5.25″ minifloppy
    B. Software that cannot be changed
    C. Flexible hardware
    D. Software embedded in hardware, such as a ROM chip

16. All of the following statements about the CMOS are true *except*:

    A. The CMOS chip is so named because it is the only chip manufactured by that process.
    B. The CMOS requires a battery to keep its contents when the computer is turned off.
    C. The CMOS holds alterations to the default BIOS settings.
    D. Resetting the BIOS to factory defaults erases the CMOS.

17. What is the term for the technology that provides circuitry for more than one processor in a single CPU package?

    A. HTT
    B. Multicore
    C. SMT
    D. Multiplicity

18. Which of the following statements about overclocking is false?

    A. Overclocking is the practice of using a clock signal that exceeds the rating for the CPU.
    B. Overclocking your CPU is always safe.
    C. You may need enhanced cooling methods when overclocking.
    D. Other components may be damaged by an overclocked CPU.

19. All of the following are true regarding ECC, *except*:

    A. ECC can detect up to two bit errors in the same memory access.
    B. ECC can correct single bit errors in a single memory access.
    C. ECC has been replaced by parity checking.
    D. The ECC algorithm is performed on each memory access.

20. Which of the following statements about standard SDRAM is *not* true?

    A. SDRAM is tied to the FSB and the processor for clocking.
    B. SDRAM is rated as PCx, where x is the clock rate of the system clock in MHz.
    C. You can find SDRAM's throughput in bytes by multiplying 8 bytes times the rated frequency.
    D. SDRAM derives its clocking from the inbound signal.

21. All of the following are terms related to Rambus memory *except*:

    A. RDRAM
    B. RDIMM
    C. RIMM
    D. Dual-channel

22. Which of the following Rambus memory pairings is *not* accurate?

    A. 16-bit: 168 pins
    B. 16-bit: two keying notches
    C. 32-bit: 232 pins
    D. 32-bit: one keying notch

23. Which of the following is *not* one of the three primary components of a hard-drive system?

    A. Modulator/Demodulator
    B. Controller
    C. Hard disk
    D. Host adapter

24. In looking for a replacement CD-RW drive for your computer, you want to make sure the CD-RW *rewrite* speed is as fast as the CD-RW *write* speed. You find a unit labeled 52X-32X-52X. How does this fulfill your requirement?

    A. Perfectly. The write and rewrite speeds are both 52X.
    B. Perfectly. The 32X refers to the speed of any type of burning.
    C. Not at all. The rewrite speed is only 32X, whereas the write speed is 52X.
    D. Incredibly. This unit writes at 32X and rewrites at 52X.

25. What is SDIO?

    A. A digital serial interface to replace USB
    B. A specification that is capable of bringing high-speed/low-power components to handheld mobile devices
    C. The underlying technology behind CD-ROM
    D. A competitor for S/PDIF

26. What are HD DVD and Blu-ray Disc?

    A. The two bestselling brand names of DVD-ROM drives from competing manufacturers
    B. Competing trade names for double-layered DVD offerings
    C. Next-generation DVD formats, capable of higher data capacities and true HDTV
    D. Computer DVD technologies that store video information only

27. With regard to power supplies, you must be careful of all of the following *except*:

    A. How the voltage selection switch is set
    B. How much of a load the system and its components place on the power supply
    C. The current that can be discharged inside the power supply's case
    D. Which way the fan rotates

28. All of the following statements about ATX, ATX12V, and EPS12V connectors are true *except*:

    A. Each one has a single multipin main connector that takes the place of P8/P9 in AT systems.
    B. The EPS12V and ATX12V main connectors are interchangeable.
    C. The ATX12V and EPS12V systems use a supplementary connector that supplies additional +12VDC leads.
    D. The ATX12V specification calls for a connector similar to P8 and P9 that supplies additional +3.3VDC and +5VDC leads.

29. Which video standard has widescreen capability and a maximum resolution of 1920 × 1200, and is capable of 32-bit color?

    A. SVGA
    B. XGA
    C. WXGA
    D. WUXGA

GO ON TO THE NEXT PAGE

30. What is dot pitch when discussing a CRT monitor?

    A. The shortest distance between two dot phosphors of the same color

    B. The angle at which the dot phosphors are struck by the electron beam, making curved monitors more brilliant at the edges than their flat-monitor counterparts

    C. Shooting arcs of light as if the pixel were thrown from one point on the monitor to another, requiring degaussing to mitigate the magnetic disturbance

    D. The perceptible movement of the screen image due to an interlaced refresh rate

31. What is the most accurate designation for a 9-pin male D-subminiature port that has one row of five pins and one row of four?

    A. DA9M

    B. DB9M

    C. DC9M

    D. DE9M

32. What is another way to refer to IEEE 1394?

    A. USB 2.0

    B. ECP

    C. FireWire

    D. Ethernet

33. All of the following statements about enhanced parallel ports are accurate *except*:

    A. They are specified by IEEE 1284.

    B. Two forms exist: ECP and EPP.

    C. They are on track to become the most common connectors for printer interfaces.

    D. They are faster than standard parallel ports.

34. Which of the following could apply to the terms *front intake*, *rear exhaust*, *CPU*, *chipset*, and *video-card chipset*?

    A. Module

    B. Chip

    C. Fan

    D. Controller

35. All of the following statements regarding ATA are true *except*:

    A. UltraDMA/133 is SATA.

    B. UltraDMA/100 supports maximum transfer rates of 100MBps.

    C. ATA-2 and higher are referred to as EIDE.

    D. ATAPI was introduced with ATA-3 to support devices other than hard drives.

36. How can you best identify pin 1 on a drive's flat ribbon cable?

    A. The number 1 is printed every inch on the side of the cable where pin 1 is located.

    B. There is a colored stripe along the side of the cable where pin 1 is located.

    C. An LED beside the connector lights when it detects pin 1 in the proper orientation.

    D. The keying in the connector always orients the cable properly.

37. Which of the following statements about SCSI termination is true?

    A. The SCSI adapter cannot be terminated.

    B. If you are in doubt about which devices to terminate, terminate them all.

    C. Only one device on the bus needs to be terminated.

    D. Termination does not follow address but rather physical position on the bus.

38. Which statement about RAID is true?

    A. RAID 0 does not provide fault tolerance.

    B. RAID 1 does not provide fault tolerance.

    C. RAID 5 does not provide fault tolerance.

    D. Fault tolerance is not a part of RAID. RAID is only designed to allow a single drive letter to span multiple drives.

39. Which of the following screwdrivers is most indispensable while working with most computers?

    A. Torx

    B. Philips

    C. Flat-blade

    D. Hex driver

40. Which of the following specific meters is not commonly included in a multimeter?

    A. Ammeter
    B. Wattmeter
    C. Voltmeter
    D. Ohmmeter

41. All of the following are benefits of a bootable floppy *except*:

    A. When the BIOS is inoperable, you can still boot to a floppy.
    B. When the hard drive is inoperable, you can still boot to a floppy.
    C. Corrupt operating systems and device-driver conflicts can be avoided by booting to a floppy.
    D. If you can boot to a floppy, you can rule out motherboard and memory issues.

42. In what way is the POST routine helpful in isolating problems?

    A. When you get to the end of the POST process, you can scroll back to check for errors reported by the components tested during POST.
    B. POST creates a log that can be reviewed for details that may isolate the problem.
    C. If a component tested by POST fails, POST usually halts at that point, indicating that the problem lies with that component.
    D. POST results are transmitted to the BIOS manufacturer over the Internet. For a fee, you can get a report of the results, possibly indicating problem areas.

43. What is the most common reason for a computer to repeatedly work for a short time and then lock up?

    A. Spilled liquids
    B. The motherboard resting on a metal standoff, shorting circuits underneath
    C. Overheating
    D. A failing power supply

44. All of the following BIOS settings are likely to get your IDE CD-ROM drive detected during boot-up *except*:

    A. None
    B. Auto
    C. ATAPI
    D. CD-ROM

45. When removing a card from a computer, what should you do if you do not intend to replace the card with another?

    A. Put a blank bracket in the slot.
    B. Leave the slot open to improve airflow.
    C. Leave the card in place but not seated.
    D. Leave the card in place, and disable it in the BIOS.

46. Which of the following is an internal component that you can purchase for a laptop without proprietary barriers?

    A. Motherboard
    B. Modem
    C. Hard drive
    D. Keyboard

47. Which of the following is a key addition to some laptop processors and chipsets when compared to processors and chipsets used in desktop computers?

    A. Internal cache
    B. An extra pipeline
    C. Higher voltage for increased performance
    D. Built-in wireless NIC

48. What is the term for the fixed resolution of an LCD display?

    A. Standard resolution
    B. Set resolution
    C. Native resolution
    D. Local resolution

49. Which of the following has never been a commonly built-in pointing device for a laptop?

    A. Mouse
    B. Touchpoint
    C. Touchpad
    D. Touch screen

GO ON TO THE NEXT PAGE

50. Which of the following options lists the CardBus component hierarchy in the correct order from highest to lowest level?

  A. Application; Card Services; Socket Services; CardBus slot

  B. Card Services; Application; Socket Services; CardBus slot

  C. Socket Services; CardBus slot; Card Services; Application

  D. Application; Socket Services; Card Services; CardBus slot

51. What is a docking station?

  A. A Wi-Fi hot spot, where laptop users gain Internet access

  B. A bay in a laptop into which an external drive chassis can be placed

  C. A device on which you can mount a laptop and to which external devices can be semipermanently attached

  D. A secure storage enclosure for a laptop

52. All of the following components must support ACPI for it to work *except*:

  A. The RAM

  B. The CPU

  C. The motherboard

  D. The operating system

53. Which of the following is the best practice for removing external components from a laptop?

  A. Stop the device first with the icon in the System Tray.

  B. It's external. Just remove it.

  C. Shut the device down in the BIOS before removing it.

  D. Uninstall the device in Device Manager before removing it.

54. Which of the following input devices is it sometimes possible to disable in Control Panel, making troubleshooting more difficult?

  A. Scanner

  B. Keyboard

  C. Pointing device

  D. Bar-code reader

55. All of the following are tasks that must be performed by an operating system *except*:

  A. Document formatting

  B. Disk and file management

  C. Device access

  D. Memory management

56. All of the following are required to support Plug and Play *except*:

  A. Plug and Play–compatible RAM

  B. A Plug and Play–compatible operating system

  C. A Plug and Play–compatible BIOS

  D. Plug and Play–compatible components

57. Which of the following Windows operating-system pairings have the most similar GUIs?

  A. 2000; XP

  B. 95; 2000

  C. 95; 98

  D. 98; 2000

58. All of the following can generally be found on the Windows Taskbar *except*:

  A. Start button

  B. Control Panel

  C. System Tray

  D. Buttons for active windows

59. If the My Computer icon does not display on the Desktop in Windows XP, how can you add it?

  A. You must have the original distribution disk to install it.

  B. Add it through the Add/Remove Windows Components utility in Add or Remove Programs.

  C. You must download it from Microsoft's website.

  D. Add it from the Desktop Items dialog under Display Properties.

60. In attempting to display your computer's IP configuration, you enter `ipconfig` in the Open field of the Run dialog and click OK. However, the information flashes and disappears before you are able to read it. What can you do to cause the display to hold until you close it?

A. As soon as the window pops up, press the Pause button on your keyboard.

B. Open a Command Prompt first, and then execute the `ipconfig` command from the command line.

C. Use the `-p` switch after the `ipconfig` command to pause the display until you press a key.

D. Select the Wait for Input check box in the Run dialog before clicking the OK button.

61. Which one of the following is *not* considered a standard Desktop icon?

A. Recycle Bin

B. My Computer

C. Control Panel

D. Network Neighborhood/My Network Places

62. All of the following methods permanently delete an object without involving the Recycle Bin *except*:

A. Hold down the Shift key while right-clicking the object and dragging it to the Recycle Bin.

B. Hold down the Shift key while dragging the object to the Recycle Bin.

C. Click the object, and then press Shift-Delete.

D. Right-click the object, and then click Delete in the shortcut menu while holding the Shift key.

63. Which of the following statements is *not* true?

A. By clicking on and dragging any of the four corners of a maximized window, you are able to resize it.

B. Restoring a maximized window usually makes it smaller.

C. A minimized window's only proof of its existence is a button on the Taskbar.

D. Maximizing, minimizing, and restoring a window can be accomplished from the window's Control box.

64. How can you achieve the same result as double-clicking the Display icon in Control Panel without doing so?

A. In any Explorer window, click Folder Options in the Tools menu.

B. Use the function-key sequence prescribed for this purpose by your system's manufacturer.

C. Right-click a blank area of the Desktop, and then click Properties.

D. Right-click My Computer, and then click Display.

65. What is the term that refers to Microsoft checking and certifying drivers as not being hazardous to the operating environment?

A. 3PC (third-party certification)

B. Driver registration

C. Driver certification

D. Driver signing

66. All of the following statements about System Restore are true *except*:

A. Windows sets restore points when certain events occur.

B. Restore points can be used to roll back the Windows configuration to a point before there were issues.

C. Windows automatically attempts to use the most recent restore point to recover from a catastrophic failure.

D. You can manually set a restore point.

67. At a command prompt, you attempt to enter the command `cd c:\program files`. The response to your attempt is `Too many parameters - files`. Which *two* of the following will allow you to accomplish your intended task?

A. Close the 16-bit Command Prompt you opened with command, open a 32-bit Command Prompt with cmd, and then try the same command.

B. Leave `files` off your command.

C. Use the command `cd c:\progra~1`.

D. Omit the space between `program` and `files`.

GO ON TO THE NEXT PAGE

68. Which Registry hive contains information about the associations of file extensions with applications?

    A. HKEY_CURRENT_USER

    B. HKEY_CLASSES_ROOT

    C. HKEY_LOCAL_MACHINE

    D. HKEY_CURRENT_CONFIG

69. What is the term used to describe the data structure that stores the contents of virtual RAM?

    A. Paging file

    B. Registry

    C. DIMM

    D. Sysvol

70. Which of the following describes the BOOT.INI system file?

    A. Starts the loading of the operating system

    B. A text file that points to the partitions where one or more operating systems are installed

    C. The core of the operating system that must remain loaded at all times, never being paged to disk

    D. Parses the system for current configuration information as the operating system starts, and creates the dynamic portion of the Registry

71. Which of the following is a utility that was offered in Windows 9x and higher but not in Windows 2000, which can be copied from Windows XP for use in Windows 2000 and is used to view and change a broad range of settings?

    A. IFCONFIG

    B. IPCONFIG

    C. MSCONFIG

    D. MSDIAG

72. Which operating system supports FAT16 and FAT32, but not NTFS?

    A. Windows 98

    B. Windows NT 4

    C. Windows 2000

    D. Windows XP

73. What is the name of the Windows utility that allows you to partition and format a hard disk?

    A. FDISK

    B. FORMAT

    C. Disk Management

    D. Device Manager

74. All of the following are advanced attributes for objects that Windows 9x did not offer *except*:

    A. Indexing

    B. Encryption

    C. Hidden

    D. Compression

75. If you find it necessary to install more than one Microsoft operating system on the same computer, how should you go about installing them?

    A. Install the oldest operating system first, and then work your way to the newest in chronological order.

    B. Installation order does not matter.

    C. You cannot install more than one operating system on the same computer.

    D. Install them all on the same partition.

76. In attempting to upgrade your Windows 2000 Professional operating system to Windows XP Professional, using a bootable CD, you find that every time you reboot with the CD in the drive, you keep coming to the Windows 2000 splash screen. Which of the following is *not* a possible reason for this result?

    A. You must press any key at a certain time during the boot process to boot to the CD-ROM, and you failed to do so.

    B. You have a copy of XP that is not able to upgrade Windows 2000.

    C. Your system's BIOS is set not to boot to the CD-ROM drive.

    D. You have a malfunction in the CD-ROM drive or a corruption of the XP disc.

77. All of the following are post-installation tasks that you may need to consider *except*:

    A. Update drivers.

    B. Run a final format on the installation drive.

    C. Install applications, and restore user data.

    D. Verify installation.

78. All of the following statements about virtual memory are true *except*:

A. Delete a swap file by setting the minimum and maximum sizes to zero.

B. In Windows 2000, increasing the size of the page file does not require you to reboot, but reducing it does.

C. Increasing the size of the swap file never reduces system performance.

D. Increasing virtual memory is rarely as good for performance as increasing RAM.

79. What is the name of the utility that allows you to display system, application, and security logs?

A. System Properties

B. Task Manager

C. Event Viewer

D. Computer Management

80. What is the name for the limited-functionality command-line utility that enables you to enter commands to repair certain problems with the operating system?

A. Command Prompt

B. CHKDSK

C. Scandisk

D. Recovery Console

81. Which one of the following is *not* a common form of printer?

A. Laser

B. Bubble-jet

C. Scanning

D. Impact

82. Which EP print process follows the charging step?

A. Writing

B. Cleaning

C. Developing

D. Fusing

83. You find that your printer squirts tiny droplets of ink onto the page in a pattern that forms characters and images. What type of printer is it?

A. Laser

B. Bubble-jet

C. Dot-matrix

D. Thermal

84. What are PCL and PostScript?

A. Page-description languages

B. Communications interfaces

C. Software drivers

D. Parallel-connector types

85. What is CCD?

A. A device that determines the resolution that a scanner can deliver to a computer by turning light into electrical impulses

B. The type of CD that a scanner with direct-CD output uses

C. The standards specification that governs the majority of all scanners in production today

D. A digital carbon copy, referring to attachments to e-mails provided by network-attached scanners

86. Which of the following dot-matrix symptoms is a result of the printer ribbon-advance gear slipping?

A. A blank line running through each line of print in the same position

B. A dark line running through each line of print in the same position

C. Lines of print with varying levels of darkness

D. Printing unintelligible garbage

87. Which laser-printer component has most likely failed in situations where all toner on the output page is loose?

A. Transfer corona wire

B. HVPS

C. Fuser

D. Cleaning blade

88. Which networking structures differ by the types of protocol they use and vastly by the geographic range they cover?

A. Switched LANs and routed LANs

B. LANs and WANs

C. T1 WANs and DS-3 WANs

D. Ethernet LANs and Token Ring LANs

89. How is an Ethernet LAN using hubs and switches described?

A. Logical star, physical bus

B. Physical star, logical ring

C. Logical mesh, physical bus

D. Physical star, logical bus

GO ON TO THE NEXT PAGE

90. Which of the following is *not* a protocol in the TCP/IP protocol suite?

    A. UDP

    B. ICMP

    C. IPX

    D. FTP

91. What are the two portions of an IP address called?

    A. Host; node

    B. Network; host

    C. Address; node

    D. Address; mask

92. What is the purpose of a subnet mask in IP addressing?

    A. By itself, it tells what subnet a node is a member of.

    B. It hides, or masks, the subnet number for security purposes.

    C. When used with the address, it marks where the network ID ends and the host ID begins.

    D. When mathematically applied to the IP address, it sets the subnet portion to all zeros and leaves the host portion visible.

93. Which of the following values is equivalent to 2^{24}?

    A. 48

    B. 256

    C. 65,536

    D. 16,777,216

94. Which of the following is the best transmission medium for long distances and when electrical interference is a factor?

    A. Coaxial

    B. Twisted pair

    C. Fiber

    D. Wireless

95. What does it mean for communications cabling to be plenum-rated?

    A. The jacket is more rugged, for installation in harsher environments.

    B. Plenum-rated cabling takes longer to burn in a fire than does PVC and is safer for open ventilation returns.

    C. PVC allows for only certain jacket colors. Plenum is a material that supports additional colors.

    D. Plenum-rated cabling has a much longer distance limitation than PVC.

96. What does the term VoIP refer to?

    A. Video transmissions are converted to IP packets for transmission over an IP network.

    B. Voice recorders with an Ethernet attachment send audio over an IP network.

    C. Voice traffic is converted to IP packets for transmission over an IP network.

    D. Variability of IP traffic ensures that no one source monopolizes the available bandwidth.

97. How does file-system security differ between FAT and NTFS file systems?

    A. File-system security is equivalent in the two files systems.

    B. FAT only allows securing of network shares. NTFS allows securing of individual files for local access as well.

    C. A user must be logged on for FAT file-system security to work. NTFS file-system security works all the time.

    D. FAT offers absolutely no security, locally or over the network.

98. All of the following are terms found in the field of data encryption *except*:

    A. Hashing

    B. Algorithm symmetry

    C. SHA

    D. PAP

99. With regard to protecting against damaging components with ESD, which of the following is *not* sound advice?

    A. Don't try to make your own antistatic wrist straps. Commercial models have a resistor to keep you from being the best path to ground.

    B. When you do not have an antistatic work area or wrist strap, just make sure to keep touching the antistatic bags that the components came in to bleed off any dangerous static charge.

    C. Don't wear an antistatic wrist strap when working with CRTs and power supplies.

    D. Keep the relative humidity in your work area from getting too low to avoid improved conditions for the development of static build-up.

100. All of the following are steps to follow in diagnosing a customer's problem *except*:

    A. Make an educated guess based on the symptoms.

    B. Have the customer reproduce the error.

    C. Identify recent changes.

    D. Have the customer describe the symptoms.

Answer Key for Practice Test 2

1. D	26. C	51. C	76. B
2. A	27. D	52. A	77. B
3. B	28. B	53. A	78. C
4. D	29. D	54. C	79. C
5. C	30. A	55. A	80. D
6. A	31. D	56. A	81. C
7. A	32. C	57. D	82. A
8. D	33. C	58. B	83. B
9. C	34. C	59. D	84. A
10. D	35. A	60. B	85. A
11. BC	36. B	61. C	86. C
12. A	37. D	62. A	87. C
13. B	38. A	63. A	88. B
14. C	39. B	64. C	89. D
15. D	40. B	65. D	90. C
16. A	41. A	66. C	91. B
17. B	42. C	67. AC	92. C
18. B	43. C	68. B	93. D
19. C	44. A	69. A	94. C
20. D	45. A	70. B	95. B
21. B	46. C	71. C	96. C
22. A	47. D	72. A	97. B
23. A	48. C	73. C	98. D
24. C	49. A	74. C	99. B
25. B	50. A	75. A	100. A

Answer Explanations for Practice Test 2

1. **D.** For any specific function, there are generally many manufacturers that offer such a device.

2. **A.** For non-integrated motherboards, NICs generally must be added as expansion cards.

3. **B.** The BTX form factor is designed in such a way as to promote heat dissipation well enough to allow passive cooling without the need for fans on the motherboard. None of the other form factors cool as well.

4. **D.** The motherboard's chipset integrates into one or more larger ICs the functions of a vast number of separate chips and circuits, which once took up considerable space. Chipsets are one of many reasons why motherboards are smaller today that originally. Chipsets do not, however, include all chips on the motherboard. There are still many chips present on the motherboard that are not part of the chipset.

5. **C.** The Northbridge portion of the chipset provides the frontside bus and effects communication between the CPU and RAM.

6. **A.** The Southbridge portion of the chipset supports I/O communications, including those of ports and expansion slots. It also relies on the Northbridge for its own functions.

7. **A.** Only ISA slots existed in the original personal computers. The other technologies were developed in the years that followed.

8. **D.** The longer a PCIe slot is, the more bandwidth it supports.

9. **C.** Speeds of PCIe slots are based on powers of 2. Because 2 raised to the 0 power equals 1, 1X is valid. 2X, 4X, 8X, 16X, and 32X are the other PCIe speed levels.

10. **D.** A variety of memory modules are in use today, and modules are inserted in slots directly on the motherboard in favor of individual chips. Although memory has been included in a multicavity module alongside the processor itself, only cache has been placed onboard the CPU.

11. **BC.** SoDIMMs come in 72- and 144-pin varieties. Earlier SIMMs had 30 pins, and SDRAM DIMMs have 168 pins.

12. **A.** Competition in the CPU market ensures that there will be multiple types of CPU in each generation. Intel and AMD, for example, often have competing models on the market at any time.

13. **B.** The Intel Celeron fits in a Socket 478, among a few others.

14. **C.** The additional 40 wires are ground wires that allow the cable to handle a higher bit rate, but because there are still only 40 data wires, the headers and connectors have only 40 contacts.

15. **D.** Firmware is so named because it is somewhere between hardware and software.

16. **A.** The CMOS chip was the first high-profile chip in personal computer systems to be manufactured by the complementary metal-oxide semiconductor process, which creates components that can be powered by a battery for long periods of time. It is the memory for changes to the BIOS, so this is an important characteristic when your system is powered down for extended periods of time. For lack of a better name, and because no other CMOS-manufactured chips were competing for the name at the time, the name of the process became the name of the chip. Not long after and still today, many other types of chip have been manufactured by this process.

17. **B.** HTT and SMT refer to an operating system's ability to support multiple processors or their equivalent, while also being able to operate on the faster modern single-core processors. Multicore refers to the fact that the core of the CPU packaging includes more than one independent processor.

18. **B.** Few things in this industry are *always* safe. Overclocking is far from being one of those things. The CPU can generate enough heat that if the heat isn't carried away from the CPU and surrounding circuitry properly and more aggressively than normal, serious damage can occur.

19. **C.** Parity checking is a more rudimentary form of error checking. ECC builds on parity checking by adding the ability to correct certain errors.

20. D. Unlike more basic DRAM, SDRAM is synchronous, which means it shares the clock of the frontside bus, or the external clock that the processor uses. This type of clocking is preferential but means that you must match the modules purchased to the rated frequency of the motherboard. SDRAM DIMMs transmit one bit per data pin per clock cycle. Because there are 64 bits, or 8 bytes, transferred in parallel by most of today's processors, you actually can determine the throughput in bytes by multiplying the clock frequency by 8 bytes, but not for DDR and higher. These technologies transfer more than one bit per cycle.

21. B. Although RIMMs resemble DIMMs, RDIMM is not the name given to the Rambus line of modules.

22. A. None of the Rambus modules match the 168-pin count of standard DIMMs. However, the 16-bit RIMMs have 184 pins like DDR DIMMs, although the keying is different.

23. A. Data is encoded onto a hard drive, not modulated. A modem is a modulator/demodulator and has nothing to do with hard drives.

24. C. CD-RW drives are marketed using a *write-rewrite-read* format based on these speeds.

25. B. The SD Input/Output (SDIO) specification is based on the technology behind SD memory cards and slots. SDIO is designed to bring the SD technology to ever-smaller mobile devices.

26. C. HD DVD and Blu-ray Disc are competing technologies vying for market share for the first generation of high-definition video disc products.

27. D. Power-supply fans always force air out the back of the computer system. Blowing air into the system would not serve to cool the components as well. Secondary chassis fans mounted on the opposite side of the case draw air into the case more powerfully than the power supply's fan is able to by itself, but the power supply's fan must still blow this forced air out the back of the system for proper cooling to occur.

28. B. The primary connector of the ATX12V specification has 20 pins. That of the EPS12V specification has 24. So does the primary connector of the ATX12V 2.0 standard, but that's a different standard from the original ATX12V mentioned in the question.

29. D. WUXGA is the only standard that satisfies all the stated characteristics. The closest alternative is WXGA, which provides for the widescreen aspect and 32-bit color but falls short with a maximum monitor resolution of only 1280 × 800.

30. A. Remember that a picture element, or pixel, is a software-based single point on the screen. Resolution, such as 1024 × 768, is derived from pixels. At the hardware level, however, there are dot phosphors, the chemical compounds lining the inside of the CRT's screen that glow red, green, or blue when struck by the cathode ray, which is a stream of electrons. The dot phosphors are arranged in a dot trio, one for each of the three primary colors. Dot pitch is the distance between neighboring dot phosphors that glow the same color.

31. D. Contrary to popular misconception, they aren't all DB connectors. Perhaps the ubiquitous, yet correctly named, DB25 parallel port started the trend. Nevertheless, there are five distinctly lettered designations in the D-subminiature series, each one defining a specific size of shell. Although the trend is to call a VGA interface a DB15-HD because of the higher density of pins in the same shell that houses only 9 pins for a serial interface, if you refer to these two interfaces by their appropriate name, DE15F and DE9M, respectively (the F and M represent gender), you can easily tell that they are the same size, based on *DE*. It becomes obvious then that the VGA interface must have its 15 pins packed in tighter than the serial interface's pins for them to both be in DE connectors. There is no need for special suffixes to signify density unless you insist on calling all D-sub connectors DB.

32. C. IEEE 1394 is more commonly known by Apple's name for it, FireWire.

33. C. Parallel ports enjoyed a long run of being the most popular printer interfaces, but today that title is steadily migrating toward USB ports.

34. C. Only *fan* works with all of these terms.

35. A. Think of UDMA as being equivalent to parallel ATA, not serial.

36. B. As odd as it may sound, never trust keying as the only guide for inserting flat ribbon-cable connectors into their headers. Every so often, you run across a header that is notched on both sides, allowing you to insert the connector either way. The colored stripe down one side of the cable is on the pin-1 side.

37. D. You must terminate exactly two devices on the SCSI bus, and these must be the devices at each end of the chain, regardless of their addresses on the bus.

38. A. Only RAID 0 defies its own name and offers no redundancy. This level of RAID builds one large volume, to which you can assign a single drive letter, from multiple drives with no parity for fault tolerance.

39. B. The vast majority of the screws in non-Compaq computers are Philips-head. Compaq was partial to Torx.

40. B. Wattage can be calculated by multiplying voltage by current, but multimeters do not measure wattage directly.

41. A. The BIOS must be in working order to be able to pass control to any bootable device, including a floppy drive.

42. C. If the correct answer is not immediately obvious, the process of elimination makes it so. There is no way to scroll the text created by the BIOS during POST. Although the operating system can be set to create a bootlog, the BIOS does not create one during POST. We haven't reached the point in the Internet age that the BIOS accesses the Web to report your POST results.

43. C. Of all the incorrect answers, a failing power supply could cause such a symptom, but heat would still be the most likely underlying cause. When the CPU overheats, it shuts down the system to prevent damaging itself.

44. A. There is a setting labeled *None*. It means that no drive is installed at that position and causes the system to not look for one. The other settings make the process fully automatic, fairly broad for ATA devices that are not hard drives, and quite specific, respectively.

45. A. You should always cover open slots on the backplane to maintain the engineered path for airflow inside the case. Leaving the slot open does not tend to cool the system but instead causes stagnant pockets of air that can heat to damaging temperatures. Never leave an unseated card in the system. There's always the possibility that it could become partially seated and short out the card, the motherboard, or both. Generally, you can disable only onboard components, not those plugged into expansion slots.

46. C. Hard drives are standardized in their size and interface. The other items often must be purchased from the manufacturer because of their proprietary nature. A modem on a PC Card is not considered internal, by the way.

47. D. Processors these days all have some sort of internal cache, or Level 1 cache, built into the CPU. The voltage on a laptop CPU is often less than that of a desktop CPU because lower voltage means less heat. Chipsets accompanying processors such as the Centrino and Celeron M are made for mobile devices and have built-in wireless NICs.

48. C. The native resolution of an LCD display is the fixed resolution that all aspect ratios must be adjusted to fit, sometimes resulting in distortion of the image.

49. A. By definition, a mouse is a separate input device, not one that is built in. The other options are input devices that are commonly built in.

50. A. The Application makes its way to the CardBus slot by directly accessing Card Services, which uses Socket Services to interface with the slot.

51. C. A docking station is a platform into which you can install a portable computer. The docking station typically contains slots for expansion cards, bays for storage devices, and connectors for peripheral devices, such as printers and monitors, resulting in a composite device somewhere between a standalone laptop and a full-fledged desktop computer. Usually, any interfaces on the laptop that are hidden by the docking station are replicated by the docking station.

52. A. ACPI is a power-management system that integrates the CPU, motherboard, and operating system, forming an intelligent power conservation and control consortium. There is no special requirement for RAM to support ACPI in order for the system to benefit from ACPI.

53. **A.** The System Tray holds an icon that you can use to stop removable devices and safely remove them without causing damage to the system or the component.

54. **C.** A complaint of a nonworking built-in pointing device does not always indicate a serious problem. Be sure to ask the user if the device ever worked. If so, then check the settings in Control Panel; but there may be other problems. If the user reports that the pointing device has never worked, it could be that they have never used it, tried it out of the blue, and found that it does not work. In this case, enabling it in Control Panel is almost certain to work.

55. **A.** Document formatting is the job of an application such as a word processor. The operating system is required to save or load the document and manage the copy of the document in memory as well as print the document, for example.

56. **A.** RAM does not need to support Plug and Play, nor is RAM Plug and Play compatible. The operating system needs to work with the BIOS and the Plug and Play compatible component for this feature to function properly.

57. **D.** The GUI of Windows 2000 was based on that of Windows 98 with only minor enhancements and the return of the right-click from the more secure Windows NT series. Windows NT appeared similar to Windows 95, and Windows XP looks very similar to Windows Me.

58. **B.** It is true that you can place almost anything you like on the Quick Launch bar beside the Start button, but Control Panel is not generally found anywhere on the Taskbar.

59. **D.** To show or hide the standard Desktop icons, double-click the Display icon in Control Panel; click the Customize Desktop button on the Desktop page; and check or clear the boxes in the Desktop Icons section for the icons you want to show or hide, respectively.

60. **B.** Certain command line–only programs need to be executed from a stable Command Prompt window, not from the Open field of the Run dialog, which executes the command in a Command Prompt window and then shuts down the window when the command finishes running. This interface is best for accessing network shares or running standalone applications, such as Command Prompt, not CLI commands (such as `ipconfig` and `ping`, to name a couple).

61. **C.** Control Panel can be accessed from multiple locations, but unless you add a shortcut there, the Desktop is not one of the standard places it can be found.

62. **A.** Through various combinations that involve the Shift key or right-clicking, permanent deletion can be performed; but combining the two is not one of the methods that works.

63. **A.** A maximized window cannot be resized without first restoring it. Once it is no longer maximized, the edges and corners become active, allowing you to interactively resize the window.

64. **C.** The Display applet in Control Panel gives you access to the Display Properties dialog pages. One shortcut that bypasses Control Panel is to right-click an otherwise unaffiliated blank spot on the Desktop and choose Properties from the shortcut menu.

65. **D.** Driver signing is Microsoft's term for the way it certifies drivers as having been tested and approved for use in the Windows environment.

66. **C.** Windows will not automatically attempt to restore your system. You have to do that yourself. Unfortunately, if the failure is bad enough, restore points will be of no use. As a companion to restore points, you should regularly back up your system. Use the option that creates a system recovery disk so that you do not need to reinstall the operating system first.

67. **AC.** The first correct option places you in the correct shell for what you are attempting. The 16-bit shell is a throwback to the old days of DOS, whereas the 32-bit version has all the enhancements. The second correct option keeps you in the 16-bit shell but changes the command structure to one that is compatible. If the long name does not fit in the 8.3 format the 16-bit shell requires, it is given an alias made up of the first six characters of the name followed by a tilde (~) and a sequential number (in case multiple files in the same folder begin with the same six characters). The first three characters of the long name's extension are used as the extension in the 16-bit shell.

68. B. HKEY_CURRENT_USER holds configuration information about the currently logged-on user. It gets its information from HKEY_USERS, which holds similar information for all users who have ever logged on to the machine. HKEY_LOCAL_MACHINE holds configuration information about the system's hardware and software. HKEY_CURRENT_CONFIG holds a smaller subset of the more popular keys found in HKEY_LOCAL_MACHINE.

69. A. Virtual RAM uses a page file, or swap file, on a contiguous area of the hard drive to swap data and instructions with RAM so the CPU always works with RAM for its needs. As a result, the operating system believes there to be more RAM than there actually is.

70. B. The BOOT.INI file is a basic text file that uses Advanced RISC Computing (ARC) syntax to specify the path where the primary operating-system files are located. Multi-boot systems have multiple ARC paths in the BOOT.INI file, one for each operating system, each one pointing to the drive and partition where an operating system can be found as well as which one should be started by default.

71. C. Microsoft brought back MSCONFIG for Windows XP after leaving it out of Windows 2000.

72. A. Windows NT 4 supports NTFS and FAT16. Windows 2000 and Windows XP support all three file systems.

73. C. The FDISK utility partitions drives, whereas the FORMAT utility formats the partitions. Device Manager does neither, and Disk Management does both.

74. C. Hidden files have been around since the early days of DOS.

75. A. Newer operating systems understand the needs of older ones. The newer operating systems can offer the boot process for the older operating systems, resources required at startup, and a mechanism to point to where the older operating system is installed and how to pass control to it. In light of this, the older operating system must already be there, or the newer operating system won't be able to work with it after the fact. Additionally, the older operating system may not recognize the new one and insist on installing itself clean, wiping out the newer operating system during installation.

76. B. XP will always upgrade 2000. Check the other situations to make sure your system is configured to boot to the CD-ROM drive and that you are not missing the opportunity to confirm booting from the CD-ROM.

77. B. Running a final format on the installation drive will destroy your installation. This is decidedly not compatible with a working installation.

78. C. It is possible to detrimentally affect performance by increasing the size of the swap file. If you do not believe that Windows is managing virtual memory in an adequate fashion, which is highly unlikely, you need to use trial and error or benchmark utilities to measure the effect of changing the size of the swap file.

79. C. Control Panel has an icon called Administrative Tools. Event Viewer is one of the tools found in the Administrative Tools folder.

80. D. The Recovery Console seems limited in functionality when compared to the full-featured Command Prompt. CHKDSK and Scandisk are not CLIs. With the Recovery Console, you have a slew of administrative utilities in a command-line format that allow you to resolve file-system problems without being able to get to the GUI, but you do not have access to all the features of the Command Prompt.

81. C. Printers fall into a very few categories, of which scanning is not one.

82. A. The electrophotographic print process follows these steps in order: cleaning, charging, writing, developing, transferring, and fusing.

83. B. The bubble-jet printer, which is a close cousin to the ink-jet family, is operating normally when it displays this behavior.

84. A. Page-description languages are programming languages that the printer driver compiles to send to the printer. The printer uses the code to construct the page in its memory and subsequently print it. If you knew how to write code directly, it is conceivable that you could create a text document containing such code and send it to the printer to produce similar results.

85. A. Charge-coupled devices essentially convert light photons to electrical impulses that can be used to drive electrical circuitry for the purpose of storing scanned material. Digital cameras and camcorders use CCDs as well.

86. C. When a dot-matrix printer's ribbon-advance gear begins to slip, at almost random times the ribbon remains in the same place too long, such that printed output becomes lighter as it wears out the ink in that portion of the ribbon. Normally advanced ribbon is not worn out as much and produces darker output.

87. C. The fuser's job is to heat the toner and melt it to the page. When this component fails, the toner remains on the surface of the page and is easily removed.

88. B. The paired networks in each option, except LANs and WANs, are too similar in type and geographical reach to satisfy this question.

89. D. Ethernet devices even today believe they are on a shared bus architecture. That's the point of CSMA/CD. However, this describes the logical view of the network. Most networks today are wired from a system of closets or telecommunications rooms out to end stations in a sort of hub-and-spoke, or star, configuration, leading to the phrase *physical star, logical bus*.

90. C. Novell's IPX is the cornerstone of an antiquated, if not defunct, TCP/IP competitor known as IPX/SPX.

91. B. Although network and node are perfectly acceptable, the only response that means the same thing is network and host.

92. C. The purpose of the subnet mask is to delineate the network and host portions of an IP address. Through the binary AND operation, the zeros in the mask turn all corresponding ones and zeros in the ANDed address into zeros as well. This enables routing and end devices to first pay attention to the destination network before becoming concerned with the end device on that network to which the address pertains. This simplifies routing in the same way that mail is delivered to a region based on the first part of the ZIP code before anyone worries about the city and postal patron that are also referenced in the complete address. The postal service ignores, or masks, the pertinent portion of the address until it is needed. Similarly, the portion of the IP address that is being masked is not removed—it's simply ignored.

93. D. It helps to memorize some milestones. For example, memorize the powers of 2 whose exponents are multiples of 10. 2^{10} is roughly equivalent to 1000. From there, the rough calculations come close to the real thing if you multiply the previous value by 1000. So, 2^{20} is roughly 1,000,000, and 2^{30} is roughly 1,000,000,000. Thus 2^{24} must be greater than 1 million but less than 1 billion.

94. C. Fiber is great for long-haul transmission and is not susceptible to electrical phenomena, such as lightning strikes, signal induction, and eavesdropping.

95. B. Occasionally, you will hear that plenum-rated cable does not burn or that it does not give off poisonous fumes. Everything burns, but at varying temperatures. Such is the case with cable that is rated to meet code that requires slow-to-burn cable in plenums, which are the type of open ventilation return systems found in some dropped ceilings or raised floors where ventilation ductwork is not used to return ambient air to the system for conditioning. The Teflon-equivalent coating of plenum-rated cabling takes longer to burn, but when it does burn, the fumes it gives off are just as deadly as those from PVC. Everyone just has a better chance of getting out before the fumes fill the air.

96. C. Voice over IP is one of the latest technologies to enjoy mainstream support. It works by taking normal analog voice and encoding it into a digital bit stream ready for packetization and transmission across an IP network.

97. B. Share-level security is OK, but when a user sits down at the machine that hosts the secured share, a FAT file system has no mechanism to prevent a user who is unable to access the share from accessing the resource on which the share is based. If you can't access a network share, you may still be able to sit down at the share's hosting machine and access the folder the share points to. But with the NTFS file system, you can secure the local file as well, potentially making sure that anyone blocked from accessing the share is also blocked from directly accessing the resource by logging on to the hosting device.

98. D. PAP, the Password Authentication Protocol, matches access credentials against an access-control list of some sort. Not only are the data transferred not encrypted, but the authentication credentials are passed as clear text as well.

99. B. Antistatic bags and foam packing materials keep static influences away from the devices they contain, but they do nothing to discharge static. Touching these materials does not make it safe to handle the components packaged inside.

100. A. Education is wonderful, but guesses can lead to errors and longer service calls that reduce a customer's confidence in the technician. Follow the standard recommended troubleshooting process for consistent success in diagnosing problems.

Answer Sheets for Practice Test 3

(Remove This Sheet and Use It to Mark Your Answers)

Section 1
Multiple Choice Questions

CUT HERE

1 (A) (B) (C) (D) (E)		51 (A) (B) (C) (D) (E)
2 (A) (B) (C) (D) (E)		52 (A) (B) (C) (D) (E)
3 (A) (B) (C) (D) (E)		53 (A) (B) (C) (D) (E)
4 (A) (B) (C) (D) (E)		54 (A) (B) (C) (D) (E)
5 (A) (B) (C) (D) (E)		55 (A) (B) (C) (D) (E)
6 (A) (B) (C) (D) (E)		56 (A) (B) (C) (D) (E)
7 (A) (B) (C) (D) (E)		57 (A) (B) (C) (D) (E)
8 (A) (B) (C) (D) (E)		58 (A) (B) (C) (D) (E)
9 (A) (B) (C) (D) (E)		59 (A) (B) (C) (D) (E)
10 (A) (B) (C) (D) (E)		60 (A) (B) (C) (D) (E)
11 (A) (B) (C) (D) (E)		61 (A) (B) (C) (D) (E)
12 (A) (B) (C) (D) (E)		62 (A) (B) (C) (D) (E)
13 (A) (B) (C) (D) (E)		63 (A) (B) (C) (D) (E)
14 (A) (B) (C) (D) (E)		64 (A) (B) (C) (D) (E)
15 (A) (B) (C) (D) (E)		65 (A) (B) (C) (D) (E)
16 (A) (B) (C) (D) (E)		66 (A) (B) (C) (D) (E)
17 (A) (B) (C) (D) (E)		67 (A) (B) (C) (D) (E)
18 (A) (B) (C) (D) (E)		68 (A) (B) (C) (D) (E)
19 (A) (B) (C) (D) (E)		69 (A) (B) (C) (D) (E)
20 (A) (B) (C) (D) (E)		70 (A) (B) (C) (D) (E)
21 (A) (B) (C) (D) (E)		71 (A) (B) (C) (D) (E)
22 (A) (B) (C) (D) (E)		72 (A) (B) (C) (D) (E)
23 (A) (B) (C) (D) (E)		73 (A) (B) (C) (D) (E)
24 (A) (B) (C) (D) (E)		74 (A) (B) (C) (D) (E)
25 (A) (B) (C) (D) (E)		75 (A) (B) (C) (D) (E)
26 (A) (B) (C) (D) (E)		76 (A) (B) (C) (D) (E)
27 (A) (B) (C) (D) (E)		77 (A) (B) (C) (D) (E)
28 (A) (B) (C) (D) (E)		78 (A) (B) (C) (D) (E)
29 (A) (B) (C) (D) (E)		79 (A) (B) (C) (D) (E)
30 (A) (B) (C) (D) (E)		80 (A) (B) (C) (D) (E)
31 (A) (B) (C) (D) (E)		81 (A) (B) (C) (D) (E)
32 (A) (B) (C) (D) (E)		82 (A) (B) (C) (D) (E)
33 (A) (B) (C) (D) (E)		83 (A) (B) (C) (D) (E)
34 (A) (B) (C) (D) (E)		84 (A) (B) (C) (D) (E)
35 (A) (B) (C) (D) (E)		85 (A) (B) (C) (D) (E)
36 (A) (B) (C) (D) (E)		86 (A) (B) (C) (D) (E)
37 (A) (B) (C) (D) (E)		87 (A) (B) (C) (D) (E)
38 (A) (B) (C) (D) (E)		88 (A) (B) (C) (D) (E)
39 (A) (B) (C) (D) (E)		89 (A) (B) (C) (D) (E)
40 (A) (B) (C) (D) (E)		90 (A) (B) (C) (D) (E)
41 (A) (B) (C) (D) (E)		91 (A) (B) (C) (D) (E)
42 (A) (B) (C) (D) (E)		92 (A) (B) (C) (D) (E)
43 (A) (B) (C) (D) (E)		93 (A) (B) (C) (D) (E)
44 (A) (B) (C) (D) (E)		94 (A) (B) (C) (D) (E)
45 (A) (B) (C) (D) (E)		95 (A) (B) (C) (D) (E)
46 (A) (B) (C) (D) (E)		96 (A) (B) (C) (D) (E)
47 (A) (B) (C) (D) (E)		97 (A) (B) (C) (D) (E)
48 (A) (B) (C) (D) (E)		98 (A) (B) (C) (D) (E)
49 (A) (B) (C) (D) (E)		99 (A) (B) (C) (D) (E)
50 (A) (B) (C) (D) (E)		100 (A) (B) (C) (D) (E)

Directions: For each of the following questions, select the choice that best answers the question or completes the statement.

1. Which of the following best describes a motherboard?

   A. An important component that connects other components together
   B. Any circuit board manufactured by IBM, the mother of all personal computers
   C. The circuit board that connects the rest of the components to the fatherboard
   D. A synonym for network interface controller card

2. Which of the following statements about integrated motherboards is most correct?

   A. The motherboard is integrated into the case and cannot be removed.
   B. The power supply is integrated into the motherboard and cannot be replaced separately.
   C. Sometimes, you can disable malfunctioning components and replace them with expansion cards.
   D. All components that were once on expansion cards are integrated into the motherboard, and no expansion slots are available.

3. Which of the following motherboard form factors places expansion cards parallel to the motherboard?

   A. NLX
   B. microATX
   C. BTX
   D. ATX

4. Which of the following statements concerning chipsets is most accurate?

   A. The chipset provides physical connecting points for all peripherals.
   B. The CPU is the largest chip in the chipset.
   C. Northbridge is the largest manufacturer of chipsets.
   D. The chipset dictates how a CPU communicates with the installed peripherals.

5. All of the following are functions of the Northbridge subset of a motherboard's chipset *except*:

   A. Manages high-speed peripheral communication
   B. Manages processor-to-memory communication
   C. Supports communication between peripherals, such as IDE, parallel and serial ports, and FDD, and the rest of the computer
   D. Utilizes a frontside bus and a backside bus

6. Which of the following is *not* supported by the Southbridge?

   A. Integrated audio
   B. AGP
   C. USB
   D. PS/2 keyboard and mouse

7. Which of the following expansion slots is *not* paired with its characteristic color?

   A. ISA: beige
   B. AGP: brown
   C. PCI: white
   D. PCIe: black

8. Which of the following is an advantage of AMR and CNR slots?

   A. Allow a motherboard to pass FCC certification more quickly
   B. Make the motherboard run more efficiently
   C. Increase the speed of the CPU
   D. Create the frontside bus without the need for a chipset

GO ON TO THE NEXT PAGE

9. Which of the following statements about PCIe slots is *not* true?

    A. PCIe slots will not accept a PCI card.

    B. The 8X slots will accept a 16X card.

    C. The 32X slots will accept a 1X card.

    D. PCIe slots are designed to replace both PCI and AGP.

10. How does a DIMM slot differ from a SIMM slot?

    A. DIMM slots have fewer pins than SIMM slots.

    B. The pins on one side of the DIMM slot are separate from the pins on the other side.

    C. SIMM slots are not keyed.

    D. DIMMs are inserted perpendicular to the slot, whereas SIMMs slide in from the side.

11. All of the following are accurate statements regarding cache memory, *except*:

    A. More expensive SRAM is used for cache.

    B. L1 cache is internal to the processor.

    C. L2 cache is external to the primary CPU circuitry.

    D. With enough cache, there is no need for RAM.

12. What is the term for the piece of hardware that passively draws heat away from a component?

    A. Fan

    B. Power supply

    C. Heat sink

    D. Thermal grease

13. Which of the following most accurately describes the purpose of the motherboard's power-supply connector?

    A. The interface that connects the motherboard to the power supply.

    B. The interface to which all internal devices connect for power.

    C. The connector that joins the secondary power supply to the primary power supply.

    D. The power supply has its own connectors. There is not one on the motherboard.

14. Which of the following is *not* a method of keyboard attachment?

    A. ATX

    B. AT

    C. PS/2

    D. USB

15. Which of the following statements about the BIOS is true?

    A. The BIOS knows about all hardware installed in the computer.

    B. Today's BIOS cannot be updated for new hardware.

    C. You cannot alter the default settings of the BIOS.

    D. The BIOS allows the processor and operating system to interact with other hardware in the computer.

16. Which *two* of the following might be used to allow manual configuration of certain settings right on the motherboard?

    A. Fuses

    B. DIP switches

    C. Jumpers

    D. Resistors

17. What is meant by the term *CPU throttling*?

    A. Multiplying the CPU's rated speed for faster production

    B. Short bursts of extra CPU cycles to avoid overheating the processor

    C. Controlling how much of the CPU's time an application receives

    D. Shutting down the CPU in times of low usage

18. What does a voltage regulator module do?

    A. Prevents power spikes from making it through the power supply and into the motherboard

    B. Allows the user to choose between 110VAC and 220VAC

    C. Plugs into the wall power outlet to regulate what the power supply receives

    D. Allows the CPU to request the voltage it needs, and then supplies that voltage

19. Which of the following is *not* a form of DRAM?

A. SDRAM

B. SRAM

C. DDR

D. RDRAM

20. All of the following statements about DDR SDRAM are accurate *except*:

A. DDR modules are named the same as SDR SDRAM modules that use the same clock rate.

B. DDR creates the effect of a clock rate that is twice as fast as that of SDR SDRAM.

C. DDR achieves a throughput of 1600MBps with a 100MHz clock rate.

D. DDR uses both edges of the bipolar clock signal to transfer data.

21. Which of the following is *not* a form of ROM?

A. PROM

B. EPROM

C. EEROM

D. EEPROM

22. Which of the following statements about Rambus memory is true?

A. To satisfy a dual channel with 16-bit modules, you need to install only a single module at a time.

B. Care must be taken when dealing with RDRAM because the 16- and 32-bit modules are not compatible but fit into the same slot.

C. All unused Rambus slots must have CT-RIMMs installed.

D. A 32-bit module is basically two 16-bit modules.

23. All of the following acronyms apply to floppy disks *except*:

A. CD

B. DD

C. ED

D. HD

24. All of the following are differences between CD-ROM and DVD-ROM technologies *except*:

A. DVD-ROM technologies are split between plus (+) and dash (−) formats, whereas CD-ROM has only dash formats.

B. DVD-ROM has a double-layered variant, unlike CD-ROM.

C. DVD-ROM technologies are better suited for video recordings than CD-ROM technologies.

D. A DVD+R disc has a maximum capacity four times that of a CD-R disc.

25. What is a thumb drive?

A. A hard drive that requires a recognized thumbprint before access can be granted

B. A USB-attached solid-state flash storage solution

C. A drive that takes disks that are roughly the size of the average human thumb

D. A trackball mouse, which requires the use of the thumb to move the cursor on the screen

26. All of the following are voltages supplied by a power supply *except*:

A. +3.3VDC

B. −3.3VDC

C. +5VDC

D. −12VDC

27. All of the following apply to internal peripheral power connectors *except*:

A. Berg and Molex

B. Red, yellow, and black wires

C. RAID

D. Keying

28. What is ATX12V 2.0?

A. A specification that adds four connectors to the main connector of ATX12V to support PCIe

B. Another name for EPS12V

C. A software upgrade to ATX12V 1.1

D. The additional connectors added on to ATX to form ATX12V

GO ON TO THE NEXT PAGE

29. What does DVI-I refer to?

    A. Integrated audio and video

    B. Integrated analog and digital video

    C. Increased digital clarity

    D. Improvised analog video that rivals the quality of pure-digital video

30. All of the following are possible points to be made in a discussion of active- and passive-matrix LCDs *except*:

    A. An active-matrix LCD provides a transistor for each pixel, whereas a passive-matrix LCD provides one for each row and one for each column.

    B. Image quality is better on an active-matrix LCD.

    C. Active-matrix LCDs can be switched to passive-matrix mode to conserve power.

    D. Passive-matrix LCDs respond more poorly to changes in the screen image.

31. Which pairing represents a modem jack that connects to a phone line and an Ethernet interface for twisted-pair?

    A. RJ-12; RJ-45

    B. RJ-11; RJ-45

    C. RJ-11; RJ-48X

    D. DE9; RJ-45

32. What is the technology that uses an RCA jack with coaxial or fiber cable for enhanced digital sound?

    A. DVI

    B. S/PDIF

    C. HDMI

    D. Minijack

33. What type of cable can be used to connect two computers back-to-back for direct transmission to one another?

    A. Standard serial

    B. Null modem

    C. USB

    D. Direct-connect

34. All of the following statements regarding the cooling of memory and hard drives are true *except*:

    A. A passive cooling solution used with one also cools the other.

    B. Passive methods, such as heat sinks, can be employed.

    C. Fans and liquid cooling systems can be used as active cooling methods.

    D. In some cases, no additional cooling above and beyond the standard methods employed by the system unit is required.

35. Which of the following statements about IDE is true?

    A. IDE supports a theoretically unlimited number of devices on a controller.

    B. When copying from one CD drive to another, it is best to have both devices on the same IDE controller.

    C. With more than two installed IDE devices, faster devices should be put on the same controller, and slower devices should be put on another controller.

    D. No hardware or software configuration is necessary when placing IDE devices on the same controller.

36. Which of the following is *not* a valid SCSI type/pin-count pairing?

    A. SCSI-1; 50-pin D-sub

    B. SCSI-2; 50-pin D-sub

    C. SCSI-2; 68-pin D-sub

    D. SCSI-3; 80-pin D-sub

37. Which of the following statements about internal and external SCSI devices is true?

    A. External devices cannot be terminated, so they must not be in a position to require termination.

    B. External devices are connected in the same fashion as internal devices, on a single cable with multiple connectors.

    C. External devices have their own power supply.

    D. External devices require no address but instead appear as one device on the bus.

38. When servicing CRT monitors, which of the following is a consideration?

   A. Keep the monitor plugged in to power to retain the protective ground.

   B. Discharge the flyback transformer's charging capacitor before attempting to service high-voltage components.

   C. Give the monitor ten minutes after turning it off to drain dangerous charges.

   D. Degauss the monitor to remove dangerous charges.

39. Which of the following is the best method for removing dust from the inside of a computer?

   A. Compressed air

   B. Vacuum

   C. Cloth

   D. Damp sponge

40. When testing resistance with a multimeter, which of the following must you take into consideration?

   A. You must set the meter to measure amps.

   B. You must set the meter to measure volts.

   C. The multimeter sends a current between the probes that could damage other components.

   D. Reversing the position of the probes will change the results.

41. Which of the following steps would not be one of the first three things to consider when troubleshooting?

   A. Check the simple stuff.

   B. Determine if the problem is hardware or software related.

   C. Define the problem.

   D. Check for user error.

42. How do beeps from the computer alert you to problems?

   A. Each BIOS manufacturer uses a published series of beep codes to signal a healthy system or a variety of problems detected during POST.

   B. Long before a problem becomes an issue, your computer's sound card will issue beep codes through your speaker system.

   C. All BIOS manufacturers follow a common set of beep codes that are standardized in the industry.

   D. Called beep codes, these signals are actually spoken English alerts of problems discovered during POST.

43. With modems that run the Hayes command set, what is the response to the command AT that indicates the modem is ready?

   A. Ready

   B. OK

   C. Next

   D. Proceed

44. You lose power to your computer while flashing an update to the BIOS. Which one of the following fixes will get you going again most easily?

   A. Start the flash process again.

   B. Take the computer to a manufacturer-approved service center.

   C. Boot up normally, and reset the BIOS from a command prompt.

   D. Reinstall the operating system.

45. If you notice that your BIOS settings do not remain and you have to set the date and time whenever you turn the power off and back on, what might be the problem?

   A. The operating system needs to be reinstalled.

   B. Device Manager needs to be reinstalled.

   C. The voltage selector switch on the power supply is set wrong.

   D. The CMOS battery needs to be replaced.

46. Which of the following is a possibility for a desktop motherboard that is generally not possible for a laptop motherboard?

   A. Adding expansion cards

   B. Adding memory

   C. Having a CPU onboard

   D. Having integrated components

47. Which one of the following is *not* a benefit of SoDIMMs for laptops?

   A. SoDIMMs are smaller than DIMMs.

   B. SoDIMMs are not proprietary.

   C. SoDIMMs are keyed to prevent incorrect insertion.

   D. Because they are standard, one SoDIMM fits all SoDIMM-compatible laptops.

GO ON TO THE NEXT PAGE

48. Regarding laptop displays, which of the following is the most reasonable expectation if you notice a dead pixel?

    A. Keep plugging away until you have a real case.

    B. The manufacturer should replace the pixel.

    C. The manufacturer should replace the display if it is under warranty.

    D. The manufacturer should replace the display regardless of the warranty coverage.

49. Which of the following should you use to clean a touch screen with a capacitive coating?

    A. Regular glass cleaner

    B. Denatured alcohol

    C. Warm soapy water

    D. A cloth dampened, but not saturated, with water

50. What is the name of the PCI-compatible technology for laptops?

    A. PCIe

    B. LapPCI

    C. Mini PCI

    D. PCI

51. Which of the following battery compositions is *not* rechargeable?

    A. NiCd

    B. NiMH

    C. LiIon

    D. Alkaline

52. What is the name of the power-saving mode that writes the contents of RAM to the hard drive before completely removing power from the system?

    A. Suspend

    B. Hibernate

    C. Soft off

    D. Mechanical off

53. All of the following statements about troubleshooting laptops are accurate *except*:

    A. Video, input, and wireless networking are all areas where laptop troubleshooting differs from desktop troubleshooting.

    B. Remove all external peripherals from the laptop before beginning to troubleshoot power issues.

    C. Making sure the laptop is plugged in is not important because it runs on batteries as well.

    D. Follow standard general troubleshooting procedures, just as you would on a desktop computer.

54. Your laptop has a wireless network adapter that appears to be active in the System Tray, but you are not able to surf the Internet unless you use a patch cord in the wired interface. Which of the following is the most likely issue?

    A. The network to which you are automatically connecting requires authentication.

    B. The SSID of the network you are connected to is not being broadcast.

    C. The wired adapter is interfering with the wireless adapter and must be disabled.

    D. The wireless adapter is disabled in Windows.

55. Which of the following statements about applications is *not* true?

    A. An application is software written to accomplish a specific task.

    B. An application relies on the operating system to perform some of its more basic tasks.

    C. An operating system is *not* a type of application.

    D. Commonly, a well-written application works on any operating system.

56. Which of the following Windows operating systems was released most recently?

    A. XP

    B. Me

    C. 2000

    D. 98

57. Which of the following represent the minimum required RAM and available hard disk space, respectively, to run Mac OS X (version 10.4)?

- **A.** 512MB; 4GB
- **B.** 256MB; 3GB
- **C.** 256MB; 2GB
- **D.** 128MB; 1GB

58. What is Microsoft's term for the area that shows only the date and time as well as icons for utilities running in the background?

- **A.** Taskbar
- **B.** Start menu
- **C.** Desktop
- **D.** System Tray

59. All of the following can be found at the top level of the Start menu of XP *except*:

- **A.** All Programs
- **B.** My Recent Documents
- **C.** Program Files folder
- **D.** Control Panel

60. Why is it not wise to turn off a Windows-based computer without going through the shut-down process first? (Choose two.)

- **A.** Microsoft is unable to collect data properly on your session.
- **B.** Running programs keep files open that can be corrupted.
- **C.** Temporary files are left on the hard drive and tie up space.
- **D.** Viruses can more easily attach themselves to your system.

61. Which of the following Desktop icons offers the most direct access to network resources?

- **A.** Recycle Bin
- **B.** My Documents
- **C.** My Computer
- **D.** My Network Places

62. All of the following methods always restore an object from the Recycle Bin to its original location *except*:

- **A.** Open the original folder, and drag the object from the Recycle Bin into the original folder.
- **B.** Drag the object out of the Recycle Bin, and release it.
- **C.** Right-click the object in the Recycle Bin, and click Restore.
- **D.** Click the object, and then click Restore This Item in the left frame.

63. Which of the following best describes Control Panel?

- **A.** A set of shortcuts to often-used programs
- **B.** A folder that holds your most recently used applications
- **C.** A folder full of unrelated utilities
- **D.** A set of applets that allows you to change the Registry without editing the Registry directly

64. In networking, which of the following is a key difference between workgroups and domains?

- **A.** Workgroups are Microsoft associations. Domains are not.
- **B.** Workgroups are loose associations between computers and remote resources. Domains are tighter associations with centralized security.
- **C.** Domains are loose associations between computers and remote resources. Workgroups are tighter associations with centralized security.
- **D.** Domains are not able to offer resources to their clients to the same extent that workgroups can.

65. What feature of Windows supports the selective activation of hardware during boot-up?

- **A.** Last known good configuration
- **B.** Hardware profiles
- **C.** Hardware selection
- **D.** Optional device activation

GO ON TO THE NEXT PAGE

66. All of the following are valid events that create restore points *except*:

   A. Every time you turn the computer on and log on to Windows

   B. Whenever an application installs itself with a supported installer

   C. Every 24 hours that your computer is on

   D. When a Windows automatic update starts to install

67. What is the name of the database where Windows 9*x* and later store most of their configuration information?

   A. ConfigDB

   B. Registry

   C. WIN.INI

   D. SYSTEM.INI

68. What is the best policy regarding editing the Registry?

   A. Be careful, and click Edit ➤ Undo as soon as you realize you made a mistake.

   B. Do so freely, but be prepared to load the last known good configuration if the system fails to boot properly.

   C. Do so only as a last resort.

   D. Do so freely. Windows repairs its own Registry to avoid catastrophes, when necessary.

69. Which *two* of the following can, by themselves, improve the situation when you receive the message that there is insufficient memory to perform an operation?

   A. Increasing the size of the hard drive or adding an additional hard drive

   B. Upgrading to a faster processor

   C. Adding more RAM

   D. Increasing the size of the swap file

70. Which of the following describes the NTOSKRNL.EXE system file?

   A. Starts the loading of the operating system

   B. A text file that points to the partitions where one or more operating systems are installed

   C. The core of the operating system that must remain loaded at all times, never being paged to disk

   D. Parses the system for current configuration information as the operating system starts, and creates the dynamic portion of the Registry

71. Which of the following most closely maps to a drive letter on a single disk?

   A. Cluster

   B. Partition

   C. Track

   D. Sector

72. Which operating system supports FAT16 and NTFS, but not FAT32?

   A. Windows 98

   B. Windows NT 4

   C. Windows 2000

   D. Windows XP

73. Which of the following best describes fragmentation?

   A. When multiple partitions are created on a single physical drive

   B. When a larger file is chained across the incontiguous gaps left by multiple smaller files

   C. When a single volume is made up of multiple physical drives

   D. The unusable disk space caused by clusters that are not used completely and cannot be shared by multiple files

74. What is the name of the Microsoft list of Windows-compatible hardware?

   A. Microsoft Compatibility List

   B. Windows Compatibility List

   C. Hardware Compatibility List

   D. Hardware Abstraction Layer

75. When choosing a file system before installation, all of the following are sound reasons for selecting one *except*:

A. Go with FAT32 over FAT16 when possible.
B. Go with NTFS unless Windows 9*x* will be installed on the same machine and will require access to the partition.
C. Go with NTFS for partitions larger than 512MB.
D. Make sure the file system is the same on all partitions on the same machine.

76. What happens between the text phase of a Windows installation and the graphical phase?

A. The computer reboots.
B. A human or answer file must be present to confirm the phase transition.
C. You must change discs.
D. The computer attempts to get online and must be able to access the Internet for the entire graphical phase.

77. Which of the following Windows upgrade paths is not valid?

A. 2000 to XP
B. NT Workstation 4 to XP
C. 95 to 2000
D. Me to 2000

78. All of the following have the tendency to increase some area of system performance *except*:

A. Enabling large system cache
B. Using many smaller partitions rather than one large partition
C. Adjusting disk caching in Internet Explorer
D. Deleting temporary files

79. What is the EXTRACT.EXE utility used for?

A. To remove a known virus from a particular file
B. To pull current system configuration information from the Registry
C. To pull redundant content out of a specific file, effectively compressing the file
D. To pull an embedded file out of a cabinet file and place it in a specified location

80. What is the name of the disk that is created through Backup in Windows XP, similar to the way the ERD is created in Windows 2000?

A. ASR
B. EBD
C. XPBD
D. NTBD

81. Which one of the following is *not* a common form of scanner?

A. Laser
B. Flatbed
C. Sheet-fed
D. Handheld

82. How many components play an active role in cleaning the waste toner from the photosensitive drum in an EP laser printer?

A. 1
B. 2
C. 3
D. 4

83. Which type of printer offers true color and works in a fashion similar to bubble-jet printers, while keeping its ink fresh longer and being less messy?

A. Dye sublimation
B. Thermal
C. Solid ink
D. Inkjet

84. Which of the following features is *not* commonly found on a multifunction printer?

A. Copying
B. CD burning
C. Scanning
D. Faxing

85. All of the following are differences between flatbed and sheet-fed scanners *except*:

A. Resolution normally suffers on sheet-fed scanners compared to flatbed scanners.
B. A flatbed scanner has a glass plate between the scan head and the object to be scanned. A sheet-fed scanner does not.
C. Speed of sheet-fed scanners normally surpasses that of flatbed scanners.
D. The scan head on a sheet-fed scanner is often stationary, whereas the scan head of a flatbed scanner moves.

GO ON TO THE NEXT PAGE

86. Which of the following fixes the majority of inkjet/bubble-jet printer issues?

   A. Power-cycle the printer.

   B. Replace the ink cartridge.

   C. Reboot the computer.

   D. Check and/or replace the data cable between the printer and the computer.

87. All of the following laser-printer components can lead to blank output pages *except*:

   A. Toner cartridge

   B. Transfer corona assembly

   C. Charging corona wire

   D. HVPS

88. What type of server acts only as a server and not also as a workstation for direct local access?

   A. Dedicated server

   B. File server

   C. Nondedicated server

   D. Print server

89. How many layers are represented in the OSI Reference Model, and what is the name of the top layer?

   A. 4; Transport

   B. 3; Network

   C. 7; Application

   D. 6; Presentation

90. What is the name for Microsoft's implementation of the IPX/SPX protocol suite?

   A. Novell

   B. NWLINK

   C. TCP/IP

   D. NetBEUI

91. How many octets is an IP address made up of, and how many bits is this equivalent to?

   A. 6; 48

   B. 32; 4

   C. 1; 32

   D. 4; 32

92. What is the highest decimal value that can be represented with 8 bits?

   A. 128

   B. 255

   C. 256

   D. 512

93. RG-*x* generally denotes what kind of transmission medium?

   A. Coaxial

   B. Twisted pair

   C. Fiber

   D. Wireless

94. Which of the following devices is considered to operate at Layer 3 of the OSI Model?

   A. Hub

   B. Bridge

   C. Switch

   D. Router

95. What type of address is embedded in the circuitry of network interfaces and normally does not change for that particular device?

   A. Physical or MAC

   B. IPX

   C. IP

   D. AppleTalk

96. What is the difference between PAP and CHAP?

   A. PAP is not an authentication protocol. CHAP is.

   B. PAP sends passwords in clear text across the link. CHAP does not.

   C. PAP is more secure and harder to hack than CHAP.

   D. PAP is the next generation of CHAP.

97. What is a firewall?

   A. Another name for a router

   B. A hardened case that prevents fire damage to the computer

   C. A hardware or software solution that isolates two or more networks from each other and permits or denies traffic based on configurable security rules

   D. Another name for a gateway

98. Given a suspected hazardous material, what is the best resource for you to discover proper handling and disposal practices?

    A. Your local recycling center

    B. The vendor of the material

    C. The material's MSDS

    D. Calling the EPA directly

99. Which of the following battery compositions is not considered hazardous waste but should still be recycled?

    A. Lead-acid

    B. NiCd

    C. Alkaline

    D. LiIon

100. All of the following are good behavior *except*:

    A. Be on time for appointments.

    B. Own up to issues you cause during your service call.

    C. Tactfully attempt to keep your customers on the schedule to which you have agreed so that your business as a whole does not suffer.

    D. Treat sensitive information that you come across with discretion.

Answer Key for Practice Test 3

1.	A	26.	B	51.	D	76.	A
2.	C	27.	C	52.	B	77.	D
3.	A	28.	A	53.	C	78.	B
4.	D	29.	B	54.	A	79.	D
5.	C	30.	C	55.	D	80.	A
6.	B	31.	B	56.	A	81.	A
7.	A	32.	B	57.	B	82.	B
8.	A	33.	B	58.	D	83.	C
9.	B	34.	A	59.	C	84.	B
10.	B	35.	C	60.	BC	85.	B
11.	D	36.	A	61.	D	86.	B
12.	C	37.	C	62.	B	87.	C
13.	A	38.	B	63.	D	88.	A
14.	A	39.	A	64.	B	89.	C
15.	D	40.	C	65.	B	90.	B
16.	BC	41.	B	66.	A	91.	D
17.	C	42.	A	67.	B	92.	B
18.	D	43.	B	68.	C	93.	A
19.	B	44.	B	69.	CD	94.	D
20.	A	45.	D	70.	C	95.	A
21.	C	46.	A	71.	B	96.	B
22.	D	47.	D	72.	B	97.	C
23.	A	48.	A	73.	B	98.	C
24.	D	49.	D	74.	C	99.	D
25.	B	50.	C	75.	D	100.	C

Answer Explanations for Practice Test 3

1. A. The motherboard is the primary circuit board of the personal computer. All other components connect to or through the motherboard, creating an integrated system that works as a unit.

2. C. Integrated motherboards are as removable as nonintegrated motherboards and still have expansion slots for adding features. So that the entire motherboard does not need to be replaced when components fail, manufacturers routinely add the option to disable onboard components in the BIOS; this also serves to avoid conflicts when similar components are added, whether as enhancements or out of personal preference.

3. A. NLX and LPX are low-profile form factors that use a riser card that is shorter in height than standard expansion cards and is installed perpendicular to the motherboard, just like an expansion card normally is. Expansion cards plug into slots on the broad side of the riser card so that their height is parallel to the motherboard instead of perpendicular (as in the case of standard form factors that require higher cases).

4. D. The CPU is not a member of the chipset, of which the Northbridge is always one element (it is not a manufacturer). The chipset supports the CPU in its communication with the rest of the system.

5. C. This function is the job of the Southbridge portion of the chipset.

6. B. Although AGP is a form of I/O technology, which is primarily what the Southbridge controls, AGP is synchronized with the frontside bus, the dominion of the Northbridge.

7. A. ISA slots are characteristically black. The recommendation is for PCIe slots to be black as well, which should not be an issue because new motherboards with PCIe slots will tend not to have ISA slots. Until the standard is ratified, expect to see PCIe slots that are yellow as well as other possible colors.

8. A. AMR and CNR slots do nothing for the rest of the system. Their role is to take communications off-board so that the motherboard can be brought to market sooner without regulatory delays.

9. B. PCIe slots are superior to PCI and AGP slots. Faster slots—those with higher numerical values in their name—can accept slower cards, but the converse is not true.

10. B. SIMM slots have a *single* row of pins, such that a SIMM module does not differentiate between the corresponding pins on opposing sides of the module. Opposing pins in DIMM slots, on the other hand, are not connected to one another and must be counted separately.

11. D. The function of cache is not the same as that of RAM. Therefore, one cannot replace the other.

12. C. Fans and power supplies, by virtue of their fans, are active in their heat dissipation, meaning they require power to draw heat away. Heat sinks do not. Although thermal grease is decisively passive, it is not hardware in the truest sense of the word and, by itself, is not used to draw heat from the component. A thin film of thermal grease closes the gaps of air between a component and its heat sink, which does draw heat through the grease. It would take a mound of messy grease to approximate the same effect afforded by a heat sink.

13. A. The power supply connects to the power-supply connector on the motherboard so that components built into and connected to the motherboard can receive power.

14. A. Although one method of keyboard connectivity was named after the motherboard form factor of the day, AT, the ATX form factor does not have its own specific type of connector.

15. D. The BIOS doesn't manage all hardware. Hardware that the BIOS does not manage for the operating system requires a device driver to be installed for the same purpose, but a device driver is less seamless and must be loaded from the hard drive during bootup. The BIOS can be updated today more than ever, through the advent of the flashable BIOS. The CMOS chip, which has existed since the early days of the personal computer, holds the alterations you make to the BIOS settings.

16. BC. Jumpers and dip switches can be used to configure settings that the BIOS does not control but they are used less as each generation of motherboards arrives on the market.

17. C. CPU throttling is more of a fairness algorithm to make sure no one application monopolizes the CPU's attention.

18. D. A voltage regulator is a variable device that alters its output based on a signal from the CPU. Older regulators were adjusted manually by jumpers or dip switches.

19. B. DRAM is dynamic RAM, and SRAM is static RAM. The two are mutually exclusive. SDRAM is still DRAM, with an emphasis on the synchronous nature of today's RAM, which times itself not on the signal but on the system clock that drives the frontside bus.

20. A. Because DDR double-pumps, using both pulses of each cycle, and SDRAM uses only half of that clocking, DDR modules are named after the throughput. SDRAM is named after the clock rate, which it uses in a one-for-one fashion. Assume a 100MHz clock rate. With an 8-byte (64-bit) bus width, SDRAM transfers 800MBps but uses the name PC100, after the clock rate. Using the same bus width but twice the bit rate per clock cycle, DDR transfers 1600MBps and uses the name PC1600, after the bit rate. This nomenclature gives DDR the appearance of 16 times the bit rate of SDRAM, which is not accurate.

21. C. Programmable ROM, erasable PROM, and electrically erasable PROM are all valid types of ROM.

22. D. Rambus memory uses 16-bit channels for communication. A 32-bit module uses two channels simultaneously, by virtue of the enhanced chipset. To physically create a 32-bit module, two 16-bit modules are combined into one package. Although it is true that all blank slots must be filled, only blank 32-bit slots require CT-RIMMs. Blank 16-bit slots call for C-RIMMs, continuity with no termination.

23. A. Floppies come in double-, high-, and extended-density formats. CD stands for compact disc, which is not a floppy diskette term.

24. D. A DVD+R disc stores up to 4.7GB of data, considerably more than four times the capacity of a 700MB CD-R disc.

25. B. Thumb drive is the industry name for a memory card mounted in a USB-attached enclosure that is often no larger than an average human thumb.

26. B. Power supplies have leads for ±5VDC and ±12VDC, but only +3VDC is present on ATX and later power supplies.

27. C. RAID is a technology that provides for multidevice volumes and fault tolerance. It has nothing to do with power connectors.

28. A. The second version of ATX12V was required when PCIe and its added power requirements hit the market after the original ATX12V specification was released.

29. B. The *I* on the end is for *integrated*. Analog and digital video formats are integrated into the same DVI connector using different pins for each.

30. C. The physical electronic technology that makes a display active or passive is mutually exclusive between the two technologies. One cannot be switched to the other.

31. B. Modular jacks are denoted by a Registered Jack (RJ) designation. RJ-12 is a form of telephony jack, but the standard POTS line interface is an RJ-11 jack. Although it's a misnomer, the 8-pin modular data jack used in twisted-pair implementations of Ethernet and certain other networking interfaces is known as an RJ-45.

32. B. The Sony/Philips Digital Interface specification is a digital audio technology. DVI and HDMI are non-coaxial video technologies. HDMI includes an optional digital audio connection as well. The 1/8″ stereo minijack is the standard connector used on sound cards.

33. B. A crossover cable is used in the Ethernet networking arena for such a direct connection between two NIC cards; but for standard serial interfaces, the similarly crossed-over cabling is known as null modem, named for the fact that a physical modem is not needed for serial communications.

34. A. Each component that uses a passive cooling mechanism uses one that caters to that component alone. Only active cooling methods are able to cool groups of components.

35. C. The devices on an IDE controller once adapted their bit rate to the slowest device. Although this is not true with newer devices and controllers, one device in a master/slave pair must wait for the other to finish its use of the channel before it can transfer data on the same channel. The result is that slower devices can cause a faster device to have to wait longer for channel access. Therefore, faster devices should be paired together, not mixed with slower devices. Furthermore, two devices that frequently transfer data between one another should be placed on different controllers so they can operate simultaneously. A good rule of thumb is to combine like devices, unless you know one such device to be vastly slower than the other. Another tip is to give each device its own controller where possible. Most motherboards have two controllers. If you have only two IDE devices, giving them their own controllers works out fine.

36. A. Although SCSI-1 external connectors do have 50 pins, the connector is a Centronics, not a D-subminiature.

37. C. External SCSI devices do not cable to the power supply and must have their own external power source. External devices routinely have two connectors that are used to attach the device to its two neighbors on the chain using separate cables. If either connector does not have a neighbor to connect to, meaning the device is the last on the chain, you must attach a terminator with the appropriate interface to the vacant connector. External devices are on a part of the SCSI bus that is a simple extension to the internal bus. Thus, all external devices require addresses on the bus as well.

38. B. Never work on a CRT monitor that is plugged in to power or has been plugged in within the past week without first discharging the flyback transformer's charging capacitor. Do so regardless, just in case gremlins plugged it in while you weren't looking. Degaussing removes magnetic influences from the shadow mask; it does nothing to remove dangerous charges from the monitor. However, unless you have specialized training, you should never open CRTs and power supplies.

39. A. Avoid water and anything that might promote static, including standard vacuum cleaners and certain cloth fabrics. Additionally, cloths and sponges can snag on components large and small, causing damage that could result in the dreaded intermittent failure. Of the options given, compressed air, when used correctly, is the best tool for cleaning dust and contaminants from the inside of a computer.

40. C. Amps are related to current, and volts to voltage. The ohm is the unit of measure for resistance, which is not polarity-sensitive. Be aware that the multimeter sends a current between the probes, so the component should not be in-circuit when measuring resistance.

41. B. After defining the problem, then checking the simple stuff, and then checking to see if it's user error, you should try restarting the computer before worrying about the nature of the problem in terms of hardware or software.

42. A. A beep code is a distinctive series of beeps heard during the initial stages of bootup. By default, the beeps come from the system speaker driven by the motherboard, not through the sound card. Each BIOS manufacturer uses a proprietary set of codes that may resemble those of other manufacturers but normally do not completely match those of their competitors.

43. B. The Hayes command set uses OK as a response to successful command execution.

44. B. In the vast majority of cases when power is lost while flashing the BIOS, you must turn the system over to a manufacturer-authorized service center. As an alternative, if you can get access to a replacement BIOS chip, which is what flashing is designed to avoid, you can start from scratch with a known-good BIOS that may or may not need upgrading. However, the channels for such "raw" BIOS chips are fairly exclusive and have given way to flash updates in favor of chip replacement. In this failed state, your system will not boot to any device, meaning that you cannot boot to a command prompt or to a disk that will allow you to begin an operating-system installation (not that it would help if you could). The BIOS is a pre-software and software-independent portion of the boot process that is not affected by the health of the operating system and other software.

45. D. The only option presented that can affect the ability of your system to maintain the date and time when AC power is not supplied to the system is the replacement of the CMOS backup battery. None of the other options affect retention of the date and time.

46. A. Laptops generally have all functions and connectors integrated in order to maintain their small form factor. Laptop motherboards, like their desktop counterparts, have CPUs that are directly mounted. Motherboards across all platforms generally allow the installation of memory for expansion. However, expansion cards (in the sense that the term is used in the desktop family) rarely can be inserted directly into a laptop. Separate from the laptop itself, docking stations sometimes have full-size expansion slots.

47. D. Although standards exist for SoDIMMs, there are multiple form factors and edge connectors with different pin counts in the line-up. They are not interchangeable.

48. A. Many manufacturers define even warrantable replacements as those having a certain percentage of dead pixels. One dead pixel will rarely raise an eyebrow. Don't expect the same level of coverage from the manufacturer when the warranty expires; the loss of pixels tends to get worse and the upkeep of the display more expensive for the consumer.

49. D. No solution is approved for use on touch screens with a capacitive coating.

50. C. Mini PCI is the name used for the laptop expansion technology that is compatible with PCI.

51. D. Alkaline is the most commonly used nonrechargeable battery composition.

52. B. Hibernation saves an exact copy of the contents of RAM to the hard drive. When power is restored, the same contents are copied back to their original location in RAM, and users can pick up where they left off. It is still wise to save your work before hibernating, just in case there are issues when resuming from hibernation.

53. C. Be aware that laptops can exhibit symptoms that appear to have nothing to do with power, but the battery is still the culprit. Attach the laptop to AC power and even go so far as to remove the battery when troubleshooting.

54. A. Although your computer can appear to have a healthy network connection, you will not gain access to the network, and hence the Internet, through the wireless connection if authentication is required but not performed.

55. D. Two broad classifications for software are applications and systems software. An operating system is not an application. Applications require the support of the operating system to function, so much so that applications are written for a specific operating system. This pairing generally precludes application portability directly to all other operating systems.

56. A. Of the operating systems listed, Windows XP is the latest.

57. B. You must have at least 256MB of RAM and 3GB of free hard disk space to run Mac OS X.

58. D. Although the Taskbar is the entire strip that holds such features as the Start button, the Quick Launch tray, and the System Tray, it is the System Tray at the right on the Taskbar that the question describes.

59. C. The Program Files folder is generally accessed through My Computer or Windows Explorer as a first-level subfolder to the root of the hard drive on which it resides.

60. BC. It is a long-established truth that if a file is being written when power is lost, that file will likely suffer corruption. Other open files can become corrupt as well. Furthermore, Windows uses the shutdown process to perform housekeeping by removing temporary files that it uses while you work on data files.

61. D. Of the options, only My Network Places gives you immediate access to network resources without additional steps beyond launching it.

62. B. The key here is the word *always*. Although you can drag the object to its original location and release it, you can also release it in a location other than where it originated.

63. D. The applets in Control Panel are shortcuts to other locations, but they are not necessarily used frequently. It is true, however, that these applets directly alter the contents of the Registry without the need to do so in Registry Editor.

64. B. Both workgroups and domains are used in Microsoft operating systems and allow clients to obtain resources from other devices. Workgroups do not have the structure and security found in domains, however.

65. B. The term *hardware profiles* refers to this capability. The last known good configuration is a selection offered after you press the F8 key during bootup. Hardware profiles are set up in the graphical portion of Windows and chosen from a menu when booting up. You can differentiate between devices to be used when docked or undocked, for instance.

66. A. Simply logging on to Windows does not create a restore point. Each of the other events, however, does create a restore point.

67. B. The Registry is the name for the database that took the place of the various .ini files that once held Windows' entire configuration.

68. C. There is no undo feature in Registry Editor. If you did not save the Registry before editing it, or you do not remember the original value that you changed, you run the risk of rendering the system inoperable. Edit the Registry only when you cannot make changes using Control Panel and only when you are absolutely certain of the procedure required to make the required changes.

69. CD. By *memory*, Windows is referring to primary memory, or RAM, not secondary memory, or disk storage. So, increasing disk capacity will not alleviate this problem. Adding RAM or the perception of RAM, by way of the virtual-memory swap file, will help get rid of this symptom.

70. C. The NTOSKRNL.EXE file houses the portion of the operating system that cannot be swapped to virtual memory or closed and stored back to disk during a Windows session. It is the core of the operating system and must always be resident in memory.

71. B. Each primary partition gets a single drive letter under normal circumstances. Extended partitions can map to multiple drive letters, but none of the other terms fits as well here.

72. B. Although NT 4 is not mentioned in the objectives for the exam, it's wise to know the abilities and limitations of all Windows operating systems for practical purposes. Additionally, you need to be able to rule out such statements in reference to more contemporary operating systems.

73. B. As you delete smaller files and then write larger ones to the same disk, Windows does not seek out a contiguous space in the disk for the larger file; it starts out early in the disk's logical structure and splits the file as necessary to write the entire contents to the disk. This act and the results are known as *fragmentation*.

74. C. The Hardware Compatibility List (HCL) is a Microsoft-published list of proven compatible devices that will not compromise the stability and integrity of the operating system.

75. D. There is no reason why all partitions should or must use the same file system. It depends on various circumstances, some of which are presented in the other options.

76. A. The computer reboots to change to the graphical phase of installation.

77. D. Windows 2000 cannot upgrade Windows Me. All other paths are valid.

78. B. The more partitions you create—especially smaller, less efficient ones that may indicate the use of the FAT file system—the longer your system can take to access content and become stable. The better choice is to use fewer, larger partitions and organize your data and applications with folders, not partitions.

79. D. The EXTRACT.EXE application is used to isolate a file from a group in a .cab file, expand the file, and place it in its usable form in the location of your choosing.

80. A. When you select the most inclusive backup set from the Backup wizard in Windows XP, you are prompted at the end to insert a blank diskette (or one that you do not mind overwriting) to create the Automated System Recovery disk that can be used to boot the machine and restore from the backup set in the event of a catastrophic failure.

81. A. Lasers are types of printers, not scanners. The other types are valid forms of scanners.

82. B. In many cases, a rubber cleaning blade scrapes the remaining toner into a used toner receptacle and a fluorescent lamp discharges the photosensitive drum, facilitating the release of the waste toner from the drum. So, the blade and fluorescent lamp have active roles in cleaning the drum. Although other implementations employ more pieces, the general concept remains that two major phases comprise the cleaning process: a physical cleaning and the discharging of the drum.

83. C. Solid-ink printers use ink that is not susceptible to the same pitfalls as that of standard bubble-jet printers, such as drying and making a mess when handled. However, the process of printing is similar between the two technologies.

84. B. Multifunction printers generally print, copy, scan, and fax. They don't usually burn CDs.

85. B. Many sheet-fed scanners also have a glass plate between the object to be scanned and the scan head. The difference is, with such sheet-fed scanners, a mechanism draws the object to be scanned into the unit and places it automatically on the glass plate.

86. B. Because the electronics and the ink-distribution mechanism reside in the ink cartridge, and because liquid-ink cartridges are susceptible to various anomalies, the vast majority of inkjet/bubble-jet issues can be resolved by replacing the cartridge.

87. C. If the charging corona wire fails, the result will be a predominantly black page, because the drum never acquires the uniform –600VDC charge that repels the similarly charged toner wherever the transfer corona wire does not reduce this uniform charge. In this case, the majority of the drum would remain at about –100VDC, thereby attracting toner to almost the entire surface of the drum.

88. A. The type of server (file, print, and so on) does not speak to whether it acts as a server only or also as a client. Dedicated servers, by definition, are not used as workstations for normal use. They act as servers only.

89. C. The seven layers of the OSI Model, from the bottom up, are Physical, Data-link, Network, Transport, Session, Presentation, and Application.

90. B. Microsoft implements the IPX/SPX protocol suite as NWLINK. The *NW* refers to NetWare, Novell's trade name for its product that once implemented IPX/SPX exclusively.

91. D. There are 8 bits in an octet, which is equivalent to a standard byte. An IPv4 address has 32 bits, which corresponds to 4 octets. The order of the numbers in the correct answer, with respect to the question, differentiates it from the answer in which these numbers are reversed.

92. B. The bit weights in a byte of binary digits, from the right, are 1, 2, 4, 8, 16, 32, 64, and 128. Turning all bits on, which sets them to 1, produces the largest possible value. The value of the byte is determined by multiplying each bit weight by the bit value in that position and then adding up all eight results. To simplify matters, you can evaluate only positions with a bit value of 1, because those that have values of 0 contribute nothing to the total value of the byte. As a result, setting all bits to 1 and adding all 8 bit weights comes to a total of 255.

93. A. Radio grade (RG) cable refers to coaxial cable.

94. D. Although routers operate at Layers 1, 2, and 3, they are considered to be Layer-3 devices, based on the highest of these layers. Hubs operate only at Layer 1, making them Layer-1 devices. Bridges and switches operate at Layers 1 and 2, making them Layer-2 devices.

95. A. A unique MAC address is assigned to each network interface by the manufacturer. The first half of the MAC address identifies the manufacturer, and the second half differentiates all interfaces created by that manufacturer. The end result is a worldwide unique address, even though it must be unique on the immediate link only. IP, IPX, and AppleTalk addresses are assigned to a network interface and can change at the whim of the administrator.

96. B. PAP is considered less secure and therefore less desirable than CHAP. PAP sends the password over the link in the clear, making it simple to eavesdrop and acquire the password. CHAP never sends the password across the link. It creates an encrypted hash by using the common password set up locally on each end of the link and the challenge from the opposite end of the link. This encrypted hash is the only thing sent over the link.

97. C. Some firewalls are basically routers with exceptional security features built in. However, not all firewalls are routers, and not all routers can be called firewalls, thus the terms are not interchangeable.

98. C. Each hazardous material has a Material Safety Data Sheet. If an MSDS does not exist for a particular material, then the material likely has no special handling procedures, and it can be considered nonhazardous.

99. D. Although LiIon is not considered a hazardous material, all batteries should be recycled to minimize effects on the environment as well as the cost of manufacturing new batteries.

100. C. Each customer should be considered individually. It is rarely in the best interest of the customer to pressure them into meeting the schedule that you have established with them. Learn to adjust your schedule while minimizing inconveniences to other customers, instead of forcing the current customer to fit into your day's schedule.

Answer Sheets for Practice Test 1

(Remove This Sheet and Use It to Mark Your Answers)

Section 1
Multiple Choice Questions

1 Ⓐ Ⓑ Ⓒ Ⓓ Ⓔ	41 Ⓐ Ⓑ Ⓒ Ⓓ Ⓔ
2 Ⓐ Ⓑ Ⓒ Ⓓ Ⓔ	42 Ⓐ Ⓑ Ⓒ Ⓓ Ⓔ
3 Ⓐ Ⓑ Ⓒ Ⓓ Ⓔ	43 Ⓐ Ⓑ Ⓒ Ⓓ Ⓔ
4 Ⓐ Ⓑ Ⓒ Ⓓ Ⓔ	44 Ⓐ Ⓑ Ⓒ Ⓓ Ⓔ
5 Ⓐ Ⓑ Ⓒ Ⓓ Ⓔ	45 Ⓐ Ⓑ Ⓒ Ⓓ Ⓔ
6 Ⓐ Ⓑ Ⓒ Ⓓ Ⓔ	46 Ⓐ Ⓑ Ⓒ Ⓓ Ⓔ
7 Ⓐ Ⓑ Ⓒ Ⓓ Ⓔ	47 Ⓐ Ⓑ Ⓒ Ⓓ Ⓔ
8 Ⓐ Ⓑ Ⓒ Ⓓ Ⓔ	48 Ⓐ Ⓑ Ⓒ Ⓓ Ⓔ
9 Ⓐ Ⓑ Ⓒ Ⓓ Ⓔ	49 Ⓐ Ⓑ Ⓒ Ⓓ Ⓔ
10 Ⓐ Ⓑ Ⓒ Ⓓ Ⓔ	50 Ⓐ Ⓑ Ⓒ Ⓓ Ⓔ
11 Ⓐ Ⓑ Ⓒ Ⓓ Ⓔ	51 Ⓐ Ⓑ Ⓒ Ⓓ Ⓔ
12 Ⓐ Ⓑ Ⓒ Ⓓ Ⓔ	52 Ⓐ Ⓑ Ⓒ Ⓓ Ⓔ
13 Ⓐ Ⓑ Ⓒ Ⓓ Ⓔ	53 Ⓐ Ⓑ Ⓒ Ⓓ Ⓔ
14 Ⓐ Ⓑ Ⓒ Ⓓ Ⓔ	54 Ⓐ Ⓑ Ⓒ Ⓓ Ⓔ
15 Ⓐ Ⓑ Ⓒ Ⓓ Ⓔ	55 Ⓐ Ⓑ Ⓒ Ⓓ Ⓔ
16 Ⓐ Ⓑ Ⓒ Ⓓ Ⓔ	56 Ⓐ Ⓑ Ⓒ Ⓓ Ⓔ
17 Ⓐ Ⓑ Ⓒ Ⓓ Ⓔ	57 Ⓐ Ⓑ Ⓒ Ⓓ Ⓔ
18 Ⓐ Ⓑ Ⓒ Ⓓ Ⓔ	58 Ⓐ Ⓑ Ⓒ Ⓓ Ⓔ
19 Ⓐ Ⓑ Ⓒ Ⓓ Ⓔ	59 Ⓐ Ⓑ Ⓒ Ⓓ Ⓔ
20 Ⓐ Ⓑ Ⓒ Ⓓ Ⓔ	60 Ⓐ Ⓑ Ⓒ Ⓓ Ⓔ
21 Ⓐ Ⓑ Ⓒ Ⓓ Ⓔ	61 Ⓐ Ⓑ Ⓒ Ⓓ Ⓔ
22 Ⓐ Ⓑ Ⓒ Ⓓ Ⓔ	62 Ⓐ Ⓑ Ⓒ Ⓓ Ⓔ
23 Ⓐ Ⓑ Ⓒ Ⓓ Ⓔ	63 Ⓐ Ⓑ Ⓒ Ⓓ Ⓔ
24 Ⓐ Ⓑ Ⓒ Ⓓ Ⓔ	64 Ⓐ Ⓑ Ⓒ Ⓓ Ⓔ
25 Ⓐ Ⓑ Ⓒ Ⓓ Ⓔ	65 Ⓐ Ⓑ Ⓒ Ⓓ Ⓔ
26 Ⓐ Ⓑ Ⓒ Ⓓ Ⓔ	66 Ⓐ Ⓑ Ⓒ Ⓓ Ⓔ
27 Ⓐ Ⓑ Ⓒ Ⓓ Ⓔ	67 Ⓐ Ⓑ Ⓒ Ⓓ Ⓔ
28 Ⓐ Ⓑ Ⓒ Ⓓ Ⓔ	68 Ⓐ Ⓑ Ⓒ Ⓓ Ⓔ
29 Ⓐ Ⓑ Ⓒ Ⓓ Ⓔ	69 Ⓐ Ⓑ Ⓒ Ⓓ Ⓔ
30 Ⓐ Ⓑ Ⓒ Ⓓ Ⓔ	70 Ⓐ Ⓑ Ⓒ Ⓓ Ⓔ
31 Ⓐ Ⓑ Ⓒ Ⓓ Ⓔ	71 Ⓐ Ⓑ Ⓒ Ⓓ Ⓔ
32 Ⓐ Ⓑ Ⓒ Ⓓ Ⓔ	72 Ⓐ Ⓑ Ⓒ Ⓓ Ⓔ
33 Ⓐ Ⓑ Ⓒ Ⓓ Ⓔ	73 Ⓐ Ⓑ Ⓒ Ⓓ Ⓔ
34 Ⓐ Ⓑ Ⓒ Ⓓ Ⓔ	74 Ⓐ Ⓑ Ⓒ Ⓓ Ⓔ
35 Ⓐ Ⓑ Ⓒ Ⓓ Ⓔ	75 Ⓐ Ⓑ Ⓒ Ⓓ Ⓔ
36 Ⓐ Ⓑ Ⓒ Ⓓ Ⓔ	76 Ⓐ Ⓑ Ⓒ Ⓓ Ⓔ
37 Ⓐ Ⓑ Ⓒ Ⓓ Ⓔ	77 Ⓐ Ⓑ Ⓒ Ⓓ Ⓔ
38 Ⓐ Ⓑ Ⓒ Ⓓ Ⓔ	78 Ⓐ Ⓑ Ⓒ Ⓓ Ⓔ
39 Ⓐ Ⓑ Ⓒ Ⓓ Ⓔ	79 Ⓐ Ⓑ Ⓒ Ⓓ Ⓔ
40 Ⓐ Ⓑ Ⓒ Ⓓ Ⓔ	80 Ⓐ Ⓑ Ⓒ Ⓓ Ⓔ

Directions: For each of the following questions, select the choice that best answers the question or completes the statement.

1. You are onsite at a customer's location and realize you have forgotten your antistatic wrist strap. Which of the following is the best solution to your problem?

   A. Tell the customer you have to run back to the office to pick up your wrist strap and you will return in an hour.
   B. Proceed with your internal computer repairs. The odds are in your favor that you will not destroy anything with ESD.
   C. Fashion an impromptu wrist strap from a spare Ethernet patch cord.
   D. Plug the computer system unit into the wall outlet, and touch the outside of the internal power supply.

2. A customer places a service call that you are dispatched on. The customer requested the latest and greatest video card to go with the cutting-edge motherboard they recently had installed. Which of the following expansion buses is the customer most likely referring to?

   A. PCI
   B. PCIe
   C. AGP
   D. ISA

3. While working on a customer's computer in their office, the power supply shorts out and starts a fire. What should you do?

   A. Use a nearby class-C fire extinguisher to put out the flame.
   B. Do nothing. These types of fires play out rapidly with little or no peripheral damage.
   C. Douse the fire with water from the nearby water cooler.
   D. Use your can of compressed air to blow out the fire.

4. A user opened a trouble ticket after receiving a new hardened laptop. The complaint is that the user sees the End and Home keys but is unable to use them in the manner to which they are accustomed. What is the most likely issue with this service call?

   A. The user must hold the Fn key while pressing these keys.
   B. This particular model of keyboard does not use these keys in the same fashion as a standard laptop or computer keyboard.
   C. To remain visually compatible with standard keyboards, these keys are present but not functional.
   D. Number Lock is on and affects how these keys are used.

5. While servicing a laser printer, you suspect the problem lies with the laser. Eager to diagnose the problem and fix it, which of the following is the best method to quickly test your theory?

   A. With the printer's case removed, watch for the laser to come on while the customer begins a print job.
   B. Insert a flexible photometer into the feed mechanism, and watch the display for confirmation that light is found in its path.
   C. Replace the EP cartridge, and print a test page.
   D. Remove the EP cartridge, and look at the element to see if it has blown.

6. Which command-line utility is best to use to ascertain the failure point between source and destination of an IP network?

   A. `ping`
   B. `nslookup`
   C. `tracert`
   D. `ipconfig`

GO ON TO THE NEXT PAGE

7. Which of the following items can be found in a substance's MSDS?

 A. The chemical model for the substance
 B. Personal protective equipment to use while handling the substance
 C. Where the substance was shipped from
 D. The number to call to arrange disposal of the substance

8. When you arrive onsite for a service call, the customer informs you that they attempted to upgrade their hard drive by using a new hard drive and an included utility to clone the old hard drive to the new one. Both drives are ATA and set for master, but the new drive does not show up when booting. Which of the following is most likely to fix the problem?

 A. Inform the customer that you cannot have more than one such drive in the system at one time, and then provide a quote for your time to back up the data on the original drive, install the operating system on the new drive, and restore the data to the new drive.
 B. Inform the customer that you are not willing to work on a system that has been tampered with, and leave the premises.
 C. Sell the customer a *Y* Molex connector, and provide power to the new drive.
 D. Don't change the jumpers on the drives, but connect them both to the same controller on the motherboard.

9. You arrive on a service call after a customer has complained of a malfunctioning floppy drive. According to the user, they recently installed additional RAM. Ever since the installation, the light on the floppy drive remains lit, and the user is unable to access any of their diskettes. What is the most likely explanation for the problem?

 A. More RAM has been installed than the system can support.
 B. Apparently, the user's diskettes have been exposed to a magnetic field, because this is the normal operation of a floppy drive.
 C. Diskettes are not meant to be inserted into a floppy drive.
 D. While working inside the system unit, the user dislodged the data cable from the floppy and reinserted it upside down.

10. While you are finishing a service call, a customer asks if you have the appropriate memory modules with you to upgrade their laptop. Which *two* of the following might be the type of module that you need?

 A. MicroDIMMs
 B. SIMMs
 C. RIMMs
 D. SoDIMMs

11. A user complains of having heard noise coming from the inside of the computer recently, but not in the two days preceding your service call. You determine that the CPU fan was the source of the problem. Which of the following is the best way to handle the situation?

 A. Replace the CPU fan.
 B. Do nothing. No noise means no problem.
 C. Solder the break in the CPU fan's electrical wire.
 D. Remove the defective CPU fan so that the remaining heat sink can remove heat from the processor without obstruction.

12. A customer complains that their computer consistently runs for a little while and then shuts down on its own. Upon arriving, you begin your inspection of the system. Which of the following is most likely the culprit?

 A. Multiple shallow dents in the system case
 B. Clumps of dust on the back of the power-supply fan and chassis vent holes
 C. A massive wad of cables behind the system and on the floor
 D. Sticky keys indicating that something has been spilled in the keyboard

13. Upon arriving onsite for a service call involving a dead system, you discover that pressing the power button causes the power-supply fan to kick over but not begin to run. The system never boots. Which of the following is a likely cause?

 A. The power cable is not completely plugged in on the power supply.
 B. The power button is defective.
 C. An adapter card has become partially seated.
 D. The system partition on the hard drive is damaged.

14. While working inside a computer system, you drop a screw into the system unit. Which of the following is the best method of retrieving the screw?

    A. Plastic tweezers

    B. Static-resistant vacuum cleaner

    C. Magnetic screwdriver

    D. Your fingers

15. A customer's monitor has recently begun displaying odd colors, mostly purples and greens. Which of the following is the most likely cause?

    A. One of the three cathode rays has stopped working.

    B. The monitor needs to be degaussed.

    C. The monitor's cable is not completely inserted into the video card's connector.

    D. The wrong video driver is being used.

16. Which of the following commands, when executed using Start ➢ Run, causes the Command Prompt window to remain open after the ping executes?

    A. `ping www.sybex.com`

    B. `cmd /k ping www.sybex.com`

    C. `cmd /c ping www.sybex.com`

    D. `cmd ping www.sybex.com`

17. Which of the following is the best utility to use to rebuild a damaged partition when running Windows XP?

    A. ASR

    B. ERD

    C. System Restore

    D. Recovery Console

18. Which of the following is the best way to clean the screen of most monitors?

    A. Spray the appropriate cleaning solution directly onto the screen, and then wipe dry with a soft, lint-free cloth.

    B. Spray the appropriate cleaning solution onto a soft, lint-free cleaning cloth, and then wipe the screen with the dampened cloth.

    C. Wipe the screen with a dry soft, lint-free cloth or one lightly dampened with clean water.

    D. Spray the screen with compressed air.

19. A customer with whom your company has a service and maintenance contract has a workstation that is uniquely installed and desk-mounted. As a result, there is no place for you to connect your antistatic wrist strap when the computer is not connected to the wall outlet, which is inaccessible to you while performing service. What is the best way to handle the ESD issues with this workstation?

    A. Wear rubber-soled shoes when working onsite for this customer.

    B. Attach your wrist strap to the computer chassis anyway, to take advantage of the enormous electron sink that large amounts of metal provide.

    C. Rub a fabric-softener sheet over your clothes before servicing the workstation.

    D. Suggest that the customer purchase an antistatic bench-top computer mat to place under the computer.

20. At the end of a service call to repair a printer, the user tells you of another issue they are having with their scanner. Every time the user scans a file and then tries to use a specific application to open the file produced, they receive the message *This file cannot be used with this software*. Only that software package has issues. What should you do?

    A. Tell the user that this will be a new service call and they must open it separately and move to the bottom of the queue. Then leave, and wait to be dispatched on the new call.

    B. Open the file with an image-editing application, and reduce the resolution or change the file type.

    C. Return the scanner's software to its default settings.

    D. Sell the user a new application that can use the file in the expected manner.

GO ON TO THE NEXT PAGE

21. You have a software utility that is able to test a computer's ability to send and receive the proper signals on a standard serial interface. Not being able to control the device on the other end of the serial connection, what is the best way to make sure that both transmit and receive signals are available on the serial interface for the software to test?

    A. Use a hardware loopback plug.
    B. Disconnect the cable from the serial interface.
    C. There is no need to do anything special. Utilities like this can control the equipment on the remote end to place them in a software loopback state.
    D. Use a null-modem cable instead of the standard serial cable.

22. The read and write heads of floppy drives, tape drives, and optical disc drives, such as CD and DVD, can become dirty, obscuring their ability to function properly. Which of the following is the correct regular preventative maintenance to avoid such a problem?

    A. Regular use of such drives keeps the heads clean and free of contaminants. If a drive has not been used recently and now produces errors, access the drive repeatedly until the data is read properly.
    B. Use a cotton swab and rubbing alcohol to clean the heads.
    C. Use a head-cleaning system designed for the drive being cleaned.
    D. Execute the Head Clean utility in Windows on a regular basis.

23. Which of the following do surge protectors guard equipment from?

    A. Direct lightning strikes
    B. Voltage spikes in dirty power sources
    C. Power lags and sags
    D. Power loss

24. During a service call to install DSL for a client, a user requests that the internal analog modem be removed from their system. After removing the adapter, you search in vain for a blank bracket to go in its place. What should you do?

    A. Temporarily cover the hole in the backplane with electrical tape until you can replace it with a bracket.
    B. Unplug the adapter, but leave it in place to cover the hole.
    C. Leave the hole open until you can return with a blank bracket.
    D. Disable the card in the BIOS, and leave it installed.

25. A user complains that their system has started getting slower. You discover that their job entails the frequent creation of documents and presentations of various sizes and that for confidentiality reasons, once these data files are finalized, they are moved to a secure server and removed from the user's hard drive. What is the best solution to attempt to speed up the system again?

    A. Search for files that the user forgot to delete after they were moved to the server and that are building up and slowing down the system.
    B. Run the ASR utility.
    C. Run System Restore.
    D. Defragment the user's hard drive.

26. Which of the following TCP/IP protocols allows you to remotely configure an IP host that is set up to allow it?

    A. SMTP
    B. FTP
    C. Telnet
    D. DNS

27. While investigating the failure of a laptop's built-in LCD display, you discover that an external monitor works fine when connected to the VGA connector on the back of the laptop. Which of the following could cause this problem?

    A. The external VGA connector is defective.
    B. The inverter board is defective.
    C. The operating system has been configured to display on the external monitor only.
    D. The rectifier board is defective.

28. During a service call to diagnose a user's inability to access the network, you notice that the laptop with which the user is attempting access has no cable attached; the built-in wireless LAN antenna is turned off; and Bluetooth is enabled and working. Which of the following is the best start to resolving the issue?

   A. You need to investigate the Bluetooth connection to the LAN, which should be providing access already.

   B. A problem with the wireless LAN caused the antenna to turn off automatically.

   C. A network cable needs to be attached to the NIC, or the wireless antenna needs to be enabled.

   D. Stop and start the computer's workstation service.

29. Which of the following methods is the best way to remove a PC Card NIC from a laptop?

   A. Double-click the Safely Remove Hardware icon in the System Tray, and then stop the device before unplugging it.

   B. Hot-swappable devices like PC Cards should be unplugged like a cable to disconnect them from the system.

   C. Use Device Manager to uninstall the driver for the device before unplugging it.

   D. Use the switch on the PC Card to turn it off before unplugging it.

30. When you arrive onsite for a service call, you are forced to run an extension cord across an aisle with moderate traffic. You have confirmed that no cable guard is available onsite for temporary use. Which of the following is the best option?

   A. Do nothing. Moderate traffic is not a case for special consideration because pedestrians are spaced apart to have enough time to see the cable before tripping over it.

   B. Be vigilant, and warn each passerby about the hazard.

   C. Make a trip to your office or a store, whichever is nearest, to procure a cable guard.

   D. Secure the cable to the floor using duct tape.

31. On a service call to diagnose a laptop that will not stay powered up, which of the following is the *least* effective way to gather information about the problem?

   A. Observe the LED on the AC adapter.

   B. Swap the AC adapter with another one.

   C. Remove the battery from the laptop.

   D. Unplug all non–power related cables and PC Cards from the laptop.

32. A user complains that their pen mouse has stopped working. Which of the following is the most probable cause of the problem?

   A. The user is applying too much pressure to the tablet, which is confusing the driver.

   B. The user's stylus is upside down.

   C. The user is using the stylus from their PDA.

   D. The user has stopped holding down the button on the stylus while moving the stylus around the tablet.

33. While onsite, you discover that the customer's power supply is defective. On closer inspection, you believe you have narrowed the problem to a fuse on the inside of the power supply. Which of the following is the best course of action to take?

   A. To save the customer money, open the power supply, replace the fuse, and then test your solution.

   B. Replace the power supply.

   C. Bypass the circuit with the fuse on the outside of the power supply using a direct connection.

   D. Tell the customer that you do not perform work on power supplies because of the inherent danger.

34. Before ending your service call to install a printer and a scanner for a client, and after documenting your progress and testing your work on the individual devices, what should you do?

   A. Confirm that the two devices communicate properly with one another.

   B. Make sure the operating system can access both devices.

   C. Educate the primary user on how to use the new devices.

   D. Configure the printer's PostScript driver.

GO ON TO THE NEXT PAGE

35. In diagnosing a software issue with the functionality of a peripheral device, you discover that the driver for that device is two years old. Which of the following methods is the best way to upgrade the driver?

    A. Use the original distribution disc for the operating system.

    B. There is nothing for you to do. The latest driver is downloaded automatically when available.

    C. Download the latest driver from the manufacturer's website.

    D. Avoid the possibility of downloading a virus, and call the manufacturer to send you the latest driver by mail.

36. Which of the following commands reliably displays a listing of the files in the first-level folder named `data` on drive E: as well as all the folders and their files below it?

    A. `dir e:\data /s`

    B. `dir e:data /s`

    C. `dir e:\data /f`

    D. `dir e:data /f`

37. Which *two* of the following are reasons to use System Restore instead of Device Driver Roll Back?

    A. You want to restore application settings as well as roll back to earlier drivers.

    B. You want to restore user data as well as roll back to earlier drivers.

    C. You want to be able to specify the destination of the restore in case you prefer certain content to be in a different location.

    D. You are not sure which driver needs to be rolled back.

38. A user has been complaining that their battery gauge is not acting in a linear fashion. It shows that the LiIon battery has 98% of its charge left and that this equates to three and a half hours of run time; but after reaching about 50%, the laptop dies quickly, and the user's overall run time is never more than 90 minutes on a full charge. What can be done to improve this situation?

    A. The battery must be placed in a deep-charge apparatus overnight to reverse the cell oxidation.

    B. Nothing can be done short of a battery replacement.

    C. This is the standard operation of LiIon batteries, and the situation cannot be rectified.

    D. The battery needs to be calibrated.

39. Where is the best place to obtain firmware updates for computers and printers?

    A. A local computer superstore

    B. Through the Postal Service

    C. The manufacturer's website

    D. Via updates that are downloaded and installed automatically through Windows Update

40. Which of the following command-line commands allows you to open a text file and make changes to its contents?

    A. `TYPE`

    B. `EDIT`

    C. `OPEN`

    D. `ALTER`

41. The network administrator tells you that they would like to be able to encrypt files on a server but cannot do so. Which of the following command-line utilities may assist in resolving this problem?

    A. There is no such utility. You can only encrypt network traffic, not files.

    B. `ENCRYPT`

    C. `SECURE`

    D. `CONVERT`

42. The HP printer you have been sent to repair displays the message *PERFORM USER MAINTENANCE*. Which *two* of the following are most likely called for in this case?

    A. Clear all paper jams.

    B. Clean spilled toner out of the printer.

    C. Install a maintenance kit.

    D. Reset the page count.

43. A user claims to have restarted the Spooler service from the command line, but when you investigate from the Services snap-in, you notice that the Spooler service is not started. What command might the user have forgotten to issue to completely restart the spooler?

    A. `net start spooler`

    B. `spooler /start`

    C. `net spooler start`

    D. `spooler restart`

44. One of the departmental printers in your company has been seeing increased usage recently and does not appear to be up to the challenge. Complaints of slow printing and inefficient use of users' time are common. What can you do that is most likely to have the greatest positive effect on the problem?

    A. Use compression to reduce the size of the print jobs.

    B. Change the pickup and exit rollers to reduce slipping.

    C. Add memory to the computers of each user who prints to that printer.

    D. Add memory to the printer.

45. Which of the following gets you to the `C:\level1\level2` directory when the currently logged directory is `C:\level1\level2\level3\level4`?

    A. `cd ..\..`

    B. `cd .\.`

    C. `cd ..`

    D. `cd \..\..`

46. Which protocol can be used as a layer of security between HTTP and TCP, creating HTTPS in the process?

    A. IPSec

    B. SSL

    C. PPTP

    D. L2TP

47. Which command would you use to begin a backup of the C: drive from the command line that backs up only files that were changed today, overwriting an existing file named todayback.bkf in the root directory of the D: drive?

    A. `backup c: /f "d:\todayback.bkf" /m daily`

    B. `backup c: "d:\todayback.bkf" /v overwrite`

    C. `ntbackup backup c: /f "d:\todayback.bkf" /m daily`

    D. `ntbackup backup c: /f "d:\todayback.bkf" /v overwrite`

48. Which of the following addresses is considered a public IP address?

    A. 172.32.0.1

    B. 172.17.0.1

    C. 192.168.0.1

    D. 10.0.0.1

49. After completing a memory upgrade from 256MB to 512MB in a client's laptop, you attempt to confirm that the upgrade was successful and that all memory in the system is accessible. You notice that all but 32MB of the total RAM installed is accessible by Windows. What is the most likely issue at play here?

    A. The memory module you installed is defective.

    B. The onboard video adapter uses shared memory.

    C. The operating system does not report virtual memory in the total.

    D. The operating system always reserves 32MB for non-application purposes.

50. Which *two* of the following are compatible enough that they commonly run over the same access points?

    A. 802.11

    B. 802.11a

    C. 802.11b

    D. 802.11g

GO ON TO THE NEXT PAGE

51. Which of the following is *not* a reason to use a keyboard cover?

   A. To reduce the chance of damage from liquid spills

   B. To reduce the effect of dust build-up

   C. To increase the precision of keystrokes

   D. To reduce wear on the keys

52. Which of the following paths in Windows XP allows you to set Automatic Updates to automatically occur at 3:00 A.M. every day?

   A. Control Panel ➤ Automatic Updates. Then, select the radio button for Automatic, and select Every Day and 3:00AM from the drop-downs.

   B. Control Panel ➤ Administrative Tools ➤ Automatic Updates. Then, select the radio button for Automatic, and select Every Day and 3:00AM from the drop-downs.

   C. Start ➤ All Programs ➤ Automatic Updates. Then, select the radio button for Automatic, and select Every Day and 3:00AM from the drop-downs.

   D. Control Panel ➤ Automatic Updates. Then, select the radio button for Download Updates, and select Every Day and 3:00AM from the drop-downs.

53. In Device Manager, what is the easiest way to find out which device is using IRQ5?

   A. You have to double-click each device and click the Resources tab to observe the IRQ it is using until you find one that is using IRQ5.

   B. Click View ➤ Devices by Connection, and find IRQ5 in the list.

   C. Click View ➤ Resources by Type, and then expand Interrupt Request.

   D. Click View ➤ Devices by Type, and find IRQ5 in the list.

54. Bob in accounting, and a few others around the company, have been complaining that they are occasionally unable to access a resource that is being shared on a Windows XP Professional system. Which of the following is the best solution to the problem?

   A. Increase the user limit for the share from the default to a number that will cover all users who may simultaneously need the resource.

   B. Place the share on a Windows Server 2003 system.

   C. Add the affected users to the permissions list for the share.

   D. Allow the Everyone group access to the share.

55. Upon entering the equipment room at a customer site, you find that a water pipe has apparently burst, and the room has about an inch of standing water on the floor. The equipment appears to be unaffected thus far, and the server you have come to work on still needs attention. What should you do?

   A. Alert the network administrator, and do no work until the water is removed.

   B. Unplug the server, and perform the required service.

   C. Soak up the water around the server or use your antistatic vacuum to remove it before performing the necessary service.

   D. Remove the server, and perform the necessary service in a dry area.

56. How do you terminate a nonresponsive application in Task Manager?

   A. On the Applications tab, right-click the application, and then click End Process Tree.

   B. On the Processes tab, click the application, and then click the End Process button.

   C. On the Applications tab, click the application, and then click the End Task button.

   D. On the Applications tab, click the application, and then press the Backspace key.

57. Which *two* of the following paths can be followed to change the share permissions for a resource on a Windows XP Professional system?

    A. Control Panel ➢ Shares ➢ Double-click share ➢ Share Permissions tab

    B. Control Panel ➢ Administrative Tools ➢ Computer Management ➢ System Tools ➢ Shared Folders ➢ Shares ➢ Double-click share ➢ Share Permissions tab

    C. Right-click shared folder ➢ Properties ➢ Sharing tab ➢ Permissions button

    D. Right-click shared folder ➢ Properties ➢ Security tab

58. Which of the following is a reason to use REGEDT32 instead of REGEDIT?

    A. You want to be able to view and edit all functions and data types in Windows 2000.

    B. REGEDT32 is for use in 32-bit operating systems. REGEDIT is for use in 16-bit operating systems.

    C. You want to import and export registration entry (`.reg`) files.

    D. You want to be able to search the Registry in Windows 2000.

59. A customer in an electrically noisy environment complains that their Ethernet network is experiencing a large number of lost packets. Which of the following will have the most positive impact on this issue?

    A. Replace copper cabling with fiber optic cabling.

    B. Replace copper cabling with wireless components.

    C. Replace twisted-pair cabling with coaxial cabling.

    D. Replace Category 5 cabling with Category 5e or 6 cabling.

60. How do you find the Settings button in System Properties that takes you to Performance Options so that you can adjust virtual memory?

    A. Hardware tab ➢ Virtual Memory section

    B. Advanced tab ➢ Virtual Memory section

    C. Advanced tab ➢ Memory Usage section

    D. Advanced tab ➢ Performance section

61. A user complains that every time they try to access a secure website, their browser stalls and then gives a client-side error message. Which of the following may correct the user's problem?

    A. Reduce the browser's security level to the lowest possible setting.

    B. Upgrade the browser to the latest version.

    C. Configure the user's firewall to permit TCP port 443 traffic.

    D. Turn off pop-up blocking on the browser.

62. A user has consistently backed up their data on an external hard drive using the ASR Wizard. Recently, the user accidentally destroyed the ASR-based backup set. They used a server share to store a manual backup set without using the ASR Wizard. During a service call, you are asked to recover a damaged partition using the resources mentioned above. How is this situation likely to turn out?

    A. Not well. The ASR Wizard backs up only disk signatures as well as volume and partition information. If the backup set was not created at the same time with the ASR disk, the ASR process will not know it exists and will not be able to use it to restore the rest of the system.

    B. Fine. Even though the backup set and the ASR disk were created at separate times, the ASR process allows you to specify where the backup set is located.

    C. Fine. Once you run the ASR process, you can use the simplified installation of Windows to restore the latest backup set.

    D. Fine. The ASR disk contains a highly compressed image of the user's applications and data.

63. What is the term for the commercial entity that connects subscribers to the World Wide Web?

    A. Telco

    B. DNS

    C. ASP

    D. ISP

GO ON TO THE NEXT PAGE

64. A client has expressed concern over suspected unauthorized access to a particular network resource. You configure the potentially compromised server to audit access attempts to the resource. Where do you need to look later to check the results of your access audit?

   A. The same place where you configured the audit

   B. In the dialog accessed by the Permissions button found in the Sharing tab of the Properties dialog for the shared folder

   C. In the System category of Event Viewer

   D. In the Security category of Event Viewer

65. After installing a wireless network adapter in a Windows XP Professional computer system, you do not see an icon for the adapter in the System Tray. What's the best way to bring up a list of wireless networks in range of the adapter so you can begin the connection process?

   A. Run the Wireless Network Setup Wizard in Control Panel.

   B. Control Panel ➢ Network Connections ➢ Double-click the wireless adapter ➢ Click View Wireless Networks

   C. Double-click My Network Places on the Desktop.

   D. Control Panel ➢ Network Connections ➢ Right-click the wireless adapter ➢ Click Properties ➢ Check the box in the General tab labeled *Show icon in notification area when connected.*

66. Upon arriving at a client's location for a service call, you are informed that the user noticed their system acting strangely after making some changes. They rebooted and logged on a couple of times, but the system is still unstable. The user has no backup of the system, and now the system boots but fails to make it to the logon screen. Which of the following could you try in order to fix the problem?

   A. Safe Mode and System Restore

   B. Last known good configuration

   C. ASR process

   D. Device Driver Roll Back

67. While conducting a service call, you are interviewing the primary user of the problematic system. The user is a bit long-winded and seems to be saying the same thing over and over again. Which of the following is the best approach in this situation?

   A. In order not to hurt the user's feelings and perhaps stress your relationship, politely interrupt and begin recounting the problem in more technical jargon so the user will realize you know what you're doing and let you get to work on the problem.

   B. Actively listen to the user until they are comfortable that they have expressed the problem, and listen for additional information each time the user repeats something. Follow up with a brief synopsis that lets the user know you understand the issue.

   C. In order not to affect the rest of your schedule, abruptly stop the user, and make it clear that you understand and need to get to work on the problem.

   D. Interrupt the user, and recount the problem as you understand it in terms the user will understand so they are confident you know what is wrong and where to start.

68. When booting up in Windows XP, a user has recently started receiving the message *Invalid system disk*. Which of the following can possibly correct the problem?

   A. Boot into Safe Mode, and perform a System Restore.

   B. Use a boot diskette.

   C. Change the boot order in the BIOS.

   D. Restore the partition from a backup.

69. During an external customer service call in a building with very thin walls, you hear a manager on the phone discussing the impending termination of a couple of acquaintances of yours in the company. What should you do?

   A. Inform the manager that you heard their side of the conversation.

   B. Warn your friends about what you heard so they can begin making other plans.

   C. Let your supervisor know what you heard so your supervisor can handle the breach in confidentiality.

   D. Pretend that you never heard a thing, and carry on with the service call.

70. What is a recovery partition?

    A. A partition that has been recovered by one or more utilities

    B. A hidden partition accessible by a recovery CD

    C. The mirrored copy of a partition that provides fault tolerance

    D. A partition that holds deleted content for a configurable period of time to aid in recovering accidentally deleted data

71. While servicing a user's computer, their phone rings. You can tell from the caller identification that it is the user's supervisor's boss. You know that the user left their office to work on something else so they would not be in your way. What should you do?

    A. Answer the call, and explain to the manager where the user is and that they are engaged in legitimate work.

    B. Answer the call, and offer to take a message.

    C. Let the call go to voicemail.

    D. Pick up the receiver and put it back down, to buy the user a little more time to return before the manager calls back.

72. A user places a service call stating that their ink-jet printer has yellow ghosting around certain colored objects and that the spacing between horizontal lines is not consistent. Which of the following makes the most sense to try?

    A. Calibrate the printer.

    B. Change the print cartridges, especially the yellow one.

    C. Replace the belt for the carriage assembly.

    D. Clean the print cartridges.

73. A customer has attempted to install 20GB of RAM in a state-of-the-art dual-processor motherboard. You make a service call to investigate why the entire 20GB is not recognized by Windows XP Professional. Which of the following is the most likely cause of this problem?

    A. Windows XP Professional can access only 4GB of RAM.

    B. The wrong type of memory modules were used.

    C. With that much memory, there is no need for virtual memory, which reduces the total amount of RAM that can be recognized.

    D. Windows XP Professional cannot access multiple processors, which is throwing off the use of the RAM.

74. Which of the following has the greatest impact on reducing repeat calls for the same problem?

    A. Document the problem and your resolution.

    B. Be courteous to the customer, and listen actively.

    C. Escalate the problem to someone with more expertise.

    D. Test your solution.

75. You have a customer who is designing their IP addressing scheme. When asked how best to accommodate more IP hosts than the number of addresses they have, what should you suggest?

    A. Static addressing

    B. Dynamic addressing

    C. Public addressing

    D. APIPA

76. Which TCP/IP protocol or utility is instrumental in concealing a company's internal network addressing scheme from the Internet?

    A. HTTPS

    B. SSL

    C. IPSec

    D. NAT

77. Each of the following is required for an IP host to access the Internet *except*:

    A. DNS server's address

    B. Gateway

    C. Subnet mask

    D. IP address

78. All of the following TCP/IP protocols are related to e-mail *except*:

    A. IMAP

    B. HTTP

    C. SMTP

    D. POP3

GO ON TO THE NEXT PAGE

79. Which of the following technologies has the potential of delivering the highest bit rate for Internet access?

    A. Broadband

    B. LAN

    C. ISDN

    D. Dial-up

80. During a service call, the user explains that a common website that must be accessed to perform their job does not seem to display correctly and often shuts down Internet Explorer, asking if they want to report the error. Suspecting scripting issues and active content, you endeavor to disable scripting for the browser and try the website again. Where in Internet Options should you go to disable scripting?

    A. Advanced tab ➤ Security section ➤ Uncheck *Allow active content to run in files on My Computer*

    B. Privacy tab ➤ Advanced button ➤ Check *Override automatic cookie handling* ➤ Click Block for *First-party Cookies* and *Third-party Cookies.*

    C. Security tab ➤ Custom Level button ➤ Scripting section ➤ Click Disable for *Active scripting* and *Scripting of Java applets*

    D. Advanced tab ➤ Browsing section ➤ Check *Disable Script Debugging (Internet Explorer)*

Answer Key for Practice Test 1

1. D	21. A	41. D	61. C
2. B	22. C	42. CD	62. C
3. A	23. B	43. A	63. D
4. A	24. A	44. D	64. D
5. C	25. D	45. A	65. B
6. C	26. C	46. B	66. A
7. B	27. B	47. C	67. B
8. C	28. C	48. A	68. C
9. D	29. A	49. B	69. D
10. AD	30. D	50. CD	70. B
11. A	31. D	51. C	71. C
12. B	32. C	52. A	72. A
13. C	33. B	53. C	73. A
14. A	34. C	54. B	74. D
15. C	35. C	55. A	75. B
16. B	36. A	56. C	76. D
17. A	37. AD	57. BC	77. A
18. B	38. D	58. A	78. B
19. D	39. C	59. A	79. B
20. B	40. B	60. D	80. C

Answer Explanations for Practice Test 1

1. D. Odds are that you *will* destroy something with ESD if you are not properly protected from doing so. However, worse than no wrist strap is a rigged-up wrist strap. Wrist straps are not simply metallic conductors that connect to ground. Such a solution will almost certainly lead to your electrocution without the proper resistance included in the system. Take great lengths to avoid putting the customer off by leaving their premises to retrieve tools or equipment. This can lead to lost confidence in you and your company. If you cannot contact someone to bring you what you need while you continue to work, consider that the outside of the power supply is a grounded shell that can dissipate static, as long as the power supply is plugged into a three-prong outlet. Once grounded, make sure you unplug the power cord from the wall outlet before beginning work, unless you have a hard switch on the power supply that removes DC power from the inside of the computer system.

2. B. Although AGP is no slouch when it comes to high-speed graphics, PCIe is the state of the art today for graphics, especially in the gaming arena. PCI could be considered a distant third, and ISA should never be considered in this day and age, even if you can find a new motherboard that has ISA slots on it.

3. A. It just so happens that class-C fire extinguishers are made specifically for electrical fires. Their chemical makeup reduces the risk of worsening the short and causing more problems, especially with circuits that are still live. Not as good at protecting life in the same situation are liquids, such as water, coffee, or soft drinks. Never use such substances to try to put out an electrical fire. Potential repercussions include expanding the scope of the electrical fire by involving other live circuits and allowing the current to travel up the stream of liquid to you and electrocute you. Leaving the fire or blowing it with compressed air, and thus fanning it, could easily result in the total loss of your surroundings before the fire department shows up to fix your lapse in judgment.

4. A. Number Lock generally does not affect these keys on a laptop, ever since the separate cursor-movement pad was added to standard keyboards. Laptop keyboards do, however, sometimes place these functions on other keys in a color related to the Fn key, meaning that the Fn key must be held to gain access to their functions.

5. C. Never try to look at any concentrated light source, such as the laser of a printer or its equivalent. Looking at the light mechanism is not like looking at a common household light bulb. You won't be able to see a telltale burnt filament and you can cause permanent damage to your eyes. Because the technician does not have access to any tool that acts as a flexible photometer, the best bet is to replace the EP cartridge with a known good unit to attempt to disprove your theory by trying to print because replacing the EP cartridge replaces a large number of components other than the laser or LED array. If it works, you've already implemented the solution, and you're that much closer to closing out the call.

6. C. The `tracert` utility performs a traceroute between the source device and the destination that you specify by address or name in the command. A traceroute sends a special UDP message to the destination, but it manipulates the Time to Live (TTL) field in the IP header so that it only gets to the first device in the path and then to one additional device each iteration of the message. Each successive device discards the message because of the expired TTL and sends an executioner's message back to the source. The source uses this message to identify the next device in the path and build a list for the user to follow. By executing a traceroute, either you find that the path through to the destination is healthy and discover the devices along the path, or you find the last device that is able to send you an executioner's message, which usually—but not always—tells you where the break in the path lies. The `ping` utility tests only the existence of the destination. It gives no details of the intermediate path other than whether it is healthy or *potentially* not healthy; you can't be sure whether a failed ping means the path is broken or the destination is simply not active. The `nslooklup` utility helps you discover problems with your name servers and general DNS functionality, and `ipconfig` tells you local settings for the device on which it is executed.

7. B. Although you won't see a model of how the atoms and molecules bind to one another, the MSDS does include the chemical formula for the substance in Section 9. The MSDS is a generic form that applies to hazardous substances in a general sense, not to any particular lot or shipment of a substance, so manufacturers, wholesalers, and distributors cannot be listed. Although you will not find a number to call in the MSDS when investigating how to dispose of a substance, Section 13 outlines any disposal consideration particular to that substance. Section 8 details suggested equipment and clothing to help protect eyes, skin, and lungs.

8. C. You absolutely can have multiple ATA drives in the system at the same time. Without making one of the drives a slave, you cannot put them both on the same controller. For them both to remain masters, they must be on different controllers. Systems that have been tampered with are potentially out of warranty, either due to warranty violation or past warranty expiration. Either way, you stand to produce revenue by working on the failed system, as long as it is agreed up front that this call is not covered under warranty. Besides, a standard disclaimer should always be signed by the customer before you perform service on any system. Of these options, supplying power to the new drive when none was supplied previously is the most likely fix.

9. D. Of course, diskettes are meant to be inserted into a floppy drive, and exceeding the maximum amount of RAM in a computer has no effect on the floppy drive. The constant steady light on a floppy drive indicates that the data cable is inverted, which is a very easy thing to do because few drive headers have single-side keying to match the connector on the cable. Often, there is a notch on both sides of the header, making it simple to put the cable on upside down.

10. AD. Laptops tend to require SoDIMMs and the even smaller MicroDIMMs for memory upgrades. SIMMs, which are the predecessors to DIMMS, and RIMMs, which carry Rambus memory, are rarely, if ever, used in today's laptops.

11. A. The noise could have been caused by something dragging across the fan as it runs. If so, part of the solution is to replace the cable or cord that may have been damaged over time, as well as the CPU fan, the motor of which has been compromised by the added resistance of running against the impediment. The noise also could have been the motor's bearings in the various stages of failing. When the noise stops, it generally means that the bearings have worn so much that the motor can no longer turn the fan, a serious problem that will lead to overheating. You cannot generally remove a CPU fan without also removing the integrated heat sink, not that you would want to. A passive cooling mechanism has only a prayer of working in BTX systems, but you should always go with the active cooling option to make sure. You save the customer money by replacing the fan versus charging them for the time to solder broken wires, and you avoid the curse of an unpredictable rigged solution.

12. B. The symptom indicates an overheating issue. Dust blocking vents and fan exhaust outlets can lead to overheating. The BIOS monitors the temperature of the CPU and the inside of the case. When the temperature reaches a lower threshold, a warning usually sounds. At an upper threshold, the system shuts itself down to avoid damage. Shallow dents would not impede the engineered flow of air in the system, although more severe dents might cause shorts with the motherboard or other circuitry, which could conceivably lead to ungraceful shutdowns. Although improper cable management is not linked with system failure, it is a potential safety hazard and should be corrected. Keyboard malfunction of any type does not lead to regular system shutdowns. Only a freak automatic series of keystrokes could shut the system down, but this would likely happen only once, if at all.

13. C. This is a classic symptom of a short on the motherboard. Because the power supply interface on the motherboard is a two-way connection, such feedback to the power supply incapacitates it. The fan generally jumps when you press the power button, but it never starts. Problems with the power button and the power cable are basically all-or-nothing in nature: They cause the system either to work or to appear completely dead with no fan movement at all. Software issues never manifest themselves in this fashion.

14. A. The least invasive, least static-conducting method should be used in this situation. Passive plastic implements are the way to go. Despite every technician's urge, magnets and computers don't mix, and the idea of using your fingers bring up concerns about static and body oils. The static-resistant vacuum is great for removing dust and contaminants that are not directly on circuit boards, but it can dislodge small components easily and cause more problems immediately or down the road—not to mention that you will have to retrieve the screw from the vacuum's belly if you need it.

15. C. Video drivers don't just go bad. If the monitor ever displayed the right colors, this wouldn't be something to investigate further. Individual cathode rays don't generally fail, and Gaussian effects don't cause such symptoms over the entire display. An improperly inserted video connector and some cheaper switching equipment, which mimics poor connectivity at times, can cause this phenomenon. Check the connection first, before switching out the monitor or trying other, more drastic remedies.

16. **B.** The /K switch causes the Command Prompt window to remain open after the command executes. The /C switch ensures that it closes, as does executing the ping command alone without preceding it by cmd. Executing the cmd command with the ping command as an argument with no switches causes cmd to ignore the ping command. It opens a Command Prompt window and does nothing further.

17. **A.** Some pre-XP operating systems used the Emergency Repair Disk (ERD). XP uses a process known as Automated System Recovery (ASR). The ASR disk is used in conjunction with the ASR process to access a backup archive for completely restoring the system to the state of the latest backup. As a result, your backup should not be stored on the same physical drive as the one you are archiving. The Recovery Console is an incredible utility for a nuts-and-bolts surgical resurrection of a failed system, but damaged partitions are best recovered using ASR when available. System Restore requires a working system and is generally best used for rolling back drivers and application settings to a state when the system was stable.

18. **B.** You shouldn't spray or apply any liquid directly to a monitor's screen. The point where the screen and monitor casing meet is not watertight. Liquids can seep into the interior of the monitor, causing a short-circuit or other expensive damage. A cloth moistened with the approved cleaner for the screen should be used to remove contaminants such as dirt and dust, which dry cloths and compressed air cannot completely remove, and oils, which require more than water to remove.

19. **D.** The appropriate bench-top computer mat will connect permanently to the appropriate ground point as well as give you a place to connect your wrist strap. This is by far the best solution among those given. Antistatic mats for the floor that you stand on will work as well. The excessive electrical resistance created by rubber-soled shoes can prevent you from completing a path to ground through your body, thus protecting you from certain forms of electrocution but inhibiting the decay of static caused by walking around as you work. A wrist strap attached to an ungrounded computer chassis tends to equalize the difference in potential between you and the chassis but not between you and external adapters and other equipment, thus allowing you to cause damage to those devices as well as to the computer through the strap. The fabric-softener solution is a neat trick for emergencies, but this is not a technologically sound resolution, and there is the possibility of building up dangerous charges even if you successfully treat all of your clothing.

20. **B.** Certain software cannot accept images with parameters that are beyond the specifications of the software. Generally, you can reduce the resolution in either on-screen pixels or printed dots per inch to allow their use. Optionally, you can change the file type from low-loss formats, such as TIFF, to others that produce smaller files, such as JPEG. Unless you will ruin your schedule for the rest of day, you should never leave the user high and dry by hiding behind your company's policy. The customer loyalty you build will outweigh the hassle incurred by adjusting your schedule. There is no reason to believe that the software that produced the image is not at its default settings. The problem is the software being used to access the scanned image. If only that software has issues, then there is no reason to make broad adjustments that could potentially affect other software that is currently working with the images. There is also no reason to assume that you can replace the user's software with a similar package that can use the image. Work on the image to make it compatible with the existing software instead of trying to find software that the image works with as is.

21. **A.** This is the exact situation for which hardware loopback plugs were created. They short, or interconnect, the transmit and receive pins as well as other complementary pins on the local interface, taking cabling and remote devices out of the equation so that you can test the local interface without unpredictable influences. Null-modem cables allow you to connect DTE devices to other DTE devices, such as one computer to another; however, they don't help in this case. Unconnected interfaces don't test properly, and these utilities are too generic to control specific remote devices.

22. **C.** Each of these drives has a corresponding relatively inexpensive head-cleaning system that is readily available in the market and is good for multiple uses before needing to be replaced. Using a swab dampened with alcohol is not an ineffective solution, but you must take care not to apply alcohol to rubber rollers and other parts that the alcohol can cause to dry and crack. Additionally, many heads are not easily accessible for this type of maintenance, and the drive must be disassembled first. If the drive is already disassembled and unable to accept media due to the disassembly or lack of power, then the proper cleaning system is not an option, and the swab method may be the only solution; but it should not be considered a regular preventive maintenance routine. Unfortunately, regular maintenance does not keep read/write heads clean (quite the opposite), and there is no Head Clean utility in Windows.

23. B. Surge protectors are not perfect and generally cannot be expected to guard against direct lightning strikes. They should be removed from the wall outlet during electrical storms to protect them and the equipment connected to them. Surge protectors do nothing in the event of power loss or brownouts. Their role is to make sure that common power spikes are clipped before they do cumulative damage to sensitive electronic equipment. You should keep an eye on the indicator, if one exists, to tell when the internal protection components are no longer able to do their job. When the protector has run its course, you should replace it immediately.

24. A. It is important for proper airflow that you cover all open slots in the backplane and in other areas of the case and chassis, and that you not run the system with the case off. The system unit is engineered under fairly tight constraints for the power supply to draw air from the various ventilation holes around the case and chassis across the internal components to cool them. Holes like those left when you remove adapters can disturb the normal flow of air across the components, leaving stagnant pockets of air that can heat to unsafe levels. Adapters generally cannot be disabled in the BIOS, and you should not leave a card unplugged in the system because it can make accidental partial contact and cause the system to fail or even damage the card or motherboard or both. Besides, the user wants the card out and may have another use planned for it. Another point that bears mentioning is that an improperly seated adapter does not completely cover the hole in the backplane, negating the value of leaving it in.

25. D. Moving files implies copying them and then deleting them in one motion. Therefore, and by definition, no files that had already been moved would be left on the user's hard drive. Regardless, a leftover or two wouldn't cause the system to slow down noticeably. Performing an ASR or System Restore turns the system back to an earlier time, to the last backup and selected restore point, respectively. The ASR process causes you to lose recent work without guaranteeing a system speed-up. System Restore does not affect data files one way or another. As files are deleted, such as during a move, empty spots are left in the file system. As new, larger files are written to the disk, they are often split up, or fragmented, across the smaller empty spots. The more fragmentation that occurs, the more time the physical drive has to spend jumping around to piece files together as they are read into memory. Running the DEFRAG utility places the fragmented pieces of a file together in the proper order on the disk, speeding up access when the time comes.

26. C. Telnet is the protocol used for this purpose. SMTP is for sending e-mail. FTP is for transferring files. DNS resolves network names to IP addresses.

27. B. Once you confirm that the internal/external-display keyboard control is not biased against the internal display, the most likely cause for the loss of image on a built-in laptop display is the failure of the inverter board, which converts the DC voltage supplied by the power adapter back to AC, which the laptop's LCD display requires. The voltages in this component are extremely high, although the amperage is not so large. Nevertheless, care should be taken when handling this component because focal burning and deep pitting of the skin can occur and, in just the right situation, even this lower amperage can be deadly. Rectifiers convert AC to DC, as in the case of the laptop's power adapter. There are no rectifiers that affect only the LCD display on laptops. Obviously, the external VGA connector on the laptop is fine if the external monitor displays the image properly. No operating-system control turns off the built-in display. Any software controls for monitor selection that may exist come from specialized utilities that operate on top of the operating system. Be aware, however, that the Multiple Monitors feature of Windows, accessible from Display Properties, can cause unpredictable results on occasion, sometimes requiring a System Restore to return the system back to a time of normal functionality and return the display to the built-in LCD. This is not a feature designed to switch between internal and external monitors.

28. C. This is a simple situation of no viable network connection. Either plug the NIC into a switch or hub or enable the wireless antenna (a manual task) if there is a wireless LAN in the vicinity. Bluetooth is designed for cord replacement, as with keyboards, mice, and peripherals, not for wireless networking.

29. A. Although it is true that these devices are hot swappable, meaning they can be inserted and removed while power is applied to the system, Windows dedicates resources to them while they are in use, making it less than elegant to simply unplug them. Use the Safely Remove Hardware utility in the System Tray to stop these devices when possible. If they do not appear in the list within the utility, unplug the PC Card with no prior action.

30. D. Avoiding leaving the work site and not being distracted by watching for pedestrians are important considerations here. Either diversion promises to annoy or disappoint the customer by prolonging the service call. However, you must do something. Even one passerby during your service call is enough to worry about. Anyone can have an obstructed view of the floor at any time. All it takes is for a person to have a cumbersome load in their arms, and a cord across the floor becomes a cruel booby-trap. If you have the duct tape with you, eliminate the possibility of a shoe slipping under the cord by creating your own temporary cable guard.

31. D. Generally, cables and PC Cards do not contribute to power issues with laptops, but they should still be removed to rule them out. However, doing so is the least likely option to provide useful diagnostic information. The AC adapter is the likely cause and most adapters have an LED that illuminates when they are working properly. However, swapping out with another power adapter of the same type that is known to be in working condition is a quick test of the adapter's viability. Occasionally, batteries can affect power to the system and interfere with a working adapter's ability to power the laptop. If removing the battery causes the system to begin working properly, change out the battery. Removing the battery is also suggested any time you are servicing a laptop, just to make sure there is no negative influence from the battery. Doing so also helps to confirm the quality of the DC power the laptop is receiving from the AC adapter.

32. C. A pen mouse has a special stylus that must be used in order for the mouse to work. Most models have buttons that are programmable for various functions, such as double-clicking and application launching, but not for making the mouse work in general. It could be that the user has started holding the pen upside down. But a change in behavior like this is not likely, and many models allow you to hold the pen upside down to erase or produce broader strokes; so that's not as likely to be the problem as the user using a passive stylus from his PDA, which most often will not actuate the sensors in the tablet. These units are also not pressure-sensitive, so even if the user changed this behavior, it would not result in a cessation of operation.

33. B. There is no need to perform any work directly on the power supply, which includes opening it or creating a hazard like bypassing a fusible link with a direct connection. Furthermore, the danger to your life is not worth a repair; it might not solve the problem even if you survive. If you tell the customer that you don't do such work, you imply that someone else may, which is highly unlikely. It also makes you look like you have a serious limitation in your ability to get the system up and running. With the price of a new power supply being what it is, hook the customer up with a new one, and get them going rather quickly in the process. You look efficient, and the customer is happy and not out too much money.

34. C. The two devices do not need to communicate directly with one another. Anything that is scanned and then printed goes through the operating system between these two phases. Part of the testing of your work should have been making sure the operating system can access both devices and that the proper print driver was configured and working. Making any changes to the drivers means that you must test your solution again to be able to claim you have tested it at all. One of the last things you should do, and only after you are sure the installation is final, is educate one or more users on the basic functionality of the equipment or software, and optionally on any specific functionality that you were requested to provide.

35. C. Don't expect Microsoft to keep drivers updated for most components. Drivers on the original distribution disc for the operating system age with the disc. The latest driver is generally available on the Internet, as long as the manufacturer is not defunct. You shouldn't be concerned with viruses coming from the website of a reputable manufacturer. If you are not comfortable with such a solution, and the user does not have a reliable antivirus application installed, advise them to allow you to install one before downloading the driver.

36. A. The key is the word *reliably*, given that you know the correct switch is /S and not /F, which is an invalid switch for the DIR command. When you issue the command, if the logged directory on drive E: is not the root directory (E:\), leaving the backslash off will not produce the desired results.

37. AD. Neither System Restore nor Device Driver Roll Back has any effect on user data, positive or negative. Anything restored or rolled back returns to its original location. You have no control over that. Device Driver Roll Back is ideal when you use a last-in, first-out approach to updating device drivers. If you test the system after updating a driver, you have a better chance to find out if it caused problems. However, despite the best hyper-vigilance, problems can arise after some time, obscuring the identity of the true culprit. In such a case, and when you need to restore application settings, System Restore shines over Device Driver Roll Back, which requires you to enter the Driver tab of Properties in Device Manager for the specific device whose driver needs to be rolled back.

38. D. Although LiIon batteries do not form a chemical memory per se, they do suffer from irreversible life-robbing oxidation. When the battery has a significant charge, this oxidation is exacerbated by heat, such as that generated by the laptop in which the battery is installed or by leaving the battery in a car exposed to ambient heat. There is no cure for this effect, and the battery has a finite life expectancy; but the effect also has a bearing on how Windows' battery gauge interprets the battery's remaining charge. Calibrating the battery, which really means calibrating Windows' gauge or synchronizing the gauge with the battery, involves allowing the battery to discharge completely once in every 30 charging cycles until the laptop loses power. Doing so keeps the gauge more accurate, and users who watch their gauge vigilantly will not be caught off guard.

39. C. Firmware, such as BIOS and internal printer software, is not something you can buy off the shelf; and Windows Update does not deal with firmware, just updates to the operating system, including security patches and driver updates. Most manufacturers that produce equipment with replaceable or flashable firmware offer the latest revisions on their websites. This is the first place you should look for updates.

40. B. The EDIT command opens a text-based editing utility that allows you to create or edit an existing text file and save your changes. The TYPE command only displays the contents of a text file. OPEN and ALTER are not command-line commands, although you might recognize OPEN from utility shells, such as FTP and TELNET.

41. D. There actually is a utility called CIPHER that encrypts and decrypts files at the command line, but the question is vague enough to allow for a utility that solves the problem without actually performing the encryption. Besides, if CIPHER worked in this situation, a network administrator would have been able to encrypt the files from within the GUI already. Nothing will allow you to encrypt files on a FAT partition, and apparently, that is the obstacle in this case. The CONVERT utility allows a one-way conversion of file systems from FAT to NTFS. The administrator probably would have known that one, too. Anyway, once you have an NTFS file system, files can be encrypted from the operating system's GUI or by using CIPHER at the prompt. The ENCRYPT and SECURE utilities don't exist.

42. CD. Clearing paper jams is not considered maintenance, which is more proactive in nature. It's more of a reaction to an event. Although cleaning toner out of a printer can be considered proactive in most cases, it's not something the printer will ask for in a message like this. You can argue that responding to any message is hardly proactive maintenance, but it's tough to deny when you're using something called a "maintenance" kit. The average maintenance kit contains items such as a fuser assembly, a transfer roller, and pickup or feed/separation rollers. Some printers reset the page count when you install a maintenance kit, but in case it doesn't work out that way, there are methods to reset the count yourself. Installing a maintenance kit before the page count reaches the threshold that spawns the warning message can make it more difficult to reset the page count, but there are usually ways to do so with little additional effort.

43. A. Restarting the spooler from the command line involves first stopping the Spooler service and then starting it. The command to stop it is net stop spooler. The command to start it is net start spooler. This process may be necessary on occasion if printing fails consistently.

44. D. Up to a point, the more memory you equip a printer with, the less average time a user has to wait for a print job to leave their computer in order to free them up to do other things. It has almost nothing to do with how much memory is in their computer. While compression can give the perception of having more memory, there is no way to control how much memory the data takes up in the printer without changing the page-description language, which was not an option here and is not always effective or welcome. While printers are rated for a certain maximum number of pages per minute, and more memory does not generally affect this rating, users are not as sensitive to the speed at which pages come out of the printer as they are with how long their system is tied up when they print, similar to how frustrated users become with web pages that are slow to load. To further the analogy, you can be dealing with the fastest website known to man but still suffer from local bottlenecks that slow it and all other sites down to a crawl. Try to impress a user of that network with the statistics of that website. It's all about the users' perception of performance when you receive complaints about slow response. In this case, increased printer memory improves this perception better than the other options.

45. A. Although it looks like so much Morse Code, each of these commands does something, but only cd ..\.. traverses two levels up toward the root, which is where you want to be. The .. represents the parent directory. A single dot (.) represents the current directory. Therefore, ..\.. means the parent of your parent. Read these the same way you do a normal directory path, from left to right. The operating system takes you to the directory represented by the first symbol, up to the first backslash, if any. Then, the operating system takes you to the next symbol, if applicable, and so on. So, the path `.\.` means "stay where you are" and then "stay where you are." You go nowhere with that one. The path `..` takes you up only one level. The path `\..\..` takes you to the root first; then, the two parent symbols (`..`) are lost because the root has no parent. You wind up at the root directory, and you might as well have issued the command `cd\` to do the same thing.

46. B. HTTPS is really just HTTP with an added layer between it and TCP for security. This security layer can be created with Secure Sockets Layer (SSL) or Transport Layer Security (TLS). HTTPS allows for secure transactions, such as credit card orders, over a decidedly insecure network. IPSec is another way to ensure end-to-end TCP/IP security; but it requires more deliberate configuration and is not used in browser security, which requires a more dynamic peering between the server and any number of randomly changing clients. PPTP and L2TP are both Layer-2 tunneling protocols that secure a link between two points on the same local network but cannot provide the end-to-end security afforded by HTTPS.

47. C. The base command is `ntbackup`, but you must specify `backup` as the operation immediately afterward, even though there is no restore operation from the command line. The next parameter is generally the top level from which to start the backup, including all files and subdirectories below (`c:`). The `/F` switch is followed by the name of the file that will hold the backup set (`"d:\todayback.bkf"`). The quotes are suggested but not required. The `/M` switch is required when you are requesting a backup type other than the default set in the GUI Backup utility. Because you can't know the default in this case, it must be specified (`daily`). A daily backup captures only those files that were altered today. The `/V` switch turns verification on or off. It has nothing to do with appending or overwriting the backup set. Overwriting is the default action. You use the `/A` switch to override it and append to the backup set.

48. A. The private-use addresses for intranets are in the following ranges:

CLASS	LOWER LIMIT	UPPER LIMIT
A	10.0.0.0	10.255.255.255
B	172.16.0.0	172.31.255.255
C	192.168.0.0	192.168.255.255

As you can see, 172.32.0.0 is just out of the Class B private range, making it public. There are other special-use addresses that can be considered private, such as the non-routable APIPA (self-configuration) range of 169.254.0.0 through 169.254.255.255. However, only the addresses in the table are considered usable for private intranets.

49. B. Some inferior onboard video adapters in laptops, and even desktop machines, use a technology known as shared video memory. The video card uses a portion of the main system RAM to hold frame buffers that are to be displayed next—in this case, 32MB. Better video adapters have their own RAM for this purpose. If you notice pixilation of moving video, you may be able to enter the BIOS routine to increase the amount of shared video memory. Be aware that doing so decreases the amount of system RAM available to the operating system and applications, sometimes reducing performance noticeably.

50. CD. The original 802.11 as well as both 802.11b and 802.11g used a transmission frequency of 2.4GHz. This means that, theoretically, access points should be able to handle signals from all three technologies, but only 802.11b and 802.11g are commonly seen working together in practice. The 802.11a specification transmits at a frequency of 5GHz and higher and is not natively compatible with access points made especially for the other standards. This does not mean that circuitry for both sets of frequencies cannot be combined in the same equipment. It can be, and hybrid access points are sold for such hodge-podge environments.

51. C. Unfortunately, keyboard covers can increase the "fat-finger" effect. These flexible plastic covers attempt to fit your keyboard model perfectly, but pressing one key can still affect neighboring keys on occasion. Even if the cover works flawlessly, it will not increase the precision of your keystrokes. Some covers are simply attractive fabric covers that you place over the keyboard at the end of the day while the system is not in use to protect against airborne contaminants. Others are waterproof plastic skins that remain in place during use to reduce the effects of spills, dust, and other contaminants on a fulltime basis. They also take the wear and tear of normal use, reducing wear on the keys themselves.

52. A. Automatic Updates is an applet in Control Panel. Within Automatic Updates, you have the choice of selecting Automatic and then setting the time to check for updates and automatically install them. Otherwise, you can choose to automatically download updates but manually install them when notified, to be notified when updates are available for manual download and installation, or to turn off Automatic Updates.

53. C. The Resources by Type view in Device Manager has an IRQ category that lists all devices that have an IRQ grouped by expansion bus and then by IRQ number. You can spot all devices using a specific IRQ without any additional action other than possibly scrolling.

54. B. Windows XP Professional, Windows 200 Professional, and Windows NT Workstation 4.0, as well as similar workstation versions of Windows, have a default hard limit of 10 simultaneous users per share, which cannot be increased. Therefore, increasing the limit from the default is not a solution because it is not possible to do so. The Server versions theoretically have no upper limit, so migration of the resource to one of these systems is the best solution. If the users have occasional success accessing the resource, permissions are not an issue.

55. A. Although this solution appears to violate the rule that you should complete the necessary service to the extent of your abilities, that rule is trumped when it comes to your safety and that of others. Even entering a room with standing water and working equipment could lead to death from electrocution. Take no chances whatsoever when liquids and electricity are involved. Stay out of the room, and leave the mitigation to trained professionals. Inform the individual or department responsible for the equipment room of the situation, and wait for the problem to be rectified.

56. C. You can click the application on the Applications tab and then press the Delete key to terminate an application, but the Backspace key does nothing. End Process Tree is a selection when you right-click a process on the Processes tab; no such selection is available on the Applications tab. The Processes tab does not list applications—it lists processes, which are smaller portions of applications. Terminating a process with the End Process button or selecting End Process after right-clicking the process is not often the most effective way to terminate an entire application. Component processes can remain, causing issues. Even the End Process Tree is not favored over using the Applications tab to end an application and all of its processes in one fell swoop.

57. BC. Computer Management is the plug-in required to access all the shares currently configured on the system. There is no Share applet in Control Panel. Alternatively, you can use the Share tab in the Properties dialog of the folder being shared to access the Permissions button and arrive at the same dialog. Although the Security tab does include permissions, they are for file-level access on an NTFS volume. It is true that you may need to adjust these at some point because most administrators leave share-level access wide open, limit who is allowed to log on locally to the system, and adjust the more granular file-level permissions to control who is allowed to access the resource locally and from across the network. Doing it this way allows the administrator to grant a mixture of access to different files within the same folder. Share permissions apply only to shared folders because files cannot be shared individually. So, managing permissions the other way around leads to everyone with access to the shared folder having access to all files and folders within. Adjusting both file-level and share permissions creates a complex access-control rule that may be difficult to troubleshoot later. Because the question mentioned share permissions, there is no justification for changing anything on the Security tab, regardless of standard practice.

58. A. This can be a tricky question if you're not completely up on your Registry editing trivia. In Windows XP and Server 2003, REGEDT32 is a small application that runs REGEDIT. So, in XP there is no reason to run REGEDT32 over REGEDIT. However, in NT-based versions of Windows all the way back to NT 3.*x*, including Windows 2000, there are marked differences. REGEDIT did start out in NT 3.*x* as a way to examine the `reg.dat` file from a 16-bit Windows operating system—but in a 32-bit NT environment (not in the 16-bit environment), making that option for this question not quite correct. Since NT 4.0, REGEDIT has been a serious utility for making changes in the active Registry. In Windows XP and Server 2003, it's the only utility that does so, with REGEDT32 being just a launch pad for REGEDIT. In Windows 2000, REGEDIT does not allow viewing and editing of all functions and data types the way REGEDT32 does. Specifically, those with more than 256 characters are not displayed by REGEDIT. Microsoft suggests that you run REGEDIT over REGEDT32 in Windows NT 4.0 and 2000 for the searching capabilities and to be able to import and export `.reg` files, not the other way around. REGEDT32 doesn't support these features in Windows NT 4.0 and 2000.

59. A. Of the choices given, only fiber optics will provide immunity from electrical interference. Coaxial cable tends to have more EMI resistance than twisted-pair cable, but in general, there is no clear path to migrate from twisted-pair to coax and stay with the same Ethernet technology. Wireless communication is susceptible to EMI and RFI as well. If you are upgrading from Fast Ethernet to Gigabit Ethernet in an environment without EMI/RFI issues, switching the cabling infrastructure from Category 5 cabling to a higher standard is required for the newer echo-cancellation encoding technique used where three pairs carry the same signal and can more easily interfere with return traffic on the lone pair; but doing so does not decrease external interference substantially.

60. D. In System Properties, you must choose the Advanced tab to find the Performance section. The Settings button therein takes you to the Performance Options dialog, where you can choose another Advanced tab to find the Virtual Memory section and the Change button that takes you to the Virtual Memory dialog. Note that two Advanced tabs are at play here, and the first one, which is in System Properties, has neither a Virtual Memory section nor a Memory Usage section. Those are under the second Advanced tab, which is under the Performance Options dialog.

61. C. This appears to be a problem with the user's system accepting HTTPS traffic, which uses TCP port 443, instead of the port 80 that HTTP uses. Opening the system's firewall (or the entire network's firewall, if this is a widespread issue) to allow HTTPS traffic should solve the problem. Such a specific outage would not be related to the browser version or to pop-up blocking, which does not target only secure sites or any primary-page sites. Reducing a browser's security level has no effect on the types of sites you can visit; doing so allows you to adjust how the browser handles scripting, downloads, and authentication.

62. C. Although it is true that the ASR wizard only backs up disk signatures as well as volume and partition information, it does create a simplified installation of Windows that you can use to restore backup sets. However, the ASR process is not interactive enough for you to specify this disjoint backup set during the recovery process; you'll have to wait until the process is complete to restore it. There's no way to fit a useful image on a diskette using today's compression technologies. It is highly recommended that you use the appropriate option in the Backup or Restore Wizard to create an ASR disk and a full system backup at the same time on a regular basis or use the ASR Wizard in the Advanced mode of the Backup Utility to do the same thing. Note that creation of the backup set alone does not automatically update the ASR disk, so doing it that way will require a slightly more manual approach in the end.

63. D. *Internet service provider* is the generic term for any entity that resells Internet access to other ISPs or directly to consumers. One such entity is the telephone company, or Telco, but it is only one of many and is not synonymous with ISP. DNS is a protocol for name-to-address resolution, and Active Server Pages (ASP) is a Microsoft protocol that uses server-side scripting to create dynamic web pages that can carry variable information from one page to another.

64. D. You configure the audit in the Security tab of the Properties dialog for the shared folder by clicking the Advanced button and then clicking the Audit tab. You must also globally enable auditing, or the audits you set will not be performed. This is definitely not where you can find results of the audit. There are also no results in the Sharing tab for you to see. The Security category in Event Viewer is where you will find entries generated by the triggers you set in the Audit tab for the resource.

65. B. Double-clicking the wireless adapter in Network Connections and then clicking on the View Wireless Networks button brings up the list of available wireless networks that are in range. The Wireless Network Setup Wizard is something very different and is not meant for simply finding wireless networks in range of the computer. My Network Places does not have a direct link to the list of available wireless networks. Showing the icon in the System Tray is a good idea to make bringing up the list of wireless networks easier in the future, but doing so does not bring up the list. However, once the icon is in the System Tray, you can right-click it and click View Available Wireless Networks or double-click the icon in the System Tray and then click the View Wireless Networks button. Alternatively, you can double-click the icon in the System Tray, click the Properties button, and then select the Wireless Networks tab where there is another button labeled View Wireless Networks as well as a list of past networks recognized that allows you to set the order of preference among them for future connection. You can also remove unused wireless networks that appear in the Preferred Networks list, which contains wireless networks to which you have attached in the past.

66. **A.** The best way to handle this problem, as well as system lock-ups, auto-restarts, and repeated bluescreen errors, is to hit F8 while booting. Doing so gives you access to the Startup Options screen, which contains a number of choices, including Safe Mode, Safe Mode with Networking, and Last Known Good Configuration (LKGC), among others. Choosing one of these two Safe Mode options is the way to start Windows with minimal drivers. You then hope that the driver causing the system instability will not be loaded, which is highly likely. Once you are in this limited Windows session, you can run System Restore normally and roll back to a time when the system ran properly. In this case, the problem with LKGC is that whenever the user logs on, the Registry location that LKGC draws from is updated with the system's current settings. Although it's considered known-good, you can tell from the question that it's really not good. Without any further changes, the system began to refuse to make it to the logon screen, hardly a known-good configuration that you would want to roll back to. You must be able to log on to Windows to perform a Device Driver Roll Back, and the ASR process requires a backup set. There is also likely no ASR disk, not that it would matter without a system backup set.

67. **B.** Although enough is enough, and we all tend to know when we've heard enough, never interrupt the user. Instead, wait until the user seems to have arrived at the end of a thought, and then use what you have gleaned from active listening to formulate questions that may direct the user to fill in any blanks that still exist, or reassure the user that you understand the problem by summarizing what you have heard and even let them know what you intend to do. Many times, more technical users feel that they must repeat themselves to get all pertinent information across. Some even use you as a sounding board as they verbally go through all possible scenarios and issues as if they are telling you something—but really they are just thinking out loud. Regardless of the reason for their ramblings, it is never OK to express distaste for the user's methods or communications skills. Doing so can only lead to strained relationships.

68. **C.** If this is a problem with the hard drive, there won't be any booting going on, so Safe Mode is out. Even a boot diskette relies on the master boot record of the hard drive to complete the bootup process. If that would work, you wouldn't receive an error message like this. The diskette gets you past problems with files like BOOT.INI, NTDETECT.COM, and NTLDR. That would be a great option if you ever receive the *NTLDR is missing* error message during boot. You can't restore the partition. You need to be able to boot the system to restore a backup. If the problem is that a nonbootable CD is in the drive, that makes the option to change the boot order in the BIOS sound logical. For the system to get hung up on a nonbootable CD that was recently inserted and forgotten in the drive, it must be higher than the hard drive in the boot order, and there must be a CD in the drive. So, change the boot order, or remove the CD (the latter of which wasn't provided as an option).

69. **D.** Mind your own business. Don't bring anyone else into the situation, even the manager you overheard. Doing so can have an even more negative impact on those involved than you imagined otherwise. Your supervisor might make an error in judgment based on what you share. The manager might change plans based on your knowledge of the situation, possibly leading to the deselecting of your company as their contractor. It is highly likely that your friends will be given plenty of time to get their affairs in order per the company's termination policy. Let the normal course of events take place without muddying the waters. Confidentiality is the most important virtue in this case.

70. **B.** Some manufacturers use a portion of your hard drive to store a compressed image of your original hard drive as it was delivered to you. A recovery CD is included in the distribution materials for you to use when you want to access the hidden partition to restore your system to factory defaults. This destroys any data on the drive, so it should be used only as a last resort, much like the ASR process. Generally, the value of being able to get back up and running quickly on a clean system outweighs the loss of storage capacity, which is often prorated in the specifications so that you are not looking for the extra capacity when the time comes. Recovery partitions take the place of cramming ever-larger images onto CDs and DVDs. A major drawback to this scheme is the case of a catastrophic failure that makes the entire hard disk inaccessible, including the recovery partition.

71. **C.** This is another case when you should not involve yourself in a customer's business. You should intrude only as far as you need to in order to complete your service call. No matter how well you think you know the user or the management of the company, answering calls on their phone or treating any of their equipment as if it was yours can never end well.

72. A. This is a classic issue with the way ink-jet printers operate. Calibration allows you to tell the printer how it needs to adjust its operation based on how the print cartridges are situated in the cartridge carrier, which along with slight differences in cartridge manufacturing can have large impacts on print quality given minute changes. Think of this as the synchronization between what the printer thinks it is doing and what you observe it doing. The two should be identical, and calibration is the way to approach that goal. Nothing you can do with the cartridges themselves or the carriage assembly will resolve this problem. In fact, each time you remove the cartridges and put the same ones back in, you run the risk of throwing the printer out of calibration. Utility-based cartridge cleaning that cleans the cartridges without the need to remove them is ideal to avoid the need for further calibration. However, cleaning addresses the problems of smearing and smudging more than the inconsistencies in printing that calibration addresses.

73. A. The motherboard is a little more than XP Professional can handle. You can either consider it room to grow or a wakeup call to upgrade to XP Professional x64 Edition, which can handle 128GB of physical RAM. XP Professional can utilize as many as two processors and as much as 4GB of RAM. The following table lists the maximum number of processors and the maximum physical RAM for the various modern Windows operating systems. Incorrect memory modules do not physically fit into the wrong slots, which would result in no memory and no booting. Again, with XP Professional, there is no way to access 20GB of physical RAM, so the virtual memory setting is immaterial, regardless of the technical relationship between physical and virtual memory.

WINDOWS OPERATING SYSTEM	MAXIMUM PROCESSORS	MAXIMUM PHYSICAL RAM
XP Professional	2	4GB
XP Professional x64 Edition	2	128GB
Server 2003 Standard Edition	4	4GB
Server 2003 Standard x64 Edition	4	32GB
Server 2003 Enterprise Edition	8	64GB
Server 2003 Enterprise x64 Edition	8	1TB
Server 2003 Datacenter Edition	32	128GB
Server 2003 Datacenter x64 Edition	32	1TB
2000 Professional	2	4GB
2000 Server	4	4GB
2000 Advanced Server	8	8GB
2000 Datacenter Server	32	32GB

74. D. If you are sure the solution you implemented solved the problem, then you can be confident that the next service call is a new problem. Even though you can never be 100 percent sure that your solution completely fixed the issue, you can be 100 percent sure that it did not. Proper testing after implementation brings out all but the best hidden weaknesses in your solution. An aloof attitude and a harried pace point to the cliché *haste makes waste*, and the waste here is your time and the customer's, as well as their money. You won't have your customer for long after assuring them their problem is resolved, only to return in the near future to address the exact same issue. Have confidence in yourself enough to stick with the problem until it's resolved, even if you have to consult with someone with more expertise while you are working. Don't hand off the customer to anyone else if you can help it, especially if you are the face of your company for that customer. Documenting the resolution is of the utmost importance. Doing so will reduce the amount of time for the second call involving the same problem, but documentation and courteousness don't help reduce the need for a second visit.

75. B. None of these choices will completely solve the customer's problem. NAT with private addressing would be ideal in a situation where there are more devices requiring Internet access than public IP addresses. However, trying to give each host a static IP address will guarantee those hosts that do not receive addresses will not be able to access the Internet. Public addressing is too vague to know what the plan is. It could be static, or it could be dynamic addressing. APIPA is not routable and is generally considered more of a response to an error than anything else. Dynamic addressing uses a DHCP server to hand out addresses to those requesting one. The hope that this scheme will work is based on the assumption that not all hosts will be powered up simultaneously. This could work with shift-based personnel but is not likely to perform any better than static addressing for highly active networks.

76. D. Although all the answers represent networking security measures, only Network Address Translation makes a private intranet appear to the Internet as a public network without divulging the internal address structure.

77. A. A user's Internet experience is seriously degraded without access to a DNS server, but it is not ruined. Every IP host must have a minimum of an IP address and subnet mask to define the network they are on and who they are on that network. In order to communicate outside their network—on the Internet, for example—a host must know the local address of the router that can get them to the remote network. This is known as a *gateway*, which is the original term for a router but can refer to various other things today, such as a protocol converter.

78. B. IMAP and SMTP are both used to send e-mail through a mail server, and POP3 is used to retrieve e-mail from a mail server. Although you might use HTTP to access an online e-mail service, such as Hotmail or Yahoo Mail, HTTP only shuttles the website's pages to you for viewing. Either SMTP or IMAP is at work behind the scenes to send the mail, and POP3 is used to retrieve your mail from the service's mail server (as well as other servers you specify) for delivery to your inbox.

79. B. In order from slowest to fastest, dial-up, ISDN, broadband, and LAN all provide access to an ISP. Although some LANs still run at speeds slow enough to be outpaced by broadband services, such as DSL, the potential of LANs runs into the tens of gigabits per second, whereas cable and DSL have barely topped 10Mbps with only hundreds of megabits on the horizon. Dial-up is limited by the FCC to 53Kbps, and ISDN is not much faster with a single BRI line offering only 128Kbps. The question is one of potential, not absolutes. Even the fastest LAN can be crippled by slow WAN technology, making it slower than some or all of the other options. However, with the faster WAN technologies, such as OC-192 at 10Gbps, the faster LANs are hard to beat.

80. C. Script support is enabled or disabled in the Security tab of Internet Options. The most reliable and granular way of controlling scripting in your browser is to set custom levels of security, allowing you to specifically enable and disable the settings that you choose.

Answer Sheets for Practice Test 2

(Remove This Sheet and Use It to Mark Your Answers)

Section 1
Multiple Choice Questions

CUT HERE

1 Ⓐ Ⓑ Ⓒ Ⓓ Ⓔ		41 Ⓐ Ⓑ Ⓒ Ⓓ Ⓔ
2 Ⓐ Ⓑ Ⓒ Ⓓ Ⓔ		42 Ⓐ Ⓑ Ⓒ Ⓓ Ⓔ
3 Ⓐ Ⓑ Ⓒ Ⓓ Ⓔ		43 Ⓐ Ⓑ Ⓒ Ⓓ Ⓔ
4 Ⓐ Ⓑ Ⓒ Ⓓ Ⓔ		44 Ⓐ Ⓑ Ⓒ Ⓓ Ⓔ
5 Ⓐ Ⓑ Ⓒ Ⓓ Ⓔ		45 Ⓐ Ⓑ Ⓒ Ⓓ Ⓔ
6 Ⓐ Ⓑ Ⓒ Ⓓ Ⓔ		46 Ⓐ Ⓑ Ⓒ Ⓓ Ⓔ
7 Ⓐ Ⓑ Ⓒ Ⓓ Ⓔ		47 Ⓐ Ⓑ Ⓒ Ⓓ Ⓔ
8 Ⓐ Ⓑ Ⓒ Ⓓ Ⓔ		48 Ⓐ Ⓑ Ⓒ Ⓓ Ⓔ
9 Ⓐ Ⓑ Ⓒ Ⓓ Ⓔ		49 Ⓐ Ⓑ Ⓒ Ⓓ Ⓔ
10 Ⓐ Ⓑ Ⓒ Ⓓ Ⓔ		50 Ⓐ Ⓑ Ⓒ Ⓓ Ⓔ
11 Ⓐ Ⓑ Ⓒ Ⓓ Ⓔ		51 Ⓐ Ⓑ Ⓒ Ⓓ Ⓔ
12 Ⓐ Ⓑ Ⓒ Ⓓ Ⓔ		52 Ⓐ Ⓑ Ⓒ Ⓓ Ⓔ
13 Ⓐ Ⓑ Ⓒ Ⓓ Ⓔ		53 Ⓐ Ⓑ Ⓒ Ⓓ Ⓔ
14 Ⓐ Ⓑ Ⓒ Ⓓ Ⓔ		54 Ⓐ Ⓑ Ⓒ Ⓓ Ⓔ
15 Ⓐ Ⓑ Ⓒ Ⓓ Ⓔ		55 Ⓐ Ⓑ Ⓒ Ⓓ Ⓔ
16 Ⓐ Ⓑ Ⓒ Ⓓ Ⓔ		56 Ⓐ Ⓑ Ⓒ Ⓓ Ⓔ
17 Ⓐ Ⓑ Ⓒ Ⓓ Ⓔ		57 Ⓐ Ⓑ Ⓒ Ⓓ Ⓔ
18 Ⓐ Ⓑ Ⓒ Ⓓ Ⓔ		58 Ⓐ Ⓑ Ⓒ Ⓓ Ⓔ
19 Ⓐ Ⓑ Ⓒ Ⓓ Ⓔ		59 Ⓐ Ⓑ Ⓒ Ⓓ Ⓔ
20 Ⓐ Ⓑ Ⓒ Ⓓ Ⓔ		60 Ⓐ Ⓑ Ⓒ Ⓓ Ⓔ
21 Ⓐ Ⓑ Ⓒ Ⓓ Ⓔ		61 Ⓐ Ⓑ Ⓒ Ⓓ Ⓔ
22 Ⓐ Ⓑ Ⓒ Ⓓ Ⓔ		62 Ⓐ Ⓑ Ⓒ Ⓓ Ⓔ
23 Ⓐ Ⓑ Ⓒ Ⓓ Ⓔ		63 Ⓐ Ⓑ Ⓒ Ⓓ Ⓔ
24 Ⓐ Ⓑ Ⓒ Ⓓ Ⓔ		64 Ⓐ Ⓑ Ⓒ Ⓓ Ⓔ
25 Ⓐ Ⓑ Ⓒ Ⓓ Ⓔ		65 Ⓐ Ⓑ Ⓒ Ⓓ Ⓔ
26 Ⓐ Ⓑ Ⓒ Ⓓ Ⓔ		66 Ⓐ Ⓑ Ⓒ Ⓓ Ⓔ
27 Ⓐ Ⓑ Ⓒ Ⓓ Ⓔ		67 Ⓐ Ⓑ Ⓒ Ⓓ Ⓔ
28 Ⓐ Ⓑ Ⓒ Ⓓ Ⓔ		68 Ⓐ Ⓑ Ⓒ Ⓓ Ⓔ
29 Ⓐ Ⓑ Ⓒ Ⓓ Ⓔ		69 Ⓐ Ⓑ Ⓒ Ⓓ Ⓔ
30 Ⓐ Ⓑ Ⓒ Ⓓ Ⓔ		70 Ⓐ Ⓑ Ⓒ Ⓓ Ⓔ
31 Ⓐ Ⓑ Ⓒ Ⓓ Ⓔ		71 Ⓐ Ⓑ Ⓒ Ⓓ Ⓔ
32 Ⓐ Ⓑ Ⓒ Ⓓ Ⓔ		72 Ⓐ Ⓑ Ⓒ Ⓓ Ⓔ
33 Ⓐ Ⓑ Ⓒ Ⓓ Ⓔ		73 Ⓐ Ⓑ Ⓒ Ⓓ Ⓔ
34 Ⓐ Ⓑ Ⓒ Ⓓ Ⓔ		74 Ⓐ Ⓑ Ⓒ Ⓓ Ⓔ
35 Ⓐ Ⓑ Ⓒ Ⓓ Ⓔ		75 Ⓐ Ⓑ Ⓒ Ⓓ Ⓔ
36 Ⓐ Ⓑ Ⓒ Ⓓ Ⓔ		76 Ⓐ Ⓑ Ⓒ Ⓓ Ⓔ
37 Ⓐ Ⓑ Ⓒ Ⓓ Ⓔ		77 Ⓐ Ⓑ Ⓒ Ⓓ Ⓔ
38 Ⓐ Ⓑ Ⓒ Ⓓ Ⓔ		78 Ⓐ Ⓑ Ⓒ Ⓓ Ⓔ
39 Ⓐ Ⓑ Ⓒ Ⓓ Ⓔ		79 Ⓐ Ⓑ Ⓒ Ⓓ Ⓔ
40 Ⓐ Ⓑ Ⓒ Ⓓ Ⓔ		80 Ⓐ Ⓑ Ⓒ Ⓓ Ⓔ

Directions: For each of the following questions, select the choice that best answers the question or completes the statement.

1. While working inside a computer, you drop a small metal part into the vent of the power supply. What should you do?

   A. Unplug the power supply and remove the screws that hold its cover on. Use plastic tweezers to remove the part.
   B. Unplug the power supply immediately and wait a couple of hours or more before attempting to remove the power supply and shake the part out.
   C. Unplug the power supply and invert the computer system to try to shake the part out through the vents it went in.
   D. Unplug the power supply and reach in for the part with a magnet, making sure not to make contact with anything. Let the attraction draw the part through the air to the magnet.

2. While you're finishing a service call, your client asks if you have the appropriate memory modules with you to upgrade their desktop computer. You discover that the computer has one available slot and uses DDR2. Which of the following is most likely the type of module that you need?

   A. MicroDIMMs
   B. SIMMs
   C. SoDIMMs
   D. DIMMs

3. While servicing a laser printer, you suspect the waste toner receptacle is full. Eager to diagnose the problem and fix it, which of the following is the best method to quickly test your theory?

   A. Empty the waste-toner receptacle.
   B. Replace the toner cartridge.
   C. Confirm that there is still fresh toner in the cartridge. If so, the waste-toner receptacle should not be full.
   D. Install a maintenance kit.

4. Upon arriving onsite for a service call involving a dead system, you discover that pressing the power button has no effect at all. The motherboard was recently upgraded, and the system hasn't worked since. Which of the following is the most likely cause?

   A. Too many adapter cards are installed for the new motherboard.
   B. The power button is defective.
   C. There is a short underneath the motherboard.
   D. The power supply is dead.

5. What's the easiest way to determine if a device is using DMA channel 2?

   A. Use Device Manager to run through each device in succession until you find the device using it.
   B. Choose View ➢ Devices by Connection in Device Manager.
   C. Choose View ➢ Resources by Type in Device Manager.
   D. Open a Command Prompt, and execute the command net show dma.

6. While diagnosing an unresponsive external LCD attached to a laptop, you feel strongly that you know exactly which internal component of the LCD is to blame. Which of the following is the best course of action?

   A. Replace the external LCD with a known working unit, and try the unresponsive LCD on a known working system.
   B. Open the LCD's case and perform diagnostics on the suspected component, or replace it and test the results.
   C. Open the case, but before performing any work, discharge the flyback transformer's charging capacitor.
   D. Remove the external monitor, and use the built-in LCD display.

GO ON TO THE NEXT PAGE

7. Which of the following items is *not* included in a substance's MSDS?

   A. The chemical formula for the substance

   B. The chemical model for the substance

   C. First-aid measures

   D. Handling and storage guidelines for the substance

8. You are adding a hard drive and a DVD burner to a system that already has a hard drive and a CD burner. All devices have ATA interfaces. What is the best way to pair the devices?

   A. Put each of the four devices on its own controller.

   B. Pair the fastest hard drive with the fastest optical drive on the same controller. Pair the slower devices on another controller.

   C. Pair the hard drives on one controller and the optical drives on another controller.

   D. Place the three fastest drives on one controller and the slowest on another controller.

9. Which of the following is the best utility to use to restore all programs and data from a damaged partition when running Windows XP?

   A. Recovery Console

   B. ERD

   C. System Restore

   D. ASR

10. Which of the following is *not* a difference between FAT32 and NTFS volumes?

   A. NTFS volumes can be larger.

   B. NTFS files can be larger.

   C. The minimum recommended volume size is greater for NTFS.

   D. FAT32 supports the 8.3 naming convention. NTFS does not.

11. Which of the following function keys is used during Windows XP setup to install third-party SCSI drivers?

   A. F2

   B. F6

   C. F8

   D. F12

12. A user reports beeping coming from their computer during use, followed shortly by an automatic shutdown of the system. Which component is most likely the cause?

   A. CPU fan

   B. Power supply

   C. System speaker

   D. BIOS

13. During a service call, you need to access the company LAN from the cubicle in which you are working. However, there is no available connection in that cube. Due to construction in the area, a cable guard is covering electrical cables running to the wall across the aisle, where there is a LAN connection. What should you do?

   A. Tell the user that you need to come back with a hub to be able to share their LAN connection.

   B. Run your network cable in the same cable guard as the electrical cables.

   C. No longer than you need the connection, run it, and be sure to remove it as soon as you are finished with it.

   D. Run the network cable separately, and secure it with your own cable guard or duct tape.

14. Which of the following methods will produce a bootable floppy diskette in Windows XP Professional that places you at an A:\> prompt after bootup?

   A. My Computer ➢ Right-click floppy drive ➢ Click Format ➢ Check *Create an MS-DOS startup disk* ➢ Click Start.

   B. At a Command Prompt, enter the command `format a: /s`.

   C. At a Command Prompt, enter the command `format a: /fs:fat`.

   D. My Computer ➢ Right-click floppy drive ➢ Click Format ➢ Check *Make bootable* ➢ Click Start.

15. Which of the following is a difference between the commands COPY and XCOPY?

   A. By using the /Y switch, you can suppress the prompt to approve the overwriting of existing files with the XCOPY command, but not with COPY.

   B. XCOPY is capable of copying a directory and all of its subdirectories in one command. COPY is not.

   C. With the COPY command, you are able to specify the source to copy from only, and the destination will have the same name in the current directory. With the XCOPY command, you must explicitly specify both source and destination.

   D. The COPY command has switches that allow you to copy based on the archive attribute bit. The XCOPY command does not.

16. A client has a system running Windows XP Professional with 4GB of RAM and does not want to upgrade to a server version of Windows. However, the client wants to be able to access 8GB of RAM. Which of the following is the best solution to this problem?

   A. Upgrade to the 64-bit version of XP Professional.

   B. Do nothing except add 4GB of RAM. It will be recognized immediately.

   C. Add a second processor to the system.

   D. There is no way to access more than 4GB of RAM with a 32-bit address bus.

17. A user is trying to transfer information between two laptops in an area without a wired network connection. Additionally, the laptops are out of range of the company's wireless network. Which of the following is the best and most convenient method to transfer the data between most standard laptops?

   A. Bluetooth
   B. Standard serial cable
   C. Infrared
   D. Burn a CD.

18. A client's computer keeps overheating and shutting down. Which of the following is *not* a probable cause?

   A. The client has four hard drives installed.
   B. The CPU fan has stalled.
   C. The chassis cover is removed.
   D. An adapter slot is open.

19. A user attempted to update the driver for their video adapter. Things apparently did not go well. The user has booted into Safe Mode and called you to help. What is the least invasive thing you can do in Safe Mode to get the system working properly again?

   A. Run ASR.
   B. Run System Restore.
   C. Use Device Driver Roll Back.
   D. Just use Safe Mode from now on.

20. While investigating the failure of a laptop's built-in LCD display, you discover that an external monitor works fine when connected to the VGA connector on the back of the laptop. Which of the following could cause this problem?

   A. The external VGA interface is defective.
   B. The LCD cutoff switch is sticking or bad.
   C. The connector on the cable from the monitor is not completely connected to the interface.
   D. The system booted up into Safe Mode.

21. While you are on a service call, a user produces a DVD-ROM and asks you to install the application on it in addition to the service you were dispatched to perform. Upon closer inspection, you notice the disc is a bootleg copy of copyrighted material. What should you do?

   A. Refuse to install the software, and immediately notify anti-piracy authorities.

   B. In order to retain the customer, install the software and ask the user to keep it between the two of you.

   C. Refuse to install the software, and notify the user's supervisor of the infraction.

   D. Politely explain that you will be unable to install the software and that using it is against the law.

22. Which class of fire extinguisher is for ordinary combustible materials only, such as paper, wood, and plastic, and should never be used on electrical or chemical fires?

   A. Class A
   B. Class B
   C. Class C
   D. Class D

GO ON TO THE NEXT PAGE

23. What is the name of the device that allows you to locally test a serial interface without dependence on a remote device?

   A. Hardware loopback plug

   B. Crossover cable

   C. Multimeter

   D. Termination plug

24. A user is interested in protecting their equipment against power spikes, which have claimed two systems already. The user is not interested in keeping the system up during power outages. They simply wish to protect their equipment against harmful power anomalies. Which of the following should you suggest to satisfy these requirements?

   A. UPS

   B. Surge protector

   C. Generator

   D. Power strip

25. Which of the following commands allows you to see the physical address of your NIC in Windows XP Professional?

   A. `winipcfg`

   B. `ipconfig /mac`

   C. `ipconfig /all`

   D. `ifconfig`

26. Which of the following commands clears only the attributes that prevent the file `test.txt` from being deleted at the command line, setting all others?

   A. `attrib test.txt -r +s -h`

   B. `attrib -r +s +h test.txt`

   C. `attrib -r -s -h test.txt`

   D. `attrib test.txt -r -s -h`

27. A user's machine has lost intranet and Internet access. Which of the following utilities executed on the user's computer is the best to determine if the default gateway is functional?

   A. NSLOOKUP

   B. Traceroute

   C. Ping

   D. IPCONFIG

28. Which of the following is the path to the System Restore utility?

   A. Start ➢ All Programs ➢ Accessories

   B. Start ➢ All Programs

   C. Start ➢ Control Panel

   D. Start ➢ All Programs ➢ Accessories ➢ System Tools

29. What command would you use to tell if your hard drive needed to be defragmented?

   A. `defrag /a`

   B. `defrag -a`

   C. `defragment -a`

   D. `defragment /v`

30. All of the following are recommended laptop troubleshooting techniques *except*:

   A. Remove unneeded peripherals.

   B. Remove the battery.

   C. Remove the AC adapter.

   D. Attach an external monitor.

31. A user reports that the Safely Remove Hardware icon does not appear in the System Tray, and the user needs to unplug their USB NIC. Which of the following is the easiest way to proceed with success?

   A. Pull the USB NIC out of the USB port.

   B. Power the system down before removing the USB NIC.

   C. Use Device Manager to uninstall the driver for the USB NIC before unplugging it.

   D. Disable the device in Device Manager.

32. You respond to a service call concerning a computer on which the System File Checker was run. It was intended that the check be done immediately, but it now runs every time the system starts. Which syntax should have been used to run the check one time immediately without needing to restart the system?

   A. `sfc`

   B. `sfc /scanonce`

   C. `sfc /scannow`

   D. `sfc /scanboot`

33. A customer complains that their computer consistently runs for a little while and then shuts down on its own. Upon arriving, you begin your inspection of the system. Which of the following is the *least* likely culprit?

  A. Dust buildup at the chassis vent holes
  B. No heat sinks on the RAM modules
  C. A stalled CPU fan, system fan, or power-supply fan
  D. Poorly routed internal cables

34. Which of the following paths takes you to Event Viewer?

  A. Start ➢ All Programs ➢ Accessories ➢ System Tools ➢ Event Viewer
  B. Start ➢ Run ➢ `mmc eviewer`
  C. Control Panel ➢ Administrative Tools ➢ Event Viewer
  D. Control Panel ➢ Event Viewer

35. A computer that boots to an ATA hard drive with only Windows XP installed (no other operating system) fails to boot because of a missing or corrupt file in the root directory of the system partition. Which of the following files could be the problem?

  A. `BOOTSECT.DOS`
  B. `NTBOOTDD.SYS`
  C. `NTLDR`
  D. `NTOSKRNL.EXE`

36. Which path takes you to a utility that you can use in conjunction with Terminal Services to create a remote session on another device as if you were local to that machine?

  A. Start ➢ All Programs ➢ Accessories ➢ System Tools
  B. Start ➢ All Programs ➢ Accessories ➢ Communications
  C. Control Panel ➢ Administrative Tools
  D. Start ➢ All Programs

37. Which of the following commands is one of the two required at the command line to restart the spooler?

  A. `net stop spooler`
  B. `net spooler /stop`
  C. `net spooler start`
  D. `net restart spooler`

38. Which *two* of the following commands obtain help for the `DIR` command?

  A. `dir help`
  B. `help dir`
  C. `dir /?`
  D. `dir /h`

39. On a service call to diagnose a dead monitor, your interview with the user yields the fact that the last thing the user did was clean the monitor. Which of the following is a possible cause of the outage?

  A. The user applied an abrasive cleaner.
  B. The user misapplied the cleaner.
  C. The user wiped the screen with the wrong type of cloth.
  D. While cleaning, the user accidentally turned the horizontal position knob too far.

40. Which of the following commands displays a listing of the hidden files and folders in the first-level folder named `data` on drive `E:` as well as all the folders and their files below it?

  A. `dir e:\data /ah`
  B. `dir e:\data /h`
  C. `dir e:\data /ar`
  D. `dir e:\data /x`

41. A user reports errors on startup related to a specific application that the user needs to continue running when XP starts. Which of the following is the best way to test your theory that a conflict with a recently installed application is to blame?

  A. Use Add or Remove Programs in Control Panel to uninstall the suspected application.
  B. Disable the automatic startup of the suspected application in MSCONFIG.
  C. Use REGEDIT to disable the suspected application.
  D. Use the Recovery Console to test your theory.

42. Which term means synchronizing a software battery gauge with the actual battery?

  A. Bsync
  B. Refreshing
  C. Reconciliation
  D. Calibration

GO ON TO THE NEXT PAGE

43. Which of the following command-line commands allows you to display the contents of a text file without opening it for editing?

   A. SHOW

   B. TYPE

   C. PRINT

   D. VIEW

44. A user opened a trouble ticket after receiving a new specialty laptop. Some of the letter keys produce numbers and other symbols. What is the most likely issue with this service call?

   A. Number Lock is on and affects how these keys are used.

   B. The keyboard is mapped to another language.

   C. The keyboard is set for scientific mode and must be set back to standard mode in Control Panel.

   D. The user must hold the Fn key while pressing these keys.

45. In attempting to use the CONVERT command to change the file system, you are not able to perform or confirm the conversion. Which of the following is most likely *not* the issue?

   A. You must reboot to finish the conversion.

   B. You are trying to convert to NTFS, and the volume is already NTFS.

   C. You are running CONVERT through Start ➢ Run and using the incorrect syntax.

   D. You executed a syntactically correct command to convert a volume from NTFS to FAT.

46. While sitting at a C:\DATA> prompt, which *two* commands are necessary to change the prompt to C:\DATA\SUB1> if the DATA subdirectory currently has no subdirectories?

   A. CD\SUB1

   B. CD SUB1

   C. MD C:\SUB1

   D. MD SUB1

47. Which of the following statements about disks, partitions, and logical drives is *not* true?

   A. A drive letter can correspond to either a partition or a logical drive.

   B. One disk can have multiple partitions.

   C. Operating systems based on NT, such as Windows 2000 and XP, can boot from any drive other than B:, regardless of its drive letter.

   D. There can be only one extended partition on a disk.

48. What is the term for a partition that has been marked in such a way as to allow it to be made bootable?

   A. Boot-ready

   B. Boot partition

   C. Primary

   D. Active

49. Which of the following gets you to the C:\level1\level2\level3 directory when the currently logged directory is C:\level1?

   A. cd level2\level3

   B. cd level3

   C. cd \level2\level3

   D. cd \level3

50. Which command creates a text file called test.txt from the command line and places you into editing mode until you enter the end-of-file character, ^Z?

   A. copy test.txt con:

   B. copy test.txt con

   C. copy con test.txt

   D. copy test.txt+con test.txt

51. Which of the following Windows XP utilities allows you to fix certain disk errors and recover readable information from bad sectors?

   A. FDISK

   B. SCANDISK

   C. CHKDSK

   D. Recovery Console

52. Which of the following is a Microsoft protocol that is compatible with a protocol suite created by Novell?

A. IPX

B. NetBEUI

C. NWLink

D. SPX

53. In general, after a memory upgrade, what must you do to get the system to recognize the memory?

A. Visit the manufacturer's website, and download the device driver for the new modules.

B. Do nothing. The system recognizes the memory automatically.

C. Be ready to provide the correct keystroke at just the right moment to enter the BIOS routine, and input the amount of total RAM installed.

D. In Windows, open System Properties, and enter the total amount of RAM installed.

54. Which of the following paths reliably takes you to a utility where you can set services to not start up when XP boots?

A. Start ➢ Administrative Tools ➢ Services

B. Start ➢ All Programs ➢ Services

C. Start ➢ All Programs ➢ Control Panel ➢ Services

D. Start ➢ Control Panel ➢ Administrative Tools ➢ Services

55. Which *two* of the following paths in Windows XP take you to Windows Explorer?

A. Right-click the Start button, and then click Explore.

B. Start ➢ All Programs ➢ Accessories ➢ Windows Explorer.

C. Start ➢ All Programs ➢ Windows Explorer.

D. Right-click an unaffiliated area of the Desktop, and then click Explore.

56. In Windows XP, which path accesses Device Manager?

A. Start ➢ All Programs ➢ Device Manager

B. Control Panel ➢ Add Hardware ➢ Device Manager

C. Control Panel ➢ System ➢ Hardware tab ➢ Device Manager

D. Control Panel ➢ Device Manager

57. What is the term for a contiguous section of hard drive used to page information in and out of RAM to give the appearance of more RAM than exists?

A. Expanded memory

B. Extended memory

C. Defragmentation

D. Virtual memory

58. Which of the following is a session-layer protocol that can be transported using NetBEUI, IPX/SPX, or TCP/IP, the names of which can be converted to IP addresses by WINS for routing over an IP network?

A. NWLink

B. AppleTalk

C. HTTP

D. NetBIOS

59. When you finish a service call, the user mentions to you that most of the sites they visit on a regular basis for their job default to the previous user of the system for login credentials. The user would like you to see if you can clear the historical information that causes this behavior. Which *two* of the following methods can you use to do so?

A. Click the Clear History button in the History section of Internet Properties.

B. Click the Delete Cookies button in the Temporary Internet Files section of Internet Properties.

C. Delete the contents of the `%SystemDrive%\temp` folder.

D. Delete the contents of the `%SystemDrive%\Documents and Settings\`*username*`\Local Settings\Temporary Internet Files` folders.

60. Which of the following has the best chance of reviving an inaccessible boot drive?

A. A boot diskette

B. System Restore

C. Device Driver Roll Back

D. Recovery Console

GO ON TO THE NEXT PAGE

61. All of the following procedures open the Task Manager utility *except*:

- **A.** Press Ctrl-Alt-Del, and then click the Task Manager button.
- **B.** Press Ctrl-Alt-Esc.
- **C.** Press Ctrl-Shift-Esc.
- **D.** Right-click an unaffiliated portion of the Taskbar, and then click Task Manager.

62. You plan to handle a number of ESD-sensitive devices in a makeshift work environment. No computer system is plugged in nearby to which you can clip your antistatic wrist strap. There are also no static mats or similar ground points nearby. Which of the following is an acceptable alternative?

- **A.** Tell the customer that you will be unable to perform any services in that environment.
- **B.** Stand perfectly still, and take the chance that an ESD will not occur.
- **C.** Plug the alligator clip of the antistatic wrist strap into the ground receptacle of a three-prong electrical outlet.
- **D.** Plug the banana clip of the antistatic wrist strap into the ground receptacle of a three-prong electrical outlet.

63. Where would you most likely find an object named HKEY_LOCAL_MACHINE?

- **A.** The Registry
- **B.** My Documents
- **C.** In the root of the system drive
- **D.** In %SystemRoot%\system32

64. If you want Windows XP to manage virtual memory for you, what should you select?

- **A.** System Managed Size
- **B.** No Paging File
- **C.** Let Windows Choose What's Best for My Computer
- **D.** Adjust for Best Performance

65. Each time you attempt to make a custom setting for the virtual memory of a computer, click the OK button, and return to check your work, the setting returns to the previous selection. Which of the following is a possible reason for this behavior?

- **A.** Group Policy prohibits you from making such a change to the virtual memory.
- **B.** You must click the Set button before clicking the OK button.
- **C.** You must click the Apply button before clicking the OK button.
- **D.** Virtual memory is not supported on your computer.

66. Which of the following RAID levels does not employ some form of striping?

- **A.** 0
- **B.** 1
- **C.** 3
- **D.** 5

67. In order to use the ASR process, you need each of the following *except*:

- **A.** The Windows XP distribution disc
- **B.** A system backup set
- **C.** The same hard drive from which the ASR materials were created
- **D.** The ASR diskette

68. How can you confirm that your motherboard is receiving DC power?

- **A.** LEDs on the motherboard are lit.
- **B.** You must use a multimeter to test one or more areas of the motherboard.
- **C.** You can't. Motherboards use AC power.
- **D.** An external monitor displays an image.

69. You arrive on a service call to find a frazzled user with Windows XP Home Edition lamenting the loss of an important data file that has been deleted. The user has tried in vain to find the file. Which of the following best describes your options for recovery?

A. Use System Restore to roll the system back to a time when the data file was there.

B. Use the ASR process to recover the data file.

C. Run Device Driver Roll Back to return the drive that held the file to its earlier state.

D. If the file is not in the Recycle Bin, and the user does not have a backup set that includes the file, there may be no way to recover the file.

70. No one at your site is able to access network resources. Your IP address scheme dictates that the DHCP server should place everyone on the 172.16.*x.x* network. However, closer inspection shows that each computer you look at has an address on the 169.254.*x.x* network. What is the likely issue here?

A. Everyone is drawing addresses from the wrong DHCP server.

B. The DHCP server is down.

C. TCP/IP has not been installed on any of the machines yet.

D. The default-gateway router is down.

71. Upon arriving at a client's location for a service call, you are informed that the user updated a driver. The user has no backup of the system, and now the system boots but fails to make it to the logon screen. Which of the following should you try first in order to fix the problem?

A. Last Known Good Configuration

B. Safe Mode and System Restore

C. ASR process

D. Device Driver Roll Back

72. Your supervisor is soliciting your advice on which authentication technology would be best for your computer systems. The supervisor is interested in a technology that, regardless of how it is implemented, requires each user to have something physical as well as to have to remember a personal password. Which of the following should you recommend?

A. Biometrics

B. Smart card

C. Key fob

D. USB token

73. During your investigation into why a computer running XP starts up differently, you discover that it has been set for selective startup. Which of the following will return the system to its normal startup behavior?

A. Click the Disable All button on the Startup tab of MSCONFIG.

B. Select the Normal Startup radio button on the General tab of MSCONFIG.

C. Execute the command net start normal at the Command Prompt.

D. Enter Startup Options during boot with the F8 key, and choose *Start Windows Normally*.

74. A user places a service call stating that their inkjet printer is smudging horizontally and vertically when it prints. Which of the following makes the most sense to try?

A. Use the printer's software utility to clean the print cartridges.

B. Calibrate the printer.

C. Replace the belt for the carriage assembly.

D. Remove the print cartridges, and clean them with a lint-free cloth.

75. While working inside a large workgroup laser printer, you need to make sure a screw you are removing does not fall down onto the fuser assembly; but you are unable to fit both hands into the area where the screw is. Which of the following is the best approach to this situation?

A. Use a static-resistant vacuum.

B. Use a magnetic screwdriver.

C. Let the screw fall, and then turn the printer upside down to remove it.

D. Use an extension magnet.

76. Which of the following is the best first step to take if you are informed that a service or device failed to start when booting Windows?

A. Perform a Device Driver Roll Back.

B. Consult the System category of Event Viewer.

C. Remove the driver.

D. Reboot Windows.

77. Which of the following has the greatest impact on reducing the amount of time spent on repeat calls and calls for similar symptoms?

    A. Test your solution.

    B. Be courteous to the customer, and listen actively.

    C. Escalate the problem to someone with more expertise.

    D. Document the problem and your resolution.

78. You call the network administrator to find out the subnet mask for one of the IP subnets in the enterprise network. They inform you that it is /28. Which of the following is /28 equivalent to?

    A. 255.255.255.0

    B. 255.255.255.192

    C. 255.255.255.240

    D. 255.255.255.252

79. Which of the following is the more robust of two protocols that facilitate the transfer of any file type from one IP host to another?

    A. Telnet

    B. FTP

    C. TFTP

    D. HTTP

80. Which *two* of the following technologies provide access rates higher than dial-up but use the same copper pair as dial-up, sometimes with little conditioning?

    A. DSL

    B. Cable

    C. ISDN

    D. Cellular

Answer Key for Practice Test 2

1. B	**21.** D	**41.** B	**61.** B
2. D	**22.** A	**42.** D	**62.** D
3. C	**23.** A	**43.** B	**63.** A
4. C	**24.** B	**44.** A	**64.** A
5. C	**25.** C	**45.** D	**65.** B
6. A	**26.** C	**46.** BD	**66.** B
7. B	**27.** C	**47.** C	**67.** C
8. C	**28.** D	**48.** D	**68.** A
9. D	**29.** B	**49.** A	**69.** D
10. D	**30.** C	**50.** C	**70.** B
11. B	**31.** A	**51.** C	**71.** A
12. A	**32.** C	**52.** C	**72.** C
13. D	**33.** B	**53.** B	**73.** B
14. A	**34.** C	**54.** D	**74.** A
15. B	**35.** C	**55.** AB	**75.** D
16. A	**36.** B	**56.** C	**76.** B
17. C	**37.** A	**57.** D	**77.** D
18. A	**38.** BC	**58.** D	**78.** C
19. C	**39.** B	**59.** BD	**79.** B
20. B	**40.** A	**60.** D	**80.** AC

Answer Explanations for Practice Test 2

1. B. The key here is to wait long enough after unplugging the power supply that the capacitors inside have time to bleed off their charge. However, this is a hypothetical situation. The hard-line on this one is to cut your losses and protect your health and wellbeing by replacing the power supply. Nevertheless, you must still wait long enough after dropping the part before even touching the power supply, to make sure there is no latent charge that could short to the case of the power supply and electrocute you when you touch it to remove the power supply. If there is still a charge inside the power supply, reaching in with anything or shaking a metal part around inside can lead to an inadvertent short and possible electrocution. Although the plastic tweezers sound like a great idea, the hand holding the tweezers is made of meat. Keep it out of a freshly unplugged power supply. In fact, do nothing for a couple of hours other than unplug the power supply. Even touching the chassis or any part of the case, let alone the power supply itself, can give you a jolt if the part is bridging the right circuit.

2. D. Only laptops tend to require SoDIMMs and the even smaller MicroDIMMs for memory upgrades, which is not to say definitively that full-size systems do not. It is highly unlikely, however. SIMMs, which are the predecessors of DIMMS, are no longer used in modern motherboards and laptops. DIMMs of differing form factors have been used with the original single-data-rate SDRAM as well as the DDR and DDR2 varieties of SDRAM.

3. C. A full waste-toner receptacle is not a common cause of issues with laser printers, although it could cause problems with the cleaning cycle. However, unless you refill your own cartridges with fresh toner, cartridges that hold both fresh and waste toners are engineered to run out of fresh toner before the waste-toner receptacle fills. As a result, the second-best answer is to replace the toner cartridge, which also replaces the waste-toner receptacle. Maintenance kits do not treat toner issues, and there is usually no way to empty the waste-toner receptacle.

4. C. You will find in the majority of cases like this that components that were once working do not cease to work simply because you upgraded the motherboard. Certainly, CPUs and memory modules must be compatible with the new motherboard, but those are not mentioned here. The new motherboard could be defective, but that's not an option either. Therefore, existing cards in any quantity, the power button, and the power supply are likely to be fine. When you change out a motherboard, be absolutely certain that you remove *all* standoffs from the chassis before installing the new motherboard. One errant brass standoff can have disastrous effects if it shorts the underside of the motherboard. Quite a few standards address the location of holes in the motherboard for securing hardware placement, but not all positions are used in every motherboard. Again, it takes only one standoff to be left where there is no longer a hole in the motherboard. Treat every motherboard installation as a fresh start, and don't try to cut corners. You can destroy components otherwise.

5. C. There is no such command as net show, and *Devices by Connection* doesn't show you what you need in Device Manager. So, between the only two valid answers, shun brute force and let the answer fall in your lap with the *Resources by Type* view in Device Manager.

6. A. Long before opening any display unit, make sure the display is really bad. Opening an LCD or CRT monitor's case is a last resort and should be left to a qualified technician because of the dangers lurking within. Flyback transformers are extremely dangerous but exist only on CRT monitors. Related to good customer relations, don't ask a user who has been using an external monitor to try to get by with the built-in monitor unless it is an extremely temporary fix and there is no functional reason why the user has been using an external monitor. In some cases, a user's job requirements necessitate the use of a monitor that exceeds the quality or capabilities of the one built into a laptop, preventing them from being productive with the internal display.

7. B. Although you won't see a model of how the atoms and molecules bind to one another, the MSDS does include the chemical formula for the substance in Section 9. Section 4 gives first-aid practices to observe when necessary, and Section 7 covers handling and storage suggestions for the substance.

8. C. The devices with the fastest response time—the hard drives—should be placed on one of the two controllers. There are only two controllers. Devices on the same controller once synchronized with one another and were limited to the performance of the slowest device. Although this is not true with newer devices and controllers, one device in a master/slave pair must wait for the other to finish its use of the channel before it can transfer data on the same channel. The result is that slower devices can cause a faster device to have to wait longer for channel access. Therefore, the slower two devices—the optical drives—should be placed together on the other controller.

9. D. Pre-XP operating systems used the Emergency Repair Disk (ERD). XP uses a process known as Automated System Recovery (ASR). The ASR disk is used in conjunction with the ASR process to access a backup archive and completely restore the system to the state of the latest backup. As a result, your backup should not be stored on the same physical drive that one you are archiving. Although the Recovery Console is an incredible utility for a nuts-and-bolts surgical resurrection of a failed system, damaged partitions are best recovered using ASR when available. System Restore requires a working system and is generally best used for rolling back drivers and application settings to a state when the system was stable.

10. D. The bottom line is that you can use the 8.3 naming convention in any Microsoft file system. It is required in FAT and exists behind the scenes of long names in FAT32. NTFS does not use it to store files, but that doesn't stop you from naming a file using the convention, which is all the option alluded to. The other options are absolutely distinguishing characteristics. Another major difference is the file-level security available in NTFS, which is not available in either version of FAT. The following table details the differences.

File System	Maximum Volume Size	Maximum File Size
FAT	4GB	2GB
FAT32	Format to 32GB; read/write to 2TB	4GB
NTFS	16TB and more	As large as the volume

11. B. It is F6 that you must press when prompted during Windows installation to install SCSI drivers. There is no browse function, so you must know where the drivers are located on the disk you specify. F2 begins the ASR process, and F8 is used during bootup, not setup, to access the Startup Options screen. F12 has no function to speak of.

12. A. Most BIOS routines include a warning threshold for CPU temperature as well as, on occasion, ambient temperature inside the case. They also include a higher cutoff temperature that causes the system to shut down to avoid damage. However, this is not a problem with the BIOS. It's a feature. For the overall health of the system, the BIOS maintains vigilance over the CPU, which generates more heat than any other component in a computer. It is most often a failure of the CPU's fan that causes the temperature to rise enough to set off the temperature warning.

13. D. Data and electrical cables don't usually mix well. Even if you have experience with running them in the same conduit or other pathway, avoid doing so. Noise interference is likely; electrocution and damage to connected data equipment are possible. Run your own connection to avoid delaying the service for the user and to avoid introducing another device into the mix, especially when their issue is network-related to begin with. Make sure you secure your cable to avoid tripping anyone, regardless of the length of time you intend to need it. Someone can trip over it while you're still in the process of running it. Don't press your luck by trying to get by for the duration of its use.

14. A. Windows XP Professional has no command-line method of creating a bootable diskette. XP still maintains the system files required to create a DOS boot disk, but you must format the diskette through the GUI. You can access the Format dialog by right-clicking the floppy icon in My Computer and selecting Format from the shortcut menu. Be sure to select the check box beside *Create an MS-DOS startup disk* in order to make the diskette bootable. Creating floppies that cause the system to boot to a particular system disk (hard drive) is a matter of copying the right files to the floppy and editing the BOOT.INI file properly. Control does not remain assigned to the floppy drive the way it does for a DOS boot disk. There is no such thing as a floppy diskette that boots to the floppy drive's prompt while running the XP operating system; MS-DOS is required for such behavior.

15. B. One of XCOPY's hallmarks is its ability to copy full trees of directory structure, using the /S and /E switches. Another is its ability to pay attention to the archive attribute bit, using the /A and /M switches, unlike the way one of the incorrect answers states that COPY had this capability. Although it is a difference, the statement is not accurate. Both commands allow implicit destinations.

16. **A.** No relationship exists between the number of processors in the system and the amount of RAM that can be accessed. It's a matter of how the operating system is written. You can't access more than 4GB of RAM with the 32-bit version of XP; but with the 64-bit version, you can access up to a whopping 128GB of RAM. Advanced operating systems employ tricks to circumvent the 4GB limitation of the 32-bit address bus width of most modern CPUs. The following table lists the maximum number of processors and the maximum physical RAM for the various modern Windows operating systems.

Windows Operating System	Maximum Processors	Maximum Physical RAM
XP Professional	2	4GB
XP Professional x64 Edition	2	128GB
Server 2003 Standard Edition	4	4GB
Server 2003 Standard x64 Edition	4	32GB
Server 2003 Enterprise Edition	8	64GB
Server 2003 Enterprise x64 Edition	8	1TB
Server 2003 Datacenter Edition	32	128GB
Server 2003 Datacenter x64 Edition	32	1TB
2000 Professional	2	4GB
2000 Server	4	4GB
2000 Advanced Server	8	8GB
2000 Datacenter Server	32	32GB

17. **C.** Of those listed, only infrared and the CD burner have a chance here without further adjustment. The serial cable must be a null modem cable, not a standard cable. Regardless, infrared is more convenient than burning a CD or using the null modem cable. Bluetooth can be used, with appropriate utilities, to perform this function, but it is more often used as a cord-replacement technology. Windows XP SP2 has the Bluetooth File Transfer Wizard, but both machines must have Bluetooth capability, which is not yet commonly built in to laptops the way infrared is. As this trend continues to change, Bluetooth will likely become the best option here.

18. **A.** To varying degrees, each option alone is capable of raising the temperature within the case. The presence of four hard drives is not enough to increase the internal temperature to a dangerous level; the other conditions are. If the case will accommodate four hard drives, it should be engineered to cool four hard drives.

19. **C.** No, don't use Safe Mode from now on. Life can't possibly be bad enough for that. Doing so will not satisfy the requirement of getting the system working properly again. To get out of Safe Mode, however, you must fix the driver issue. The most straightforward and noninvasive method for doing that when you know the driver to blame is Device Driver Roll Back, which is accessed through Device Manager. ASR and System Restore are overkill in this situation. ASR will roll *everything* back to the time when the backup was performed with the creation of the ASR disk, and System Restore will roll back all drivers and application settings to the restore point you choose. You cannot be certain that this driver will be the only thing affected on this user's machine when you run either of these utilities. Save these big guns for when more needs to be rolled back or for when you are not sure what needs rolling back.

20. **B.** The LCD cutoff switch is a tiny plunger switch on the keyboard panel of a laptop that the lid trips when you close it. If this switch goes bad or sticks, the LCD display can appear to be defective. Try to release the switch before replacing it. Also consider the function key–actuated control, and don't forget that something more serious, such as the inverter board, may be wrong with the display. Nothing going on with the external monitor tends to affect the built-in display. Booting up in Safe Mode is no different than using normal mode, except that it favors the built-in display over the external display and uses only the default VGA driver, not the specialized driver for your display hardware, leading to poorer graphics. Nevertheless, if the external monitor works, having booted into Safe Mode is not your culprit.

21. D. This is a hot topic, and although you must weigh the intent of the user against the fact that it is against the law to use unauthorized software, in this case you cannot be sure that the law has been broken (yet). Tell the user you need to install the software from the original CD because it is generally regarded as legal to make at least one exact copy of a distribution disc in order to protect your investment against damage to the original, provided the holder of the copy is the registered owner of the original. This will gracefully allow the user to produce the legal disc or withdraw their request. You must not be party to knowingly installing software from the same distribution disc in more than one location simultaneously, unless the customer's company holds a site license for the software and you can confirm that the company has not reached the maximum number of installed copies. Your role is to refuse to install such software, educate the user about the fact that such behavior is illegal, and even offer to destroy the illegal copy for the user. Make sure the user understands that illegal software could cost their company in fines and lost productivity; upgrades and security updates normally cannot be installed on a bootlegged installation. In this case, especially if the user does not appear to be a habitual offender, bringing management or law enforcement into the picture may lead to a strained relationship and questionable confidentiality on your part. Nevertheless, if you feel the law is being broken intentionally and without remorse, you have a civic duty to report the crime, which is not victimless. The market suffers from higher prices for the product, and the integrity of the software can be unfairly brought into question by observers if it fails to function normally.

22. A. Class A fire extinguishers are often water-based and gas pressurized. Using one on an electrical or chemical fire can spread the fire instead of put it out. Class B extinguishers are for fires caused by combustible liquids, such as gasoline. Class C extinguishers are for electrical fires, and class D extinguishers are for types of fires that are seen most often in laboratories and that are caused by combustible metals such as potassium, sodium, lithium, magnesium, and titanium. Dry-chemical fire extinguishers that are rated for a combination of classes, except D, are also common but leave a dangerous and harmful residue that must be cleaned up afterward. Carbon-dioxide extinguishers can be effective on class B and C fires but generally only worsen class A fires. One of their advantages is their lack of residue. Be sure to match the extinguisher to the property being protected and the potential cause of the fire.

23. A. Hardware loopback plugs short the transmit and receive pins as well as other complementary pins on the local interface, taking cabling and remote devices out of the equation so that you can test the local interface without unpredictable influences. In the serial-interface world, a crossover cable is known as a null-modem cable; it allows you to connect a DTE device to another DTE device, such as one computer to another. Terminators absorb any signal that makes it to the end of a circuit and do not assist in testing. Multimeters are indispensable for testing but do not perform the function referred to here.

24. B. Surge protectors are not perfect and should be removed from the wall outlet during electrical storms to protect them and the equipment connected to them. They have varistors that take the brunt of the inconsistencies found in "dirty" power but do nothing for power loss or brownouts. Their role is to make sure that common power spikes are clipped before they do cumulative damage to sensitive electronic equipment. You should keep an eye on the indicator, if one exists, to tell when the internal protection components are no longer able to do their job. When the protector has run its course, you should replace it immediately. Some UPS units protect equipment in the same way by using the raw power input to constantly charge the battery, which provides the attached equipment with pure power that remains consistent. However, the user does not need the power preservation that a UPS provides. A generator is like a UPS without the power conditioning and only provides power during a power outage. Generators do nothing under normal circumstances to match the capabilities of a surge protector. Power strips are passive outlet multipliers that offer no protection at all.

25. C. The `winipcfg` utility has not been available since the Windows 9x generation. To view similar information, you must abandon the GUI approach and execute the `ipconfig` command at the Command Prompt with the `/all` switch. There is no `/mac` switch for the `ipconfig` command. `ifconfig` is a UNIX command and is not available in Windows.

26. C. With respect to the read-only (r), system (s), and hidden (h) attributes, setting each one alone or setting any combination of the three prevents a file from being deleted at the command line. You must clear all three in order to delete the file. Because you were not told which attributes were set, you have to play it safe and clear them all, which is easy to do because a minus (−) does not toggle the setting. It clears it or keeps it cleared. Issuing the command `attrib /?` shows that the switches must come before the filename.

27. C. Executing a ping with the default gateway (local router) as the destination is the most logical choice here. Regardless of the number of switches or hubs between the user's computer and the egress router, a ping is a Layer 3 message to which Layer 1 and Layer 2 devices are transparent. Therefore, a ping gets right down to business and involves no other devices in your query. If it is successful, you know the router is healthy. If not, the user's machine, the router, or anything in between, including cabling, may be faulty. A traceroute can yield the same results but is overkill compared to a ping. Traceroutes are designed to identify all Layer 3 devices between the source and destination. In this case, there are none. NSLOOKUP is for DNS issues or tests. IPCONFIG will only tell you the address of your default gateway, not whether it is responsive.

28. D. The System Restore utility is in the System Tools folder under Accessories and cannot be accessed from Control Panel.

29. B. The command `defrag -a` analyzes the currently logged drive and reports on its need for defragmentation. Leaving the switch off performs the defragmentation.

30. C. Although occasionally you will need to swap out the AC adapter during troubleshooting, removing the AC adapter alone is not generally considered a worthwhile troubleshooting step. Doing so requires that the laptop run solely on battery power, which is not recommended. In fact, a common step is to remove the battery because it can adversely affect power delivery to the laptop. Adapters are ordinarily either good or bad, whereas batteries can appear good but actually affect the power and functionality of the laptop. Switch out adapters and remove batteries when troubleshooting. Be aware that batteries can cause problems that do not appear to be related to power. Just as the battery can cause puzzling symptoms, so can many removable peripherals. If you don't need them during troubleshooting, remove them. The external monitor is ideal to diagnose built-in video issues.

31. A. Because it's a NIC, there is a remote possibility of conjuring the BSOD, but there is no real danger to the operating system or file structure from removing the NIC. That makes this option the easiest one that will likely result in success. However, storage devices such as thumb drives or external hard drives can lose data if you do not stop them first. In that case, create a shortcut that executes `rundll32.exe shell32.dll,control_rundll hotplug.dll`, which brings up the missing Safely Remove Hardware dialog. There is no guarantee, however, that the system will allow you to stop the storage device this way. It may tell you that the device is still in use. Occasionally, shutting down the system is the only way to get Windows to close all file handles and clear all buffers, allowing you to safely remove the device without data loss. You should never need to uninstall the driver to remove a device, but for nonstorage devices, disabling them for the current or all hardware profiles in Device Manager does stop the devices. It's USB, though—just pull out the nonstorage peripheral.

32. C. The `scannow` switch of the `sfc` command causes a scan to be run immediately without the need to restart the system. Apparently, the user or administrator ran the command with the `scanboot` switch. Although the `scanonce` switch sounds feasible, it also requires a restart. The only difference is that once a single scan is performed, that's the end of it. Executing the command without a switch is the same as requesting help for the command by executing `sfc /?`. It does not run a scan.

33. B. Clumps of dust, dead fans, and blockages of normal airflow are all causes of overheating to the point of a computer shutting itself down for safety. Although some memory modules, especially Rambus modules, call for heat sinks, lack of memory heat sinks is less likely to be the cause of such catastrophic overheating.

34. C. The Event Viewer can be found in Administrative Tools, which can be found in Control Panel. There is no separate applet in Control Panel for Event Viewer, and Event Viewer is not a System Tools accessory.

35. C. There are three keys to this question: ATA hard drive, only XP, and root directory. The file `NTBOOTDD.SYS` doesn't exist if the system partition (the one booted to) is not on a SCSI drive. Although `BOOTSECT.DOS` exists in the root directory, it is not used unless you have a dual- or multiple-boot scenario with DOS or Windows 9x as one or more of the operating systems. Although `NTOSKRNL.EXE` is a necessary file for a successful boot, it does not reside in the root directory. It can be found in the `%SystemRoot%` folder (most often `\WINNT`). NTLDR, however, is located in the root directory and is required in all boot situations.

36. B. The utility is Remote Desktop Connection, and it resides in the Communications Accessories folder.

37. **A.** Restarting the spooler from the command line involves first stopping the Spooler service and then starting it. The command to stop it is `net stop spooler`. The command to start it is `net start spooler`. This process may be necessary on occasion if printing fails consistently.

38. **BC.** The `help` command and the `/?` switch are two ways to obtain command-line assistance with almost any command. There is no `/h` switch for the `DIR` command, and `/h` does not generally produce help for commands.

39. **B.** Applying the wrong cleaner or using the wrong cloth does not make the monitor appear dead. It can, however, destroy the screen's finish. Nevertheless, the image still appears in some degraded fashion. Turning the brightness control and, in some cases, the contrast control can lead to the appearance of a dead monitor, but position knobs cannot adjust the image far enough to make it disappear form the screen. What likely happened was that the user sprayed the appropriate cleaner directly onto the screen, and it dripped into the circuitry of the monitor and caused a short. The monitor may be a total loss.

40. **A.** When you use the `dir` command without any switches, files and folders with the hidden or system attribute are not displayed. To specify the attributes that files and folders must have to be displayed, you must use the `/A` switch followed immediately by or separated by a colon from one or more attribute letters. The letter for hidden objects is H. Therefore, the correct command is `dir e:\data /ah`. The `/ar` switch displays only read-only objects. The `/x` switch displays short names for non-8.3 filenames as well as the long name for each object. There is no `/h` switch for the `dir` command. To limit output to files and folders that have both the hidden and system attributes set, for example, the correct switch is `/ahs` or `/a:hs`.

41. **B.** The Startup tab in MSCONFIG is ideal for performing selective startup by disabling the automatic startup of specific applications and then performing a reboot until you have exhausted all options or until you have proven that a specific application is causing a conflict. Uninstalling the application is not recommended, because it may not be the culprit. Reinstalling the application can be time consuming, and you must consider the danger of data loss. REGEDIT should be used only as a last resort because changes are immediate and system instability can result with no warning prior to the failed bootup, sometimes necessitating reinstallation of the operating system and severe data loss. The Recovery Console is meant for low-level file system recovery operations, not application-conflict testing.

42. **D.** Although LiIon batteries do not form a chemical memory per se, they do suffer from irreversible life-robbing oxidation. When the battery has a significant charge, the oxidation is exacerbated by heat, such as that generated by the laptop in which the battery is installed or by leaving the battery in the car exposed to ambient heat. Although there is no cure for this effect and the fact that the battery has a finite life expectancy, the effect also has a bearing on how Windows' battery gauge interprets the battery's remaining charge. Calibrating the battery, which is really calibrating Windows' gauge or synchronizing the gauge with the battery, involves allowing the battery to discharge completely once in every 30 charging cycles until the laptop loses power. Doing so keeps the gauge more accurate, and users who watch their gauge vigilantly will not be caught off guard.

43. **B.** The `TYPE` command displays the contents of a text file on the screen. The `PRINT` command sends a similar file to the printer. The `VIEW` and `SHOW` commands do not exist.

44. **A.** Some laptops function differently with respect to the Number Lock key. Often, Number Lock must be on before the Fn key can be used to access the numeric functions of the keys they share. With Number Lock off, these keys cannot be made to type their numeric values. However, in some cases, turning on Number Lock alone makes these keys type nothing other than their numeric values. This is something to check before you dig any deeper elsewhere. It's less likely that a language overlay will have this effect, and you may be thinking about Calculator with the scientific and standard settings.

45. **D.** The `CONVERT` utility allows a one-way conversion of file systems from FAT to NTFS. Therefore, there's no way to execute a syntactically correct command to convert from NTFS to FAT, making that option impossible. If the `CONVERT` utility cannot gain exclusive control over the volume, it may require a reboot to complete the conversion. If you execute the `CONVERT D: /FS:NTFS` command, and `D:` is already an NTFS volume, you receive an error and the utility ends. Running the utility using Run in the Start menu can work; but entering an incorrect command causes a Command Prompt window to flash open and disappear, perhaps leading you to believe something productive happened when, in fact, nothing did.

46. BD. From the question, you can discern that the first-level subdirectory on the C: drive named DATA, which has no subdirectories of its own, is the currently logged directory. The MD, or MKDIR, command creates directories. The CD, or CHDIR, command changes the currently logged directory to the one you specify. The RD, or RMDIR, command removes directories. With no subdirectories under DATA yet, you must create the SUB1 directory before you can make it the currently logged directory. The MD SUB1 command creates the SUB1 directory within the currently logged directory. This is equivalent to each of the following: MD C:\DATA\SUB1, MD \DATA\SUB1, MD .\SUB1, MD ..\DATA\SUB1, and so on. The first command in the list uses what is considered an absolute path—one that works from any logged directory because both the drive and the root-based path are specified (the first backslash, which specifies the root directory, is included). The other commands use relative paths that draw upon the currently logged directory, currently logged drive, or both to fill in the details left out. The command MD C:\SUB1 may look similar, but it uses an absolute path that does not create a subdirectory in the DATA directory. It specifies that a first-level directory named SUB1 be created on the C: drive directly in the root, which will be on the same level as the DATA directory, not beneath it as the question requires. The CD SUB1 command, when executed next, draws on the C: and \DATA parameters of the currently logged directory and causes the prompt (C:\DATA\SUB1>) to reflect the newly logged directory, satisfying the requirements of the question. The command CD\SUB1 uses a relative path that draws on only C: because the leading backslash directs the command not to draw on the currently logged directory and instead to start at the root and find the SUB1 directory, which is not at the root. It's under the DATA directory. Note that dropping the backslash produces the correct answer and causes the command to draw on the currently logged directory. Using CD in place of MD in each of the alternative commands listed earlier works in this case as well.

47. C. The correct answer is almost a true statement. Since NT came along, the business of booting only from drive C: has been relaxed. It's not even a limitation of the drive letter. The drive you boot to can be anything other than B:, which is reserved for the second floppy drive. Even when you swap in the BIOS, the system still thinks it is booting from A: when it boots from the second floppy. The issue with this answer, then, is that only primary partitions are bootable. A logical drive created on an extended partition is not bootable. So, it's not the *drive letter* part that makes it incorrect. It's the *any drive* part.

48. D. To be bootable, a partition must be marked active. Only primary partitions can be marked active, but there can be as many as three primary partitions with only one being active at a time. So, neither *active* nor *primary* is synonymous with *bootable*, but you would not mark a partition as active without the intent of making it bootable. Once the partition is marked active, some form of formatting must be performed to transfer the system files to the partition. The *boot* partition, in Microsoft parlance, is the partition that contains the system files that complete the boot process and run Windows for the remainder of the session. Counterintuitively, the bootable partition is called the *system* partition. *Boot-ready* is not a valid term.

49. A. What's needed here is a relative path that gets you from the currently logged folder to another one two levels deeper and beneath the current one. This means you do not have to specify an absolute path that includes the drive letter; but if you do, it must start at the root and include all four subdirectories. None of the options do this. Relative paths do not start with a backslash, which eliminates half the options. Therefore, the command that works is cd level2\level3. The command cd level3 has a relative path but suggests that the subdirectory level3 is directly below level1, which is not true. The command with the absolute path that works is cd \level1\level2\level3\level4. Feel free to add C: in front of any of these commands, but it's redundant and assumed when left off.

50. C. The con: device represents the keyboard for input and the video display for output. It can be used in the COPY command to represent input from the keyboard when placed in the source position of the command. Because source comes before destination in commands that copy from one location to another, versions with con: last are incorrect. The con: device can be specified in the COPY command without the colon, making COPY CON TEST.TXT the correct answer. The command COPY TEST.TXT+CON TEST.TXT appends input from the keyboard to the test.txt file and writes the results to the same file.

51. C. SCANDISK is not offered with XP, but CHKDSK is, and it offers the features listed in the question by using the /F and /R switches, respectively. FDISK manages partitions, and the Recovery Console gives you access to CHKDSK but does not fix errors and recover data in and of itself.

52. **C.** Novell's protocol suite is called IPX/SPX. IPX and SPX are the primary protocols of this suite. Microsoft's compatible version is known as NWLink. The *NW* evokes *NetWare*, which is Novell's trade name for its product line that used to include IPX/SPX. NetBEUI is a Microsoft protocol but is not equivalent to IPX/SPX.

53. **B.** *In general*, and on occasion, you need to allow the BIOS routine to run and save the new settings, but it's equally or more prevalent to need to do nothing at all. In cases where the BIOS routine needs to run, you do not have to watch for the opportunity to enter the BIOS routine; it detects a memory mismatch and stalls until you press a specific key to enter the routine or bypass it. Once in the routine, you do not need to input any information. Everything is automatically detected. You just need to save the settings once they are automatically updated. In the past, especially in old IBM machines, you had to insert a diskette and run a utility to update the BIOS with the new RAM size, but the utility still automatically recognized the RAM. There are no drivers for RAM because memory is BIOS-managed, not operating system–managed, which also means there is nothing you need to do in Windows to have the RAM recognized.

54. **D.** The Services utility is found in Administrative Tools, which may be available from various locations. Some of these locations are listed in the wrong answers to this question, but you can always find Administrative Tools in Control Panel.

55. **AB.** Windows Explorer is basically the GUI environment of Windows. The `explorer.exe` process runs as long as Windows is running properly. However, within the GUI, Windows Explorer is also a utility similar to My Computer, adding a directory tree to its view. Both utilities are based on `explorer.exe`. To confirm that, run each one individually, go to the Applications tab, right-click the related application for the utility you're running this time, and click Go To Process. Notice that you are taken directly to the Processes tab, and the `explorer.exe` process is highlighted.

56. **C.** The Device Manager button is on the Hardware tab in System Properties, which is labeled System in Control Panel.

57. **D.** Expanded memory is physical memory that pages content into RAM when needed. It has nothing to do with the hard drive. Extended memory is linear physical memory that extends from around the 1MB mark upward. All systems today technically have extended memory, but modern Windows operating systems no longer use this designation. Defragmentation makes files on a hard drive contiguous but has nothing to do with the contiguous swap file, or paging file, of virtual memory, which is never allowed to become fragmented.

58. **D.** NetBIOS is an API that specifies device names in a Microsoft environment. It corresponds to the session layer of the OSI model and requires lower-layer protocols to transport it. NetBEUI is a non-routable transport/network-layer protocol that allows NetBIOS to be networked locally on a LAN. NetBIOS can be routed when converted and transported over the routable IPX/SPX and TCP/IP. NWLink is Microsoft's implementation of IPX/SPX. HTTP is a TCP/IP-only protocol at the application layer. AppleTalk is a suite of protocols similar to IPX/SPX and TCP/IP that work together at the various layers to perform the same type of data communications function.

59. **BD.** Cookies are temporary files that allow an Internet merchant to use a distributed method to store information specific to your account on your own computer so that the merchant does not have to store such information for each account on their server. Whenever you access a website that has stored a cookie on your computer, the website uses the cookie to predict information that you would otherwise need to enter. Although this can add efficiency to day-to-day web browsing for the appropriate user, it can also be highly inefficient for the wrong user. To clear these cookies for the currently logged user, open the Internet Options dialog from the Tools menu in Internet Explorer or double-click the Internet applet in Control Panel, and then click the Delete Cookies button on the General tab. Another option that produces the same effect is to navigate to the local folder for the currently logged user under Documents and Settings. Therein is a hidden folder called Local Settings. Cookies for this user are stored in the Temporary Internet Files folder found within; delete this folder's contents. Clearing the history does not clear cookies; doing so only clears the history of recently visited websites.

60. **D.** The best choice of those given is to run the Recovery Console and execute commands such as `fixmbr` and `fixboot` to repair the master boot record and the partition boot sector, respectively. A boot diskette is not able to boot up on its own. It points to an actual bootable partition, which is what's missing in this case. System Restore and Device Driver Roll Back both require access to the operating system, which is missing in action here.

61. B. Pressing Ctrl-Alt-Esc has the same effect as Alt-Esc, which cycles among nonminimized windows on the Desktop, including dialogs that do not appear on the Taskbar. The other three methods bring up Task Manager.

62. D. Do your best not to leave the customer high and dry. If you are near an electrical outlet and the alligator clip on your antistatic wrist strap comes off to reveal a tensioning banana clip, the clip should plug tightly into the ground receptacle of the outlet. Do not plug the alligator clip into the receptacle. It is not meant to fit there, and it can pop loose or make contact with some other part of the receptacle accidentally. It is not reasonable to believe that you can stand still enough to not generate a static charge. It's also important to recognize that motion is not the only thing that builds static. Too many other environmental concerns go into generating a static charge to try to go this route.

63. A. HKEY_LOCAL_MACHINE is one of five Registry hives, not a folder found on a hard drive. Use REGEDIT to see the contents of this hive.

64. A. In the Virtual Memory dialog, you have three choices: Custom Size, System Managed Size, and No Paging File. System Managed Size creates or keeps the paging file, which is a must for virtual memory to exist, and uses an algorithm to choose the optimal size for the paging file. Let Windows Choose What's Best for My Computer and Adjust for Best Performance are selections on the Visual Effects tab of the Performance Options dialog and have nothing to do with virtual memory.

65. B. You must click the Set button in the Virtual Memory dialog before you click OK to close the dialog. Failing to do so has the same affect as clicking the Cancel button, which ignores your changes even if you clicked the Set button first. The necessary sequence to save your changes is Set and then OK. If Group Policy were an issue here, you would not be able to think you had made changes to begin with; and all Windows computers that allow you to see the virtual-memory settings support virtual memory. One of the distracters in this question plays on the common misconception that in dialogs with both an Apply button and an OK button, you must first click Apply (which really means "save my changes and keep the dialog open") before clicking OK (which means "save my changes and close the dialog"). You need to click OK only if you're done making changes. There is no Apply button in the Virtual Memory dialog.

66. B. RAID 0 is a striped array without fault tolerance. It is a way to create a larger volume without using a single larger disk. Just as with a single larger disk, the striped array is an "all for one" situation. If one disk in the array fails, the whole array is lost. This is analogous to the single disk developing an error in only a portion of the disk that makes the entire disk unusable. RAID 3 and RAID 5 are similar in that they are both fault tolerant, they both stripe data, and they both require a minimum of three disks in the array. They differ in their method of storing parity information: RAID 3 stores all parity information on a single disk, whereas RAID 5 stripes the parity information in with the data across all disks. RAID 1 supports mirroring and duplexing, which is fault tolerance, but there is no striping or parity—just exact copies of the data stored on another disk, possibly connected to another controller.

67. C. The ASR process is ideal for situations in which the physical drive is not available, whether due to total loss or just for data transfer. Of course, if the original drive is healthy and available, there is nothing wrong with using the same drive. An ASR recovery requires any destination hard drive, the ASR diskette, a corresponding backup set (which should be as complete as possible), and the original Windows XP distribution disc. You begin the ASR process by pressing the F2 key at the prompted moment after booting with the XP distribution disc, as if you were installing the operating system. ASR sets up a limited Windows installation and then looks for the backup set referenced by the ASR diskette to restore the system to its original state.

68. A. Motherboards use DC power, and many today have one or more LEDs that notify you that various portions of the motherboard are in operation or that the motherboard has power applied so you do not perform service on it without first removing power. You *can* use a multimeter to determine whether the motherboard is receiving power, but the word *must* is a bit strong. Most monitors can display an image without being plugged into a video adapter, which means that an image on a monitor does not guarantee a working or powered motherboard.

69. D. Unfortunately, in this case, if you cannot find the file in the Recycle Bin and the user has not been diligent with data backups, the file may be lost forever. Although there are third-party utilities that can go deeper into the file system if that physical location on the disk has not been reused, CompTIA does not mention these in its objectives, and the success of such utilities is never guaranteed. System Restore is useful only for driver and application-settings rollback, not data recovery. The ASR process is not available on XP Home Edition; and in environments where it is available, if only the ASR disk was created, and no data backup was created in conjunction with it, you will wind up with a simplified installation of Windows. A complete backup set is required to return the system to its pre-backup state. As you may already know, drivers have nothing to do with drives—the words just sound similar. Device Driver Roll Back will have no effect here.

70. B. Whenever a Microsoft device is set to obtain an IP address automatically, and a DHCP server does not respond to that device's request for an IP address, the device auto-configures itself from the Class B network 169.254.0.0. This is called Automatic Private IP Addressing (APIPA). Routers do not route packets to or from this private network. It would be detrimental if they did; in such a case, auto-configured devices with routers between them would confuse the router because different interfaces on the same router must be on different IP networks. DHCP servers do not hand out APIPA addresses, so drawing from the wrong DHCP server would not lead to devices having these addresses. However, a downed DHCP server will cause all devices to auto-configure with APIPA addresses. Unless the router acting as the default gateway is also acting as the DHCP server and handing out IP addresses, its failure will limit network access beyond its local interface but will not cause the devices on the network to auto-configure. TCP/IP must be installed in order for a device to auto-configure with addresses in the 169.254.0.0 network, so that can't be the problem. For XP devices, TCP/IP is integrated and cannot be uninstalled, only restarted.

71. A. The best way to handle this problem, as well as system lockups, auto-restarts, and repeated bluescreen errors, is to hit F8 while booting to access the Startup Options screen. This screen contains a number of choices, including Safe Mode, Safe Mode with Networking, and Last Known Good Configuration (LKGC), among others. Whenever the user logs on, the Registry location that LKGC draws from is updated with the system's current settings. Because the system last made it to this point and the user logged on before the suspect driver was updated, there is an excellent chance that LKGC will be successful in returning the system to a working state. If LKGC does not work, you can boot into Safe Mode and perform a System Restore. You may not want to do this first because doing so changes the LKGC settings, and a valid restore point may not be set, leaving a clean install with total data loss as one of your only options. You must be able to log on to Windows normally to perform a Device Driver Roll Back, and the ASR process requires a backup set unless you want to create a simple installation of Windows. Without a backup set, this won't do much.

72. C. In this case, only the key fob meets the requirements set forth. The card is self-contained and does not communicate externally. Therefore, each one must be set up before being deployed, so that it can be synchronized with the authentication server using a key that is shared between the card and server but never transmitted for eavesdroppers to steal. Because the card and server use the same algorithm, they can keep up with one another without further synchronization. With a key fob, the user must enter a PIN into the card in order for the card to produce a pseudorandom string. (Only the user can change the PIN.) The user then inputs the string into the authentication software utility, and it is compared against the rolling set of codes that the authentication server considers currently valid for that key fob. These codes are generated by a one-way algorithm, which means the shared secret cannot be reverse-engineered from any of the valid strings. The server tracks more than one but a very few of these, in case you forget you have requested a string and request another. With each of the other technologies, you need to have only, for example, a fingerprint or retina to scan, a smart card to swipe or insert, or a USB token to plug in. Although it depends on the implementation, there is no need for a separate password— the simple possession of the thing being authenticated is enough. Regardless of how it is implemented, the key fob adds an additional level of security, in case the card falls into the wrong hands.

73. B. The MSCONFIG utility can be used to selectively enable and disable applications during startup. The Startup tab is used to check or uncheck items, and the General tab is used to return operation to normal. The `net start` command is used to start services from the Command Prompt. The `normal` parameter is not valid because it implies that a service by this name exists, and it does not. The Startup Options screen has a *Start Windows Normally* option in Windows XP (*Boot Normally* in Windows 2000), but booting that way is as if you never pressed F8 to enter the Startup Options screen. The selective startup settings you make in MSCONFIG take effect by booting this way as well.

74. **A.** Utility-based cartridge cleaning that cleans the cartridges without the need to remove them is ideal to avoid the need for further calibration. Cleaning addresses the problems of smearing and smudging more than the inconsistencies in printing that calibration addresses. Think of calibration as the synchronization between what the printer thinks it is doing and what you observe it doing. Each time you remove the cartridges and put the same ones back in, you run the risk of throwing the printer out of calibration. Cleaning the cartridges this way can require calibration. Use this method if the software-managed cleaning does not work. The fact that smudging occurs horizontally could indicate an issue with the carriage assembly, although this would manifest itself more as printing everything in one place or possibly elongated horizontally. The fact that it also occurs vertically rules out the carriage assembly and points more toward build-up on the cartridges.

75. **D.** an extension magnet is ideal for working in tight spots where magnetic fields are not a problem, such as inside nonworking printers and scanners. It is thin enough to reach where a hand cannot. Place the magnet on the screw as you loosen it; when the screw breaks free, it will be less likely to fall into the depths. Extension magnets are more advisable than magnetized screwdrivers because you know the magnet is magnetic, but you may forget that the screwdriver is. Be sure you keep the extension magnet away from disks and other areas to which it is a hazard. Vacuums are not ideal in this situation because toner can be smaller than the filter on the vacuum, which will then act as a toner-blower of sorts, blowing toner out the exhaust port. Additionally, the vacuum will obstruct your view in the tight spot and may not catch the screw when it breaks free, not to mention the fact that you'll have to go fishing for each screw you capture that way. Don't count on flipping a workgroup printer over to dislodge a screw (which is potentially already damaging the sensitive fuser assembly) without hurting yourself or damaging property.

76. **B.** Look in the System category of Event Viewer to discover the service or device that failed. Only then can you formulate the appropriate next step to begin solving the problem. Rebooting will likely give you the same error message. Rebooting is not a suggested fix for such problems. Without finding out which driver has the problem—if the issue even is a driver—you cannot perform a Device Driver Roll Back or remove the driver.

77. **D.** Documenting the resolution is of the utmost importance. Doing so will reduce the amount of time for the second or similar calls involving the same problem. Although courteousness doesn't necessarily speed up your visit, it's a highly recommended trait for the customer-facing technician. Concerning proper testing, if you are sure the solution you implement solved the problem, you can be confident that the next service call is a new problem. Proper testing after implementation brings out all but the most hidden weaknesses in your solution. Therefore, plan for repeat visits and similar calls for other users. Have enough confidence in yourself to stick with the problem until it's resolved, even if you have to consult with someone with more expertise while you are working. Don't hand the customer off to anyone else if you can help it, especially if you are the face of your company for that customer.

78. **C.** Classless Interdomain Routing (CIDR) notation (/x) is shorthand for subnet masks written in dotted-decimal notation (x.x.x.x). Each binary one in the dotted-decimal form of the subnet mask is counted. Because ones always come before zeros in a subnet mask, and the two never mix, the number of ones is referred to as a *prefix*. The total count of ones is placed after the slash in CIDR notation. The converse of this rule means that a prefix of /28 corresponds to 255.255.255.240. Each 255 contributes eight binary ones to the count (255 = 11111111), for a subtotal of 24 ones. The 240 (11110000) contributes four more for a total of 28; hence the /28 prefix.

79. **B.** The File Transfer Protocol (FTP) and the Trivial File Transfer Protocol (TFTP) both transfer files between two IP hosts, but FTP is the more robust of the two protocols. FTP uses TCP for guaranteed delivery, so applications written as front-ends for FTP can be complex and feature-rich. TFTP employs UDP and is limited to best-effort delivery. TFTP is indicated only for situations where the user verifies the results of the transfer, such as downloading or uploading router and switch configurations. Telnet is used for remote configuration; and HTTP can be thought of as a sort of file-transfer protocol, but only for certain types of files that fulfill HTTP's primary function of transferring hypertext pages (which are made of text and links) to other files.

80. **AC.** DSL and its older cousin, ISDN BRI, are delivered on a single copper pair. The same pair that POTS is delivered on can be conditioned to carry these higher-rate services. Cable (DOCSIS) is delivered on CATV plant, not a Telco cable pair. Cellular, as its name implies, is a wireless networking technology that rides on the same signals as the cellular phone calls that are so prevalent today.

Answer Sheets for Practice Test 1

(Remove This Sheet and Use It to Mark Your Answers)

Section 1
Multiple Choice Questions

1 Ⓐ Ⓑ Ⓒ Ⓓ Ⓔ	41 Ⓐ Ⓑ Ⓒ Ⓓ Ⓔ
2 Ⓐ Ⓑ Ⓒ Ⓓ Ⓔ	42 Ⓐ Ⓑ Ⓒ Ⓓ Ⓔ
3 Ⓐ Ⓑ Ⓒ Ⓓ Ⓔ	43 Ⓐ Ⓑ Ⓒ Ⓓ Ⓔ
4 Ⓐ Ⓑ Ⓒ Ⓓ Ⓔ	44 Ⓐ Ⓑ Ⓒ Ⓓ Ⓔ
5 Ⓐ Ⓑ Ⓒ Ⓓ Ⓔ	45 Ⓐ Ⓑ Ⓒ Ⓓ Ⓔ
6 Ⓐ Ⓑ Ⓒ Ⓓ Ⓔ	46 Ⓐ Ⓑ Ⓒ Ⓓ Ⓔ
7 Ⓐ Ⓑ Ⓒ Ⓓ Ⓔ	47 Ⓐ Ⓑ Ⓒ Ⓓ Ⓔ
8 Ⓐ Ⓑ Ⓒ Ⓓ Ⓔ	48 Ⓐ Ⓑ Ⓒ Ⓓ Ⓔ
9 Ⓐ Ⓑ Ⓒ Ⓓ Ⓔ	49 Ⓐ Ⓑ Ⓒ Ⓓ Ⓔ
10 Ⓐ Ⓑ Ⓒ Ⓓ Ⓔ	50 Ⓐ Ⓑ Ⓒ Ⓓ Ⓔ
11 Ⓐ Ⓑ Ⓒ Ⓓ Ⓔ	51 Ⓐ Ⓑ Ⓒ Ⓓ Ⓔ
12 Ⓐ Ⓑ Ⓒ Ⓓ Ⓔ	52 Ⓐ Ⓑ Ⓒ Ⓓ Ⓔ
13 Ⓐ Ⓑ Ⓒ Ⓓ Ⓔ	53 Ⓐ Ⓑ Ⓒ Ⓓ Ⓔ
14 Ⓐ Ⓑ Ⓒ Ⓓ Ⓔ	54 Ⓐ Ⓑ Ⓒ Ⓓ Ⓔ
15 Ⓐ Ⓑ Ⓒ Ⓓ Ⓔ	55 Ⓐ Ⓑ Ⓒ Ⓓ Ⓔ
16 Ⓐ Ⓑ Ⓒ Ⓓ Ⓔ	56 Ⓐ Ⓑ Ⓒ Ⓓ Ⓔ
17 Ⓐ Ⓑ Ⓒ Ⓓ Ⓔ	57 Ⓐ Ⓑ Ⓒ Ⓓ Ⓔ
18 Ⓐ Ⓑ Ⓒ Ⓓ Ⓔ	58 Ⓐ Ⓑ Ⓒ Ⓓ Ⓔ
19 Ⓐ Ⓑ Ⓒ Ⓓ Ⓔ	59 Ⓐ Ⓑ Ⓒ Ⓓ Ⓔ
20 Ⓐ Ⓑ Ⓒ Ⓓ Ⓔ	60 Ⓐ Ⓑ Ⓒ Ⓓ Ⓔ
21 Ⓐ Ⓑ Ⓒ Ⓓ Ⓔ	61 Ⓐ Ⓑ Ⓒ Ⓓ Ⓔ
22 Ⓐ Ⓑ Ⓒ Ⓓ Ⓔ	62 Ⓐ Ⓑ Ⓒ Ⓓ Ⓔ
23 Ⓐ Ⓑ Ⓒ Ⓓ Ⓔ	63 Ⓐ Ⓑ Ⓒ Ⓓ Ⓔ
24 Ⓐ Ⓑ Ⓒ Ⓓ Ⓔ	64 Ⓐ Ⓑ Ⓒ Ⓓ Ⓔ
25 Ⓐ Ⓑ Ⓒ Ⓓ Ⓔ	65 Ⓐ Ⓑ Ⓒ Ⓓ Ⓔ
26 Ⓐ Ⓑ Ⓒ Ⓓ Ⓔ	66 Ⓐ Ⓑ Ⓒ Ⓓ Ⓔ
27 Ⓐ Ⓑ Ⓒ Ⓓ Ⓔ	67 Ⓐ Ⓑ Ⓒ Ⓓ Ⓔ
28 Ⓐ Ⓑ Ⓒ Ⓓ Ⓔ	68 Ⓐ Ⓑ Ⓒ Ⓓ Ⓔ
29 Ⓐ Ⓑ Ⓒ Ⓓ Ⓔ	69 Ⓐ Ⓑ Ⓒ Ⓓ Ⓔ
30 Ⓐ Ⓑ Ⓒ Ⓓ Ⓔ	70 Ⓐ Ⓑ Ⓒ Ⓓ Ⓔ
31 Ⓐ Ⓑ Ⓒ Ⓓ Ⓔ	71 Ⓐ Ⓑ Ⓒ Ⓓ Ⓔ
32 Ⓐ Ⓑ Ⓒ Ⓓ Ⓔ	72 Ⓐ Ⓑ Ⓒ Ⓓ Ⓔ
33 Ⓐ Ⓑ Ⓒ Ⓓ Ⓔ	73 Ⓐ Ⓑ Ⓒ Ⓓ Ⓔ
34 Ⓐ Ⓑ Ⓒ Ⓓ Ⓔ	74 Ⓐ Ⓑ Ⓒ Ⓓ Ⓔ
35 Ⓐ Ⓑ Ⓒ Ⓓ Ⓔ	75 Ⓐ Ⓑ Ⓒ Ⓓ Ⓔ
36 Ⓐ Ⓑ Ⓒ Ⓓ Ⓔ	76 Ⓐ Ⓑ Ⓒ Ⓓ Ⓔ
37 Ⓐ Ⓑ Ⓒ Ⓓ Ⓔ	77 Ⓐ Ⓑ Ⓒ Ⓓ Ⓔ
38 Ⓐ Ⓑ Ⓒ Ⓓ Ⓔ	78 Ⓐ Ⓑ Ⓒ Ⓓ Ⓔ
39 Ⓐ Ⓑ Ⓒ Ⓓ Ⓔ	79 Ⓐ Ⓑ Ⓒ Ⓓ Ⓔ
40 Ⓐ Ⓑ Ⓒ Ⓓ Ⓔ	80 Ⓐ Ⓑ Ⓒ Ⓓ Ⓔ

Directions: For each of the following questions, select the choice that best answers the question or completes the statement.

1. You are in your small shop and realize your onsite technician has taken your anti-static wrist strap. Which of the following is the best solution to your problem?

   A. Delay work until the technician returns your strap.

   B. Proceed with your internal computer repairs. The odds are in your favor that you will not destroy anything with ESD.

   C. Fashion an impromptu wrist strap from a spare Ethernet patch cord.

   D. Plug the computer system unit into the wall outlet, and touch the outside of the internal power supply.

2. While diagnosing a failed system, you discover the computer's power supply is defective. On closer inspection, you believe you have narrowed the problem to a fuse on the inside of the power supply. Which of the following is the best course of action to take?

   A. To save the customer money, open the power supply, replace the fuse, and then test your solution.

   B. Replace the power supply.

   C. Bypass the circuit with the fuse on the outside of the power supply using a direct connection.

   D. Tell the customer that you do not perform work on power supplies because of the inherent danger.

3. While working on a customer's computer in your shop, the power supply shorts out and starts a fire. What should you do?

   A. Use a nearby class-C fire extinguisher to put out the flame.

   B. Do nothing. These types of fire play out rapidly with little to no peripheral damage.

   C. Douse the fire with water from the nearby water cooler.

   D. Use your can of compressed air to blow out the fire.

4. While servicing a laser printer, you suspect the problem lies with the laser. Eager to diagnose the problem and fix it, which of the following is the best method to quickly test your theory?

   A. With the printer's case removed, watch for the laser to come on while the customer begins a print job.

   B. Insert a flexible photometer into the feed mechanism, and watch the display for confirmation that light is found in its path.

   C. Replace the EP cartridge, and print a test page.

   D. Remove the EP cartridge, and look at the element to see if it has blown.

5. Upon entering your shop one morning, you find that a water pipe has apparently burst, and the room has about an inch of standing water on the floor. The equipment appears to be unaffected thus far, and the server you were going to work on first is at the edge of the room near the door where you enter. What should you do?

   A. Alert your supervisor as well as any other pertinent authorities, and do no work until the water is removed.

   B. Unplug the server, and perform the required service.

   C. Soak up the water around the server or use your anti-static vacuum to remove it before performing the necessary service.

   D. Remove the server, and perform the necessary service in a dry area.

6. When choosing a new motherboard, which of the following expansion slots are you least likely to find?

   A. PCI

   B. PCIe

   C. AGP

   D. EISA

GO ON TO THE NEXT PAGE

7. Which of the following items can be found in a substance's MSDS?

    A. The chemical model for the substance

    B. Personal protective equipment to use while handling the substance

    C. Where the substance was shipped from

    D. The number to call to arrange for disposal of the substance

8. A customer drops off their computer and informs you that they attempted to upgrade the hard drive by using a new hard drive and an included utility to clone the old hard drive to the new one. Both drives are ATA and set for master, but the new drive does not show up when booting. Which of the following is most likely to fix the problem?

    A. Inform the customer that you cannot have more than one ATA drive in the system at one time, and then provide a quote for your time to back up the data on the original drive, install the operating system on the new drive, and restore the data to the new drive.

    B. Inform the customer that you are not willing to work on a system that has been tampered with.

    C. Sell the customer a *Y* Molex connector, and provide power to the new drive.

    D. Don't change the jumpers on the drives, but connect them both to the same controller on the motherboard.

9. You receive a computer for service that is taking an extremely long time to boot up after a large number of applications were installed. Which of the following would most likely speed up the customer's boot process while still allowing them to use the applications?

    A. Disable some of the applications on the Startup tab in MSCONFIG.

    B. Uninstall some of the applications.

    C. Increase virtual memory.

    D. Swap out for a larger hard drive.

10. Which *two* of the following may be the type of memory module that you need to upgrade a laptop?

    A. MicroDIMMs

    B. SIMMs

    C. RIMMs

    D. SoDIMMs

11. A customer brings you their computer and requests the latest and greatest video card to go with the cutting-edge motherboard they recently had installed. Which of the following expansion buses is the customer most likely referring to?

    A. PCI

    B. PCIe

    C. AGP

    D. ISA

12. A customer complains of having heard an unusual noise coming from the inside of the computer recently, but not during the two preceding days. You determine that the CPU fan was the source of the problem. Which of the following is the best way to handle the situation?

    A. Replace the CPU fan.

    B. Do nothing. No noise means no problem.

    C. Solder the break in the CPU fan's electrical wire.

    D. Remove the defective CPU fan so that the remaining heat sink can remove heat from the processor without obstruction.

13. A customer complains that their computer consistently runs for a little while and then shuts down on its own. Which of the following is most likely the culprit?

    A. Multiple shallow dents in the system case

    B. Clumps of dust on the back of the power-supply fan and chassis vent holes

    C. A massive wad of cables the customer told you was behind the system and on the floor

    D. Sticky keys indicating something has been spilled in the keyboard

14. While diagnosing a dead system, you discover that pressing the power button causes the power supply fan to kick over but not begin to run. The system never boots. Which of the following is a likely cause?

    A. The power cable is not completely plugged in on the power supply.

    B. The power button is defective.

    C. An adapter card has become partially seated.

    D. The system partition on the hard drive is damaged.

15. You are working on a computer that restarts automatically each time the owner shuts down their Windows XP system. Which of the following paths can you follow to prevent this behavior?

    A. Go to the Advanced page of System Properties, and click the Settings button in the Startup and Recovery section. Then, clear the Automatically Restart check box.

    B. Enter the BIOS setup routine; find the advanced section; and change the automatic restart field, or similar, to *disabled*.

    C. Tell the owner to use the power button to shut down the system from now on.

    D. Click the Hardware Profiles button on the Hardware tab of System Properties. Then, select the Wait Until I Select a Hardware Profile radio button.

16. A customer's monitor has recently begun displaying odd colors, mostly purples and greens. Which of the following is the most likely cause?

    A. One of the three cathode rays has stopped working.

    B. The monitor needs to be degaussed.

    C. The monitor's cable is not completely inserted into the video card's connector.

    D. The wrong video driver is being used.

17. A customer brings in a system with a malfunctioning floppy drive. According to the customer, they recently installed additional RAM. Ever since the installation, the light on the floppy drive remains lit, and the customer is unable to access any diskettes. What is the most likely explanation for the problem?

    A. More RAM has been installed than the system can support.

    B. Apparently the customer's diskettes have been exposed to a magnetic field, because this is the normal operation of a floppy drive.

    C. Diskettes are not meant to be inserted into a floppy drive.

    D. While working inside the system unit, the customer dislodged the data cable from the floppy and reinserted it upside down.

18. In diagnosing a software issue with the functionality of a peripheral device, you discover that the driver for that device is two years old. Which of the following methods is the best way to upgrade the driver?

    A. Use the original distribution disc for the operating system.

    B. There is nothing for you to do. The latest driver is downloaded automatically when available.

    C. Download the latest driver from the manufacturer's website.

    D. Avoid the possibility of downloading a virus by calling the manufacturer to send you the latest driver my mail.

19. Which of the following is the best way to clean the screen of most monitors?

    A. Spray the appropriate cleaning solution directly onto the screen, and wipe dry with a soft, lint-free cloth.

    B. Spray the appropriate cleaning solution onto a soft, lint-free cleaning cloth, and then wipe the screen with the dampened cloth.

    C. Wipe the screen with a dry soft, lint-free cloth or one lightly dampened with clean water.

    D. Spray the screen with compressed air.

20. What's the best way to control ESD when electrical outlets are difficult to come by?

    A. Wear rubber-soled shoes.

    B. Attach your wrist strap to the computer chassis to take advantage of the enormous electron sink that large amounts of metal provide.

    C. Rub a fabric-softener sheet over your clothes.

    D. Purchase an antistatic bench-top computer mat to place under the computer you are working on.

21. While working inside a computer system, you drop a screw into the system unit. Which of the following is the best method of retrieving the screw?

    A. Plastic tweezers

    B. Static resistant vacuum cleaner

    C. Magnetic screwdriver

    D. Your fingers

GO ON TO THE NEXT PAGE

22. You have a software utility that is able to test a computer's ability to send and receive the proper signals on a standard serial interface. Not having access to a remote device, what is the best way to make sure that both transmit and receive signals are available on the serial interface for the software to test?

    A. Use a hardware loopback plug.
    B. Disconnect the cable from the serial interface.
    C. There is no need to do anything special. Utilities like this can control the serial interface to place it in a software loopback state.
    D. Use a null-modem cable instead of the standard serial cable.

23. Which of the following do surge protectors guard equipment from?

    A. Direct lightning strikes
    B. Voltage spikes in dirty power sources
    C. Power lags and sags
    D. Power loss

24. Which of the following is *not* a reason to use a keyboard cover?

    A. To reduce the chance of damage from liquid spills
    B. To reduce the effect of dust build-up
    C. To increase the precision of keystrokes
    D. To reduce wear on the keys

25. A customer brings their system to you and requests that the internal analog modem be removed. After removing the adapter, you search in vain for a blank bracket to go in its place. What should you do?

    A. Temporarily cover the hole in the backplane with electrical tape until you can replace it with a bracket.
    B. Without plugging it in, put the adapter back in place to cover the hole.
    C. Leave the hole open until you can find a blank bracket, and call the customer to come get it.
    D. Disable the card in the BIOS, and leave it installed.

26. The read and write heads of floppy drives, tape drives, and optical disc drives, such as CD and DVD, can become dirty, obscuring their ability to function properly. Which of the following is the correct regular preventative maintenance to avoid such a problem?

    A. Regular use of such drives keeps the heads clean and free of contaminants. If a drive has not been used recently and now produces errors, access it repeatedly until the data is read properly.
    B. Use a cotton swab and rubbing alcohol to clean the heads.
    C. Use a head-cleaning system designed for the drive being cleaned.
    D. Execute the Head Clean utility in Windows on a regular basis.

27. A customer has complained that their system has started getting slower. You discover that their job entails the frequent creation of documents and presentations of various sizes and that for confidentiality reasons, once these data files are finalized, they are moved to a secure server and removed from the customer's hard drive. What is the best solution to attempt to speed up the system again?

    A. Search for files that the customer forgot to delete after they were moved to the server, which are building up and slowing down the system.
    B. Run the ASR utility.
    C. Run System Restore.
    D. Defragment the customer's hard drive.

28. While investigating the failure of a laptop's built-in LCD display, you discover that an external monitor works fine when connected to the VGA connector on the back of the laptop. Upon closer inspection, you find that you can see the image on the LCD screen faintly, but only in certain light. Which of the following could cause this problem?

    A. The external VGA connector is defective.
    B. The inverter board is defective.
    C. The operating system has been configured to display on the external monitor only.
    D. The rectifier board is defective.

29. Which of the following is the service in Windows XP that allows you to install a wireless NIC and immediately find available wireless networks?

   A.   Wireless Zero Configuration
   B.   Windows Zero Configuration
   C.   Configuration-free Networking
   D.   Ad Hoc wireless mode

30. Which of the following methods is the best way to remove a PC Card NIC from a laptop?

   A.   Double-click the Safely Remove Hardware icon in the System Tray, and then stop the device before unplugging it.
   B.   Hot-swappable devices like PC Cards should be unplugged like a cable to disconnect them from the system.
   C.   Use Device Manager to uninstall the driver for the device before unplugging it.
   D.   Use the switch on the PC Card to turn it off before unplugging it.

31. While diagnosing a laptop that will not stay powered up, which of the following is the least effective way to gather information about the problem?

   A.   Observe the LED on the AC adapter.
   B.   Swap the AC adapter with another one.
   C.   Remove the battery from the laptop.
   D.   Unplug all non-power-related cables and PC Cards from the laptop.

32. A customer complains that their pen mouse has stopped working. Which of the following is the most probable cause of the problem?

   A.   The user is applying too much pressure to the tablet, which is confusing the driver.
   B.   The stylus is upside down.
   C.   The customer is using the stylus from their PDA.
   D.   The user has stopped holding down the button on the stylus while moving the stylus around the tablet.

33. A customer brings you a new, hardened laptop. Their complaint is that they see the End and Home keys but are unable to use them in a manner to which they are accustomed. What is the most likely issue with this service request?

   A.   The user must hold the Fn key while pressing these keys.
   B.   This particular model of keyboard does not use these keys in the same fashion as a standard laptop or computer keyboard.
   C.   To remain visually compatible with standard keyboards, these keys are present but not functional.
   D.   Number Lock is on and affects how these keys are used.

34. Which switch specified during the execution of `WINNT32.EXE` installs the Recovery Console?

   A.   `/CMD`
   B.   `/RCONS`
   C.   `/RECCONS`
   D.   `/CMDCONS`

35. Which of the following is the first step you should take when troubleshooting a computer hardware or software issue?

   A.   Evaluate your results.
   B.   Determine who is at fault.
   C.   Gather information.
   D.   Document your work.

36. What does it mean for a computer to support SLI mode?

   A.   It is capable of accepting two or more 16X PCIe video cards and allowing them to share the video processing load.
   B.   It has an AMD K6-SLI processor installed.
   C.   A Windows operating system has booted into normal mode, as opposed to Safe Mode.
   D.   The appropriate chipset is installed to allow symmetric multiprocessing.

GO ON TO THE NEXT PAGE

37. A customer has been complaining that their battery gauge is not acting in a linear fashion. It shows that the LiIon battery has 98% of its charge left and that this equates to three and a half hours of run time; but after reaching about 50% of its charge, the laptop dies quickly. Overall run time is never more than 90 minutes on a full charge. What can be done to improve this situation?

   A. The battery must be placed in a deep-charge apparatus overnight to reverse the cell oxidation.

   B. Nothing can be done, short of a battery replacement.

   C. This is the standard operation of LiIon batteries, and the situation cannot be rectified.

   D. The battery needs to be calibrated.

38. Where is the best place to obtain firmware updates for computers and printers?

   A. A local computer superstore.

   B. Through the Postal Service.

   C. The manufacturer's website.

   D. Updates are downloaded and installed automatically through Windows Update.

39. Which of the following is the highest-quality LCD technology?

   A. Passive matrix

   B. Active matrix

   C. Dual scan

   D. Triple scan

40. A customer brings you their scanner and complains that every time they scan a file and then try to use a specific application to open the file produced, they receive the message *This file cannot be used with this software*. Only that software package has issues. What should you do?

   A. Quote the customer a new scanner.

   B. Open the file with an image-editing application, and reduce the resolution or change the file type.

   C. Return the scanner's software to its default settings.

   D. Sell the customer a new application that can use the file in the expected manner.

41. Which of the following should be done before removing a network share?

   A. Lock the file system.

   B. Reboot the server.

   C. Disconnect all users of the resource.

   D. Announce the loss of the shared resource across the network.

42. The HP printer you are repairing displays the message *PERFORM USER MAINTENANCE*. Which *two* of the following are most likely called for in this case?

   A. Clear all paper jams.

   B. Clean spilled toner out of the printer.

   C. Install a maintenance kit.

   D. Reset the page count.

43. What is the term that describes a network naming convention that can be written generically as *hostname**path* or *server**sharename*?

   A. UNC

   B. NCSU

   C. NetBIOS

   D. ARC

44. Why will an 8x AGP card not fit into a 3.3V AGP slot on a motherboard?

   A. The 3.3V slot is not long enough.

   B. The 3.3V slot is not deep enough.

   C. An 8x AGP card is a 3.3V AGP card and fits perfectly.

   D. The keying of one of the specifications does not match the other.

45. Which key can you hold down to temporarily disable the autorun feature while inserting devices, such as discs and USB thumb drives, without permanently disabling autorun through the Registry?

   A. Shift

   B. Ctrl

   C. Alt

   D. Esc

46. Which of the following impacts proper airflow and cooling most in a desktop computer system?

   A. The number of properly mounted hard drives

   B. Slot covers

   C. The size of the chassis

   D. The number of installed expansion cards

47. Which of the following is improper cable routing inside the case of a desktop computer system most likely to cause?

    A. A tripping hazard
    B. Components that fail to work
    C. Overheating
    D. Automatic system restarts

48. You receive a computer that has a power-supply fan that does not turn when you press the power button on the case. Which of the following is most likely to solve this problem?

    A. Replace the power supply.
    B. Replace the power-supply fan.
    C. Replace the motherboard.
    D. Replace the power button.

49. After completing a memory upgrade from 256MB to 512MB in a client's laptop, you attempt to confirm that the upgrade was successful and that all memory in the system is accessible. You notice that all but 32MB of the total RAM installed is accessible by Windows. What is the most likely issue at play here?

    A. The memory module you installed is defective.
    B. The onboard video adapter uses shared memory.
    C. The operating system does not report virtual memory in the total.
    D. The operating system always reserves 32MB for non-application purposes.

50. Which of the following is something that should be cleaned or replaced during routine maintenance of a laser printer?

    A. Fuser
    B. Corona wires
    C. Toner cartridge
    D. Ozone filter

51. Which of the following should you do before servicing a laser printer?

    A. Allow the fuser to cool.
    B. Allow the laser to discharge.
    C. Allow the toner to settle.
    D. Allow the page count to reach the maintenance threshold.

52. What is the last thing you should do when repairing a printer?

    A. Instruct the customer on how to use the printer.
    B. Clean the paper path.
    C. Print a test page.
    D. Reinsert the toner cartridge or ink cartridges.

53. In Device Manager, what is the easiest way to find out which device is using IRQ5?

    A. Double-click each device, and click the Resources tab to observe the IRQ it is using until you find one that is using IRQ5.
    B. Click View ➢ Devices by Connection, and find IRQ5 in the list.
    C. Click View ➢ Resources by Type, and then expand Interrupt Request.
    D. Click View ➢ Devices by Type, and find IRQ5 in the list.

54. A computer and printer are brought into your shop with the vague report that what they print is not acceptable. Which of the following is the best first step to figure out the characteristics of the problem?

    A. Print a test page from the attached computer.
    B. Print a test page from the printer's console.
    C. Calibrate the printer.
    D. Change the toner or ink cartridges.

55. When diagnosing an issue you are confident is linked to the motherboard, which of the following is *not* something you should be concerned with looking for?

    A. Damage to the motherboard
    B. Loose socketed chips
    C. Improperly seated cards
    D. Routing of the internal cables

56. What is the first thing you should do for a computer that the owner claims has become progressively slower over the past couple of weeks?

    A. Defragment the hard drive.
    B. Reinstall Windows.
    C. Run antivirus and anti-spyware scans.
    D. Run `CHKDSK` and `SFC`.

GO ON TO THE NEXT PAGE

57. Which of the following is the closest distance to the maximum range of a Bluetooth device from the computer-attached receiver?

    A. 3 feet

    B. 30 feet

    C. 300 feet

    D. 3000 feet

58. After connecting a new scanner to their computer, a customer brings in the scanner and computer and asks you to get the scanner to be recognized—an event that did not occur automatically in this case. What can you use to manually get the operating system to recognize the scanner?

    A. The Scanners and Cameras Wizard

    B. Device Manager

    C. The Add Hardware Wizard

    D. The Add Printer Wizard

59. Where do you go in Windows XP to force a user to press Ctrl-Alt-Del to reach the logon screen?

    A. The Advanced tab of the User Accounts applet in Control Panel

    B. User Profiles on the Advanced tab of System Properties

    C. The Windows logon screen

    D. Taskbar and Start Menu Properties

60. You receive a computer that boots only into Safe Mode because of a known driver issue. Which of the following can you try, to return the system to normal operation?

    A. Uninstall the device in Device Manager.

    B. Press the F8 key during bootup, and select *Last Known Good Configuration*.

    C. Physically remove the offending device.

    D. Disable the device in Device Manager.

61. Which of the following best describes an IDE header found on a motherboard?

    A. Beige, two rows of 20 pins each

    B. Black, two rows of 20 pins each

    C. Blue, two rows of 17 pins each

    D. Black, two rows of 62 pins each

62. After replacing a video expansion card with a superior model, you notice the resolution is worse than before with no options to increase it. Which of the following is the best solution to this problem?

    A. Reinstall the old adapter alongside the new adapter.

    B. Assign the old driver to the new adapter in Device Manager.

    C. Install or update the driver for the new video adapter.

    D. Enable the new video adapter in the BIOS.

63. Which of the following is an example of biometric authentication?

    A. Smart card

    B. USB token

    C. Username and password

    D. Retinal scan

64. Which of the following is the optimal DDR for a motherboard with a 400MHz FSB?

    A. PC400

    B. PC800

    C. PC3200

    D. PC2-3200

65. You receive a computer for service with a 200GB Ultra DMA/100 hard drive that the owner claims is not verifying at this speed with benchmark utilities. If you can confirm the slower performance in the shop, which of the following is the most likely cause?

    A. The drive is attached with a 40-pin cable.

    B. The drive is attached with a 40-conductor cable.

    C. The drive-cable's connector is not completely attached to the drive, the motherboard, or both.

    D. The drive is set for slave.

66. A laptop on which you are diagnosing a video problem boots up; but it initially flashes dark horizontal lines of various sizes, and then the video goes away and never returns. Which of the following is the most likely fix for this problem?

   A. Replace the LCD.

   B. Replace the inverter.

   C. Use the keyboard key sequence to activate the LCD instead of or in addition to the external monitor.

   D. Boot into Safe Mode, and update the video driver.

67. You receive a desktop computer for service but cannot get past the POST because of a system password that is requested early in the boot process. The owner is unavailable and is expecting the computer back at the end of the day. Which of the following can you try, to reset the password?

   A. Enter the BIOS, and turn off password authentication.

   B. Use the jumper on the motherboard to clear the CMOS.

   C. Hold the Esc key while booting to bypass the password.

   D. Edit the PASSWORD.INI file in the root of the system partition.

68. How can you best test a NIC without another network device to connect to?

   A. Device Manager

   B. Network Neighborhood or My Network Places

   C. Loopback plug

   D. Multimeter

69. What do inkjet, bubble-jet, and solid-ink printers have in common?

   A. Their cartridges are usually interchangeable.

   B. If you refill your own cartridges, you can use the same ink for each one.

   C. Any driver that works for one works for the others as well.

   D. They all shoot ink onto the page without touching the page.

70. A customer brings in a new printer that they have never used with the complaint that every time they start the printer, it emits an annoying noise and does not print. What should you do?

   A. Replace the print cartridges.

   B. Remove the packing tape.

   C. Install more memory in the printer.

   D. Replace the carriage motor.

71. Which *two* of the following connectors might you expect to see on a parallel printer cable?

   A. Centronics 36-pin

   B. USB Type A

   C. D-sub 25-pin

   D. D-sub 9-pin

72. A customer complains that their inkjet printer has yellow ghosting around certain colored objects and that the spacing between horizontal lines is not consistent. Which of the following makes the most sense to try?

   A. Calibrate the printer.

   B. Change the print cartridges, especially the yellow one.

   C. Replace the belt for the carriage assembly.

   D. Clean the print cartridges.

73. One of the departmental printers in your customer's company has been seeing increased usage recently and does not appear to be up to the challenge. Complaints of slow printing and inefficient use of users' time are common. What can you do that is most likely to have the greatest positive effect on the problem?

   A. Use compression to reduce the size of the print jobs.

   B. Change the pickup and exit rollers to reduce slipping.

   C. Add memory to the computers of each user who prints to that printer.

   D. Add memory to the printer.

74. Which is the term for a technology that transmits one bit at a time?

   A. Digital

   B. Analog

   C. Parallel

   D. Serial

GO ON TO THE NEXT PAGE

75. You receive from an athletic club a laser printer that experiences frequent paper jams. Which of the following is the most likely cause for these jams?

    A. The pickup rollers are worn and must be replaced.

    B. Humidity is causing the paper to stick together.

    C. The toner cartridge needs to be replaced.

    D. The fuser roller is marred.

76. Which of the following fans is considered an intake-oriented fan?

    A. Front chassis fan

    B. Power supply fan

    C. CPU fan

    D. Auxiliary rear chassis fan

77. Which of the following is the best permanent boot order for a customer who expects to boot regularly from each device?

    A. HDD; FDD; CD

    B. CD; FDD; HDD

    C. FDD; CD; HDD

    D. FDD; HDD; CD

78. All of the following are important considerations when cleaning a flatbed scanner's platen screen *except*:

    A. Use a lint-free cloth.

    B. Clean with strokes from the edge of the glass to the center.

    C. Do not apply cleaning solution directly to the glass.

    D. Blow the surface clean first to remove larger particles.

79. Which of the following is a standard tool for you to test a printer and scanner connected to the same computer?

    A. Loopback plug

    B. Test pattern

    C. USB direct connection

    D. Head cleaner

80. You receive a laptop with a touchpad, the touch stick disabled, and no external mouse. Without any interaction, the mouse cursor moves randomly around the screen. Which of the following is the first thing you should try?

    A. Enable the touch stick.

    B. Attach an external mouse.

    C. Clean the touchpad.

    D. Replace the rubber cover for the touch stick.

Answer Key for Practice Test 1

1. D	21. A	41. D	61. B
2. B	22. A	42. CD	62. C
3. A	23. B	43. A	63. D
4. C	24. C	44. D	64. C
5. A	25. A	45. A	65. B
6. D	26. C	46. B	66. A
7. B	27. D	47. C	67. B
8. C	28. B	48. A	68. C
9. A	29. A	49. B	69. D
10. AD	30. A	50. D	70. B
11. B	31. D	51. A	71. AC
12. A	32. C	52. C	72. A
13. B	33. A	53. C	73. D
14. C	34. D	54. B	74. D
15. A	35. C	55. D	75. B
16. C	36. A	56. C	76. A
17. D	37. D	57. B	77. C
18. C	38. C	58. A	78. B
19. B	39. B	59. A	79. B
20. D	40. B	60. D	80. C

Answer Explanations for Practice Test 1

1. D. Odds are that you *will* destroy something with ESD if you are not properly protected from doing so. However, worse than no wrist strap is a rigged-up wrist strap. Wrist straps are not simply metallic conductors that connect to ground. Such a solution will almost certainly lead to your electrocution without the proper resistance included in the system. Take great lengths to avoid putting off working when there is a suitable workaround. This can lead to lost confidence in you and your company due to missed commitments. If you cannot contact someone to bring you what you need while you continue to work, consider that the outside of the power supply is a grounded shell that can dissipate static, as long as the power supply is plugged into a three-prong outlet. Make sure you unplug the power cord from the wall outlet before beginning work, unless you have a hard switch on the power supply that removes DC power from the inside of the computer system.

2. B. There is no need to perform any work directly on the power supply, which includes opening it or creating a hazard like bypassing a fusible link with a direct connection. If you tell the customer that you don't do such work, you imply that some else might, which is highly unlikely. It also makes you look like you have a serious limitation in your ability to get them up and running again. With the price of a new power supply being what it is, hook the customer up with a new one and get them going quickly in the process. You look efficient, and the customer is happy and not out too much money.

3. A. It just so happens that the nearby class-C fire extinguisher is made specifically for electrical fires. Its chemical makeup reduces the risk of worsening the short and causing more problems, especially with circuits that are still live. Not as good at protecting life in the same situation are liquids, such as water, coffee, or soft drinks. Never use such substances to try to put out an electrical fire. Potential repercussions include expanding the scope of the electrical fire by involving other live circuits and allowing the current to travel up the stream of liquid to you and electrocute you. Leaving the fire or blowing it with compressed air, and thus fanning it, could easily result in the total loss of your surroundings before the fire department shows up to fix your lapse in judgment.

4. C. Never try to look at any concentrated light source, such as the laser of a printer or its equivalent light source. Looking at the light mechanism is not like looking at a common household light bulb. You won't be able to see a telltale burnt filament. Because the technician has no access to a tool that acts as a flexible photometer, the best bet is to replace the EP cartridge with a known good unit to test your theory by trying to print. If it works, you've already implemented the solution, and you're that much closer to closing out the call.

5. A. Although this solution appears to violate the rule that you should complete the necessary service to the extent of your abilities, that rule is trumped when it comes to the safety of you and others. Even entering a room with standing water and working equipment could lead to death from electrocution. Take no chances whatsoever when liquids and electricity are involved. Stay out of the room, and leave the mitigation to trained professionals. Inform your supervisor about the situation, or follow your organization's published emergency procedure, and wait for the problem to be rectified.

6. D. EISA is one of the older expansion-slot technologies, to be outdone only by MCA and the daddy of them all, ISA. If you have a motherboard with an EISA slot on it, watch out for that 486 processor (if you're lucky). AGP, PCI, and PCIe are still readily available on today's motherboards.

7. B. You won't see a model of how the atoms and molecules bind to one another, but the MSDS does include the chemical formula for the substance in Section 9. The MSDS is a generic form that applies to hazardous substances in a general sense, not to any particular lot or shipment of the substance, so manufacturers, wholesalers, and distributors cannot be listed. Although you will not find a number to call in the MSDS when investigating how to dispose of a substance, Section 13 outlines any disposal consideration particular to that substance. Section 8 details suggested equipment and clothing to help protect eyes, skin, and lungs.

8. C. You absolutely can have multiple ATA drives in the system at the same time. Without making one of the drives a slave, you cannot put them both on the same controller. For them both to remain masters, they must be on different controllers. Systems that have been tampered with are potentially out of warranty, either due to warranty violation or because they are past warranty expiration. Either way, you stand to produce revenue by working on the failed system, as long as it is agreed up front that this call is not covered under warranty. Besides, the customer should always sign a standard disclaimer before you perform service on any system. Of these options, supplying power to the new drive when none was supplied previously is the most likely fix.

9. A. Of the options given, only adjusting the entries on the Startup tab in MSCONFIG will allow the customer to speed up the boot process and keep all the applications. The other options either have no effect or leave the customer with a subset of the original applications. Although the applications do not start up with Windows, they are still installed and available for use when the customer executes them.

10. AD. Laptops tend to require SoDIMMs and the even smaller MicroDIMMs for memory upgrades. SIMMs, which are the predecessors to DIMMS and Rambus RIMMs, are rarely, if ever, used in today's laptops.

11. B. Although AGP is no slouch when it comes to high-speed graphics, PCIe, with or without multi-adapter SLI mode, is the state of the art today for graphics, especially in the gaming arena. PCI could be considered a distant third, and ISA should never be considered in this day and age, even if you can find a new motherboard that still has ISA slots on it.

12. A. The noise could have been caused by something dragging across the fan as it runs. If so, part of the solution is to replace the cable or cord that may have been damaged over time, as well as the CPU fan, the motor of which has been compromised by the added resistance of running against the impediment. The noise also could have been the motor's bearings in the various stages of failing. When the noise stops, it generally means that the bearings have worn so much that the motor can no longer turn the fan, a serious problem that will lead to overheating. While some fans can be removed from their associated heat sink, you would not want to leave the system with only the heat sink to cool the CPU. A passive cooling mechanism has only a prayer of working in BTX systems, but you should always go with the active cooling option to make sure. You save the customer money by replacing the fan, compared to charging them for the time to solder broken wires, and you avoid the curse of an unpredictable rigged solution.

13. B. The symptom indicates an overheating issue. Dust blocking vents and fan exhaust outlets can lead to overheating. The BIOS monitors the temperature of the CPU and the inside of the case. When the temperature reaches a lower threshold, a warning usually sounds. At an upper threshold, the system shuts itself down to avoid damage. Shallow dents will not impede the engineered flow of air in the system, although more severe dents may cause shorts with the motherboard or other circuitry, which could conceivably lead to ungraceful shutdowns. Although improper cable management is not linked with system failure, it is a potential safety hazard and should be corrected. Keyboard malfunction of any type does not lead to regular system shutdowns. A freak automatic series of keystrokes could shut down the system, but this would likely happen only once, if at all.

14. C. This is a classic symptom of a short on the motherboard, which could be caused by a partially seated expansion card. Because the power supply interface on the motherboard is a two-way connection, such feedback to the power supply incapacitates it. The fan generally jumps but never starts when you press the power button. Problems with the power button and the power cable are basically all-or-nothing in nature: They cause the system either to work or to appear completely dead with no fan movement at all. Software issues never manifest themselves in this fashion.

15. A. Whenever an error that usually causes a BSoD event occurs during shutdown, an event is logged and can be viewed later in Event Viewer. If the Automatically Restart check box is checked in System Properties, the computer will restart for any such event. When such an event occurs during shutdown, you are unable to examine the blue screen's details or even tell that the event occurred. The confusion that ensues leads to service calls to diagnose the restart on shutdown. Clearing the check box causes the system to pause on the blue screen so that you may be able to troubleshoot the problem and perhaps repair the offending driver. There is no such feature in the BIOS as the one mentioned here, nor is there any setting in the BIOS that can assist with this issue. Powering down with the power button is not an acceptable option because it encourages the customer to shut down Windows improperly, leaving temporary files scattered on the hard drive and compromising the operating system's stability. The option to alter how hardware profiles are handled affects how the system boots up, not how it shuts down.

16. C. Video drivers don't just go bad. If the monitor was ever displaying the right colors, this wouldn't be something to investigate further. Individual cathode rays don't generally fail, and Gaussian effects don't cause such symptoms over the entire display. An improperly inserted video connector and some cheaper switching equipment, which mimics poor connectivity at times, can cause this phenomenon. Check the connection first, before switching out the monitor or other more drastic remedies. Because the customer may suspect the monitor is the culprit, you may not have the computer system unit to work from. If the monitor exhibits no symptoms, you may be inclined to believe the problem is in the computer. Have the customer take the monitor back and try it again, being careful to properly connect the video cable, bypassing switching equipment if the problem persists. Tell the customer to bring in the entire system if nothing alleviates the problem. As an alternative, if available, send a field technician back with the monitor to check things out.

17. D. Of course, diskettes are meant to be inserted into a floppy drive, and exceeding the maximum amount of RAM in a computer has no effect on the floppy drive. The constant steady light on a floppy drive indicates that the data cable is inverted, which is an easy thing to do because few drive headers have single-side keying to match the connector on the cable. Often, there is a notch on both sides of the header, making it easy to put the cable on upside down.

18. C. Don't expect Microsoft to keep drivers updated for most components. Drivers on the original distribution disc for the operating system age with the disc. The latest driver is generally available on the Internet, as long as the manufacturer is not defunct. You shouldn't be concerned with viruses coming from the website of a reputable manufacturer. If you are not comfortable with such a solution, and the customer does not have a reliable antivirus application installed, advise them to allow you to install one before downloading the driver, which is the best way to obtain the latest device driver, among other things.

19. B. You shouldn't spray or apply any liquid directly to a monitor's screen. The point where the screen and monitor casing meet is not watertight. Liquids can seep into the interior of the monitor, causing a short-circuit or other expensive damage. A cloth moistened with the approved cleaner for the screen should be used to remove contaminants such as dirt and dust, which dry cloths and compressed air cannot completely remove, and oils, which require more than water to remove.

20. D. The appropriate bench-top computer mat will connect permanently to the appropriate ground point as well as give you a place to connect your wrist strap. This is by far the best solution among those given. Anti-static mats for the floor that you stand on will work as well. The excessive electrical resistance created by rubber-soled shoes can protect you from completing a path to ground through your body, thus protecting you from certain forms of electrocution but inhibiting the decay of static caused by walking around as you work. A wrist strap attached to an ungrounded computer chassis tends to equalize the difference in potential between you and the chassis but not between you and external adapters and other equipment, allowing you to cause damage to those devices as well as to the computer through the strap. The fabric-softener solution is a neat trick for emergencies, but this is not a technologically sound resolution, and there is still the possibility of building up dangerous charges even if you successfully treat all of your clothing.

21. A. The most non-invasive, least static-conducting method should be used in this situation. Passive plastic implements are the way to go. Despite every technician's urge, magnets and computers don't mix, and your fingers bring up concerns about static and body oils. The vacuum is great for removing dust and contaminants that are not directly on circuit boards, but it can dislodge small components easily and cause more problems immediately or down the road—not to mention that you will have to retrieve the screw from the vacuum's belly if you need it.

22. A. This is the exact situation for which hardware loopback plugs were created. They short the transmit and receive pins as well as other complementary pins on the local interface, taking cabling and remote devices out of the equation so that you can test the local interface without unpredictable influences. Null-modem cables allow you to connect DTE devices to other DTE devices, such as one computer to another. They don't help in this case. Unconnected interfaces don't test properly, and these utilities are too generic to overcome this state.

23. B. Surge protectors are not perfect. They should be removed from the wall outlet during electrical storms to protect them and the equipment connected to them. Surge protectors do nothing for power loss or brownouts. Their role is to make sure that common power spikes are clipped before they do cumulative damage to sensitive electronic equipment. You should keep an eye on the indicator, if one exists, to tell when the internal protection components are no longer able to do their job. When the protector has run its course, you should replace it immediately.

24. C. Unfortunately, keyboard covers can increase the "fat-finger" effect. These flexible plastic covers attempt to fit the keyboard model you have perfectly, but pressing one key can still affect neighboring keys on occasion. Even if the cover works perfectly, it will not increase the precision of your keystrokes. Some covers are simply attractive fabric covers that you place over the keyboard at the end of the day while the system is not in use to protect against airborne contaminants. Others are waterproof plastic skins that remain in place during use to reduce the effects of spills, dust, and other contaminants on a fulltime basis. They also take the wear and tear of normal use, reducing wear on the keys themselves.

25. A. It is important for proper airflow that you cover all open slots in the backplane and in other areas of the case and chassis, including not running the system with the case off. The system unit is engineered under fairly tight constraints for the power supply to draw air from the various ventilation holes around the case and chassis across the internal components to cool them. Holes like those left when you remove adapters can disturb the normal flow of air across the components, leaving stagnant pockets of air than can heat to unsafe levels. Adapters generally cannot be disabled in the BIOS, and you should not leave a card unplugged in the system because it can make accidental partial contact and cause the system to fail or even damage the card or motherboard or both. Besides, the customer wants the card out and may have another use planned for it. Another point that bears mentioning is that an improperly seated adapter does not completely cover the hole in the backplane, negating the value of leaving it in.

26. C. Each of these drives has a corresponding relatively inexpensive head-cleaning system that is readily available in the market and is good for multiple uses before it needs to be replaced. Using a swab dampened with alcohol is not an ineffective solution, but you must take care not to apply alcohol to rubber rollers and other parts that the alcohol can cause to dry and crack. Additionally, many heads are not easily accessible for this type of maintenance, and the drive must be disassembled first. If the drive is already disassembled and unable to accept media due to the disassembly or lack of power, then the proper cleaning system is not an option, and the swab method may be the only solution; but it should not be considered a regular preventive maintenance routine. Unfortunately, regular use does not keep read/write heads clean (quite the opposite), and there is no Head Clean utility in Windows.

27. D. Moving files implies copying them and then deleting them in one motion. Therefore, and by definition, there aren't any files left on the customer's hard drive that have already been moved. Regardless, a leftover or two wouldn't cause the system to slow down noticeably. Performing an ASR or System Restore will turn the system back to an earlier time, to the last backup and selected restore point, respectively. The ASR process causes you to lose recent work without guaranteeing a system speed-up. System Restore does not affect data files one way or another. As files are deleted, such as during a move, empty spots are left in the file system. As new, larger files are written to the disk, they are often split up, or fragmented, across the smaller empty spots. The more fragmentation that occurs, the more time the physical drive has to spend jumping around to piece files together as they are read into memory. Running the DEFRAG utility places the fragmented pieces of a file together in the proper order on the disk, speeding up access when the time comes.

28. B. Once you confirm that the internal/external-display keyboard control is not biased against the internal display, the most likely cause for the dimming of the image on a built-in laptop display is the failure of the inverter board. The inverter board powers the backlight by converting the DC voltage supplied by the power adapter back to AC, which the laptop's LCD backlight requires. The voltages in this component are extremely high, although the amperage is not so large. Nevertheless, care should be taken when handling this component because focal burning and deep pitting of the skin can occur; in just the right situation, even this lower amperage can be deadly. Rectifiers convert AC to DC, as in the case of the laptop's power adapter. No rectifiers affect only the LCD display on laptops. Obviously, the external VGA connector on the laptop is fine if the external monitor displays the image properly. No operating-system control turns off the built-in display. Any software controls for monitor selection that may exist come from specialized utilities that operate on top of the operating system. Be aware, however, that the Multiple Monitors feature of Windows, accessible from Display Properties, can cause unpredictable results on occasion, sometimes requiring a System Restore to return the system back to a time of normal functionality and return the display to the built-in LCD. This is not a feature designed to switch between internal and external monitors.

29. A. Wireless Zero Configuration (WZC) is the service and associated utility integrated into Windows XP that allows you to do nothing more than install a wireless NIC to immediately detect available wireless networks that are broadcasting their SSIDs. If you need to disable this feature, for whatever reason, you can stop the WZC service, but be aware that doing so also affects your ability to use 802.1x for wired network connections. The only other valid option given is Ad Hoc mode, which is an alternative to infrastructure mode when connecting devices in a wireless LAN. Ad Hoc mode does not use access points; infrastructure mode does.

30. A. Although it is true that these devices are hot swappable, meaning they can be inserted and removed while power is applied to the system, Windows dedicates resources to them while they are in use, making it less than elegant to unplug them. Use the Safely Remove Hardware utility in the System Tray to stop these devices when possible. If they do not appear in the list within the utility, unplug the PC Card with no prior action.

31. D. Generally, cables and PC Cards do not contribute to power issues with laptops, but they should still be removed to rule them out. The AC adapter is the likely cause, and most have an LED that illuminates when they are working properly. However, swapping out with another power adapter of the same type that is known to be in working condition is a quick test of the adapter's viability. Occasionally, batteries can affect power to the system and interfere with a working adapter's ability to power the laptop. If removing the battery causes the system to begin working properly, change out the battery. Removing the battery is also suggested any time you are servicing a laptop, just to make sure there is no negative influence from the battery. Doing so also helps to confirm the quality of the DC power the laptop is receiving from the AC adapter. A multimeter comes in handy if you suspect the AC adapter is not putting out the correct DC voltage.

32. C. Pen mice have special styli that must be used in order for the mouse to work. Most models have buttons that are programmable for various functions, such as double-clicking and application launching, but not usually for making the mouse work in general. It could be that the customer has started holding the pen upside down; but such a change in behavior is not likely, and many models allow you to hold the pen upside down to erase or produce broader strokes. So, that's not as likely to be the problem as their using a passive stylus from their PDA, which most often will not actuate the sensors in the tablet. These units are also not pressure-sensitive, so even if the user changed this behavior, it would not result in a cessation of operation.

33. A. Number Lock generally does not affect these keys on a laptop, ever since the separate cursor-movement pad was added to standard keyboards. Laptop keyboards do, however, sometimes place these functions on other keys in a color related to the Fn key, meaning that the Fn key must be held to gain access to their functions.

34. D. When you execute the `WINNT32.EXE` program from its location (such as the `I386` folder in the root of the distribution CD) on a functioning XP installation and use the `/CMDCONS` switch, the Recovery Console is installed as one of the startup options along with your primary operating system and any additional operating systems and environments offered in the text-mode startup menu that appears early during bootup. Note that XP must already be installed and that the use of the `/CMDCONS` switch does not reinstall XP; it only installs the Recovery Console. The `/CMD` switch is the only other valid switch listed, but its function is to execute a command of your choosing before the final phase of Setup.

35. C. Perhaps you could consider laying blame to be part of the information-gathering process. However, it's not a good idea to get that kind of tension stirred up in an already volatile and frustrating situation. Figure out what's going on, develop some theories, try the most likely of them first, and then document your results—successes and failures. They'll come in handy down the line.

36. A. Scalable Link Interface (SLI) mode refers to a computer system's ability to accept two or more 16X PCIe video cards and tie them together in such a way as to divide the graphical processing load evenly between or among them. None of the other options describes SLI mode.

37. D. Although LiIon batteries do not form a chemical memory per se, they do suffer from irreversible life-robbing oxidation. When the battery has a significant charge, this oxidation is exacerbated by heat, such as that generated by the laptop in which the battery is installed or by leaving the battery in the car exposed to ambient heat. There is no cure for this effect and the fact that the battery has a finite life expectancy. The effect also has a bearing on how Windows' battery gauge interprets the battery's remaining charge. Calibrating the battery, which really means calibrating Windows' gauge or synchronizing the gauge with the battery, involves allowing the battery to discharge completely once in every 30 charging cycles until the laptop loses power. Doing so will keep the gauge more accurate, and the user who watches their gauge vigilantly will not be caught off guard.

38. C. Firmware, such as BIOS and internal printer software, is not something you can buy off the shelf; and Windows Update does not deal with firmware, just updates to the operating system, including security patches and driver updates. Most manufacturers that produce equipment with replaceable or flashable firmware offer the latest revisions on their website. This is the first place you should look for updates.

39. B. Active-matrix LCD technology is the highest quality available today. It is characterized by a very wide angle of view and a clear image due to the implementation of a thin-film transistor per pixel. Dual-scan is a form of passive-matrix technology, which uses row and column signals to change the state of a particular pixel with less than stunning results compared to those of active-matrix displays. Dual-scan displays divide the image into two halves, each of which is traced simultaneously, increasing the refresh rate over standard passive-matrix displays. There is no such thing as triple-scan technology.

40. B. Certain software cannot accept images with parameters that are beyond the specifications of the software. Generally, you can reduce the resolution in either on-screen pixels or printed dots per inch to allow their use. Optionally, you can change the file type from low-loss formats, such as TIFF, to others that produce smaller files, such as JPEG. In this case, up-selling the customer is probably not the correct approach, assuming the suggested solution works. There is no reason to believe that the software that produced the image is not at its default settings. The problem is more the software they are using to access the scanned image. If only that software has issues, then there is no reason to make broad adjustments that could potentially affect other software that is currently working with the images. There is also no reason to assume that you can replace the customer's hardware or software with a similar package that can use the image. Work on the image to make it compatible with the existing software and scanner instead of trying to find software or a scanner that the image works with as is.

41. D. You should always give users time to complete what they are doing with a shared resource before you take it out of commission. Five minutes is generally enough, but longer is the prerogative of the technician taking the resource offline. Locking the file system is not something a technician can do, and the other two options would be just as rude as removing the share without making an announcement. Rebooting would be even more rude because it would affect a larger number of shares and users.

42. CD. Clearing paper jams is not considered maintenance, which is more proactive in nature. It's more of a reaction to an event. Although cleaning toner out of a printer can be considered proactive in most cases, it's not something the printer will ask for in a message like this. You can argue that responding to any message is hardly proactive maintenance, but it's tough to deny when you're using something called a "maintenance" kit. The average maintenance kit contains items such as a fuser assembly, a transfer roller, and pickup or feed/separation rollers. Some printers reset the page count when you install a maintenance kit, but in case it doesn't work out that way, there are methods to reset the count yourself. Installing a maintenance kit before the page count reaches the threshold that spawns the warning message can make it more difficult to reset the page count, but there are usually ways to do so with little additional effort.

43. A. A Universal Naming Convention (UNC) name begins with a double-backslash, which is followed by the hostname of the server that hosts the shared resource, followed by a backslash and the path to the resource, starting with the share name (generically, *hostname**path*). NCSU is the North Carolina State University, a fierce rival of the University of North Carolina at Chapel Hill (also UNC), not a naming convention. NetBIOS is not a naming convention but a protocol adopted by Microsoft to provide names, such as the hostname and share name in this example, to devices and resources on the network. The Advanced RISC Computing (ARC) convention is what Microsoft uses to name boot devices in the `BOOT.INI` file. For example, `multi(0)disk(0)rdisk(0)partition(2)\WINNT` is an ARC name pointing to the `\WINNT` folder on the second partition (cardinal numbering) of the first non-SCSI device (ordinal numbering) as containing the system files used to complete the boot process, none of which are CompTIA A+ topics.

44. D. The 8x AGP specification uses a 0.8V signal and works off of a 1.5V power supply from the motherboard. The length and depth of 8x AGP and the 3.3V AGP technologies (1x and 2x) are identical. Only keying prevents the 8x card from inserting into the older 3.3V slots. If either the card or slot is poorly made, allowing cross-insertion, damage to the card or motherboard can result, so always make sure you truly have matching AGP components. The slot that 8x and 4x cards fits in is known as a 1.5V slot. All 0.8V 8x AGP cards must be manufactured to tolerate the 1.5V power from the motherboard without resulting in component destruction, but 3.3V slots are off-limits for 8x and 4x cards. Universal slots, which have no keying, are designed to accommodate all AGP cards and operate at an acceptable voltage, based on the card and the version of the AGP specification. The latest version is 3.0, which matches each card's voltage perfectly. In summary, as long as you are not dealing with the rarer AGP Pro, all AGP cards are the same size. Only keying keeps the higher-speed cards from fitting in the lower-speed, higher-voltage slots, which would almost certainly cause damage to the components.

45. A. Holding down the Shift key while inserting such media disables the autorun feature, which searches for an autorun information file on the inserted media that points to a routine to run automatically.

46. B. It's easy to fall for any one of these options, but by far, slot covers left off the backplane circumvent proper airflow and cooling the most. Each of the other options have been allowed for and engineered into the system. Although the more devices and expansion cards you install, the more challenging it is for the system to move the air, a missing slot cover can short-circuit proper airflow considerably more. Larger chassis come with larger power supplies and usually additional chassis fans to alleviate the adverse effect on cooling that results from being able to fit more devices into the system.

47. C. Improper cable routing can lead directly to improper airflow inside the case, which can result in the computer system's overheating. Cable routing has no impact on automatic restarts and is not likely to affect the functionality of the connected component, as long as the connectors are secure. Being internal cables, there is no danger of tripping over them; these cables do not appear outside the case where people would be walking.

48. A. By and large, dead power-supply fans mean dead power supplies. Occasionally, the motherboard or something attached to it can produce feedback to the power supply that makes it react as if it had no load on it, which can cause the fan not to run. If you replace the power supply and have the same results, begin by removing all the cards from the motherboard. If the problem persists, try removing all cables that attach to the motherboard. Finally, if the problem persists, try a new motherboard. The power switch fails even more rarely. Starting out by changing the switch is likely to be an exercise in frustration and futility, but keep it in mind if all else fails.

49. B. Some inferior onboard video adapters in laptops, and even desktop machines, use a technology known as shared video memory. The video card uses a portion of the main system RAM to hold frame buffers that are to be displayed next—in this case, 32MB. Better video adapters have their own RAM for this purpose. If you notice pixilation of moving video, you may be able to enter the BIOS routine to increase the amount of shared video memory. Be aware that doing so decreases the amount of system RAM available to the operating system and applications and sometimes reduces performance noticeably.

50. D. Anything that filters builds up whatever it filters, degrading its performance. If the filter cannot be cleaned, replace it. Because it's difficult to tell the remaining life of a filter, each one should be cleaned or replaced each time routine maintenance is performed. Of the other options, the closest to being a possible answer is the toner cartridge; but because the toner cartridge cannot be cleaned, and because replacing it is not cheap, especially when the EP drum is part of the same assembly, you should avoid changing it out on a schedule. Wait until the need to replace an item like this is triggered by an event, such as running out of toner.

51. A. The fuser can become scorching hot. You should try to ascertain how long the printer has been powered down and how long it was in operation beforehand. The toner is in a containment chamber and does not need to settle. The laser does not carry a charge and is safe when the printer is powered down and unplugged. Applying maintenance kits is the only thing that needs to be synchronized with page-count thresholds. Most printers will tell you in an obvious way when the maintenance kit needs to be installed.

52. C. Printing is what printers do. When they do it well, they are not in need of repair. Printing a final test page successfully and with the appropriate quality indicates your repair worked. The toner or ink cartridges must be installed before you can test the printer. Presumably, if you are repairing a printer, then it was once in service, and the customer knows how to use it. That would be the last step for an IT technician or the equivalent to do when installing a printer for a customer. Cleaning the paper path is usually a maintenance task and must be done with certain parts of the printer opened or removed. Many steps must be performed after cleaning the paper path, even if it was part of the repair process, which is possible but not likely.

53. C. The *Resources by Type* view in Device Manager has an IRQ category that lists all devices that have an IRQ grouped by expansion bus and then by IRQ number. You can spot all devices using a specific IRQ without any additional action other than possibly scrolling.

54. B. The key here is not to start "fixing" the problem before you've diagnosed it. Changing and calibrating cartridges before you even know what's going on with the printer is premature. Additionally, don't add unnecessary variables into the mix. Make sure the printer can produce its own printed page before predisposing your diagnosis to point the finger at a potentially working printer driver. If and when the printer ejects a perfect internally generated page, you can add the computer and its peculiarities to the hunt.

55. **D.** If you are certain there is a motherboard issue, cable routing does not produce symptoms that could lead you to suspect the motherboard. It tends to cause overheating and system shutdown, which can lead you to suspect fans and the power supply, but not the motherboard. Damage to the motherboard, such as fractures and severed traces, as well as chip creep (the gradual ejection of socketed chips through numerous heating and cooling cycles) can lead to motherboard failures. Additionally, poorly inserted cards can short out the motherboard by way of the expansion bus, leading to a condition that appears to be a failed motherboard.

56. **C.** A machine that runs noticeably more slowly over a short period of time is not likely suffering as much from a fragmented file system as from an attack of viruses or spyware. Fragmentation occurs over time, and the effects are not obvious because of the slower onset. The CHKDSK and SFC utilities should be run every so often but do not have an impact on slow systems. These utilities help to prevent inconsistencies in the file system that may leave your system files, applications, and data inaccessible, even to the point of disabling you operating system. So, although executing these utilities on a regular basis is wise, doing so in this situation is not the solution. Although reinstalling the operating system will fix problems with viruses and spyware, it's overkill and should not be necessary with the proper scans.

57. **B.** Bluetooth, a short-range cord-replacement technology used with computer systems to allow wireless connection of peripherals, such as keyboard and mouse, has a maximum range of 10 meters, or about 32 feet.

58. **A.** Although you can add a printer with the Add Printer and Add Hardware Wizards, the only way to manually add a scanner is with the Scanners and Cameras Wizard. Device Manager is ideal for scanning for new hardware and disabling devices as well as updating and uninstalling drivers. It's not used to manually add drivers.

59. **A.** This feature is turned on and off in the User Accounts applet found in Control Panel. A check box on the Advanced tab, when checked, forces the use of Ctrl-Alt-Del to get to the genuine Windows logon screen. Although it adds an extra step, it's a good idea to require this because Trojan horse attacks can use a fake logon screen to trick you into entering your username and password. However, no Trojan horse has the ability to survive the Ctrl-Alt-Del key sequence, which always takes you to the genuine Windows logon screen, ensuring that Windows is the only entity receiving your information.

60. **D.** Thanks to the ability to disable a device through its driver in Device Manager, even in Safe Mode, there is no need to uninstall the device or its driver. The problem with LKGC is that when you log on in Safe Mode, the Registry location that LKGC draws from is updated with the system's current settings. Although it's considered known-good, you can tell from the question that it's really not good.

61. **B.** An A+ depot technician should be able to visually recognize standard connectors and components on a motherboard. IDE headers are black for standard ATA and blue for Ultra DMA (UDMA). They all have 40 pins arranged in two rows of 20 each. PCI slots are white, not black, and have two rows of 62 pins each. Floppy connectors are black, not blue, and have two rows of 17 pins each.

62. **C.** This is an issue with the new video adapter not being compatible with the old video driver. Because of the incompatibility, Windows uses a standard driver to get the operating system running and an image on your screen. The problem is that the default driver is minimal in its functionality. If a compatible driver is already installed, it is possible that the installed version is not optimal for the operating system. Installing the appropriate driver, or updating the installed correct driver to the latest designed to work with the operating system you are using, generally fixes this issue. Having two adapters installed will constitute a conflict or, at least, require two separate drivers. Reinstalling the old adapter doesn't do anything for the new adapter. The Device Manager and BIOS options are not valid.

63. **D.** Biometric authentication uses some form of biological measurement that can be regarded as unique to compare against a database of scans from all authorized users. Examples include retinal, fingerprint, and voice scans. None of the other options rely on biological scans of any sort.

64. **C.** Know your memory for this one. For DDR, the FSB frequency is twice the system clock frequency, which is 200MHz, in this case. That's purely academic because you want to use the FSB frequency in your calculations to find the data transfer rate, which will tell you the model of memory module you need. With a 400MHz FSB, each pin between the CPU and memory can transfer 400Mbps, which means each set of eight pins can transfer 400MBps. Because Pentium-class and higher processors transfer 64 bits, or 8 bytes, at a time, the total transfer rate is 3200MBps. DDR and DDR2 chips are named after the FSB frequency. In this case, the modules would use

DDR-400 chips, which are different from PC400, which describes a module, not a chip. DDR and DDR2 modules are named after the total transfer rate. In this case, the modules you need are known as PC3200 modules. PC2-3200 modules are for DDR2 and use DDR2-400 chips. Such chips rely on an FSB of 400MHz, which is quadruple a system clock of 100MHz. This explanation started out by computing that the system clock used in this question is 200MHz, which DDR doubles, not quadruples. Although you cannot tell that PC3200 is faster than PC2-3200 by looking at the FSB frequency, which is 400MHz for both, knowing how to derive the system clock rate from the FSB frequency will lead you to this conclusion. Noting the nomenclature is easier than mulling over the system clock rate. If the module name starts with *PC2*, it's for DDR2, not DDR. In summary, a quick way to solve problems like this is to multiply the FSB frequency by 8. This technique works for DDR and DDR2.

65. B. This is a standard issue when you connect an Ultra-DMA drive that operates at any data rate with a 40-conductor cable, which is acceptable for use only with standard ATA drives and Ultra-DMA/33 drives. The increased frequency used to transfer data across the cable with Ultra DMA/66 and higher produces enough noise interference that each data lead is compromised by its neighbors. The additional 40 conductors are ground leads that reduce the effect of the capacitive coupling among the original 40 leads by being interleaved between them so that the data leads are not adjacent to one another. The connector on the cable and the header on the motherboard or host adapter is a different color from the connector used with standard ATA, but the pin count and configuration are identical, retaining the 40-pin arrangement. Connector attachment generally produces an all-or-nothing functionality for the drive. Partial attachment does not slow down the drive down: It causes it to stop working. Ultra DMA specifies a master and slave function for each controller, so having one drive set for slave, as long as the other is set for master, is not an issue.

66. A. This symptom points to an issue with the ability of the LCD to activate the pixels in the active or passive matrix. There is no field fix for this problem, except to replace the offending LCD. The fact that you can see the lines on the screen indicates the backlight from the inverter is present. The fact that you are seeing the lines also indicates the LCD is active and you do not need to try to switch to it from the external monitor. In light of each of the foregoing points, there is no driver issue here. Besides, the LCD's Windows driver does not affect the black-screen portion of the boot process. It wouldn't hurt to be sure that there is no software issue, so feel free to attach an external monitor to prove the operating system is OK; but the writing is on the wall with these symptoms: bad LCD.

67. B. The system password authentication blocks *any* progress until you enter the correct password (which is case-sensitive, by the way). This block also keeps you out of the BIOS and out of the file system. If holding the Esc key or editing an `.INI` file could bypass the system password, it wouldn't be worth setting the password to begin with.

68. C. Windows doesn't offer a way to verify the external functionality of a NIC card without a network device, such as hub, a switch, a router, or another computer attached. There is no easy way to use a multimeter to test a NIC interface. Even if you could test the transmit functionality, you can't generate traffic with the multimeter in order to test the receive portion of the interface. By far the easiest and most ingenious tool is the Ethernet loopback plug, which you can purchase or make for yourself. To make your own, start with a blank eight-pin modular plug (commonly referred to as an RJ-45 plug). Tie pins 1 and 3 together, and tie pins 2 and 6 together. This causes the NIC to receive its own signal and light its link light, which tells you immediately that the NIC is operating properly at Layer 1. Through the use of utilities, you can perform more in-depth testing of the NIC's ability to function properly.

69. D. Each of these types of printer sprays its ink onto the page without striking or touching the page, unlike impact (print head) and laser printers (fuser). You'd be lucky if the same ink cartridge or software driver could be used across any two inkjet models from the same manufacturer, much less across printer technologies and brands. You shouldn't refill cartridges; doing so can cause damage to the printer without warning and degrade its performance in the short run. Even if you do, inkjet and bubble-jet printers use a liquid ink, and solid-ink printers use a solid-base ink that is melted just before application to the page.

70. B. New printers and scanners often come with moving and removable parts taped to the chassis so that they do not move during shipping. Most often, the pieces of tape or their tips are colored for easy recognition. Make sure all tape is removed before attempting to power up the device and use it. Another thing to look for with new scanners is a mechanical lock for the scanning head. This cam must be turned and released before powering the scanner up and using it. Check all of these items before diving in to replace components.

71. **AC.** Standard parallel printer cables have a male Centronics 36-pin connector on the printer end and a male D-sub 25-pin connector on the computer end. Some printers use a mini-Centronics connector, but USB interfaces and 9-pin D-sub connectors have never been used with parallel printer connections.

72. **A.** This is a classic issue with the way inkjet printers operate. Calibration allows you to tell the printer how it needs to adjust its operation based on how the print cartridges are situated in the cartridge carrier, which along with slight differences in cartridge manufacturing can have a significant impact on print quality given minute changes. Think of this as the synchronization between what the printer thinks it is doing and what you observe it doing. The two should be identical, and calibration is the way to approach that goal. Nothing you can do with the cartridges themselves or the carriage assembly will resolve this problem. Each time you remove the cartridges and put the same ones back in, you run the risk of throwing the printer out of calibration. Utility-based cartridge cleaning that cleans the cartridges without the need to remove them is ideal to avoid the need for further calibration. However, cleaning addresses the problems of smearing and smudging more than the inconsistencies in printing that calibration addresses.

73. **D.** Up to a point, the more memory you equip a printer with, the less average time a user has to wait for a print job to leave their computer in order to free them up to do other things. It has almost nothing to do with how much memory is in the computer. Compression can give the perception of having more memory, but there is no way to control how much memory the data takes up in the printer without changing the page-description language, which is not an option here and is not always effective or welcome. Although printers are rated for a certain maximum number of pages per minute, and more memory does not generally affect this rating, users are not as sensitive to the speed at which pages come out of the printer as they are to how long their system is tied up when they print; it's similar to the frustration users experience when web pages are slow to load. To further the analogy, you can be dealing with the fastest website known to humanity but still suffer from local bottlenecks that slow it and all other sites to a crawl—just try to impress a user of that network with the statistics of that website. It's all about the users' perception of performance when you receive complaints about slow response. In this case, increased printer memory improves this perception better than the other options.

74. **D.** Serial is the term that means transmitting one bit at a time. In contrast, parallel transmission transfers more than one bit simultaneously. Digital and analog refer to the method of encoding that places the signal on the medium, not how many bits are transferred per transmission.

75. **B.** Humidity is one of the biggest enemies of loose-leaf paper loaded in a hopper, and certain venues can produce more humidity than others. The page expands, and the fibers of the paper do not lie flat and can interact with one another, causing multiple pages to load at the same time. Suggest that the customer place the printer in a climate-controlled location in the athletic club, away from swimming pools, saunas, and outside access, among other places. Worn pickup rollers are more likely to miss the page than to take more than one, as long as humidity is not a factor. Physical shock to a printer can cause it to require service sooner, but picking up more than one sheet of paper at a time is not a likely symptom. A marred fuser roller will leave marks on the printed page where there should be none, but a marred fuser roller does not contribute to paper jams.

76. **A.** The front chassis fan is designed to draw air into the chassis to flow across the internal components, cooling them before being blown out the back of the chassis by the power supply's fan and any rear auxiliary fans that are installed. It also supplies fresh, cooler air for the CPU fan, which blows downward with an exhaust orientation toward the CPU, pushing air off the surface of the processor and keeping the hotter air between the fins of the heat sink moving outward from the center of the heat sink. This hotter air is then swept away and removed from the interior of the case by the airflow circuit created by the exhaust fans in the power supply and on the back of the chassis.

77. **C.** When analyzing boot order, always consider the possibility that the hard drive is functional. If the directive is to boot from any other device, the hard drive must fall after the boot device in the order or it will boot the system instead. The advantage of booting to removable media is that you can remove the media if you would rather not boot to that device: You don't have to change the boot order. The question is which removable media you should place first in the list. In reality, it's a toss-up, and if you chose to boot to the CD before the floppy, that would work fine. The nuance of booting to the floppy first is that when you have a bootable diskette in the drive, you don't want to wait for the timeout required to check the CD drive for bootable media—especially if a bootable CD is loaded. If so, it will take longer while the BIOS waits for you to press a key to boot from the CD. Once it is done waiting for the input from you that never comes, it will move on to the floppy. If you reverse the order,

floppy then CD, and you wish to boot to the CD, the floppy check is much quicker. If you wish to boot from the floppy instead, you don't have to endure the CD check.

78. B. Although it sounds logical to avoid wiping the platen glass toward the edges, if you follow the advice of the other options, doing so shouldn't be a problem. Certainly, don't actively and intently wipe toward the edge so as to push the lint-free cloth with cleaner applied first (or better yet, a professionally prepared pre-moistened wipe saturated with the proper amount of cleaner) hard against the seam. However, the proper amount of cleaner applied to the cloth you are using is safe enough to allow you to clean the platen glass much the way you would clean a window. Deliberate, possibly circular motions are acceptable, as long as you do not leave lint or push around damaging particles that may permanently etch the glass and affect the quality of future scanned images.

79. B. A test pattern can be printed from the console of most printers. With the test pattern, you can discover if any part of the printer's capabilities is operating suboptimally. You can scan the same test pattern to determine whether the scanner is capable of capturing a wide variety of colors and patterns. You can then adjust the resolution to provide optimal results or repair any part of the scanner that proves to be defective based on its performance with this standard object. There is no such thing as a USB direct connection, and loopbacks are for testing interfaces, not entire peripheral devices. Head cleaning may be necessary based on what you find during your diagnosis with the test pattern.

80. C. This is often an issue when the touchpad becomes dirty enough to register false impulses on the pad. Cleaning the touchpad should rectify the problem. Adding or enabling other devices does not disable the touchpad, so the problem will remain. Because the touch stick is disabled, changing its cover is not the solution.

Answer Sheets for Practice Test 2

(Remove This Sheet and Use It to Mark Your Answers)

Section 1
Multiple Choice Questions

CUT HERE

1 Ⓐ Ⓑ Ⓒ Ⓓ Ⓔ	41 Ⓐ Ⓑ Ⓒ Ⓓ Ⓔ
2 Ⓐ Ⓑ Ⓒ Ⓓ Ⓔ	42 Ⓐ Ⓑ Ⓒ Ⓓ Ⓔ
3 Ⓐ Ⓑ Ⓒ Ⓓ Ⓔ	43 Ⓐ Ⓑ Ⓒ Ⓓ Ⓔ
4 Ⓐ Ⓑ Ⓒ Ⓓ Ⓔ	44 Ⓐ Ⓑ Ⓒ Ⓓ Ⓔ
5 Ⓐ Ⓑ Ⓒ Ⓓ Ⓔ	45 Ⓐ Ⓑ Ⓒ Ⓓ Ⓔ
6 Ⓐ Ⓑ Ⓒ Ⓓ Ⓔ	46 Ⓐ Ⓑ Ⓒ Ⓓ Ⓔ
7 Ⓐ Ⓑ Ⓒ Ⓓ Ⓔ	47 Ⓐ Ⓑ Ⓒ Ⓓ Ⓔ
8 Ⓐ Ⓑ Ⓒ Ⓓ Ⓔ	48 Ⓐ Ⓑ Ⓒ Ⓓ Ⓔ
9 Ⓐ Ⓑ Ⓒ Ⓓ Ⓔ	49 Ⓐ Ⓑ Ⓒ Ⓓ Ⓔ
10 Ⓐ Ⓑ Ⓒ Ⓓ Ⓔ	50 Ⓐ Ⓑ Ⓒ Ⓓ Ⓔ
11 Ⓐ Ⓑ Ⓒ Ⓓ Ⓔ	51 Ⓐ Ⓑ Ⓒ Ⓓ Ⓔ
12 Ⓐ Ⓑ Ⓒ Ⓓ Ⓔ	52 Ⓐ Ⓑ Ⓒ Ⓓ Ⓔ
13 Ⓐ Ⓑ Ⓒ Ⓓ Ⓔ	53 Ⓐ Ⓑ Ⓒ Ⓓ Ⓔ
14 Ⓐ Ⓑ Ⓒ Ⓓ Ⓔ	54 Ⓐ Ⓑ Ⓒ Ⓓ Ⓔ
15 Ⓐ Ⓑ Ⓒ Ⓓ Ⓔ	55 Ⓐ Ⓑ Ⓒ Ⓓ Ⓔ
16 Ⓐ Ⓑ Ⓒ Ⓓ Ⓔ	56 Ⓐ Ⓑ Ⓒ Ⓓ Ⓔ
17 Ⓐ Ⓑ Ⓒ Ⓓ Ⓔ	57 Ⓐ Ⓑ Ⓒ Ⓓ Ⓔ
18 Ⓐ Ⓑ Ⓒ Ⓓ Ⓔ	58 Ⓐ Ⓑ Ⓒ Ⓓ Ⓔ
19 Ⓐ Ⓑ Ⓒ Ⓓ Ⓔ	59 Ⓐ Ⓑ Ⓒ Ⓓ Ⓔ
20 Ⓐ Ⓑ Ⓒ Ⓓ Ⓔ	60 Ⓐ Ⓑ Ⓒ Ⓓ Ⓔ
21 Ⓐ Ⓑ Ⓒ Ⓓ Ⓔ	61 Ⓐ Ⓑ Ⓒ Ⓓ Ⓔ
22 Ⓐ Ⓑ Ⓒ Ⓓ Ⓔ	62 Ⓐ Ⓑ Ⓒ Ⓓ Ⓔ
23 Ⓐ Ⓑ Ⓒ Ⓓ Ⓔ	63 Ⓐ Ⓑ Ⓒ Ⓓ Ⓔ
24 Ⓐ Ⓑ Ⓒ Ⓓ Ⓔ	64 Ⓐ Ⓑ Ⓒ Ⓓ Ⓔ
25 Ⓐ Ⓑ Ⓒ Ⓓ Ⓔ	65 Ⓐ Ⓑ Ⓒ Ⓓ Ⓔ
26 Ⓐ Ⓑ Ⓒ Ⓓ Ⓔ	66 Ⓐ Ⓑ Ⓒ Ⓓ Ⓔ
27 Ⓐ Ⓑ Ⓒ Ⓓ Ⓔ	67 Ⓐ Ⓑ Ⓒ Ⓓ Ⓔ
28 Ⓐ Ⓑ Ⓒ Ⓓ Ⓔ	68 Ⓐ Ⓑ Ⓒ Ⓓ Ⓔ
29 Ⓐ Ⓑ Ⓒ Ⓓ Ⓔ	69 Ⓐ Ⓑ Ⓒ Ⓓ Ⓔ
30 Ⓐ Ⓑ Ⓒ Ⓓ Ⓔ	70 Ⓐ Ⓑ Ⓒ Ⓓ Ⓔ
31 Ⓐ Ⓑ Ⓒ Ⓓ Ⓔ	71 Ⓐ Ⓑ Ⓒ Ⓓ Ⓔ
32 Ⓐ Ⓑ Ⓒ Ⓓ Ⓔ	72 Ⓐ Ⓑ Ⓒ Ⓓ Ⓔ
33 Ⓐ Ⓑ Ⓒ Ⓓ Ⓔ	73 Ⓐ Ⓑ Ⓒ Ⓓ Ⓔ
34 Ⓐ Ⓑ Ⓒ Ⓓ Ⓔ	74 Ⓐ Ⓑ Ⓒ Ⓓ Ⓔ
35 Ⓐ Ⓑ Ⓒ Ⓓ Ⓔ	75 Ⓐ Ⓑ Ⓒ Ⓓ Ⓔ
36 Ⓐ Ⓑ Ⓒ Ⓓ Ⓔ	76 Ⓐ Ⓑ Ⓒ Ⓓ Ⓔ
37 Ⓐ Ⓑ Ⓒ Ⓓ Ⓔ	77 Ⓐ Ⓑ Ⓒ Ⓓ Ⓔ
38 Ⓐ Ⓑ Ⓒ Ⓓ Ⓔ	78 Ⓐ Ⓑ Ⓒ Ⓓ Ⓔ
39 Ⓐ Ⓑ Ⓒ Ⓓ Ⓔ	79 Ⓐ Ⓑ Ⓒ Ⓓ Ⓔ
40 Ⓐ Ⓑ Ⓒ Ⓓ Ⓔ	80 Ⓐ Ⓑ Ⓒ Ⓓ Ⓔ

Directions: For each of the following questions, select the choice that best answers the question or completes the statement.

1. You plan to be handling a number of ESD-sensitive devices in a makeshift work environment. There is no computer system plugged in nearby for you to clip your antistatic wrist strap to. There are also no static mats or similar ground points nearby. Which of the following is an acceptable alternative?

   A. Tell your supervisor that you will be unable to perform any services in that environment.

   B. Stand perfectly still, and take the chance that an ESD will not occur.

   C. Plug the alligator clip of the antistatic wrist strap into the ground receptacle of a three-prong electrical outlet.

   D. Plug the banana clip of the antistatic wrist strap into the ground receptacle of a three-prong electrical outlet.

2. While working inside a computer, you drop a small metal part into the vent of the power supply. What should you do?

   A. Unplug the power supply, and remove the screws that hold its cover on. Use plastic tweezers to remove the part.

   B. Unplug the power supply immediately, and wait a couple of hours or more before attempting to remove the power supply and shake the part out.

   C. Unplug the power supply, and invert the computer system to try to shake the part out through the vents it went in.

   D. Unplug the power supply, and reach in for the part with a magnet, making sure not to make contact with anything. Let the attraction draw the part through the air to the magnet.

3. Which class of fire extinguisher is for ordinary combustible materials only, such as paper, wood, and plastic, and should never be used on electrical or chemical fires?

   A. Class A

   B. Class B

   C. Class C

   D. Class D

4. While servicing a laser printer, you suspect the waste-toner receptacle of the toner cartridge is full. Eager to diagnose the problem and fix it, which of the following is the best method to quickly test your theory?

   A. Empty the waste-toner receptacle.

   B. Replace the toner cartridge.

   C. Confirm that there is still fresh toner in the cartridge. If so, the waste-toner receptacle should not be full.

   D. Install a maintenance kit.

5. While diagnosing an unresponsive external LCD attached to a laptop, you feel strongly that you know exactly which internal component of the LCD is to blame. Which of the following is the best course of action?

   A. Replace the external LCD with a known working unit, and try the unresponsive LCD on a known working system.

   B. Open the LCD's case, and perform diagnostics on the suspected component; or replace it, and test the results.

   C. Open the case, but before performing any work, discharge the flyback transformer's charging capacitor.

   D. Remove the external monitor, and use the built-in LCD display.

GO ON TO THE NEXT PAGE

6. You need to access the LAN with a customer's computer from your new workbench. However, no network connection is set up there yet. Due to construction in the area, an existing cable guard covers electrical cables running to the wall across the hall where there is a LAN connection. What should you do?

   A. Go buy a hub to be able to share the LAN connection.

   B. Run your network cable in the same cable guard as the electrical cables.

   C. Given that you won't need the connection for long, run it and be sure to remove it as soon as you are finished with it.

   D. Run the network cable separately, and secure it with your own cable guard or duct tape.

7. Which of the following items is *not* included in a substance's MSDS?

   A. The chemical formula for the substance

   B. The chemical model for the substance

   C. First-aid measures

   D. Handling and storage of the substance

8. You are adding a hard drive and a DVD burner to a system that already has a hard drive and a CD burner. All devices have ATA interfaces. What is the best way to pair the devices?

   A. Put each of the four devices on its own controller.

   B. Pair the fastest hard drive with the fastest optical drive on the same controller. Pair the slower devices on another controller.

   C. Pair the hard drives on one controller and the optical drives on another controller.

   D. Place the three fastest drives on one controller and the slowest on another controller.

9. A customer drops off their computer and reports experiencing network connectivity issues and an IP address of 169.254.12.169. Which of the following is the most appropriate thing you should encourage the customer to check?

   A. Is there a network connection icon in the notification area?

   B. Is the LED lit on their NIC?

   C. Can they ping their default gateway?

   D. Can they reach their destination by IP address instead of by name?

10. While performing a memory upgrade on a desktop computer, you discover that the computer has one available slot and uses DDR2. Which of the following is most likely the type of module that you need?

   A. MicroDIMM

   B. SIMM

   C. SoDIMM

   D. DIMM

11. Which of the following function keys is used during Windows XP setup to install third-party SCSI drivers?

   A. F2

   B. F6

   C. F8

   D. F12

12. A customer reports beeping coming from their computer during use, followed shortly by an automatic shutdown of the system. Which component is most likely the cause?

   A. CPU fan

   B. Power supply

   C. System speaker

   D. BIOS

13. A customer complains that their computer consistently runs for a little while and then shuts down on its own. Upon beginning your inspection of the system, which of the following are you *least* likely to find to be the culprit?

   A. Dust buildup at the chassis vent holes

   B. No heat sinks on the RAM modules

   C. A stalled CPU fan, system fan, or power-supply fan

   D. Poorly routed internal cables

14. During your diagnosis of a dead system, you discover that pressing the power button has no effect. The motherboard was recently upgraded, and the system hasn't worked since. Which of the following is the most likely cause?

   A. Too many adapter cards are installed for the new motherboard.

   B. The power button is defective.

   C. There is a short underneath the motherboard.

   D. The power supply is dead.

15. Which *two* of the following printer technologies use heat during the process of printing a page?

A. Laser
B. Thermal
C. Inkjet
D. Impact

16. If you need to transfer information between two laptops in an area without a wired network connection, and no wireless network is installed in range of your shop, which of the following is the best and most convenient method to transfer the data between most standard laptops?

A. Bluetooth
B. Standard serial cable
C. Infrared
D. Burn a CD.

17. A customer complains of odd colors in various areas of their CRT monitor. You set up their system and notice the same thing. Which of the following can you do to rectify the problem?

A. Degauss the monitor.
B. Connect an external monitor to see if the problem shows up there as well.
C. Power-cycle the monitor.
D. Reboot the system.

18. A customer drops off their inkjet printer and complains that it fails to print blue every so often. There are no smudges or smears to speak of, just the occasional loss of blue. Which of the following best explains the cause of the problem?

A. The blue print cartridge is dirty.
B. The blue print cartridge is clogged.
C. The driver has failed.
D. The interface on the computer or the printer has corroded.

19. While checking in a dead monitor, your interview with the customer yields the fact that the last thing the customer did was clean the monitor. Which of the following is a possible cause of the outage?

A. The customer applied an abrasive cleaner.
B. The customer misapplied the cleaner.
C. The customer wiped the screen with the wrong type of cloth.
D. While cleaning, the customer accidentally turned the horizontal position knob too far.

20. Which of the following battery chemistries is credited with the longest run time in laptops?

A. LiIon
B. NiMH
C. Alkaline
D. NiCd

21. You are working on an inkjet printer that is smudging horizontally and vertically when it prints. Which of the following makes the most sense to try?

A. Use the printer's software utility to clean the print cartridges.
B. Calibrate the printer.
C. Replace the belt for the carriage assembly.
D. Remove the print cartridges, and clean them with a lint-free cloth.

22. What is the name of the device that allows you to locally test a serial interface without dependence on a remote device?

A. Hardware loopback plug
B. Crossover cable
C. Multimeter
D. Termination plug

23. A customer is interested in protecting their equipment against power spikes, which have claimed two of their systems already. They are not interested in keeping their system up during power outages. They simply wish to protect their equipment against harmful power anomalies. Which of the following should you suggest to satisfy their requirements?

A. UPS
B. Surge protector
C. Generator
D. Power strip

24. Your supervisor is soliciting your advice on which authentication technology you think would be best for a customer's computer systems. They are interested in one that requires each user to have something physical as well as to have to remember a personal password. Which of the following should you recommend?

A. Biometrics
B. Smart card
C. Token card
D. USB token

GO ON TO THE NEXT PAGE

25. A customer's computer keeps overheating and shutting down. Which of the following is *not* a probable cause?

    A. The customer has four hard drives installed.
    B. The CPU fan has stalled.
    C. The chassis cover is removed.
    D. An adapter slot is open.

26. Which of the following should you do first for a keyboard with nonfunctioning keys?

    A. Try a new keyboard.
    B. Replace the keys that are not functional.
    C. Clean the keyboard.
    D. Try the keyboard on another system.

27. All of the following are advisable materials to use when controlling static electricity *except*:

    A. Tile floors
    B. Static mats
    C. Antistatic wrist straps
    D. Carpet

28. While investigating the failure of a laptop's built-in LCD display, you discover that an external monitor works fine when connected to the VGA connector on the back of the laptop. Which of the following could cause this problem?

    A. The external VGA interface is defective.
    B. The LCD cutoff switch is sticking or bad.
    C. The connector on the cable from the monitor is not completely connected to the interface.
    D. The system booted up into Safe Mode.

29. All of the following are recommended laptop troubleshooting techniques *except*:

    A. Remove unneeded peripherals.
    B. Remove the battery.
    C. Remove the AC adapter.
    D. Attach an external monitor.

30. A customer reports that the Safely Remove Hardware icon does not appear in their System Tray, and they need to know how to unplug their USB NIC. Which of the following is the easiest way for them to proceed with success?

    A. Pull the USB NIC out of the USB port.
    B. Power the system down before removing the USB NIC.
    C. Use Device Manager to uninstall the driver for the USB NIC before unplugging it.
    D. Disable the device in Device Manager.

31. In which of the following cases should you *not* use an antistatic wrist strap?

    A. When working with components from an antistatic bag
    B. While standing on a static mat
    C. When the system unit is sitting on a static mat
    D. When working inside a CRT monitor

32. Which *two* of the following paths take you to Event Viewer?

    A. Start ➢ All Programs ➢ Accessories ➢ System Tools ➢ Event Viewer
    B. Start ➢ Run ➢ `eventvwr.msc`
    C. Control Panel ➢ Administrative Tools ➢ Event Viewer
    D. Control Panel ➢ Event Viewer

33. A customer brought in a new specialty laptop. Some of their letter keys produce numbers and other symbols. What is the most likely issue with this service call?

    A. Number Lock is on and affects how these keys are used.
    B. They have their keyboard mapped to another language.
    C. The keyboard is set for scientific mode and must be set back to standard mode in Control Panel.
    D. They must hold the Fn key while pressing these keys.

34. Which of the following motherboard sockets have 2 rows of 84 pins and latches on each end to secure the inserted component?

    A. IDE
    B. DIMM
    C. AGP
    D. PCIe

35. Which of the following processors might call for being installed in a Socket 478?

   A. Xeon
   B. AMD K6
   C. Pentium 4
   D. Pentium M

36. Which of the following processors might call for being installed in a Socket 462?

   A. Athlon
   B. Pentium 4
   C. Pentium Pro
   D. Itanium

37. What is the term that means synchronizing a software battery gauge with the actual battery?

   A. Bsync
   B. Refreshing
   C. Reconciliation
   D. Calibration

38. Which of the following processors might call for being installed in a PAC611?

   A. Opteron
   B. Itanium
   C. Itanium 2
   D. Pentium D dual-core

39. Which of the following is most closely associated with an SECC?

   A. DDR2
   B. Slot 1
   C. PCIe adapter
   D. AMD processors

40. Which of the following best describes an AGP slot found on a motherboard?

   A. White, two rows of 66 pins each, one key
   B. Brown, two rows of 66 pins each, one key
   C. Brown, two rows of 66 pins each, two keys
   D. Black, two rows of 49 pins each, one key

41. If you are disposing of a laptop, which of the following provides the best advice as to what you should do with the battery?

   A. Place the battery in a separate bag or container before throwing it in the trash.
   B. Disassemble the battery, and take the chemical component to a recycling facility. Throw the case away.
   C. The battery must be burned to reduce the hazard to the environment.
   D. Follow the instructions on the battery.

42. Which of the following statements about disks, partitions, and logical drives is *not* true?

   A. A drive letter can correspond to either a partition or a logical drive.
   B. One disk can have multiple partitions.
   C. Operating systems based on NT, such as Windows 2000 and XP, can boot from any drive other than B:, regardless of its drive letter.
   D. There can be only one extended partition on a disk.

43. Which of the following is advisable before servicing a laptop?

   A. Remove the AC adapter.
   B. Remove the pluggable drive.
   C. Boot into Safe Mode.
   D. Enter the BIOS setup routine.

44. Which of the following terms is most closely associated with RAID 1?

   A. Striping
   B. Volume extension
   C. Non-fault tolerant
   D. Mirroring

45. What is meant by the term *disk array*?

   A. Multiple disk drives working together to form a single volume
   B. Multiple disk drives working independently within the same system
   C. A single drive assembly with multiple disk platters
   D. A series of dissimilar disk drives within the same system

GO ON TO THE NEXT PAGE

46. Which of the following should you do before swapping batteries in a laptop?

    A. Remove the AC adapter.

    B. Turn off the laptop.

    C. Stop the battery with Safely Remove Hardware.

    D. Fully charge the replacement battery.

47. Which of the following is a valid use of a multimeter?

    A. Testing the voltage present on the power connector of a laptop

    B. Checking the refresh rate of a CRT monitor

    C. Testing the output of a laptop's power adapter

    D. Checking the remaining charge of an installed laptop battery

48. Which of the following is the best plan for disposing of laser-printer consumables?

    A. Consult the printer manufacturer's documentation or the pamphlet accompanying the replacement cartridge or container.

    B. Dispose of the consumables in a toilet.

    C. Use a vacuum with a HEPA filter to remove the waste product from its container.

    D. Throw the container holding the waste product in a trash receptacle.

49. In general, after a memory upgrade, what must you do to get the system to recognize the memory?

    A. Visit the manufacturer's website, and download the device driver for the new modules.

    B. Do nothing. The system recognizes the memory automatically.

    C. Be ready to provide the correct keystroke at just the right moment to enter the BIOS routine and input the amount of total RAM installed.

    D. In Windows, open System Properties, and enter the total amount of RAM installed.

50. A customer brings in a new scanner that they are unable to use. They report that the scanner will not produce any usable output and makes unusual noises during the scanning process. Which of the following should you do first?

    A. Check to make sure the customer has the correct power adapter for the scanner.

    B. Ask the customer to bring in their computer so you can check the driver they are using.

    C. Power up the scanner, and try to scan something from a computer in your shop.

    D. Check the scanning-head locking mechanism.

51. Which of the following media is used by Bluetooth?

    A. Radio waves

    B. Fiber optics

    C. Copper

    D. Sonic waves

52. Which of the following is closest to the maximum range for IEEE 802.11b?

    A. 3 feet

    B. 30 feet

    C. 300 feet

    D. 3000 feet

53. Which of the following would *not* be part of the regular maintenance of a laser printer?

    A. Cleaning the paper path

    B. Cleaning or replacing the pickup rollers

    C. Cleaning or replacing the fuser

    D. Cleaning or replacing the ozone and fan filters

54. Which of the following RAID levels does not employ some form of striping?

    A. 0

    B. 1

    C. 3

    D. 5

55. Which motherboard slots or connectors are usually black and have 34 pins and the occasional keying?

    A. AGP

    B. PCI

    C. IDE

    D. FDD

56. For an overheating system, which of the following is the most likely factor?

    A. The installed operating system

    B. Internal cable routing

    C. A greasy substance on the CPU

    D. The front chassis fan blowing air into the case instead of out

57. Which *two* of the following are the most likely locations to find settings for a computer's power-management features?

    A. Utility disc

    B. Operating system

    C. BIOS

    D. Web client session to the power-management device

58. You diagnose a dead motherboard and need to replace it with a new one. You notice that when you remove the motherboard, all peripheral interfaces come with it. Which of the following is the best description of the type of motherboard you should replace it with?

    A. An integrated motherboard

    B. A non-integrated motherboard

    C. A motherboard with the latest processor

    D. An ATX motherboard

59. How many pins does a SATA power connector have?

    A. 4

    B. 7

    C. 12

    D. 15

60. You install a sound card in a desktop system but find that you hear no sound even after rebooting. Which of the following should you do first?

    A. Remove and reinstall the sound card.

    B. Select *Use this device (enable)* in Device Manager.

    C. Enable the sound card in the BIOS.

    D. Run the setup utility provided with the sound card.

61. After installing a brand-new hard drive, you find the old power connector does not appear to fit the drive. Which *two* of the following are the most likely to produce this result?

    A. The new drive is a SCSI drive.

    B. The new drive is a SATA drive.

    C. The new drive derives its power from the data cable and does not require a separate power cable.

    D. You are trying to insert the power cable upside down.

62. Which type of cabling do you need to connect directly to a 1000BaseT NIC?

    A. Fiber

    B. Coax

    C. Twisted pair

    D. Twinax

63. Which of the following commands reliably formats drive `E:` as a FAT32 partition?

    A. `format e: /f:fat32`

    B. `format e: /fat32`

    C. `format e: /fs:fat32`

    D. `format e:`

64. How can you confirm that your motherboard is receiving DC power?

    A. LEDs on the motherboard are lit.

    B. You must use a multimeter to test one or more areas of the motherboard.

    C. You can't. Motherboards use AC power.

    D. An external monitor displays an image.

65. In which *two* of the following motherboard slots will an AGP 8x adapter fit?

    A. 0.8V-keyed slot

    B. 1.5V-keyed slot

    C. 3.3V-keyed slot

    D. Universal-keyed slot

66. Which of the following memory types will fit in a slot that has 240 pins and one key?

    A. DDR2

    B. DDR

    C. Single-data-rate SDRAM

    D. Rambus

GO ON TO THE NEXT PAGE

67. During an upgrade, which of the following is most likely the least expensive, valid option if you find the processor socket on the motherboard is larger than the processor you intend to insert into it?

   A. If the processor fits in the innermost holes of the socket, it will work.

   B. Replace the motherboard.

   C. Replace the processor.

   D. Use an adapter between the processor and the motherboard.

68. What is the minimum number of physical drives required for RAID 3 and RAID 5?

   A. 1

   B. 2

   C. 3

   D. 4

69. Which of the following is the *least* likely result of dust build-up inside a computer system?

   A. Overheating

   B. Short circuiting

   C. Mechanical restriction

   D. Loss of stored data

70. The same technology used in cellular telephony can readily be used to create which of the following?

   A. A local area network

   B. A wide area network link

   C. A metropolitan area network

   D. A campus area network

71. Which LCD video technology uses a row and column signal to specify the particular pixel to be altered, as opposed to supplying each pixel with its own controllable transistor?

   A. CRT

   B. Passive matrix

   C. Active matrix

   D. Inverted

72. A customer brings in their inkjet printer and states that it intermittently prints dark splotches ad fails to complete the line of print. Which of the following makes the most sense to try?

   A. Use the printer's software utility to clean the print cartridges.

   B. Calibrate the printer.

   C. Replace the belt for the carriage assembly.

   D. Remove the print cartridges, and clean them with a lint-free cloth.

73. While working inside a large workgroup laser printer, you need to make sure that a screw you are removing does not fall down onto the fuser assembly, but you are unable to fit both hands into the area where the screw is. Which of the following is the best approach to this situation?

   A. Use a static-resistant vacuum.

   B. Use a magnetic screwdriver.

   C. Let the screw fall, and then turn the printer upside down to remove it.

   D. Use an extension magnet.

74. Which of the following devices uses a light source, mirrors, and the equivalent of a camera to perform its function?

   A. Impact printer

   B. Laser printer

   C. Inkjet printer

   D. Scanner

75. What is the term that refers to the feature characterized by the starting of a program upon the insertion of a disc or thumb drive? An .INF file by the same name can be found in the root directory of the media.

   A. Autoplay

   B. Autorun

   C. Boot

   D. Startup

76. What type of port is used to connect a printer to a computer with a parallel cable?

   A. Direct port

   B. Network port

   C. Local port

   D. TCP/IP port

77. You arrive one morning at your repair shop to find a scanner with a service ticket attached that states only that the scanner does not work properly. Which of the following methods of gathering information should you try first?

    A. Hook the scanner to one of the shop computers.

    B. Power up the scanner without connecting it to a computer.

    C. Contact the customer.

    D. Visually inspect the scanner.

78. You receive a laser printer for service that prints a recurring mark in regular intervals on the page. Which of the following components should you clean or replace?

    A. Pickup rollers

    B. Fuser

    C. Transfer corona

    D. Toner cartridge

79. What is the term for a physical device that produces a pseudorandom alphanumeric sequence after the owner enters a PIN?

    A. Key fob

    B. Smart card

    C. Token

    D. USB key

80. Which of the following is the first level of security for a non-networked computer that contains sensitive corporate information?

    A. User account

    B. Share permission level

    C. Physical security

    D. Forced authentication from the screensaver

Answer Key for Practice Test 2

1. D		**21.** A		**41.** D		**61.** BD	
2. B		**22.** A		**42.** C		**62.** C	
3. A		**23.** B		**43.** A		**63.** C	
4. C		**24.** C		**44.** D		**64.** A	
5. A		**25.** A		**45.** A		**65.** BD	
6. D		**26.** C		**46.** B		**66.** A	
7. B		**27.** D		**47.** C		**67.** B	
8. C		**28.** B		**48.** A		**68.** C	
9. B		**29.** C		**49.** B		**69.** D	
10. D		**30.** A		**50.** D		**70.** B	
11. B		**31.** D		**51.** A		**71.** B	
12. A		**32.** BC		**52.** C		**72.** C	
13. B		**33.** A		**53.** C		**73.** D	
14. C		**34.** B		**54.** B		**74.** D	
15. AB		**35.** C		**55.** D		**75.** B	
16. C		**36.** A		**56.** B		**76.** C	
17. A		**37.** D		**57.** BC		**77.** C	
18. B		**38.** C		**58.** A		**78.** B	
19. B		**39.** B		**59.** D		**79.** A	
20. A		**40.** B		**60.** D		**80.** C	

Answer Explanations for Practice Test 2

1. **D.** Do your best to not leave the customer high and dry. If you are near an electrical outlet, and the alligator clip on your antistatic wrist strap comes off to reveal a tensioning banana clip, the clip should plug tightly into the ground receptacle of the outlet. Do not plug the alligator clip into the receptacle: It is not meant to fit in there and can pop loose or make contact with some other part of the receptacle accidentally. It is not reasonable to believe you can stand still enough to not generate a static charge. It's also important to recognize that motion is not the only thing that builds static. Too many other environmental concerns go into generating a static charge to try to go this route.

2. **B.** The key here is to wait long enough after unplugging the power supply that the capacitors inside have time to bleed off their charge. If there is still a charge inside the power supply, reaching in with anything or shaking a metal part around inside can lead to an inadvertent short and possible electrocution. Although the plastic tweezers sound like a great idea, the hand holding the tweezers is made of meat. Keep it out of a freshly unplugged power supply. In fact, do nothing for a couple of hours other than unplug the power supply. Even touching the chassis or any part of the case, let alone the power supply itself, can give you a jolt if the part is bridging the right circuit.

3. **A.** Class A fire extinguishers are water-based and gas-pressurized. Using one on an electrical or chemical fire can spread the fire instead of putting it out. Class B extinguishers are for fires caused by combustible liquids, such as gasoline. Class C extinguishers are for electrical fires, and class D extinguishers are for fires seen most often in laboratories, caused by combustible metals such as potassium, sodium, lithium, magnesium, and titanium. Dry-chemical fire extinguishers that are rated for a combination of classes, except D, are also common but leave a dangerous and harmful residue that must be cleaned up afterward. Carbon-dioxide extinguishers can be effective on class B and C fires but generally only worsen class A fires. One of their advantages is their lack of residue. Be sure to match the extinguisher to the property being protected and the potential cause of fire.

4. **C.** A full waste-toner receptacle is not a common cause of issues with laser printers, although it could cause problems with the cleaning cycle. However, unless you refill your own cartridges with fresh toner, cartridges that hold both fresh and waste toners are engineered to run out of fresh toner before the waste-toner receptacle fills. As a result, the second best answer is to replace the fresh-toner cartridge, which also replaces the waste-toner receptacle. Maintenance kits do not treat toner issues, and there is usually no way to empty the waste-toner receptacle.

5. **A.** Long before opening any display unit, make sure the display is really bad. Opening an LCD or CRT monitor's case is a last resort and should be left to a qualified technician because of the dangers lurking within. Flyback transformers are extremely dangerous but exist only on CRT monitors. Related to good customer relations, don't ask a customer who has been using an external monitor to try to get by with the built-in monitor unless it is an extremely temporary fix and there is no functional reason why the customer has been using an external monitor. In some cases, a customer's job requirements necessitate the use of a monitor that exceeds the quality or capabilities of the one that is built into a laptop, preventing them from being productive with the internal display.

6. **D.** Data and electrical cables don't usually mix well. Even if you have experience with running them in the same conduit or other pathway, avoid it. Noise interference is likely; electrocution and damage to connected data equipment are possible. Run your own connection to avoid delaying servicing your customers' equipment and to avoid introducing another device into the mix, especially when the computer you are working on has an issue that is network-related to begin with. Make sure you secure your cable to avoid tripping anyone, regardless of the length of time you intend to need it. Someone can trip over it while you're still in the process of running it. Don't press your luck by trying to get by for the duration of its use.

7. **B.** Although you won't see a model of how the atoms and molecules bind to one another, the MSDS does include the chemical formula for the substance in Section 9. Section 4 gives first-aid practices to observe when necessary, and Section 7 covers handling and storage suggestions for the substance.

8. **C.** The devices with the fastest response time—the hard drives—should be placed on one of the two controllers. There are only two controllers. Devices on the same controller once synchronized with one another and were limited to the performance of the slowest device. Although this is not true with newer devices and controllers, one device in a master/slave pair must wait for the other to finish its use of the channel before it can transfer data on

the same channel. The result is that slower devices can cause a faster device to have to wait longer for channel access. Therefore, the slower two devices—the optical drives—should be placed together on the other controller.

9. **B.** This issue is caused when the local device is set to obtain its IP address automatically and no DHCP server is available from which to acquire an address. APIPA is the term used for this type of auto-configuration from the 169.254.0.0 reserved Class B network. There can be many reasons why the computer is not acquiring an address from a DHCP server, most of which you will need to inform the customer about checking themselves. The best clue on the computer comes from the lack of an illuminated LED on the NIC, which can point to the NIC or the device to which it is directly connected, such as a hub or switch. If the NIC appears normal, the problem lies outside the computer. However, a nonfunctional default gateway is not likely the issue unless it doubles as the DHCP server. Regardless, pinging the default gateway is not possible when it does not have an auto-configured address. It constitutes poor design to allow any interface on a router to auto-configure, so it's not likely to be reachable when your computer has one of these addresses. Any existing icon in the notification area (System Tray) will remain there when the computer uses APIPA to configure itself, so that's not a reliable troubleshooting method. Because the problem lies with the local device giving itself an address with a local scope, DNS resolution is not an issue and does not need to be tested. When your computer has one of these addresses, attempting to contact a remote device by name or address is virtually guaranteed to fail.

10. **D.** Only laptops tend to require SoDIMMs and the even smaller MicroDIMMs for memory upgrades, which is not to say definitively that full-size systems do not. It is highly unlikely, however. SIMMs, which are the predecessors of DIMMS, are no longer used in modern motherboards and laptops. DIMMs of differing form factors have been used with the original single-data-rate SDRAM as well as the DDR and DDR2 varieties of SDRAM.

11. **B.** You must press F6 when prompted during Windows installation to install SCSI drivers. There is no browse function, so you must know where the drivers are located on the disk you specify. F2 begins the ASR process, and F8 is used during bootup, not setup, to access the Startup Options screen. F12 has no function to speak of.

12. **A.** Most BIOS routines include a warning threshold for CPU temperature as well as, on occasion, ambient temperature inside the case. They also include a higher cutoff temperature that causes the system to shut down to avoid damage. However, this is not a problem with the BIOS. It's a feature. For the overall health of the system, the BIOS maintains vigilance over the CPU, which generates more heat than any other component in a computer. It is most often a failure of the CPU's fan that causes the temperature to rise enough to set off the temperature warning.

13. **B.** Clumps of dust, dead fans, and blockages of normal airflow are all causes of overheating to the point of a computer shutting itself down for safety. Although some memory modules, especially Rambus modules, call for heat sinks, lack of memory heat sinks is less likely to be the cause of such catastrophic overheating.

14. **C.** You will find in the majority of cases like this that components that were once working do not cease to work simply because you upgraded the motherboard. Certainly, CPUs and memory modules must be compatible with the new motherboard, but those are not mentioned here. The new motherboard could be defective, but that's not an option either. Therefore, existing cards in any quantity, the power button, and the power supply are likely to be fine. When you change out a motherboard, be absolutely certain that you remove *all* standoffs from the chassis before installing the new motherboard. One errant brass standoff can have disastrous effects if it shorts the underside of the motherboard. Although quite a few standards cover the location of holes in the motherboard for securing hardware placement, not all positions are used in every motherboard. Again, it takes only one standoff to be left where there is no longer a hole in the motherboard. Treat every motherboard installation as a fresh start; don't try to cut corners. You can destroy quite a few components otherwise.

15. **AB.** Although bubble-jet printers heat the ink to form a bubble, other inkjet printers use different methods to print. Beyond a doubt, the fuser in a laser printer and the print head in a thermal printer use heat to function. Impact printers strike a ribbon in front of the paper to leave an imprint.

16. **C.** Of those listed, only infrared and the CD burner have a chance here without further adjustment. The serial cable must be a null modem cable, not a standard cable. Regardless, infrared is more convenient than burning a CD or using the null modem cable. Bluetooth can be used, with appropriate utilities, to perform this function, but it is more often used as a cord-replacement technology. Windows XP SP2 has the Bluetooth File Transfer Wizard,

but both machines must have Bluetooth capability, which is not yet commonly built in to laptops the way infrared is. As this trend continues to change, Bluetooth will likely become the best option here.

17. A. This is a common result of the Gaussian effect. The shadow mask on the CRT monitor can develop a magnetic field and cause the cathode rays to be bent before striking the dot phosphors, causing them to excite the wrong dots. This results in discoloration, often in the form of a rainbow or oil-slick effect. Degaussing the monitor is the way to reverse this effect. If you're working with a CRT, you're already dealing with an external monitor, and although switching one external monitor out for another is not a bad troubleshooting technique, doing so is not the appropriate first step here. Because the Gaussian effect follows the monitor and not the computer, you may believe you've solved the issue, but all you've done is condemn an innocent monitor and set yourself up for a repeat visit from the customer when the new monitor begins exhibiting the same symptoms down the road. Rebooting the system won't have any effect, and power-cycling the monitor will have only a slight effect. Each time the monitor powers on, it performs a less-effective degaussing, which won't boast the longer-lasting result of a controlled degaussing. One note about degaussing: Don't perform more than one in a short period of time. Doing so can damage the monitor.

18. B. By far the most likely cause of this problem is a clogged cartridge. Clogged cartridges can cause intermittent failures. A dirty cartridge has a build-up of materials, such as ink, paper, and dust, and causes smudging or streaking. Cleaning will generally solve both problems, but a clogged cartridge may be harder to fix with software or physical cleaning. If the clog is bad enough, replacing the cartridge may be the only solution. Working drivers don't fail often. If they do, they fail big—not by dropping out a single color intermittently, but by making it easy to believe that there *is* life on Mars and that the inhabitants are communicating through your printer. Corroded contacts are rare as well, especially in all but the harshest of environments. Their failure would likely be complete, or at least back to the Martians again.

19. B. Applying the wrong cleaner or using the wrong cloth does not make the monitor appear dead. It can, however, destroy the screen's finish. Nevertheless, the image still appears, although possibly in a degraded fashion. Turning the brightness control and, in some cases, the contrast control can lead to the appearance of a dead monitor, but position knobs cannot adjust the image far enough to make it disappear from the screen. What likely happened was that the customer sprayed the appropriate cleaner directly onto the screen, and it dripped into the circuitry of the monitor and caused a short. The monitor may be a total loss.

20. A. In order of higher energy density to lower, the technologies are alkaline, LiIon, NiMH, and NiCd. Energy density and capacities, measured in milliamp-hours (mAh), can be misleading. They are fairly proportional to run time, but only if you match the application to the battery chemistry. When the wrong battery is used, its stats don't mean much. Alkaline batteries can be rated at 2500mAh and higher; but when subjected to high-current drains, these batteries do not last as long as a LiIon battery with less than half the capacity. Therefore, in a hypothetical laptop application, you can expect LiIon to outlast the other technologies.

21. A. Utility-based cartridge cleaning that cleans the cartridges without your having to remove them is ideal to avoid the need for further calibration. Cleaning solves the problems of smearing and smudging more than the inconsistencies in printing that calibration addresses. Think of calibration as the synchronization between what the printer thinks it is doing and what you observe it doing. Each time you remove the cartridges and put the same ones back in, you run the risk of throwing the printer out of calibration. Cleaning the cartridges this way can require calibration. Use this method if the software-managed cleaning does not work. The fact that smudging occurs horizontally may indicate an issue with the carriage assembly, although this would manifest itself more as printing everything in one place or possibly elongated horizontally. The fact that it also occurs vertically rules out the carriage assembly and points more toward build-up on the cartridges.

22. A. Hardware loopback plugs short the transmit and receive pins as well as other complementary pins on the local interface, taking cabling and remote devices out of the equation so that you can test the local interface without unpredictable influences. In the serial-interface world, a crossover cable is known as a null-modem cable, which allows you to connect a DTE device to another DTE device, such as one computer to another. Terminators absorb any signal that makes it to the end of a circuit and do not assist in testing. Multimeters are indispensable for testing, but they do not perform the function referred to here.

23. B. Surge protectors are not perfect and should be removed from the wall outlet during electrical storms to protect them and the equipment connected to them. They have varistors that take the brunt of the various inconsistencies found in "dirty" power but do nothing for power loss or brownouts. Their role is to make sure that common power spikes are clipped before they do cumulative damage to sensitive electronic equipment. You should keep an eye on the indicator, if one exists, to tell when the internal protection components are no longer able to do their job. When the protector has run its course, you should replace it immediately. Some UPS units protect equipment in the same way by using the raw power input to constantly charge the battery, which provides the attached equipment with pure power that remains consistent. However, the customer does not need the power preservation that a UPS provides. A generator is like a UPS without the power conditioning and provides power only during a power outage. Generators do nothing under normal circumstances to match the capabilities of a surge protector. Power strips are passive outlet multipliers that offer no protection at all.

24. C. In this case, the token card, also known as a key fob, is the only one that meets the requirements set forth. The card is self-contained and does not communicate externally. Therefore, each one must be set up before being deployed, so that it can be synchronized with the authentication server using a key that is shared between the card and server but never transmitted for eavesdroppers to steal. Because the card and server use the same algorithm, they can keep up with one another without further synchronization. In order for a token card to produce a pseudorandom string, the user must enter into the card a PIN that only the user can change. The user then inputs the string into the authentication software utility, and it is compared against the authentication server's rolling set of codes that it considers currently valid for that token card. These codes were generated by a one-way algorithm, which means the shared secret cannot be reverse-engineered from any of the valid strings. The server tracks more than one but a very few of these, in case you forget you have requested a string and request another. With each of the other technologies, you need only have, for example, the fingerprint or retina to scan, the smart card to swipe or insert, or the USB token to plug in. There is no need to have a separate password. The simple possession of the thing being authenticated is enough. The token card adds an additional level of security, in case the card falls into the wrong hands.

25. A. To varying degrees, each option alone is capable of raising the temperature within the case. The presence of four hard drives cannot increase the internal temperature to a dangerous level; the other conditions can. If the case will accommodate four hard drives, it should be engineered to cool four hard drives.

26. C. When a subset of the keys on a keyboard do not function, you may be looking at a bad keyboard. But you should try to clean the keyboard before replacing it, because more often than not, the keyboard is fine; it just has contaminated contacts under the keys that do not work. The part of the keys that you touch is not the problem. Replacing the keys themselves will not rectify the symptoms. Trying the keyboard on another computer suggests that the problem is with the connector or motherboard, which is highly unlikely. Such issues manifest themselves in a complete failure of the keyboard, not just select keys.

27. D. Carpet s never a wise choice for a workshop where static-sensitive devices will be handled. Floors made of tile do not contribute to static build-up in humans. Adding static mats and always using antistatic wrist straps further decreases the likelihood of destroying static-sensitive components.

28. B. The LCD cutoff switch is a tiny plunger switch on the keyboard panel of a laptop that the lid trips when you close it. If this switch goes bad or sticks, the LCD display can appear to be defective. Try to release the switch before replacing it. Also consider the function key–actuated control, and don't forget that something more serious, such as the inverter board, could be wrong with the display. Nothing going on with the external monitor tends to affect the built-in display. Booting up in Safe Mode is no different than normal mode, except that it favors the built-in display over the external.

29. C. Although occasionally you will need to swap out the AC adapter during troubleshooting, removing the AC adapter alone is not generally considered a worthwhile troubleshooting step. Doing so requires that the laptop run solely on battery power, which is not recommended. In fact, a common step is to remove the battery because it can adversely affect power delivery to the laptop. Adapters are ordinarily either good or bad, whereas batteries can appear good but affect the power and functionality of the laptop. Switch out adapters and remove batteries when troubleshooting. Be aware that batteries can cause problems that do not appear to be related to power. Just as the battery can cause puzzling symptoms, so can many removable peripherals. If you don't need them during troubleshooting, remove them. The external monitor is ideal to diagnose built-in video issues.

30. A. Because it's a NIC, there is a remote possibility of conjuring the BSOD, but there is no real danger to the operating system or file structure from removing the NIC. That makes this option the easiest that will likely result in success. However, storage devices such as thumb drives or external hard drives can lose data if you do not stop them first. In that case, create a shortcut that executes `rundll32.exe shell32.dll,control_rundll hotplug.dll`, which brings up the missing Safely Remove Hardware dialog. There is no guarantee, however, that the system will allow you to stop the storage device this way. It may tell you that it is still in use. Occasionally, shutting down the system is the only way to get Windows to close all file handles and clear all buffers, allowing you to safely remove the device without data loss. You should never need to uninstall the driver to remove a device, but for nonstorage devices, disabling them for the current or all hardware profiles in Device Manager does stop the device. It's USB, though: Pull out the nonstorage peripheral.

31. D. As a general rule, *never* wear an antistatic wrist strap when working inside a CRT monitor. If you make contact with the capacitor that charges the flyback transformer, you will most likely electrocute yourself. If you wear the strap on one hand and touch the capacitor with the other hand, the current could travel through your heart, stopping it. Antistatic plastic bags that static-sensitive components come in are excellent at creating a barrier to protect the components from outside static, but they do nothing to protect the components once they are removed from the bags. You must make sure you are not carrying a static charge when you handle such devices. Although you or the computer may be on a static mat, you should still wear an antistatic wrist strap to ensure proper static dissipation. You can usually snap your wrist strap directly onto a bench-top static mat. If you have a floor mat, you should consider connecting a heel strap to it.

32. BC. The Event Viewer can be found in Administrative Tools, which can be found in Control Panel. There is no separate applet in Control Panel for Event Viewer, and Event Viewer is not a System Tools accessory. The MSC file is called EVENTVWR.MSC and can be executed from a Command Prompt. Search for *.msc on your hard drive to find additional consoles that can be brought up from a prompt.

33. A. Some laptops function differently with respect to the Number Lock key. Often, Number Lock must be on before the Fn key can be used to access the numeric functions of the keys they share. With Number Lock off, these keys cannot be made to type their numeric values. However, in some cases, turning Number Lock on alone makes these keys type nothing other than their numeric values. This is something to check before digging any deeper elsewhere. It's less likely that a language overlay would have this effect, and you may be thinking about Calculator with the scientific and standard settings.

34. B. Of those listed, only DIMM sockets have 168 pins and latches that secure the modules in place. The other sockets or headers do not have locking mechanisms.

35. C. Know all your sockets, slots, and processors. The Socket 478 has been used with the Pentium 4, Pentium 4 Extreme Edition, and Celeron processors. The Xeon is most commonly associated with the Socket 603, AMD K6 with the Socket 7, and Pentium M with the Socket 479.

36. A. The AMD Athlon and Socket 462 are most commonly used together. The Socket 462 may also be referred to as a Socket A (think *A* for *AMD*). The Pentium 4, Pentium Pro, and Itanium are most closely associated with the Socket 478, Socket 8, and PAC418, respectively.

37. D. Although LiIon batteries do not form a chemical memory per se, they do suffer from irreversible life-robbing oxidation. When the battery has a significant charge, this oxidation is exacerbated by heat, such as that generated by the laptop in which the battery is installed or by leaving the battery in the car exposed to ambient heat. There is no cure for this effect and the fact that the battery has a finite life expectancy, but the effect also has a bearing on how Windows' battery gauge interprets the battery's remaining charge. Calibrating the battery, which really means calibrating Windows' gauge or synchronizing the gauge with the battery, involves letting the battery discharge completely once in every 30 charging cycles until the laptop loses power. Doing so will keep the gauge more accurate, and users who watch their gauge vigilantly will not be caught off guard.

38. C. The Itanium 2 and PAC611 are most commonly used together. The Opteron, Itanium, and Pentium D are most closely associated with the Socket 940, PAC418, and Socket T (LGA 775), respectively.

39. B. SECC stands for Single Edge Connector Cartridge. It refers to a processor slot, such as Slot 1, provided for processors such as the Pentium II and Pentium III—not any of AMD's line of processors, and definitely not for nonprocessor hardware.

40. B. Most non-Pro AGP slots are brown and have a single key at most, whether the 3.3V or 1.5V/0.8V key, and two rows of 66 pins for a total of 132 pins. Universal AGP slots do not have a key. PCI slots are white with a single key and two rows of 62 pins each. ISA slots are black and have a single key and two rows of 49 pins each.

41. D. You should not throw *any* battery in the trash; nor should you disassemble or burn batteries. A local battery recycling center is probably the best place to take your batteries, but the best option here is to follow the instructions printed on the battery. If no specific instructions appear on the battery, check the laptop manufacturer's manual or website.

42. C. The correct answer is almost true. Since NT came along, the business of booting only from drive C: has been relaxed. It's not even a limitation of the drive letter. The drive you boot to can be anything other than B:, which is reserved for the second floppy drive. Even when you swap in the BIOS, the system still thinks it is booting from A: when it boots from the second floppy. The issue with this answer, then, is that only primary partitions are bootable. A logical drive created on an extended partition is not bootable. So, it's not the *drive letter* part that makes it incorrect: It's the *any drive* part.

43. A. Do not work on the inside of a laptop with the AC adapter plugged in. Some components, such as the inverter, pose a serious hazard to your safety when power is applied. Also remove all batteries before servicing laptops. It is fine to leave pluggable drives and PC Card devices installed, unless your servicing relates to them. Leaving the system in any state of boot assumes that power is applied to the laptop, which again is not safe.

44. D. RAID 1 uses mirroring and optional duplexing of controllers to provide a level of fault tolerance that requires the most commitment of all the fault-tolerant RAID implementations in terms of drive usage. Unlike RAID 5, for instance, RAID 1 does not use striping. Unlike the non-fault tolerant RAID 0, RAID 1 is not used for creating larger volumes out of multiple drives.

45. A. A disk array is any series of physical drives in the same system that work together to form a single volume, with or without the benefit of fault tolerance. The term *array* appears in the expansion of the acronym RAID.

46. B. You should never plug or unplug a laptop battery with power applied to the laptop. LiIon batteries, especially, constantly walk a tightrope between working perfectly and exploding. Any unfortunate mishap with improperly mating the contacts of the battery with those of the laptop could have disastrous consequences. The unexpected surge to the control circuitry built into the battery is not a good thing either. If you turn off the laptop before removing or inserting a battery, there is no reason to remove the AC adapter. Although they are removable devices, laptop batteries do not appear in the Safely Remove Hardware list and do not need to be "stopped" before you remove them—but then, neither do other devices that *do* appear in the list if you power down the laptop first. There is no problem with inserting a completely drained battery in a laptop. The laptop is designed to charge any system battery that you insert.

47. C. If you need to check the DC output of a laptop's AC adapter, a multimeter is an ideal tool. Consult the specifications on the adapter or in the manufacturer's documentation to determine the expected output. The power connector of a laptop is for power input only. Checking voltage levels there will not produce any results. Monitor refresh rates should be checked through the operating system. A multimeter is not capable of indicating refresh rates or other frequencies. If you would like to check the remaining charge on a battery, it must be removed for access to its contacts before testing. You cannot use a multimeter to do so while the battery is installed.

48. A. Much of the waste product generated by the use of laser-printer consumables (mostly toner) is recyclable. Consult the materials accompanying the new toner for advice on how to return or recycle the waste toner. Any of the other options are highly inadvisable.

49. B. On occasion, you need to allow the BIOS routine to run and save the new settings, but it's equally or more prevalent to need to do nothing at all. In cases where the BIOS routine needs to run, you do not need to watch for the opportunity to enter the BIOS routine; it detects a memory mismatch and stalls until you press a specific key to enter the routine or bypass it. Once in the routine, you do not need to input any information. Everything is automatically detected. You just need to save the settings once they are automatically updated. Once upon a time, especially in old IBM machines, you needed to insert a diskette and run a utility to update the BIOS with the new RAM size, but the utility still automatically recognized the RAM. There are no drivers for RAM because memory is BIOS-managed, not operating system-managed, which also means there is nothing you need to do in Windows to have the RAM recognized.

50. D. In order to protect the moving parts during shipment, most scanners have a locking mechanism that immobilizes the scanning head. This lock must be released before normal use, or you will hear a straining noise during head actuation, possibly leading to damage of the scanning-head motor over time. It is not likely that this symptom has anything to do with the scanner's power adapter or the computer it is attached to. Although you may do well to install the scanner on a computer that you have available in your shop, check the disposition of the head-locking mechanism first. It could save you the hassle of going through the installation process. However, you should check out the scanner completely with a local computer before handing it back to the customer. Doing so will help to avoid a repeat service visit.

51. A. Bluetooth is a cord-replacement and low-end networking technology that uses radio frequency waves to transmit information from a wireless device to a receiver attached to a computer.

52. C. The maximum ranges for the various IEEE 802.11 wireless specifications depend on the bit rate currently being used. The highest rates are limited to distances shorter than the maximum for each specification. With that said, 802.11a, 802.11b, 802.11g, and 802.11n have maximum approximate indoor ranges of 100 feet, 300 feet, 100 feet, and 150 feet, respectively.

53. C. The fuser has a finite life indicated by page count or signs of physical damage, whichever comes first. Although it's part of a maintenance kit, it's not something you replace during routine maintenance. Fusers are not made to be cleaned by a technician. They are cleaned during normal use by a plastic scraping blade. The other items should be cleaned or replaced each time the printer undergoes routine maintenance.

54. B. RAID 0 is a striped array without fault tolerance. It is simply a way to create a larger volume without using a single larger disk. Just as with a single larger disk, the striped array is an all-for-one situation. If one disk in the array fails, the whole array is lost. This is analogous to the single disk developing an error in only a portion of the disk that makes the entire disk unusable. RAID 3 and RAID 5 are similar in that they are both fault tolerant, they both stripe data, and they both require a minimum of three disks in the array. They differ in their method of storing parity information. RAID 3 stores all parity information on a single disk. RAID 5 stripes the parity information in with the data across all disks. RAID 1 supports mirroring and duplexing, which is fault tolerance, but there is no striping or parity—just exact copies of the data stored on another disk, possibly connected to another controller.

55. D. You'll spot floppy connectors on the motherboard as rectangular, often black connectors with two rows of 17 pins. Keying can be in the form of a missing pin close to pin 1 and a notch in the shell that receives the cable's connector. Don't count on such keying, however; and learn to scrutinize the silkscreen writing on the motherboard or consult the motherboard's manual, if available, to locate pin 1 on the connector.

56. B. Improper cable routing can inhibit the proper flow of air through the inside of the system, which is crucial for replacing the warmer inside air with cooler outside air before it heats to a temperature that could cause damage to sensitive components. The level of heat generated by a computer has never been attributed to the operating system. Thermal transfer grease on the CPU helps to move the heat generated by the CPU to the heat sink which the grease helps to couple with the CPU. The front chassis fan *should* be arranged for the intake of air into the system. The air is meant to pass from the front of the case, across the heat-generating internal components, and out the rear chassis fan and power-supply fan. A front-chassis fan set to blow air out of the front of the system would not be effective at dissipating heat because it would conflict with the rear fans and cause the airflow circuit to never truly be completed.

57. BC. The Power Options applet in Control Panel and the BIOS setup routine both have settings for your system's power management. Third-party utilities and access to remote devices are not necessary because power management refers to how the computer manages its power consumption and conservation. No remote device is responsible for system power management.

58. A. From the description, you are dealing with an integrated motherboard, one in which some or all of the internal peripheral components that are used in the complete system and that have external interfaces are mounted directly to the motherboard. Contrast this broad category of motherboards with non-integrated motherboards. There is no guarantee from the information given that choosing a motherboard with the latest processor or one that adheres to the ATX form factor will be what you need in this instance, but it is highly likely that the replacement motherboard will need to have some or all of the previously integrated components built in.

59. D. Serial ATA power cables have 3 each of +3.3V, +5V, and +12V leads; 5 ground leads; and a staggered spin-up lead. Common connectors with 4, 7, and 12 pins are Molex power (larger, non-SATA drives use them), SATA data, and the collective P8/P9, respectively.

60. D. Most sound cards ship with a setup disc that may or may not be required for the operating system to recognize the adapter. If Windows does not recognize the card automatically, try installing the drivers from the menu that displays when you insert the disc. You may even have to find the setup.exe file in the root of the disc to start the utility if it does not automatically start. Removing and reinstalling the card is more work than it is worth for the expected payoff. Unless you have made changes in Device Manager, there is no reason to expect that the usage setting is not already where it should be. The BIOS is normally set to allow any new cards to be recognized and begin working by default. Entering the BIOS routine should not be necessary.

61. BD. It's possible that a new drive will be a Serial ATA drive, which often has a different power connector that is not compatible with Parallel ATA drives and other larger drives, such as CD and DVD drives. If it's a SATA or PATA drive, you can only insert the power connector one way. If you invert the connector, it is not keyed to fit that way. SCSI drives usually have the same Molex power connector found on PATA drives. Changing out ATA drives for SCSI drives is not usually an issue for power connectivity. Even on the newest drives, data and power are generally supplied through separate cables.

62. C. In the Ethernet world, any variety with a suffix that includes a *T* indicates a physical-layer dependency on twisted-pair copper cabling. The 1000BaseT specification is no different.

63. C. The switch /FS:FAT32 is required to be sure that the partition is formatted as FAT32. The other two choices are /FS:FAT to format the partition as FAT and /FS:NTFS to format it as NTFS. The only other valid form given as an option is FORMAT E:, which reformats the partition using its existing file system, which may not be FAT32.

64. A. Motherboards use DC power. Many today have one or more LEDs that notify you that various portions of the motherboard are in operation or that the motherboard has power applied, so you do not perform service on it without first removing power. You *can* use a multimeter to determine if the motherboard is receiving power, but the word *must* is a bit strong. Most monitors can display an image without being plugged into a video adapter, which means that an image on a monitor does not guarantee a working or powered motherboard.

65. BD. An 8x AGP video adapter uses 0.8V signaling but is powered by 1.5V and thus fits in a 1.5V-keyed slot. The slot must be compliant with version 3.0 of the AGP specification in order for the card to get the 0.8V signal it requires to function, but it will physically fit into a slot manufactured under an earlier version. Universal slots have no keying and accept any non–Pro AGP adapter. Again, in order to work, the slot must be version 3.0–compliant. It does, however, fit. The key is at the wrong end in a 3.3V slot for 1.5V-keyed adapters such as the 8x card, and there is no such thing as 0.8V keying. Again, the 0.8V adapters use 1.5V-keyed slots. In order to function, these 1.5V-keyed slots must be able to offer 0.8V signaling, and only the AGP version 3.0-compliant slots can do so.

66. A. DDR2 DIMMs have 240 pins and one keying notch. DDR DIMMs have one keying notch as well but only 184 pins. SDR SDRAM modules have 168 pins and two keying notches. Rambus RIMMs have 168, 184, 232, or 242 pins and two notches.

67. B. Although it is not an exact science, and the answer is easily arguable, there are a few important things to know or learn here, as well as a stub for some lively debate. If you see this exact question anywhere else, click the Comment button and give 'em both barrels. It's not a fair question, but the key in this forum is to think and learn. With that said, the rationale for replacing the motherboard instead of the processor is that for the same level of motherboard and processor, the motherboard is usually less expensive. Because the processor is smaller than the motherboard's CPU socket, it stands to reason that the motherboard is higher-end than the processor. Although it doesn't always make sense to move backward in technology to save a few bucks, the question explicitly asks for the least expensive valid option. There is almost no chance that a processor will fit in a subset of the holes in a motherboard socket and even less of a chance that the processor will work. Because of the way the function of the chipset ties into the processor, it isn't feasible to devise an adapter to fit different processors in the same motherboard socket.

68. C. The *A* in RAID stands for *array*. You can't have an array of only 1 disk. RAID 0 and RAID 1 can be implemented with as few as two disks, but at least three disks are required for the redundant striping levels of RAID, such as RAID 3 and RAID 5.

69. D. For permanent loss of stored data, drives and their media would have to be affected by the dust. Because hard disk drives are sealed against unfiltered air exchange with the outside, there is little chance that an unopened hard drive will experience data loss. Optical discs, such as CDs and DVDs, are not touched by read and write mechanisms, so damage is unlikely to occur with these discs. Floppy diskettes are the most likely to be affected by dust because the read/write heads come in contact with the media; but the most likely effect is the inability to read or write to the diskette, not loss of information already stored. Any ramifications of overheating, shorting, and mechanical restriction are temporary in nature unless they cause the system to reboot before the current nonstored data has been saved. With overheating, however, the system is more likely to warn you about an impending disaster beforehand; and with mechanical restriction, such as a blocked fan, you will usually hear telltale signs of the restriction before the fan stops completely. When fans slow down and stop, the system overheats, causing a warning to alert you to the problem. Any shorting due to conductive materials in the dust will probably manifest itself at power-on before there is any data to lose. Regardless, no permanent data loss is likely.

70. B. Cellular connections can be employed as WAN links in certain cases. The data rates available using cellular technology are not as high as those available with many of the terrestrial technologies, such as T-carrier circuits, Frame Relay, ATM, DOCSIS, and DSL, which limits their use comparatively. Cellular lends itself more to point-to-point service, as seen in many WAN links, not the mesh layouts common with LANs, MANs, and CANs.

71. B. Passive-matrix technology uses row and column signals to change the state of a particular pixel with less than stunning results compared to active-matrix displays. Active-matrix LCD technology is the highest quality available today. It is characterized by a wide angle of view and a clear image due to the implementation of a thin-film transistor per pixel. CRT is the technology of tube-based, non-LCD monitors. *Inverted* is not a term in the video arena, but it may be argued that the term can be derived from the inverter that LCD displays use to convert the DC current back to AC for powering the backlight.

72. C. When the mechanism that drives the print cartridges in an inkjet printer begins to fail, the same content is printed; it just tends to print in one spot, causing a dark splotch. The failed mechanism could be the drive motor or the belt that the motor drives. Utility-based cartridge cleaning that cleans the cartridges without your needing to remove them is ideal to avoid the need for further calibration. Cleaning solves the problems of smearing and smudging more than the inconsistencies in printing that calibration addresses. Think of calibration as the synchronization between what the printer thinks it is doing and what you observe it doing. Each time you remove the cartridges and put the same ones back in, you run the risk of throwing the printer out of calibration. Cleaning the cartridges this way can require calibration. Use this method if the software-managed cleaning does not work. The fact that smudging was not reported by the user tends to rule out cleaning as a fix.

73. D. Extension magnets are ideal for working in tight spots where magnetic fields are not a problem, such as inside nonworking printers and scanners. They are thin enough to make it to where a hand cannot reach. Place the magnet on the screw as you loosen it; when the screw breaks free, it will be less likely to fall into the depths. Extension magnets are more advisable than magnetized screwdrivers because you know the magnet is magnetic, but you may forget that the screwdriver is. Just make sure you keep the extension magnet away from disks and other areas to which it is a hazard. Vacuums are not ideal in this situation because toner can be smaller than the filter on the vacuum, which will then act as a toner-blower of sorts, blowing toner out the exhaust port. Additionally, the vacuum will obstruct your view in the tight spot and may not catch the screw when it breaks free—not to mention the fact that you'll have to go fishing for each screw you capture that way. Don't count on flipping a workgroup printer over to dislodge a screw (which is potentially already damaging the sensitive fuser assembly) without hurting yourself or damaging property.

74. D. Although laser printers use a light source to change the charge on a developing drum to hold toner wherever the image to be printed falls, they do not use cameras to do their job. Scanners, on the other hand, use mirrors and devices similar to cameras to capture the object image and digitize it for transfer to the computer. Impact and inkjet printers do not use any of these components.

75. B. The AUTORUN.INF file in the root directory of the removable media contains sequential lines that tell the operating system what steps to take and which additional files to execute to start an installation utility or other program each time the media is inserted. *Autoplay* is the term used for audio CDs that play their content automatically upon insertion. There is no standard BOOT.INF file, but there is a BOOT.INI file that has less to do with removable media per se and more to do with the use of the ARC syntax to direct the operating system to the rest of the system files for completing the boot process. Although there is no common STARTUP.INF file to speak of, the STARTUP.EXE file is often the one called by the autorun process. `Startup` is also a folder that holds applications that should start automatically each time Windows starts.

76. C. Windows uses the term *local port* to refer to direct connections made to printers. *Direct port* is not a standard term. A network printer, not a network port, is advertised over the network through the Windows Browser service or Active Directory. You can also use this path to connect to a printer using its UNC name or, for Internet printing, a URL. A TCP/IP port is one that you can create through the local-port path when the printer is not being advertised, but you know the IP address, DNS name, or NetBIOS name of the printer.

77. C. Although all the options are valid methods of gathering data regarding the issues with the scanner, without knowing the complaint of the customer, you validate the shortcomings of the person who checked in the scanner and run the risk of fixing everything except the problem that brought the scanner to you in the first place. Doing so may guarantee a repeat service request and a loss of confidence in your shop, regardless of who is at fault for the lapse.

78. B. This is a problem with the fuser roller. Any damage to the surface of the fuser can cause toner to collect and transfer to the paper each time the fuser roller touches the paper in that position. A similar problem can occur with the developer roller.

79. A. A key fob is a small electronic security device that the owner can easily identify as missing (read "stolen"), unlike a stolen password, which may be used by the thief concurrently with the owner for an extended period of time before the theft is discovered. It is not the PIN that the user enters into the software interface, but the alphanumeric code that the key fob produces when the correct PIN is entered into the key fob. *Token* is a generic term used in various scenarios, but not for the device described in the question. Smart cards and USB keys are devices used for direct access to a system or location without the implication of further authentication. The key fob adds another level of security to the model.

80. C. The system should be behind locked doors, a form of physical security and the first level of security to avoid physical sabotage. Because the computer is not networked, such authentication and permissions are not necessary because there are no shares without networking. However, local authentication is the next level of security, so the system should require logging on and authentication to resume from a screensaver. Other considerations include file-level security (only on NTFS partitions) once a user is allowed access to the file system.

Answer Sheets for Practice Test 1

(Remove This Sheet and Use It to Mark Your Answers)

Section 1
Multiple Choice Questions

1 Ⓐ Ⓑ Ⓒ Ⓓ Ⓔ	41 Ⓐ Ⓑ Ⓒ Ⓓ Ⓔ
2 Ⓐ Ⓑ Ⓒ Ⓓ Ⓔ	42 Ⓐ Ⓑ Ⓒ Ⓓ Ⓔ
3 Ⓐ Ⓑ Ⓒ Ⓓ Ⓔ	43 Ⓐ Ⓑ Ⓒ Ⓓ Ⓔ
4 Ⓐ Ⓑ Ⓒ Ⓓ Ⓔ	44 Ⓐ Ⓑ Ⓒ Ⓓ Ⓔ
5 Ⓐ Ⓑ Ⓒ Ⓓ Ⓔ	45 Ⓐ Ⓑ Ⓒ Ⓓ Ⓔ
6 Ⓐ Ⓑ Ⓒ Ⓓ Ⓔ	46 Ⓐ Ⓑ Ⓒ Ⓓ Ⓔ
7 Ⓐ Ⓑ Ⓒ Ⓓ Ⓔ	47 Ⓐ Ⓑ Ⓒ Ⓓ Ⓔ
8 Ⓐ Ⓑ Ⓒ Ⓓ Ⓔ	48 Ⓐ Ⓑ Ⓒ Ⓓ Ⓔ
9 Ⓐ Ⓑ Ⓒ Ⓓ Ⓔ	49 Ⓐ Ⓑ Ⓒ Ⓓ Ⓔ
10 Ⓐ Ⓑ Ⓒ Ⓓ Ⓔ	50 Ⓐ Ⓑ Ⓒ Ⓓ Ⓔ
11 Ⓐ Ⓑ Ⓒ Ⓓ Ⓔ	51 Ⓐ Ⓑ Ⓒ Ⓓ Ⓔ
12 Ⓐ Ⓑ Ⓒ Ⓓ Ⓔ	52 Ⓐ Ⓑ Ⓒ Ⓓ Ⓔ
13 Ⓐ Ⓑ Ⓒ Ⓓ Ⓔ	53 Ⓐ Ⓑ Ⓒ Ⓓ Ⓔ
14 Ⓐ Ⓑ Ⓒ Ⓓ Ⓔ	54 Ⓐ Ⓑ Ⓒ Ⓓ Ⓔ
15 Ⓐ Ⓑ Ⓒ Ⓓ Ⓔ	55 Ⓐ Ⓑ Ⓒ Ⓓ Ⓔ
16 Ⓐ Ⓑ Ⓒ Ⓓ Ⓔ	56 Ⓐ Ⓑ Ⓒ Ⓓ Ⓔ
17 Ⓐ Ⓑ Ⓒ Ⓓ Ⓔ	57 Ⓐ Ⓑ Ⓒ Ⓓ Ⓔ
18 Ⓐ Ⓑ Ⓒ Ⓓ Ⓔ	58 Ⓐ Ⓑ Ⓒ Ⓓ Ⓔ
19 Ⓐ Ⓑ Ⓒ Ⓓ Ⓔ	59 Ⓐ Ⓑ Ⓒ Ⓓ Ⓔ
20 Ⓐ Ⓑ Ⓒ Ⓓ Ⓔ	60 Ⓐ Ⓑ Ⓒ Ⓓ Ⓔ
21 Ⓐ Ⓑ Ⓒ Ⓓ Ⓔ	61 Ⓐ Ⓑ Ⓒ Ⓓ Ⓔ
22 Ⓐ Ⓑ Ⓒ Ⓓ Ⓔ	62 Ⓐ Ⓑ Ⓒ Ⓓ Ⓔ
23 Ⓐ Ⓑ Ⓒ Ⓓ Ⓔ	63 Ⓐ Ⓑ Ⓒ Ⓓ Ⓔ
24 Ⓐ Ⓑ Ⓒ Ⓓ Ⓔ	64 Ⓐ Ⓑ Ⓒ Ⓓ Ⓔ
25 Ⓐ Ⓑ Ⓒ Ⓓ Ⓔ	65 Ⓐ Ⓑ Ⓒ Ⓓ Ⓔ
26 Ⓐ Ⓑ Ⓒ Ⓓ Ⓔ	66 Ⓐ Ⓑ Ⓒ Ⓓ Ⓔ
27 Ⓐ Ⓑ Ⓒ Ⓓ Ⓔ	67 Ⓐ Ⓑ Ⓒ Ⓓ Ⓔ
28 Ⓐ Ⓑ Ⓒ Ⓓ Ⓔ	68 Ⓐ Ⓑ Ⓒ Ⓓ Ⓔ
29 Ⓐ Ⓑ Ⓒ Ⓓ Ⓔ	69 Ⓐ Ⓑ Ⓒ Ⓓ Ⓔ
30 Ⓐ Ⓑ Ⓒ Ⓓ Ⓔ	70 Ⓐ Ⓑ Ⓒ Ⓓ Ⓔ
31 Ⓐ Ⓑ Ⓒ Ⓓ Ⓔ	71 Ⓐ Ⓑ Ⓒ Ⓓ Ⓔ
32 Ⓐ Ⓑ Ⓒ Ⓓ Ⓔ	72 Ⓐ Ⓑ Ⓒ Ⓓ Ⓔ
33 Ⓐ Ⓑ Ⓒ Ⓓ Ⓔ	73 Ⓐ Ⓑ Ⓒ Ⓓ Ⓔ
34 Ⓐ Ⓑ Ⓒ Ⓓ Ⓔ	74 Ⓐ Ⓑ Ⓒ Ⓓ Ⓔ
35 Ⓐ Ⓑ Ⓒ Ⓓ Ⓔ	75 Ⓐ Ⓑ Ⓒ Ⓓ Ⓔ
36 Ⓐ Ⓑ Ⓒ Ⓓ Ⓔ	76 Ⓐ Ⓑ Ⓒ Ⓓ Ⓔ
37 Ⓐ Ⓑ Ⓒ Ⓓ Ⓔ	77 Ⓐ Ⓑ Ⓒ Ⓓ Ⓔ
38 Ⓐ Ⓑ Ⓒ Ⓓ Ⓔ	78 Ⓐ Ⓑ Ⓒ Ⓓ Ⓔ
39 Ⓐ Ⓑ Ⓒ Ⓓ Ⓔ	79 Ⓐ Ⓑ Ⓒ Ⓓ Ⓔ
40 Ⓐ Ⓑ Ⓒ Ⓓ Ⓔ	80 Ⓐ Ⓑ Ⓒ Ⓓ Ⓔ

Directions: For each of the following questions, select the choice that best answers the question or completes the statement.

1. A user running Windows XP SP1a calls, complaining that they are unable to connect to a wireless access point secured with WPA. Which of the following is the likely issue?

   A. The user has the wrong SSID.
   B. No WPA client is built into XP SP1a.
   C. The user has entered a 64-bit key when a 128-bit key is required.
   D. The user's MAC address is not in the filter list of allowable addresses.

2. Which of the following is the best utility to use to rebuild a damaged partition when running Windows XP?

   A. ASR
   B. ERD
   C. System Restore
   D. Recovery Console

3. Which *two* of the following items are required to establish connectivity with a WEP-secured access point?

   A. SSID
   B. Your MAC address
   C. Key
   D. IP address of the access point

4. Which of the following should be the first step you take when the printer status is *Ready* and there are print jobs in the printer's queue, but the printer does not print?

   A. Turn off the printer.
   B. Clear the print jobs from the queue.
   C. Reboot the computer.
   D. Restart the Print Spooler service.

5. While diagnosing a laser printer with a user over the phone, you suspect that the problem lies with the laser. Which of the following is the best method to have the user quickly test your theory?

   A. Have the user remove the printer's case and watch for the laser to come on after beginning a print job.
   B. Have the user insert a flexible photometer into the feed mechanism and watch the display for confirmation that light is found in its path.
   C. Have the user replace the EP cartridge and print a test page.
   D. Have the user remove the EP cartridge and look at the element to see if it has blown.

6. In diagnosing a software issue with the functionality of a peripheral device over Remote Desktop, you discover that the driver for that device is two years old. Which of the following methods is the best way to upgrade the driver?

   A. Use the original distribution disc for the operating system.
   B. There is nothing for you to do. The latest driver is downloaded automatically when available.
   C. Download the latest driver from the manufacturer's website.
   D. Avoid the possibility of downloading a virus by calling the manufacturer to send you the latest driver by mail.

GO ON TO THE NEXT PAGE

7. While conducting a Remote Desktop session to diagnose why an error message pops up immediately when the user tries to print, you notice that the user has no printers installed. When you click the *Add a printer* link in the left frame of the Printers and Faxes utility, an error message pops up, telling you that the operation could not be completed. Which of the following is the cause of the issue?

   A. The user has no print drivers to be able to install printers.
   B. The spooler is full.
   C. The printer is offline.
   D. The Print Spooler service is stopped.

8. The read and write heads of floppy drives, tape drives, and optical disc drives, such as CD and DVD, can become dirty, obscuring their ability to function properly. Which of the following is the correct regular preventative maintenance to avoid such a problem?

   A. Regular use of such drives keeps the heads clean and free of contaminants. If a drive has not been used recently and now produces errors, access it repeatedly until the data is read properly.
   B. Use a cotton swab and rubbing alcohol to clean the heads.
   C. Use a head-cleaning system designed for the drive being cleaned.
   D. Execute the Head Clean utility in Windows on a regular basis.

9. A user calls in, complaining that their computer is taking an extremely long time to boot up after they installed a large number of applications. Which of the following will most likely speed up the user's boot process while still allowing them to use the applications?

   A. Disable some of the applications on the Startup tab in MSCONFIG.
   B. Uninstall some of the applications.
   C. Increase virtual memory.
   D. Swap out for a larger hard drive.

10. A user calls to report a dead system. They say that pressing the power button produces a sound from the rear of the system unit, but the system never boots. Which of the following is a likely cause?

   A. The power cable is not completely plugged in on the power supply.
   B. The power button is defective.
   C. An adapter card has become partially seated.
   D. The system partition on the hard drive is damaged.

11. A customer calls to ask your advice about the latest and greatest video card to go with the cutting-edge motherboard they recently had installed. Which of the following expansion buses is the user most likely referring to?

   A. PCI
   B. PCIe
   C. AGP
   D. ISA

12. Which of the following is *not* an integrated security feature in Windows XP SP2?

   A. Windows Firewall
   B. Automatic Updates
   C. Windows Security Center
   D. Microsoft Baseline Security Analyzer (MBSA)

13. When issued from the `C:\folder1\folder2\folder3>` prompt, what does the command `cd\` followed by the command `rd folder1` accomplish?

   A. It reads and displays the contents of `folder1`.
   B. It deletes `folder1` and its files but leaves `folder2` and `folder3` intact.
   C. It generates an error message and nothing else.
   D. It removes the entire directory tree (directories and files), beneath and including `folder1`.

14. A customer complains that their computer consistently runs for a little while and then shuts down on its own. Which of the following should you advise the customer to look for?

    A. Multiple shallow dents in the system case

    B. Clumps of dust on the back of the power-supply fan and chassis vent holes

    C. A massive wad of cables behind the system and on the floor

    D. Sticky keys indicating that something has been spilled in the keyboard

15. You receive a call from a customer who complains of a malfunctioning floppy drive. According to the user, they recently installed additional RAM. Ever since the installation, the light on the floppy drive has remained lit, and the user is unable to access any of their diskettes. What is the most likely explanation for the problem?

    A. More RAM has been installed than the system can support.

    B. Apparently the user's diskettes have been exposed to a magnetic field, because this is the normal operation of a floppy drive.

    C. Diskettes are not meant to be inserted into a floppy drive.

    D. While working inside the system unit, the user dislodged the data cable from the floppy and reinserted it upside down.

16. Which page in System Properties allows you to adjust how the system handles unsigned drivers and searching the Windows Update website to download drivers for newly installed devices?

    A. Advanced

    B. Automatic Updates

    C. General

    D. Hardware

17. You receive a call from a user who is illogically irate and using profanity. Which of the following should you do to handle the situation?

    A. Hang up the phone.

    B. Tell the user in a controlled voice that you would like to assist them if they can relate the problem to you.

    C. Put the user on hold, and notify your supervisor about the situation.

    D. Let the user vent as long as they need to, and then try to help them.

18. What does the command `md folder2\folder3` accomplish at the `C:\folder1>` prompt when `folder1` is an empty directory?

    A. It creates a directory named `folder2` under `folder1` and a directory named `folder3` under `folder2`.

    B. It generates an error message and nothing else.

    C. It creates a directory named `folder2` under `folder1` and then produces an error message.

    D. It moves the directory `folder2` and all of its contents to a directory in the same location named `folder3`.

19. Which of the following is a true statement?

    A. A hub does not examine Ethernet frames, whereas a switch bases filtering and forwarding decisions on Ethernet headers.

    B. A router does not examine Ethernet frames, whereas a switch bases filtering and forwarding decisions on their headers.

    C. A switch repeats every bit it receives without regard for their meaning.

    D. Hubs, switches, and routers have uplink ports designed specifically to chain multiple like devices together.

20. A user calls and informs you that they attempted to upgrade their hard drive by using a new hard drive and an included utility to clone the old hard drive to the new one. Both drives are ATA and set for master, but the new drive does not show up when booting. Which of the following is most likely to fix the problem?

    A. Inform the user that they cannot have more than one ATA drive in the system at one time; and suggest that they back up the data on the original drive, install the operating system on the new drive, and then restore the data to the new drive.

    B. Inform the user that you are not willing to assist with a system that has been tampered with, and end the call.

    C. Suggest that the user obtain a *Y* Molex connector to provide power to the new drive.

    D. Suggest that the user not change the jumpers on the drives but connect them both to the same controller on the motherboard.

GO ON TO THE NEXT PAGE

21. A user calls to request assistance with compressing a file on their hard drive. The user is running Windows XP on a FAT partition and does not want to move the file from its current location. Which of the following accurately describes the solution?

   A. It can't be done without a third-party utility.
   B. Right-click the files, click Properties, click the Advanced button, and select the check box labeled *Compress Contents to Save Disk Space*.
   C. Individual files cannot be compressed. The entire partition must be compressed.
   D. Files on a FAT partition are already compressed.

22. Which of the following is *not* a function of the DISKPART utility?

   A. Convert a basic disk to dynamic.
   B. Convert a dynamic disk to basic.
   C. Break or create a mirrored volume.
   D. Convert a FAT32 partition to NTFS.

23. A user reports that their monitor has recently begun displaying odd colors, mostly purples and greens. Which of the following is the most likely cause?

   A. One of the three cathode rays has stopped working.
   B. The monitor needs to be degaussed.
   C. The monitor's cable is not completely inserted into the video card's connector.
   D. The wrong video driver is being used.

24. Which of the following addresses is considered a public IP address?

   A. 172.32.0.1
   B. 172.17.0.1
   C. 192.168.0.1
   D. 10.0.0.1

25. How do you find the Settings button in System Properties that takes you to Performance Options so that you can adjust virtual memory?

   A. Hardware tab ➤ Virtual Memory section
   B. Advanced tab ➤ Virtual Memory section
   C. Advanced tab ➤ Memory Usage section
   D. Advanced tab ➤ Performance section

26. Which of the following commands starts a utility that should be run regularly, that alters how files are placed on the hard drive, and that adjusts the file system tables to reflect this change without removing files?

   A. CHKDSK
   B. DEFRAG
   C. SFC
   D. FDISK

27. Which of the following protocols allows access to e-mail or bulletin-board messages that remain on a server, permitting the user to access remote message stores as if they were local?

   A. POP
   B. IMAP
   C. SMTP
   D. MAPI

28. Which of the following switches causes CHKDSK to attempt to recover readable information from bad sectors?

   A. /C
   B. /F
   C. /X
   D. /R

29. A user calls to report the failure of their laptop's built-in LCD display. You have the user connect an external monitor to the VGA connector on the back of the laptop, and it works fine. Which of the following could cause this problem?

   A. The external VGA connector is defective.
   B. The inverter board is defective.
   C. The operating system has been configured to display on the external monitor only.
   D. The rectifier board is defective.

30. Which of the following would a network administrator most likely use to manage a large number of devices from a Microsoft computer to perform remote configuration tasks, such as setting permissions, turning error logging on or off, getting a list of installed applications, restarting a remote computer to apply changes, and changing virtual memory settings?

   A. WZC
   B. SNMP
   C. WMI
   D. Telnet

31. Which of the following commands reliably formats drive `E:` as a FAT partition?

A. `format e: /f:fat`
B. `format e: /fat`
C. `format e: /fs:fat`
D. `format e:`

32. A user calls to complain that their inkjet printer has yellow ghosting around certain colored objects and that the spacing between horizontal lines is not consistent. Which of the following makes the most sense to try?

A. Calibrate the printer.
B. Change the print cartridges, especially the yellow one.
C. Replace the belt for the carriage assembly.
D. Clean the print cartridges.

33. Which of the following utilities can be used to remove older files without the need to search them out individually?

A. Disk Cleanup
B. Disk Management
C. CHKDSK
D. DEFRAG

34. A user calls and complains that their battery gauge is not acting in a linear fashion. It shows that the LiIon battery has 98% of its charge left and that this equates to three and a half hours of run time; but after reaching about 50%, the laptop dies quickly. Overall run time is never more than 90 minutes on a full charge. What can be done to improve this situation?

A. The battery must be placed in a deep-charge apparatus overnight to reverse the cell oxidation.
B. Nothing can be done short of a battery replacement.
C. This is the standard operation of LiIon batteries, and the situation cannot be rectified.
D. The battery needs to be calibrated.

35. Bob in accounting, and a few others around the company, have been complaining that they are occasionally unable to access a resource that is being shared on a Windows XP Professional system. Which if the following is the best solution to the problem?

A. Increase the user limit for the share from the default to a number that will cover all who may simultaneously need the resource.
B. Place the share on a Windows Server 2003 system.
C. Add the affected users to the permissions list for the share.
D. Allow the Everyone group access to the share.

36. What is the term for the commercial entity that connects subscribers to the World Wide Web?

A. Telco
B. DNS
C. ASP
D. ISP

37. A user complains of having heard an unusual noise coming from the inside of the computer recently, but not during the two days preceding their call. You determine that the CPU fan was the source of the problem. Which of the following is the best way to help the user?

A. Replace the CPU fan.
B. Do nothing. No noise means no problem.
C. Solder the break in the CPU fan's electrical wire.
D. Remove the defective CPU fan so that the remaining heat sink can remove heat from the processor without obstruction.

38. Which of the following TCP/IP protocols allows you to remotely configure an IP host that is set up to allow it?

A. SMTP
B. FTP
C. Telnet
D. DNS

39. All of the following TCP/IP protocols are related to e-mail *except*:

A. IMAP
B. HTTP
C. SMTP
D. POP3

GO ON TO THE NEXT PAGE

40. During a phone interview with a user to diagnose their inability to access the network, you learn that the laptop they are attempting to access has no cable attached, the built-in wireless LAN antenna is turned off, and Bluetooth is enabled and working. Which of the following is the best start to resolving the issue?

   A. You need to dispatch a technician to investigate the Bluetooth connection to the LAN, which should be providing access already.

   B. There is a problem with the wireless LAN, which caused the antenna to turn off automatically.

   C. A network cable needs to be attached to the NIC, or the wireless antenna needs to be enabled.

   D. Have the user stop and start the computer's workstation service.

41. Which command-line utility is best to use to ascertain the failure point between the source and destination of an IP network?

   A. `ping`
   B. `nslookup`
   C. `tracert`
   D. `ipconfig`

42. Which of the following command-line commands allows you to open a text file and make changes to its contents?

   A. `TYPE`
   B. `EDIT`
   C. `OPEN`
   D. `ALTER`

43. Which of the following is the service in Windows XP that allows you to install a wireless NIC and immediately find available wireless networks?

   A. Wireless Zero Configuration
   B. Windows Zero Configuration
   C. Configuration-free Networking
   D. Ad Hoc wireless mode

44. A caller has expressed concern over suspected unauthorized access to a particular network resource. You walk them through configuring the potentially compromised server to audit access attempts to the resource. Where does the user need to look later to check the results of the access audit?

   A. The same place where they configured the audit

   B. In the dialog accessed by the Permissions button found in the Sharing tab of the Properties dialog for the shared folder

   C. In the System category of Event Viewer

   D. In the Security category of Event Viewer

45. Which of the following commands changes the name of the file `trash.txt` to `keep.txt` at the command line?

   A. `rename trash keep`
   B. `move trash.txt keep.txt /r`
   C. `ren trash.txt keep.txt`
   D. `copy trash.txt keep.txt /d`

46. A user calls and complains that their Windows XP Professional workstation is running slower than desired. When you ask if they are interested in upgrading the workstation's memory, the user informs you that they have confirmed that their memory is already maxed out. Which of the following selections in Performance Options has the best chance of improving the system's performance?

   A. Adjust for Best Appearance
   B. Background Services
   C. Adjust for Best Performance
   D. System Cache

47. Which protocol can be used as a layer of security between HTTP and TCP, creating HTTPS in the process?

   A. IPSec
   B. SSL
   C. PPTP
   D. L2TP

48. A customer states that every time they scan a file and then try to use a specific application to open the file produced, they receive the message *This file cannot be used with this software*. Only that software package has issues. What should you do?

A. Tell the customer that this is a new issue, and the new request must move to the bottom of the queue. Then hang up.

B. Recommend that the customer open the file with an image-editing application and reduce the resolution or change the file type.

C. Walk the customer through returning the scanner's software to its default settings.

D. Sell the customer a new application that can use the file in the expected manner.

49. You receive a call about an HP printer that displays the message *PERFORM USER MAINTENANCE*. Which *two* of the following are most likely called for in this case?

A. Clear all paper jams.

B. Clean spilled toner out of the printer.

C. Install a maintenance kit.

D. Reset the page count.

50. A user calls to complain that their computer restarts automatically each time they shut down their Windows XP system. Which of the following paths can you suggest taking to prevent this behavior?

A. Go to the Advanced page of System Properties, and click the Settings button in the Startup and Recovery section. Then, clear the Automatically Restart check box.

B. Enter the BIOS setup routine; find the Advanced section; and change the Automatic Restart field, or similar, to *disabled*.

C. Tell the user to use the power button to shut down the system.

D. Click the Hardware Profiles button on the Hardware tab of System Properties. Then, select the *Wait Until I Select a Hardware Profile* radio button.

51. Which switch specified during the execution of WINNT32.EXE installs the Recovery Console?

A. /CMD

B. /RCONS

C. /RECCONS

D. /CMDCONS

52. Which of the following gets you to the C:\level1\level2 directory when the currently logged directory is C:\level1\level2\level3\level4?

A. cd ..\..

B. cd .\.

C. cd ..

D. cd \..\..

53. Which *two* of the following paths can be followed to change the share permissions for a resource on a Windows XP Professional system?

A. Control Panel ➢ Shares ➢ Double-click share ➢ Share Permissions tab

B. Control Panel ➢ Administrative Tools ➢ Computer Management ➢ System Tools ➢ Shared Folders ➢ Shares ➢ Double-click share ➢ Share Permissions tab

C. Right-click shared folder ➢ Properties ➢ Sharing tab ➢ Permissions button

D. Right-click shared folder ➢ Properties ➢ Security tab

54. Which command would you use to begin a backup of the C: drive from the command line that backs up only files that were changed today, overwriting an existing file named todayback.bkf in the root directory of the D: drive?

A. backup c: /f "d:\todayback.bkf" /m daily

B. backup c: "d:\todayback.bkf" /v overwrite

C. ntbackup backup c: /f "d:\todayback.bkf" /m daily

D. ntbackup backup c: /f "d:\todayback.bkf" /v overwrite

GO ON TO THE NEXT PAGE

55. A customer has attempted to install 20GB of RAM in a state-of-the-art dual-processor motherboard. You receive a call complaining that the entire 20GB is not recognized by Windows XP Professional. Which of the following is the most likely cause of this problem?

   A. Windows XP Professional can access only 4GB of RAM.

   B. The customer used the wrong type of memory modules.

   C. With that much memory, there is no need for virtual memory, which reduces the total amount of RAM that can be recognized.

   D. Windows XP Professional cannot access multiple processors, which is throwing off the use of the RAM.

56. All of the following are examples of added security for wireless networks *except*:

   A. Not broadcasting the SSID
   B. Enabling MAC address filtering
   C. Minimizing unused wireless connections
   D. Enabling ICS

57. Which of the following paths in Windows XP allows you to set Automatic Updates to automatically occur at 3:00AM every day?

   A. Control Panel ➢ Automatic Updates. Then, select the radio button for Automatic, and select Every Day and 3:00AM from the drop-downs.

   B. Control Panel ➢ Administrative Tools ➢ Automatic Updates. Then, select the radio button for Automatic, and select Every Day and 3:00AM from the drop-downs.

   C. Start ➢ All Programs ➢ Automatic Updates. Then, select the radio button for Automatic, and select Every Day and 3:00AM from the drop-downs.

   D. Control Panel ➢ Automatic Updates. Then, select the radio button for Download Updates, and select Every Day and 3:00AM from the drop-downs.

58. In Device Manager, what is the easiest way to find out which device is using IRQ5?

   A. Double-click each device and click the Resources tab to observe the IRQ it is using until you find one that is using IRQ5.

   B. Click View ➢ Devices by Connection, and find IRQ5 in the list.

   C. Click View ➢ Resources by Type, and then expand Interrupt Request.

   D. Click View➢ Devices by Type, and find IRQ5 in the list.

59. Which of the following is a reason to use REGEDT32 instead of REGEDIT?

   A. It lets you view and edit all functions and data types in Windows 2000.

   B. REGEDT32 is for use in 32-bit operating systems. REGEDIT is for use in 16-bit operating systems.

   C. You can import and export registration entry (.reg) files.

   D. It lets you search the Registry in Windows 2000.

60. How do you terminate a nonresponsive application in Task Manager?

   A. On the Applications tab, right-click the application, and then click End Process Tree.

   B. On the Processes tab, click the application, and then click the End Process button.

   C. On the Applications tab, click the application, and then click the End Task button.

   D. On the Applications tab, click the application, and then press the Backspace key.

61. Which of the following commands reliably displays a listing of the files in the first-level folder named data on drive E: as well as all the folders and their files below it?

   A. `dir e:\data /s`
   B. `dir e:data /s`
   C. `dir e:\data /f`
   D. `dir e:data /f`

62. A customer in an electrically noisy environment complains that their Ethernet network is experiencing a large number of lost packets. Which of the following will have the most positive impact on this issue?

   A. Replace copper cabling with fiber-optic cabling.

   B. Replace copper cabling with wireless components.

   C. Replace twisted-pair cabling with coaxial cabling.

   D. Replace Category 5 cabling with Category 5e or 6 cabling.

63. While taking a call from a user, they are a bit long-winded and seem to be saying the same thing over and over again. Which of the following is the best approach in this situation?

   A. In order not to hurt the user's feelings and perhaps stress your relationship, politely interrupt and begin recounting the problem in more technical jargon so the user will realize you know what you're doing and will let you get to work on the problem.

   B. Actively listen to the user until they are comfortable that they have expressed the problem, and listen for additional information each time they repeat something. Follow up with a brief synopsis that lets the user know you understand the issue.

   C. At the first opportunity, begin asking closed-ended questions to make the user's answers short and concise.

   D. Interrupt the user, and recount the problem as you understand it in terms the user will understand so they are confident that you know what is wrong and where to start.

64. A user claims to have restarted the Spooler service from the command line, but when you investigate from the Services snap-in over Remote Desktop, you notice that the Spooler service is not started. What command may the user have forgotten to issue to completely restart the spooler?

   A. `net start spooler`

   B. `spooler /start`

   C. `net spooler start`

   D. `spooler restart`

65. A user complains that every time they try to access a secure website, their browser stalls and then gives a client-side error message. Which of the following may correct the problem?

   A. Reduce their browser's security level to the lowest possible setting.

   B. Upgrade the browser to the latest version.

   C. Configure the firewall to permit TCP port 443 traffic.

   D. Turn off pop-up blocking on the browser.

66. You answer a call from a user in the company with a computer running Windows XP Home that has been a standalone device for years in a remote location of the premises. The need has arisen for the machine to gain network access, but the user has not found anyone who has been able to add the computer to the corporate domain. How should you proceed?

   A. Because the user seems to have gotten the runaround already, put them in touch with a domain administrator who can add the computer to the domain immediately.

   B. Walk the user through the appropriate procedure to add their computer to the domain.

   C. Explain to the user that XP Home computers cannot join a domain.

   D. Explain to the user that by logging into the domain on startup, they place the computer on the domain automatically.

67. Which *two* of the following are reasons to use System Restore instead of Device Driver Roll Back?

   A. You want to restore application settings as well as roll back to earlier drivers.

   B. You want to restore user data as well as roll back to earlier drivers.

   C. You want to be able to specify the destination of the restore in case you prefer certain content to be in a different location.

   D. You are not sure which driver needs to be rolled back.

GO ON TO THE NEXT PAGE

68. You obtain credentials to diagnose a customer issue. Later, without being noticed, you observe a coworker using those credentials to access the customer's network to surf the Internet. What should you do?

    A. Confront the coworker, and tell them that what they are doing is wrong.

    B. Do nothing. Your coworker cannot possibly use enough bandwidth to impact the customer's network negatively.

    C. Tell the customer what you have found.

    D. Tell your supervisor about the infraction.

69. After installing a wireless network adapter in a Windows XP Professional computer system, the user calls and states that they do not see an icon for the adapter in the System Tray. What's the best way to bring up a list of wireless networks in range of the adapter so you can begin the connection process?

    A. Run the Wireless Network Setup Wizard in Control Panel.

    B. Control Panel ➢ Network Connections ➢ Double-click the wireless adapter ➢ Click View Wireless Networks.

    C. Double-click My Network Places on the Desktop.

    D. Control Panel ➢ Network Connections ➢ Right-click the wireless adapter ➢ Click Properties ➢ Check the box in the General tab labeled *Show icon in notification area when connected*.

70. A user calls and informs you that they noticed their system acting strangely after they made some changes. They rebooted and logged on a couple of times, but the system is still unstable. The user has no backup of their system, and now the system boots but fails to make it to the logon screen. Which of the following can you suggest in order to fix the problem?

    A. Safe Mode and System Restore

    B. Last Known Good Configuration

    C. ASR process

    D. Device Driver Roll Back

71. Which of the following commands, when executed using Start ➢ Run, causes the Command Prompt window to remain open after the ping executes?

    A. `ping www.sybex.com`

    B. `cmd /k ping www.sybex.com`

    C. `cmd /c ping www.sybex.com`

    D. `cmd ping www.sybex.com`

72. When booting up in Windows XP, a user has recently started receiving the message *Invalid system disk*. Which of the following can possibly correct the problem?

    A. Boot into Safe Mode, and perform a System Restore.

    B. Use a boot diskette.

    C. Change the boot order in the BIOS.

    D. Restore the partition from a backup.

73. A user has complained that their system has started getting slower. You discover that their job entails the frequent creation of documents and presentations of various sizes and that for confidentiality reasons, once these data files are finalized, they are moved to a secure server and removed from the user's hard drive. What is the best solution to attempt to speed up the system again?

    A. Search for files that the user forgot to delete after they were moved to the server and that are accumulating and slowing down the system.

    B. Run the ASR utility.

    C. Run System Restore.

    D. Defragment the user's hard drive.

74. What is a recovery partition?

    A. A partition that has been recovered by one or more utilities

    B. A hidden partition accessible by a recovery CD

    C. The mirrored copy of a partition that provides fault tolerance

    D. A partition that holds deleted content for a configurable period of time to aid in recovering accidentally deleted data

75. A few moments after attempting to create a Remote Desktop Connection to the system at 172.16.10.112 on the same IP subnet as you, you receive an error message: *The client could not connect to the remote system.* Which of the following could be the cause of the failure?

A. The default gateway is down.
B. The DNS server is down.
C. Remote Desktop has not been added to the Exceptions page in Windows Firewall on your system.
D. You entered the wrong IP address.

76. Which of the following has the greatest impact on reducing repeat calls for the same problem?

A. Document the problem and your resolution.
B. Be courteous to the customer, and listen actively.
C. Escalate the problem to someone with more expertise.
D. Test your solution.

77. You have a customer who is designing their IP addressing scheme. When asked how best to accommodate more IP hosts than the number of addresses they have, what should you suggest?

A. Static addressing
B. Dynamic addressing
C. Public addressing
D. APIPA

78. Each of the following is required for an IP host to access the Internet *except*:

A. DNS server's address
B. Gateway
C. Subnet mask
D. IP address

79. Which of the following technologies has the potential to deliver the highest bit rate for Internet access?

A. Broadband
B. LAN
C. ISDN
D. Dial-up

80. Which of the following is the first step you should take when troubleshooting a computer hardware or software issue?

A. Evaluate your results.
B. Find the responsible party so it doesn't look like your doing.
C. Gather information.
D. Document your work.

Answer Key for Practice Test 1

1. B	**21.** A	**41.** C	**61.** A
2. A	**22.** D	**42.** B	**62.** A
3. AC	**23.** C	**43.** A	**63.** B
4. B	**24.** A	**44.** D	**64.** A
5. C	**25.** D	**45.** C	**65.** C
6. C	**26.** B	**46.** C	**66.** C
7. D	**27.** B	**47.** B	**67.** AD
8. C	**28.** D	**48.** B	**68.** D
9. A	**29.** B	**49.** CD	**69.** B
10. C	**30.** C	**50.** A	**70.** A
11. B	**31.** C	**51.** D	**71.** B
12. D	**32.** A	**52.** A	**72.** C
13. C	**33.** A	**53.** BC	**73.** D
14. B	**34.** D	**54.** C	**74.** B
15. D	**35.** B	**55.** A	**75.** D
16. D	**36.** D	**56.** D	**76.** D
17. B	**37.** A	**57.** A	**77.** B
18. A	**38.** C	**58.** C	**78.** A
19. A	**39.** B	**59.** A	**79.** B
20. C	**40.** C	**60.** C	**80.** C

Answer Explanations for Practice Test 1

1. B. Three out of four of these options are viable issues, but the fact that WPA compatibility was not integrated into Windows XP until SP2 is the likely problem. The other options, including the key length, which is not an issue for WPA, are issues with WEP as well.

2. A. Some pre-XP operating systems used the Emergency Repair Disk (ERD). XP uses a process known as Automated System Recovery (ASR). The ASR disk is used in conjunction with the ASR process to access a backup archive for completely restoring the system to the state of the latest backup. As a result, your backup should not be stored on the same physical drive as the one you are archiving. Although the Recovery Console is an incredible utility for a nuts-and-bolts surgical resurrection of a failed system, damaged partitions are best recovered using ASR when available. System Restore requires a working system and is generally best used for rolling back drivers and application settings to a state when the system was stable.

3. AC. No addresses are required from you to connect to an access point. You do need to know the SSID of the network to which you wish to connect, especially if it is not being broadcast. However, you also must be able to recognize it in a group of available SSIDs if it is one of many being broadcast. WEP requires you to enter a key that matches the length and value of the key that was set up on the access point. WEP key lengths are 64 and 128 bits. The longer keys are more secure.

4. B. Turning off the printer does not clear the print queue. The queue is part of the spooler, which exists on the computer or print server. Although the server and spooler may be integrated into the printer, the spooler generally maintains its contents through a power cycle. This includes rebooting the computer with the spooler on it. The specific queue should be cleared through its software interface found on the System Tray when jobs exist in the queue, either by choosing Printer ➤ Cancel All Documents or by individually clicking each document in the queue and choosing Document ➤ Cancel. Believe it or not, documents in the print queue survive restarting the Print Spooler service, so that won't work. In fact, if clearing the queue wasn't necessary before, it almost certainly is after restarting the Spooler service—on *all* printers, unless you prefer to manually go through and restart each job in each queue (click a document in the queue, and then choose Document ➤ Restart). To get rid of a terminally clogged print queue, you must clear the jobs manually.

5. C. Never try to look at any concentrated light source, such as the laser of a printer or its equivalent light source. Looking at the light mechanism is not like looking at a common household light bulb. You won't be able to see a telltale burnt filament. Because no tool the user has access to acts as a flexible photometer, the best bet is to replace the EP cartridge with a known good unit and test your theory by trying to print. If it works, you've already implemented the solution, and you're that much closer to finishing the call.

6. C. Don't expect Microsoft to keep drivers updated for most components. Drivers on the original distribution disc for the operating system age with the disc. The latest driver is generally available on the Internet, as long as the manufacturer is not defunct. You shouldn't be concerned with viruses coming from the website of a reputable manufacturer. If you are not comfortable with such a solution, and the user does not have a reliable antivirus application installed, advise them to allow you to install one before downloading the driver, which is the best way to obtain the latest device driver, among other things.

7. D. This is what happens when the Print Spooler service has not been started. All printers disappear from the Printers and Faxes utility if it is not already open for viewing, and you receive an error message before the print job has the opportunity to make it to the spooler. Windows has a base of print drivers built in, but even if it didn't, the Add Printer Wizard does not rely on the existence of drivers to run. It relies on the Print Spooler service to run. Recall that you are given the opportunity to supply your own driver from an external source while adding a printer. A full spooler would not manifest itself in this manner. You might not even receive an error, but your application would stall until the spooler made room for the job. The printer being offline makes the spooler fill, but it doesn't cause these effects.

8. C. Each of these drives has a corresponding relatively inexpensive head-cleaning system that is readily available in the market and is good for multiple uses before it must be replaced. Using a swab dampened with alcohol is not an ineffective solution, but you must take care not to apply alcohol to rubber rollers and other parts that the alcohol can cause to dry and crack. Additionally, many heads are not easily accessible for this type of maintenance, and the drive must be disassembled first. If the drive is already disassembled and unable to accept media due to the disassembly or lack of power, then the proper cleaning system is not an option, and the swab method may be the only solution; but it should not be considered a regular preventive maintenance routine. Unfortunately, regular maintenance does not keep read/write heads clean—quite the opposite—and Windows has no Head Clean utility.

9. A. Of the options given, only adjusting the entries on the Startup tab in MSCONFIG will allow the user to speed up the boot process and keep all the applications. The other options either have no effect or leave the user with a subset of the original applications. Although the applications do not start up with Windows, they are still installed and available for use when the user executes them.

10. C. This is a classic symptom of a short on the motherboard. Because the power supply interface on the motherboard is a two-way connection, such feedback to the power supply incapacitates it. The fan generally jumps when you press the power button but never starts. Problems with the power button and the power cable are all-or-nothing in nature: They cause the system either to work or to appear completely dead with no fan movement at all. Software issues never manifest themselves in this fashion.

11. B. Although AGP is no slouch when it comes to high-speed graphics, PCIe is the state of the art today for graphics, especially in the gaming arena. PCI could be considered a distant third. ISA should never be considered in this day and age, even if you can find a new motherboard that still has ISA slots on it.

12. D. Automatic Updates also existed in earlier versions of XP and are crucial for users who may otherwise forget to check for critical security-related Windows Updates. Windows Firewall can be found in the Security Center. Both are new with XP SP2. Security Center can be found in Control Panel. The MBSA must be downloaded for any operating system with which you wish to use it.

13. C. All the `rd folder1` command does in this case is generate an error message without removing any directories. The `rd` command and its longer form, `rmdir`, remove directories when the syntax of the command permits their removal. In this case, the attempt to remove `folder1` fails because it is not empty, evidenced by the prompt at which the question states you started. There is no way to remove a parent directory and keep child directories. One way to accomplish this is to move all subdirectories to the same level as the directory you wish to remove, delete all files in the directory you wish to remove, and then remove the empty directory. If your intent is to remove `folder1` and all of its files and subdirectories, issue the command `rd folder1 /S` from the `C:\>` prompt. The `/S` switch tells the operating system to remove the entire directory tree starting with and including `folder1`, even non-empty directories and their contents—a dangerous command in the wrong hands.

14. B. The symptom indicates an overheating issue. Dust blocking vents and fan exhaust outlets can lead to overheating. The BIOS monitors the temperature of the CPU and the inside of the case. When the temperature reaches a lower threshold, a warning usually sounds. At an upper threshold, the system shuts itself down to avoid damage. Shallow dents will not impede the engineered flow of air in the system, although more severe dents may cause shorts with the motherboard or other circuitry, which can conceivably lead to ungraceful shutdowns. Although improper cable management is not linked with system failure, it is a potential safety hazard and should be corrected. Keyboard malfunction of any type does not lead to regular system shutdowns. Only a freak automatic series of keystrokes could shut down the system, but this would likely happen only once, if at all.

15. D. Of course, diskettes are meant to be inserted into a floppy drive, and exceeding the maximum amount of RAM in a computer has no effect on the floppy drive. The constant steady light on a floppy drive indicates that the data cable is inverted, which is an easy thing to do because few drive headers have single-side keying to match the connector on the cable. Often, there is a notch on both sides of the header, making it easy to put the cable on upside down.

16. D. The Drivers section of the Hardware page has the Driver Signing and Windows Update buttons, which take you to dialogs where you can adjust how Windows handles issues with unsigned drivers and downloading drivers for new devices. The Advanced page has options for performance, user profiles, startup and recovery, environment variables, and error reporting. The Automatic Updates page sets the way Windows accesses the Windows Update website for security updates and driver updates for existing devices; but it has nothing to do with how drivers for new devices are downloaded, which is what the question asks. There's not much to do on the General page, unless an OEM decides to add additional functionality.

17. B. These scenarios are always tough, and you can't use one approach for all calls along the same vein. However, you can be predisposed to handle each scenario in one standard way and shift gears on the fly when necessary. In this case, avoid making the user angrier, and don't personalize the affront by attacking back. Hanging up or putting the user on hold is likely to incite them further. Rest assured, most people are resourceful enough to be able to retaliate for such perceived abuse. Because you have no idea what has set off the user and pushed them down such an illogical path, you cannot address the situation head on. You should also avoid allowing an uncontrollable rant, which could fuel the user into an even more harried frenzy. Also avoid minimizing the user's situation, even if your intent is to calm them down. Doing so offers false hope of an outcome that you cannot foresee. If joining the rant and telling the user everything will be OK are the two extremes, then you want to situate yourself somewhere in the middle. Without being rude or dismissive, find an opening to tell the user that you are there to help; be patient until the user calms down enough for you to be able to begin getting useful information from them.

18. A. The `md` command and its longer form, `mkdir`, create directories (make directory); they do not move directories. Recent versions of the Command Prompt create all nonexistent directories in the path, right down to the lowest level specified in the command, starting from the left. A relative path like this one starts in the current directory, `C:\folder1`, and creates the leftmost directory specified in the command therein, if it does not already exist. It then transfers focus to the newly created directory and creates the next directory specified in the command therein, and so on, until the end of the command. The question states that the `folder1` directory is empty, so both `folder2` and its subdirectory, `folder3`, are created by this command.

19. A. Here's how these three devices work: Hubs are Layer 1 devices that are basically multiport repeaters. Every bit that enters on every port is repeated onto every other port. Collisions are caused by devices attached to two or more ports transmitting simultaneously. CSMA/CD is designed to minimize collisions. Hubs know bit values only: They do not understand how these bits go together to form frames. Frames are the specialty of switches, although routers know about frames as well. Switches are Layer 2 devices in that they use information from the Layer 2 frame's Ethernet headers to learn the location of devices and make individual decisions about whether to forward, filter, or flood frames on each port except the port the frame came in on. Of course, switches are active devices like hubs, meaning they send out rejuvenated bits as well. Hubs and switches often have uplink ports that are used to chain similar devices together to increase port count. You can chain together only a certain number of hubs, and a switch resets the hub count. Routers don't need uplink ports and do not have them. They connect to other devices with full-featured network interfaces. Routers are Layer 3 devices that understand data at the bit level, the frame level, and the packet level. They bring the data in as bits and process the frames that are meant for them by looking inside at the routable packets to determine the best path to send them along. Therefore, routers must indeed examine Ethernet frames on their Ethernet interfaces.

20. C. You absolutely can have multiple ATA drives in the system at the same time. Without making one of the drives a slave, you cannot put them both on the same controller. For them both to remain masters, they must be on different controllers. Systems that have been tampered with are potentially out of warranty, due to either warranty violation or passed warranty expiration. Either way, you stand to produce revenue by working on the failed system, as long as it is agreed up front that this call is not covered under warranty. Besides, the customer should always sign a standard disclaimer before you perform service on any system. Of these options, supplying power to the new drive when none was supplied previously is the most likely fix.

21. A. The option that describes how to compress files and folders is accurate, but only for NTFS partitions. The same goes for encrypting files and folders. Files on a FAT/FAT32 partition are not natively compressed. To compress files on a FAT/FAT32 partition in Windows XP without moving them, you need a third-party utility. If you don't mind moving the files into a new compressed folder, Microsoft now offers a native feature known as *Compressed (zipped) Folders*, which works on FAT partitions as well. Once you create a compressed folder, copying files into the folder compresses them with no effect on performance when accessing such files. This method of compression is not compatible with UNIX and Linux, however. Of course, you can convert the partition to NTFS before compressing the files, but then the parameters of the question have changed. In the case of an NTFS partition, however, individual files can be compressed and encrypted without the need to do so for the entire partition.

22. D. `DISKPART` is a command-line utility that can accept direct input or be executed with scripts as input. A vast number of tasks can be carried out with `DISKPART`, but you cannot use it to convert from FAT32 to NTFS. Use the `CONVERT` command for that.

23. C. Video drivers don't just go bad. If the monitor ever displayed the right colors, this wouldn't be something to investigate further. Individual cathode rays don't generally fail, and Gaussian effects don't cause such symptoms over the entire display. An improperly inserted video connector and some cheaper switching equipment, which mimics poor connectivity at times, can cause this phenomenon. Have the user check the connection first, before advising that they switch out the monitor or take more drastic action.

24. A. The private-use addresses for intranets are in the following ranges:

Class	Lower Limit	Upper Limit
A	10.0.0.0	10.255.255.255
B	172.16.0.0	172.31.255.255
C	192.168.0.0	192.168.255.255

As you can see, 172.32.0.0 is just out of the Class B private range, making it public. There are other special-use addresses that can be considered private, such as the nonroutable APIPA (self-configuration) range of 169.254.0.0 through 169.254.255.255. However, only the addresses in the table are considered useable for private intranets.

25. D. In System Properties, you must choose the Advanced tab to find the Performance section. The Settings button therein takes you to the Performance Options dialog, where you can choose another Advanced tab to find the Virtual Memory section and the Change button that takes you to the Virtual Memory dialog. Note that two Advanced tabs are at play here, and the first one, in System Properties, has neither a Virtual Memory section nor a Memory Usage section. Those are under the second Advanced tab, which is under the Performance Options dialog.

26. B. Defragmentation of the hard drive changes the file system's indexing of the files on the drive without removing files. It moves files around and pulls their pieces together, each of which had to be indexed in the file system's table. A contiguous file requires less attention in the table than the same file chained across the drive. It's quicker to read from the drive, as well. CHKDSK is capable of recovering information, removing corrupt data, and marking problem areas on the drive. Its primary job is not to move information around and re-index the file system's tables. SFC is the finder of lost and damaged system files, also not a match. FDISK does not exist in modern operating systems but in older operating systems; it is deadly to data. Repartitioning a drive certainly re-indexes the tables, but doing so destroys all existing data in the process.

27. B. IMAP is the TCP/IP protocol that allows such untethered access to a user's stored messages as well as allowing the user to send messages through the server connection without having anything stored locally. In contrast to POP, IMAP lets you access your mail from anywhere on any device without scattering downloaded messages across multiple inboxes. SMTP is for sending mail only. The Messaging Application Programming Interface (MAPI) is a set of functions that developers can use to create mail-enabled applications in a Microsoft environment. Be careful not to confuse IMAP and MAPI, which have the same letters in their acronyms.

28. D. The /R switch causes CHKDSK to attempt to recover readable information from sectors that it marks as bad to avoid their future use and potential data loss. Use of the /R switch implies the /F switch, which by itself fixes errors such as lost clusters and file-system inconsistencies. The /X switch causes any network links to the volume to be broken before proceeding. The /C switch skips a certain set of checks on an NTFS volume in such a way so as to speed up the process somewhat.

29. B. Once you confirm that the internal/external-display keyboard control is not biased against the internal display, the most likely cause for the loss of image on a built-in laptop display is the failure of the inverter board, which converts the DC voltage supplied by the power adapter back to the AC the laptop's LCD display requires. The voltages in this component are extremely high, although the amperage is not so large. Nevertheless, care should be taken when handling this component because focal burning and deep pitting of the skin can occur; in just the right situation, even this lower amperage can be deadly. Rectifiers convert AC to DC, as in the case of the laptop's power adapter. No rectifiers affect only the LCD display on laptops. Obviously, the external VGA connector on the laptop is fine if the external monitor displays the image properly. No operating-system control turns off the built-in display. Any software controls for monitor selection that may exist come from specialized utilities that operate on top of the operating system. Be aware, however, that the Multiple Monitors feature of Windows, accessible from Display Properties, can cause unpredictable results on occasion, sometimes requiring a System Restore to return the system to a time of normal functionality and return the display to the built-in LCD. This is not a feature designed to switch between internal and external monitors.

30. C. Windows Management Instrumentation (WMI) is a set of Microsoft protocols for managing devices and applications in a network from a Windows machine. WMI is integrated into Windows Millennium Edition (Me), Windows 2000, Windows XP, and Windows Server 2003. It can be downloaded for Windows 98 and Windows NT 4.0, SP4, and up. WZC is a service and utility for detecting wireless networks with minimal user intervention. SNMP can be a portion of the WMI experience, but it is not the basis for WMI. Windows systems are not natively set up to allow SNMP to do all the things listed in the question. Telnet is used to remotely configure TCP/IP systems that are set up to allow remote configuration. Few Microsoft systems are set up as Telnet servers.

31. C. The switch `/fs:fat` is required to be sure that the partition is formatted as FAT. The other two choices you have are `/fs:fat32` to format the partition as FAT32 and `/fs:ntfs` to format it as NTFS. The only other valid form given as an option is `format e:`, which reformats the partition using its existing file system, which may not be FAT.

32. A. This is a classic issue with the way inkjet printers operate. Calibration allows you to tell the printer how it needs to adjust its operation based on how the print cartridges are situated in the cartridge carrier, which along with slight differences in cartridge manufacturing can have large impacts on print quality given minute changes. Think of this as the synchronization between what the printer thinks it is doing and what you observe it doing. The two should be identical, and calibration is the way to approach that goal. Nothing you can do with the cartridges themselves or the carriage assembly will resolve this problem. In fact, each time you remove the cartridges and put the same ones back in, you run the risk of throwing the printer out of calibration. Utility-based cartridge cleaning that cleans the cartridges without the need to remove them is ideal to avoid the need for further calibration. However, cleaning addresses the problems of smearing and smudging more than the inconsistencies in printing that calibration deals with.

33. A. Disk Cleanup is a utility that scours the file structure for a variety of objects that are commonly expendable, such as downloaded program files, different types of temporary and offline files, and files in the Recycle Bin. When it finds them, it gives you the ability to pick and choose which to keep and which to delete in order to gain back disk space. Disk Cleanup also offers to compress old files to save additional space. Disk Management is a utility to manage the partitions on your drives. `CHKDSK` fixes file system errors, and `DEFRAG` defragments files on your hard drives.

34. D. Although LiIon batteries do not form a chemical memory per se, they do suffer from irreversible life-robbing oxidation. When the battery has a significant charge, this oxidation is exacerbated by heat, such as that generated by the laptop in which the battery is installed or by leaving the battery in a car exposed to ambient heat. Although there is no cure for this effect and the fact that the battery has a finite life expectancy, the effect also has a bearing on how Windows' battery gauge interprets the battery's remaining charge. Calibrating the battery, which really means calibrating Windows' gauge or synchronizing the gauge with the battery, involves allowing the battery to discharge completely once in every 30 charging cycles until the laptop loses power. Doing so will keep the gauge more accurate, and the user who watches their gauge vigilantly will not be caught off guard. If the battery will not charge adequately, however, it should be replaced and recycled.

35. B. Windows XP Professional, Windows 200 Professional, and Windows NT Workstation 4.0, as well as similar workstation versions of Windows, by default have a hard limit of 10 simultaneous users per share that cannot be increased. Therefore, increasing the limit from the default is not a solution, because it is not possible to do so. The Server versions theoretically have no upper limit, so migration of the resource to one of these systems is the best solution. If the users have occasional success accessing the resource, permissions are not an issue here.

36. D. *Internet service provider* is the generic term for any entity that resells Internet access to other ISPs or directly to consumers. One such entity is the telephone company, or Telco, but it is only one of many and is not synonymous with ISP. DNS is a protocol for name-to-address resolution, and Active Server Pages (ASP) is a Microsoft protocol that uses server-side scripting to create dynamic web pages that can carry variable information from one page to another.

37. A. The noise could have been caused by something dragging across the fan as it runs. In that case, part of the solution is to replace the cable or cord that may have been damaged over time, as well as the CPU fan, the motor of which has been compromised by the added resistance of running against the impediment. The noise also could have been the motor's bearings in the various stages of failing. When the noise stops, it generally means that the bearings have worn so much that the motor can no longer turn the fan—a serious problem that will lead to overheating. You generally cannot remove a CPU fan without also removing the integrated heat sink, not that you would want to do so without replacing the fan with a working one. A passive cooling mechanism has only a prayer of working in BTX systems, but you should always go with the active cooling option to make sure. Regardless, the solution is to replace the fan. If the heat sink comes with it as an integrated component, just make sure the replacement has a heat sink as well. The fan alone should not be mounted directly to the CPU. The customer saves money and reduces the chance for more widespread damage by replacing the fan over being encouraged to solder broken wires.

38. C. Telnet is the protocol used for this purpose. SMTP is for sending e-mail. FTP is for transferring files. DNS resolves network names to IP addresses.

39. B. SMTP is used for sending e-mail through a mail server; IMAP and POP3 are used to retrieve e-mail from a mail server. Although you may use HTTP to access an online e-mail service, such as Hotmail or Yahoo Mail, HTTP only shuttles the website's pages to you for viewing. Either SMTP is at work behind the scenes to send the mail; IMAP or POP3 is used to retrieve your mail from the service's mail server, as well as other servers that you specify, for delivery into your inbox.

40. C. This is a simple situation of no viable network connection. Either have the user plug the NIC into a switch or hub, or enable the wireless antenna (a manual task) if there is a wireless LAN in the vicinity. Bluetooth is designed for cord replacement, as with keyboards, mice, and peripherals, not for wireless networking.

41. C. The `tracert` utility performs a traceroute between the source device and the destination that you specify by address or name in the command. A traceroute sends a series of special UDP messages to the destination, but it manipulates the Time to Live (TTL) field in the IP header so that it only gets to the first device in the path and then to one additional device for each iteration of the message. Each successive device discards the message because of the expired TTL and sends an executioner's message back to the source. The source uses this message to identify the next device in the path and build a list for the user to follow. By executing a traceroute, either you find that the path to the destination is healthy and discover the devices along the path, or you find the last device that is able to send you an executioner's message, which usually, but not always, tells you where the break in the path lies. The `ping` utility only tests the existence of the destination. It gives no details about the intermediate path other than that it is healthy or *potentially* not healthy; you can't be sure with a failed `ping` if the path is broken or the destination simply is not active. The `nslooklup` utility helps you discover problems with your name servers and general DNS functionality, and `ipconfig` only tells you local settings for the device on which it is executed.

42. B. The `EDIT` command opens a text-based editing utility that allows you to create or edit an existing text file and save your changes. The `TYPE` command only displays the contents of a text file. `OPEN` and `ALTER` are not command-line commands, although you may recognize `OPEN` from utility shells, such as `FTP` and `TELNET`.

43. A. Wireless Zero Configuration (WZC) is the service and associated utility integrated into Windows XP that allows you to do nothing more than install a wireless NIC to immediately detect available wireless networks that are broadcasting their SSIDs. If you need to disable this feature, for whatever reason, you can stop the WZC service, but be aware that doing so also affects your ability to use 802.1x for wired network connections. The only other valid option given is Ad Hoc mode, which is an alternative to infrastructure mode when connecting devices in a wireless LAN. Ad Hoc mode does not use access points; Infrastructure mode does.

44. D. You configure the audit in the Security tab of the Properties dialog for the shared folder by clicking the Advanced button and then clicking the Audit tab. This is definitely not where you can find results of the audit. There are also no results in the Sharing tab for you to see. The Security category in Event Viewer is where you find entries generated by the triggers you set in the Audit tab for the resource.

45. C. You can use either the `ren` or `rename` form of that command or the `move` command to change the name of a file or folder and keep it in the same folder. The `move` command is preferred when you change the location of the object, regardless of whether you keep the same name. However, there is no `/r` switch for the `move` command. Regardless of the form of the `rename` command that you use, you must specify the exact existing and new name for the object. No part of its name is assumed, only the path, so the extension must be included. Each of these commands assumes the focus of the files in the currently logged directory. The `copy` command has no switch that causes it to delete the source file after the destination file is created. The `/d` switch creates the destination file decrypted, regardless of whether copying rules would normally encrypt the destination file.

46. **C.** Without the ability to upgrade the system's memory, and without being given the option to tweak virtual memory, the best option offered is to enter System Properties and make your way to the Advanced page. There, you need to click the Settings button in the Performance section to open the Performance Options. On the Visual Effects page in that dialog is a list of items that affect how Windows manages the appearance of your Windows sessions. You can let Windows choose what's best; you can turn on all the bells and whistles by selecting Adjust for Best Appearance; you can turn them all off by selecting Adjust for Best Performance; or you can customize which ones are on and which ones are off to match your preference. As its name suggests, Adjust for Best Performance forcibly boosts the system's performance when compared to the other options and does so with the least amount of effort. The Background Services and System Cache options appear on the Advanced page of Performance Options. Background Services, found in the Processor Scheduling section, configures Windows to give equal attention to all running programs, whereas the alternative, Programs, gives priority to the program running in the foreground. System Cache, found in the Memory Usage section, is preferable if the system is being used as a server, but the question states that the user's system is a workstation. Programs is the alternative in this section as well.

47. **B.** HTTPS is just HTTP with an added layer between it and TCP for security. This security layer can be created with Secure Sockets Layer (SSL) or Transport Layer Security (TLS). HTTPS allows for secure transactions, such as credit-card orders, over a decidedly insecure network. IPSec is another way to ensure end-to-end TCP/IP security; but it requires more deliberate configuration and is not used in browser security, which requires a more dynamic peering between the server and any number of randomly changing clients. PPTP and L2TP are both Layer-2 tunneling protocols that secure a link between two points on the same local network but cannot provide the end-to-end security afforded by HTTPS.

48. **B.** Certain software cannot accept images with parameters that are beyond the specifications of the software. Generally, you can reduce the resolution in either on-screen pixels or printed dots per inch to allow their use. Optionally, you can change the file type from low-loss formats, such as TIFF, to others that produce smaller files, such as JPEG. A remote-support technician generally begins a new issue on the spot, but regardless, you should never leave the user high and dry by hiding behind your company's policy. The customer loyalty you build will outweigh the hassle incurred by any adjustments you have to make. There is no reason to believe that the software that produced the image is not at its default settings. The problem is more the software used to access the scanned image. If only that software has issues, then there is no reason to make broad adjustments that may potentially affect other software that is currently working with the images. There is also no reason to assume that you can replace the customer's software with a similar package that can use the image. Work on the image to make it compatible with the existing software instead of trying to find software that the image works with as is.

49. **CD.** Clearing paper jams is not considered maintenance, which is more proactive in nature. It's more of a reaction to an event. Although cleaning toner out of a printer can be considered proactive in most cases, it's not something the printer will ask for in a message like this. You can argue that responding to any message is hardly proactive maintenance, but it's tough to deny when you're using something called a "maintenance" kit. The average maintenance kit contains items such as a fuser assembly, a transfer roller, and pickup or feed/separation rollers. Some printers reset the page count when you install a maintenance kit, but in case it doesn't work out that way, there are methods to reset the count yourself. Installing a maintenance kit before the page count reaches the threshold that spawns the warning message can make it more difficult to reset the page count, but there are usually ways to do so with little additional effort.

50. **A.** Whenever an error that usually causes a BSoD event occurs during shutdown, an event is logged and can be viewed later in Event Viewer. If the *Automatically Restart* check box is checked in System Properties, the computer restarts for any such event. When such an event occurs during shutdown, you are unable to examine the blue screen's details or even tell that the event occurred. The confusion that ensues leads to service calls to diagnose the restart on shutdown. Clearing the check box causes the system to pause on the blue screen so that

you may be able to troubleshoot the problem and perhaps repair the offending driver. There is no such feature in the BIOS as the one mentioned here, nor is there any setting in the BIOS that can assist with this issue. Powering down with the power button is not an acceptable option because it encourages the user to not shut down Windows properly, leaving temporary files scattered on the hard drive and compromising the operating system's stability. The option to alter how hardware profiles are handled affects how the system boots up, not how it shuts down.

51. D. When you execute the WINNT32.EXE program from its location (such as from the I386 folder in the root of the distribution CD) on a functioning XP installation and use the /CMDCONS switch, the Recovery Console is installed as one of the startup options along with your primary operating system and any additional operating systems and environments offered in the text-mode startup menu that appears early during bootup. Note that XP must already be installed and that the use of the /CMDCONS switch does not reinstall XP; it only installs the Recovery Console. The /CMD switch is the only other valid switch listed, but its function is to execute a command of your choosing before the final phase of Setup.

52. A. Although they look like so much Morse code, each of these commands does something; but only cd ..\.. traverses two levels up toward the root, which is where you want to be. The .. represents the parent directory. A single dot (.) represents the current directory. Therefore, ..\.. means the parent of your parent. Read these the same way you would a normal directory path, from left to right. The operating system takes you to the directory represented by the first symbol, up to the first backslash, if any. Then, the operating system takes you to the next symbol, if applicable, and so on. So, the path .\. means "stay where you are" and then "stay where you are." You go nowhere with that one. The path .. takes you up only one level. The path \..\.. takes you to the root first; then, the two parent symbols (..) are lost because the root has no parent. You wind up at the root directory, and you may as well have issued the command cd \ to do the same thing.

53. BC. Computer Management is the plug-in required to access all the shares currently configured on the system. Control Panel has no Share applet. Alternatively, you can use the Share tab in the Properties dialog of the folder being shared to access the Permissions button and arrive at the same dialog. Although the Security tab does include permissions, they are for file-level access on an NTFS volume. It is true that you may need to adjust these at some point because most administrators leave share-level access wide open, limit who is allowed to log on locally to the system, and adjust the more granular file-level permissions to control who is allowed to access the resource locally and from across the network. Doing it this way allows the administrator to grant a mixture of access to different files within the same folder. Share permissions apply only to shared folders because files cannot be shared individually. So, managing permissions the other way around leads to everyone with access to the shared folder having access to all files and folders within. Adjusting both file-level and share permissions creates a complex access-control rule that may be difficult to troubleshoot later. Because the question mentioned share permissions, there is no justification for changing anything on the Security tab, regardless of standard practice.

54. C. The base command is ntbackup, but you must specify backup as the operation immediately afterward, even though there is no restore operation from the command line. The next parameter is generally the top level from which to start the backup, including all files and subdirectories below (c:). The /f switch is followed by the name of the file that will hold the backup set ("d:\todayback.bkf"). The quotes are suggested but not required. The /m switch is required when you are requesting a backup type other than the default set in the GUI Backup utility. Because you can't know the default in this case, it must be specified (daily). A daily backup captures only those files that were altered today. The /v switch turns verification on or off. It has nothing to do with appending or overwriting the backup set. Overwriting is the default action. You use the /a switch to override it and append to the backup set.

55. A. The motherboard is a little more than XP Professional can handle. You can consider it either room to grow or a wakeup call to upgrade to XP Professional x64 Edition, which can handle 128GB of physical RAM. XP Professional can utilize as many as two processors and as much as 4GB of RAM. The following table lists the maximum number of processors and the maximum physical RAM for the various modern Windows operating systems. Incorrect memory modules do not physically fit into the wrong slots, which would result in no memory and no booting. Again, with XP Professional, there is no way to access 20GB of physical RAM, so the virtual memory setting is immaterial, regardless of the technical relationship between physical and virtual memory.

Windows Operating System	Maximum Processors	Maximum Physical RAM
XP Professional	2	4GB
XP Professional x64 Edition	2	128GB
Server 2003 Standard Edition	4	4GB
Server 2003 Standard x64 Edition	4	32GB
Server 2003 Enterprise Edition	8	64GB
Server 2003 Enterprise x64 Edition	8	1TB
Server 2003 Datacenter Edition	32	128GB
Server 2003 Datacenter x64 Edition	32	1TB
2000 Professional	2	4GB
2000 Server	4	4GB
2000 Advanced Server	8	8GB
2000 Datacenter Server	32	32GB

56. D. Internet Connection Sharing (ICS) can be viewed as a security compromise. Allowing other devices to pass through your device for access to the Internet opens your device to malicious activity. Not broadcasting the SSID, the wireless network's name, takes away another level of access that attackers must guess or find out using less conventional methods. Filtering on MAC addresses allows you to decide exactly which devices are allowed onto the network and even which ones specifically should be denied. Placing a limit on the number of wireless connections that are allowed simultaneously can ensure that when all legitimate connections are established, anyone else will have a difficult time gaining access. This is not as powerful as MAC address filtering, but it is worthwhile.

57. A. Automatic Updates is an applet in Control Panel, as well as a page in System Properties. Within Automatic Updates, you have the choice of selecting Automatic and then setting the time to check for updates and automatically install them. Otherwise, you can choose to automatically download but manually install updates when notified, to notify you to manually download and install updates, or to turn off Automatic Updates. Windows updates are essential for security and to remain current. Updates should be checked for regularly, either manually or automatically.

58. C. The *Resources by Type* view in Device Manager has an IRQ category that lists all devices that have an IRQ grouped by expansion bus and then by IRQ number. You can spot all devices using a specific IRQ without any additional action (other than possible scrolling).

59. A. This can be a tricky question if you're not completely up on your Registry editing trivia. In Windows XP and Server 2003, REGEDT32 is a small application that runs REGEDIT. So, in XP there is no reason to run REGEDT32 over REGEDIT. However, in Windows 200 and earlier NT-based versions of Windows all the way back to NT 3.*x*, there are marked differences. REGEDIT started out in NT 3.*x* as a way to examine the `reg.dat` file from a 16-bit Windows operating system—but in a 32-bit NT environment, not in the 16-bit environment, making that option for this question not quite correct. Since NT 4.0, REGEDIT has been a serious utility for making changes in the active Registry. In Windows XP and Server 2003, it's the only utility that does so, with REGEDT32 being a launch pad for REGEDIT. In Windows 2000, REGEDIT does not allow viewing and editing of all functions and data types the way REGEDT32 does. Microsoft suggests that you run REGEDIT over REGEDT32 in Windows NT 4.0 and 2000 for the searching capabilities and to be able to import and export `.reg` files, not the other way around. REGEDT32 doesn't support these features in Windows NT 4.0 and 2000.

60. C. Although you can click the application on the Applications tab and then press the Delete key to terminate an application, the Backspace key does nothing. End Process Tree is a selection when you right-click a process on the Processes tab; no such selection is available on the Applications tab. The Processes tab does not list applications: It lists processes, which are smaller portions of applications. Terminating a process with the End Process button or selecting End Process after right-clicking the process is not often the most effective way to terminate an entire application. Component processes can remain, causing issues. Even the End Process Tree is not favored over using the Applications tab to end an entire application and all of its processes in one fell swoop.

61. A. The key is the word *reliably*, given you know the correct switch is /s and not /f, which is an invalid switch for the dir command. If the logged directory on drive E: when you issue the command is not the root directory, leaving off the backslash will not produce the desired results.

62. A. Of the choices given, only fiber optics provides immunity from electrical interference. Coaxial cable tends to have more EMI resistance than twisted-pair cable, but in general, there is no clear path to migrate from twisted-pair to coax and stay with the same Ethernet technology. Wireless communications are susceptible to EMI and RFI as well. If you are upgrading from Fast Ethernet to Gigabit Ethernet in an environment without EMI/RFI issues, switching the cabling infrastructure from Category 5 cabling to a higher standard is required for the newer echo-cancellation encoding technique used where three pairs carry the same signal and can more easily interfere with return traffic on the lone pair, but doing so does not decrease external interference substantially.

63. B. Although enough is enough, and we all know when we've heard enough, never interrupt the user. Instead, wait until the user seems to have arrived at the end of a thought, and then use what you have gleaned from active listening to formulate questions that may direct the user to fill in any blanks that still exist; or reassure the user that you understand their problem by summarizing what you have heard and even let them know what you intend to do. Many times, more technical users feel that they must repeat themselves to get all pertinent information across. Some will use you as a sounding board: They will verbally go through all possible scenarios and issues as if they are telling you something, when really they are thinking out loud. Regardless of the reason for their ramblings, it is never OK to express distaste in the user's methods or communications skills. Doing so can only lead to strained relationships. The problem with closed-ended questions is that they limit the interviewee to certain answers and are only as useful as the interviewer is comprehensive. Besides, if you've ever seen one of those law series on television, you know closed-ended questions won't stop someone from rambling, even with a judge in the room.

64. A. Restarting the spooler from the command line involves first stopping the Spooler service and then starting it. The command to stop it is net stop spooler. The command to start it is net start spooler. This procedure may be necessary on occasion if printing fails consistently.

65. C. This appears to be a problem with the user's system accepting HTTPS traffic, which uses TCP port 443 instead of the port 80 that HTTP uses. Opening up their system's firewall (or the entire network's firewall, if this is a widespread issue) to allow HTTPS traffic should solve the problem. Such a specific outage would not be related to the browser version or to pop-up blocking, which does not target only secure sites or primary-page sites. Reducing a browser's security level has no effect on the types of sites you can visit; doing so allows you to adjust how the browser handles scripting, downloads, and authentication.

66. C. Neither you nor anyone else will be able to add a Windows XP Home computer to a domain without a third-party product. If the computer does not join the domain, the user cannot authenticate against the domain controllers during log on, and logon will be local to the computer. This does not mean that the computer cannot access network resources: Plenty of tricks can get that going. It does mean that this particular computer cannot use pass-through authentication to access network resources by authenticating on the domain during logon and receiving a set of tokens for all resources the user is allowed to access. Instead, accessing resources will take a bit of finagling. For example, a mapped network drive can be created for each shared folder with the domain credentials entered individually for each mapped drive each time the user logs on. Among other limitations, the computer cannot receive scheduled internal network pushes to stay current.

67. AD. Neither System Restore nor Device Driver Roll Back has any effect on user data, positive or negative. Anything restored or rolled back returns to its original location. You have no control over that. Device Driver Roll Back is ideal when you use a last-in, first-out approach to updating device drivers. If you test the system after updating a driver, you have a better chance to find out if it caused problems. However, despite the best hyper-vigilance, problems can arise after some time, obscuring the identity of the true culprit. In such a case, and when you need to restore application settings, System Restore shines over Device Driver Roll Back, which requires you to enter the Drivers tab of Properties in Device Manager for the exact device whose driver needs to be rolled back.

68. D. Because there appears to be a gray area here, you should not make the decision yourself. Let your supervisor do that. Confronting the coworker and telling the customer what has happened are decisions your supervisor is better equipped to handle. Empirically, if you notice a security breach or weakness, you should inform the customer immediately, unless it is your company's policy to take such information to your supervisor for communication to the customer. The coworker's involvement makes this scenario less clear. The argument that this is a victimless crime is moot. The credentials your coworker is using make it look like someone else is gaining access, possibly jeopardizing the owner of the credentials. Additionally, if the customer discovers the breach, your company is easily on the hook for future disputes about damages incurred by someone using those credentials, even if it was not your coworker. Therefore, the situation is bigger than your loyalty to your coworker. The good name and even the future of the company you work for may be at stake.

69. B. Double-clicking the wireless adapter in Network Connections and then clicking on the View Wireless Networks button brings up the list of available wireless networks that are in range. The Wireless Network Setup Wizard is something very different and is not meant for simply finding wireless networks in range of the computer. My Network Places does not have a direct link to the list of available wireless networks. Showing the icon in the System Tray is a good idea to make bringing up the list of wireless networks easier in the future, but doing so does not bring up the list. However, once the icon is in the System Tray, you can right-click it and click View Available Wireless Networks or double-click the icon in the System Tray and then click the View Wireless Networks button. Alternatively, you can double-click the icon in the System Tray, click the Properties button, and then select the Wireless Networks tab where there is another button labeled View Wireless Networks as well as a list of past networks recognized that allows you to set the order of preference among them for future connection. You can also remove unused wireless networks that appear in the Preferred Networks list, which contains wireless networks to which you have attached in the past.

70. A. The best way to handle this problem, as well as system lock-ups, auto-restarts, and repeated bluescreen errors, is to hit F8 while booting. Doing so gives you access to the Startup Options screen, which contains a number of choices, including Safe Mode, Safe Mode with Networking, and Last Known Good Configuration (LKGC), among others. Choosing one of these two Safe Mode options is the way to start Windows with minimal drivers. You then hope that the driver causing the system instability will not be loaded, which is highly likely. Once you are in this limited Windows session, you can run System Restore normally and roll back to a time when the system ran properly. In this case, the problem with LKGC is that whenever the user logs on, the Registry location that LKGC draws from is updated with the system's current settings. Although it's considered known-good, you can tell from the question that it's really not good. Without any further changes, the system began to refuse to make it to the logon screen, hardly a known-good configuration that you would want to roll back to. You must be able to log on to Windows to perform a Device Driver Roll Back, and the ASR process requires a backup set. There is also likely no ASR disk, not that it would matter without a system backup set.

71. B. The /k switch causes the Command Prompt window to remain open after the command executes. The /c switch ensures that it closes, just as executing the ping command alone does without preceding it by cmd. Executing the cmd command with the ping command as an argument with no switches causes cmd to ignore the ping command. It opens a Command Prompt window and does nothing further.

72. C. If this is a problem with the hard drive, no booting will be going on, so Safe Mode is out. Even a boot diskette relies on the master boot record of the hard drive to complete the bootup process. If that would work, you wouldn't receive an error message like this. The diskette gets you past problems with files like BOOT.INI, NTDETECT.COM, and NTLDR. That would be a great option if you received the *NTLDR is missing* error message during boot. You can't restore the partition: You must be able to boot the system to restore a backup. If the problem is a nonbootable CD in the drive, that makes the option to change the boot order in the BIOS sound logical. For the system to get hung up on a nonbootable CD that was recently inserted and forgotten in the drive, it must be higher than the hard drive in the boot order, and a CD must be in the drive. So, change the boot order or remove the CD, which wasn't an option given.

73. D. Moving files implies copying them and then deleting them in one motion. Therefore, and by definition, no files that were already moved are left on the user's hard drive. Regardless, a leftover or two wouldn't cause the system to slow down noticeably. Performing an ASR or System Restore turns the system back to an earlier time: to the last backup and the selected restore point, respectively. The ASR process causes you to lose recent work without guaranteeing a system speed-up. System Restore does not affect data files one way or another. As files are deleted, such as during a move, empty spots are left in the file system. As new, larger files are written to the disk, they are often split up, or fragmented, across the smaller empty spots. The more fragmentation that occurs, the more time the physical drive has to spend jumping around to piece files together as they are read into memory. Running the DEFRAG utility places the fragmented pieces of a file together in the proper order on the disk, speeding up access when the time comes.

74. B. Some manufacturers use a portion of your hard drive to store a compressed image of your original hard drive as it was delivered to you. A recovery CD is included in the distribution materials for you to use when you want to access the hidden partition to restore your system to factory defaults. This destroys any data on the drive, so it should be used only as a last resort, much like the ASR process. Generally, the value of being able to get back up and running quickly on a clean system outweighs the loss of storage capacity, which is often prorated in the specifications so that you are not looking for the extra capacity when the time comes. Recovery partitions take the place of cramming ever-larger images onto CDs and DVDs. A major drawback to this scheme is the case of a catastrophic failure that makes the entire hard disk inaccessible, including the recovery partition.

75. D. This error can mean a number of things, including that the remote system is not prepared to accept Remote Desktop connections due to causes such as the Windows Firewall/ICS service not running or having Remote Desktop connections blocked by Windows Firewall. Commonly, however, an improperly entered IP address or computer name is the cause for this error. Windows Firewall blocks inbound Remote Desktop requests, not outbound, invalidating that option. The fact that you are trying to connect to a system on your own IP subnet precludes the gateway from being the issue. The fact that you are attempting to connect by IP address precludes DNS problems from the list of possible problems.

76. D. If you are sure the solution you implemented solved the problem, then you can be confident that the next service call is about a new issue. Even though you can never be 100 percent sure that your solution completely solved the problem, you can be 100 percent sure that it did not. Proper testing after implementation brings out all but the most hidden weaknesses in your solution. An aloof attitude and a harried pace point to the cliché *haste makes waste*, and the waste here is your time and the customer's, as well as their money. You won't have your customer for long after assuring them their problem is resolved only to receive a call in the near future for the same issue. Have enough confidence in yourself to stick with the problem until it's resolved, even if you have to consult with someone with more expertise while you are working. Don't hand the customer off to anyone else if you can help it. Documenting the resolution is of the utmost importance. Doing so will reduce the amount of time for the second call involving the same problem, but documentation and courtesy don't help reduce the need for a second call.

77. B. None of these choices will completely solve the customer's problem. NAT with private addressing would be ideal in a situation where there are more devices requiring Internet access than public IP addresses. However, trying to give each host a static IP address will guarantee those hosts that do not receive addresses will not be able to access the Internet. Public addressing is too vague to know what the plan is; it could be static or it could be dynamic addressing. APIPA is not routable and is generally considered more of a response to an error than anything else. Dynamic addressing uses a DHCP server to hand out addresses to those requesting one. The hope that this scheme will work is based on the assumption that not all hosts will be powered up simultaneously. This could work with shift-based personnel but is not likely to perform any better than static addressing for highly active networks.

78. A. Although a user's Internet experience is seriously degraded without access to a DNS server, it is not ruined. Every IP host must have a minimum of an IP address and subnet mask to define the network they are on and who they are on that network. In order to communicate outside their network—on the Internet, for example—a host must know the local address of the router that can get them to the remote network. This is known as a *gateway*, which is the original term for a router.

79. B. In order from slowest to fastest, dial-up, ISDN, broadband, and LAN all provide access to an ISP. Although some LANs still run at speeds slow enough to be outpaced by broadband services, such as DSL, the potential of LANs runs into the tens of gigabits per second, whereas cable and DSL have barely topped 10Mbps with only hundreds of megabits on the horizon. Dial-up is limited by the FCC to 53Kbps, and ISDN is not much faster with a single BRI line offering only 128Kbps. The question is one of potential, not absolutes. Even the fastest LAN can be crippled by slow WAN technology, making it slower than some or all of the other options. However, with the faster WAN technologies, such as OC-192 at 10Gbps, the faster LANs are hard to beat.

80. C. Perhaps you could consider laying blame to be part of the information-gathering process. However, it is not a good idea to stir up that kind of tension in an already volatile and frustrating situation. Figure out what's going on; develop some theories; try the most likely of them first, and then document your results—successes and failures. They will come in handy down the line.

Answer Sheets for Practice Test 2

(Remove This Sheet and Use It to Mark Your Answers)

Section 1
Multiple Choice Questions

CUT HERE

1 Ⓐ Ⓑ Ⓒ Ⓓ Ⓔ		41 Ⓐ Ⓑ Ⓒ Ⓓ Ⓔ
2 Ⓐ Ⓑ Ⓒ Ⓓ Ⓔ		42 Ⓐ Ⓑ Ⓒ Ⓓ Ⓔ
3 Ⓐ Ⓑ Ⓒ Ⓓ Ⓔ		43 Ⓐ Ⓑ Ⓒ Ⓓ Ⓔ
4 Ⓐ Ⓑ Ⓒ Ⓓ Ⓔ		44 Ⓐ Ⓑ Ⓒ Ⓓ Ⓔ
5 Ⓐ Ⓑ Ⓒ Ⓓ Ⓔ		45 Ⓐ Ⓑ Ⓒ Ⓓ Ⓔ
6 Ⓐ Ⓑ Ⓒ Ⓓ Ⓔ		46 Ⓐ Ⓑ Ⓒ Ⓓ Ⓔ
7 Ⓐ Ⓑ Ⓒ Ⓓ Ⓔ		47 Ⓐ Ⓑ Ⓒ Ⓓ Ⓔ
8 Ⓐ Ⓑ Ⓒ Ⓓ Ⓔ		48 Ⓐ Ⓑ Ⓒ Ⓓ Ⓔ
9 Ⓐ Ⓑ Ⓒ Ⓓ Ⓔ		49 Ⓐ Ⓑ Ⓒ Ⓓ Ⓔ
10 Ⓐ Ⓑ Ⓒ Ⓓ Ⓔ		50 Ⓐ Ⓑ Ⓒ Ⓓ Ⓔ
11 Ⓐ Ⓑ Ⓒ Ⓓ Ⓔ		51 Ⓐ Ⓑ Ⓒ Ⓓ Ⓔ
12 Ⓐ Ⓑ Ⓒ Ⓓ Ⓔ		52 Ⓐ Ⓑ Ⓒ Ⓓ Ⓔ
13 Ⓐ Ⓑ Ⓒ Ⓓ Ⓔ		53 Ⓐ Ⓑ Ⓒ Ⓓ Ⓔ
14 Ⓐ Ⓑ Ⓒ Ⓓ Ⓔ		54 Ⓐ Ⓑ Ⓒ Ⓓ Ⓔ
15 Ⓐ Ⓑ Ⓒ Ⓓ Ⓔ		55 Ⓐ Ⓑ Ⓒ Ⓓ Ⓔ
16 Ⓐ Ⓑ Ⓒ Ⓓ Ⓔ		56 Ⓐ Ⓑ Ⓒ Ⓓ Ⓔ
17 Ⓐ Ⓑ Ⓒ Ⓓ Ⓔ		57 Ⓐ Ⓑ Ⓒ Ⓓ Ⓔ
18 Ⓐ Ⓑ Ⓒ Ⓓ Ⓔ		58 Ⓐ Ⓑ Ⓒ Ⓓ Ⓔ
19 Ⓐ Ⓑ Ⓒ Ⓓ Ⓔ		59 Ⓐ Ⓑ Ⓒ Ⓓ Ⓔ
20 Ⓐ Ⓑ Ⓒ Ⓓ Ⓔ		60 Ⓐ Ⓑ Ⓒ Ⓓ Ⓔ
21 Ⓐ Ⓑ Ⓒ Ⓓ Ⓔ		61 Ⓐ Ⓑ Ⓒ Ⓓ Ⓔ
22 Ⓐ Ⓑ Ⓒ Ⓓ Ⓔ		62 Ⓐ Ⓑ Ⓒ Ⓓ Ⓔ
23 Ⓐ Ⓑ Ⓒ Ⓓ Ⓔ		63 Ⓐ Ⓑ Ⓒ Ⓓ Ⓔ
24 Ⓐ Ⓑ Ⓒ Ⓓ Ⓔ		64 Ⓐ Ⓑ Ⓒ Ⓓ Ⓔ
25 Ⓐ Ⓑ Ⓒ Ⓓ Ⓔ		65 Ⓐ Ⓑ Ⓒ Ⓓ Ⓔ
26 Ⓐ Ⓑ Ⓒ Ⓓ Ⓔ		66 Ⓐ Ⓑ Ⓒ Ⓓ Ⓔ
27 Ⓐ Ⓑ Ⓒ Ⓓ Ⓔ		67 Ⓐ Ⓑ Ⓒ Ⓓ Ⓔ
28 Ⓐ Ⓑ Ⓒ Ⓓ Ⓔ		68 Ⓐ Ⓑ Ⓒ Ⓓ Ⓔ
29 Ⓐ Ⓑ Ⓒ Ⓓ Ⓔ		69 Ⓐ Ⓑ Ⓒ Ⓓ Ⓔ
30 Ⓐ Ⓑ Ⓒ Ⓓ Ⓔ		70 Ⓐ Ⓑ Ⓒ Ⓓ Ⓔ
31 Ⓐ Ⓑ Ⓒ Ⓓ Ⓔ		71 Ⓐ Ⓑ Ⓒ Ⓓ Ⓔ
32 Ⓐ Ⓑ Ⓒ Ⓓ Ⓔ		72 Ⓐ Ⓑ Ⓒ Ⓓ Ⓔ
33 Ⓐ Ⓑ Ⓒ Ⓓ Ⓔ		73 Ⓐ Ⓑ Ⓒ Ⓓ Ⓔ
34 Ⓐ Ⓑ Ⓒ Ⓓ Ⓔ		74 Ⓐ Ⓑ Ⓒ Ⓓ Ⓔ
35 Ⓐ Ⓑ Ⓒ Ⓓ Ⓔ		75 Ⓐ Ⓑ Ⓒ Ⓓ Ⓔ
36 Ⓐ Ⓑ Ⓒ Ⓓ Ⓔ		76 Ⓐ Ⓑ Ⓒ Ⓓ Ⓔ
37 Ⓐ Ⓑ Ⓒ Ⓓ Ⓔ		77 Ⓐ Ⓑ Ⓒ Ⓓ Ⓔ
38 Ⓐ Ⓑ Ⓒ Ⓓ Ⓔ		78 Ⓐ Ⓑ Ⓒ Ⓓ Ⓔ
39 Ⓐ Ⓑ Ⓒ Ⓓ Ⓔ		79 Ⓐ Ⓑ Ⓒ Ⓓ Ⓔ
40 Ⓐ Ⓑ Ⓒ Ⓓ Ⓔ		80 Ⓐ Ⓑ Ⓒ Ⓓ Ⓔ

Directions: For each of the following questions, select the choice that best answers the question or completes the statement.

1. Which of the following is an example of social engineering?

   A. A technician hacks into a server by using a password-cracking utility.
   B. A technician intentionally renders a server inoperable by hacking the Registry.
   C. A technician talks a coworker into asking their supervisor for increased administrative privileges.
   D. A technician hears a director giving her credentials to the helpdesk and later uses the same credentials to have a new laptop delivered to a coworker.

2. What should you do if tape backups appear to be going well and produce no errors, but the backups are useless and do not pass verification?

   A. Increase the privileges of the backup operator.
   B. Clean the heads of the tape drive.
   C. Replace the tapes.
   D. Use tapes with larger capacity.

3. Which *two* of the following printer technologies use heat during the process of printing a page?

   A. Laser
   B. Thermal
   C. Inkjet
   D. Impact

4. While diagnosing a problem with a laser printer, you suspect the waste-toner receptacle is full. Eager to diagnose the problem and fix it, which of the following is the best method to quickly test your theory?

   A. Have the user empty the waste-toner receptacle.
   B. Have the user replace the toner cartridge.
   C. Have the user confirm that there is still fresh toner in the cartridge. If so, the waste-toner receptacle should not be full.
   D. Dispatch a technician to install a maintenance kit.

5. While diagnosing an unresponsive external LCD attached to a laptop, you feel strongly that you know exactly which internal component of the LCD is to blame. Which of the following is the best course of action?

   A. Request that the user replace the external LCD with a known working unit and try the unresponsive LCD on a known working system.
   B. Have a technician open the LCD's case and perform diagnostics on the suspected component or replace it and test the results.
   C. Have a technician open the case, but before performing any work, discharge the flyback transformer's charging capacitor.
   D. Ask the user to remove the external monitor and use the built-in LCD display.

6. Which of the following best describes the purpose of the `ping` utility?

   A. It tests the availability of a remote IP device and the network in between as well as identifies all intermediate devices.
   B. It identifies the addressing of the local device.
   C. It returns the MAC address of the remote device.
   D. It tests the availability of a remote IP device and the network in between.

7. While on a call with a user experiencing network connectivity issues, you guide the user through identifying their IP address, which is 169.254.12.169. Which of the following is the most appropriate piece of information you should try to obtain from the user?

   A. Is there a network connection icon in the notification area?
   B. Is the LED lit on the user's NIC?
   C. Can the user ping his default gateway?
   D. Can the user reach his destination by IP address instead of by name?

GO ON TO THE NEXT PAGE

8. A user calls and tells you they are adding a hard drive and a DVD burner to a system that already has a hard drive and a CD burner. The user informs you that all devices have ATA interfaces and asks how they can get the devices to work together. What is the best way to pair the devices?

    A. Put each of the four devices on its own controller.

    B. Pair the fastest hard drive with the fastest optical drive on the same controller. Pair the slower devices on another controller.

    C. Pair the hard drives on one controller and the optical drives on another controller.

    D. Place the three fastest drives on one controller and the slowest on another controller.

9. Which of the following is the best utility to use to restore all programs and data from a damaged partition when running Windows XP?

    A. Recovery Console

    B. ERD

    C. System Restore

    D. ASR

10. If you attempt to ping any other device on the local subnet, the ping succeeds. If you attempt to ping any device on a different subnet, the ping always fails. Which of the following is the most likely cause?

    A. The local Windows Firewall is misconfigured.

    B. The DHCP server is down.

    C. The subnet mask on the local computer is wrong.

    D. The local router's routing table is incomplete.

11. Which of the following function keys is used during Windows XP setup to install third-party SCSI drivers?

    A. F2

    B. F6

    C. F8

    D. F12

12. A user reports beeping coming from their computer during use, followed shortly by an automatic shutdown of the system. Which component is most likely the cause?

    A. CPU fan

    B. Power supply

    C. System speaker

    D. BIOS

13. A customer complains that their computer consistently runs for a little while and then shuts down on its own. Which of the following is *least* likely the culprit?

    A. Dust buildup at the chassis vent holes

    B. No heat sinks on the RAM modules

    C. A stalled CPU, system, or power-supply fan

    D. Poorly routed internal cables

14. A user calls to report a dead system and tells you that pressing the power button has no effect. The motherboard was recently upgraded, and the system hasn't worked since. Which of the following is the most likely cause?

    A. Too many adapter cards are installed for the new motherboard.

    B. The power button is defective.

    C. There is a short underneath the motherboard.

    D. The power supply is dead.

15. A client has a system running Windows XP Professional with 4GB of RAM and does not want to upgrade to a server version of Windows. However, the client wants to be able to access 8GB of RAM. Which of the following is the best solution to this problem?

    A. Upgrade to the 64-bit version of XP Professional.

    B. Do nothing except add the additional 4GB of RAM. It will be recognized immediately.

    C. Add a second processor to the system.

    D. There is no way to access more than 4GB of RAM with a 32-bit address bus.

16. A user is trying to transfer information between two laptops in an area without a wired network connection. Additionally, the laptops are out of range of the company's wireless network. Which of the following is the best and most convenient method to transfer the data between most standard laptops?

    A. Bluetooth

    B. Standard serial cable

    C. Infrared

    D. Burn a CD.

17. Which of the following is *not* a difference between FAT32 and NTFS volumes?

    A. NTFS volumes can be larger.

    B. NTFS files can be larger.

    C. The minimum recommended volume size is greater for NTFS.

    D. FAT32 supports the 8.3 naming convention. NTFS does not.

18. A user attempted to update the driver for their video adapter. Things apparently did not go well. The user has booted into Safe Mode and called you for help. What is the least invasive thing you can have the user do in Safe Mode to get the system working properly again?

    A. Run ASR.

    B. Run System Restore.

    C. Use Device Driver Roll Back.

    D. Just use Safe Mode from now on.

19. Which of the following could prevent a ping that uses the destination's IP address from succeeding on the local subnet?

    A. The default router being down

    B. Windows Firewall on the remote device

    C. A misconfigured dedicated firewall somewhere on the network

    D. The DNS server being down

20. A user calls to report a problem using a DVD-ROM to install an application. When you ask the user to describe the disc, you can tell from the description that the disc is a bootleg copy of copyrighted material. What should you do?

    A. Refuse to assist in the installation of the software, and immediately notify antipiracy authorities.

    B. In order to retain the customer, assist in installing the software, and ask the user to keep it between the two of you.

    C. Refuse to assist in installing the software, and notify the user's supervisor of the infraction.

    D. Politely explain that you will be unable to assist the user in installing the software and that using it is against the law.

21. Which of the following methods will produce a bootable floppy diskette in Windows XP Professional that places you at an `A:\>` prompt after bootup?

    A. My Computer ➢ Right-click floppy drive ➢ Click Format ➢ Check *Create an MS-DOS startup disk* ➢ Click Start.

    B. At a Command Prompt, enter the command `format a: /s`.

    C. At a Command Prompt, enter the command `format a: /fs:fat`.

    D. My Computer ➢ Right-click floppy drive ➢ Click Format ➢ Check *Make bootable* ➢ Click Start.

22. A user calls to complain about odd colors in various areas of their monitor. You determine that the user has a CRT display. Which of the following can you suggest to rectify the user's problem?

    A. Have the user degauss the monitor.

    B. Have the user connect an external monitor to see if the problem shows up there as well.

    C. Have the user power-cycle the monitor.

    D. Have the user reboot the system.

GO ON TO THE NEXT PAGE

23. A user is interested in protecting their equipment against power spikes, which have claimed two of their systems already. The user is not interested in keeping the system up during power outages. They simply wish to protect their equipment against harmful power anomalies. Which of the following should you suggest to satisfy the user's requirements?

   A. UPS

   B. Surge protector

   C. Generator

   D. Power strip

24. Which of the following commands allows you to see the physical address of your NIC in Windows XP Professional?

   A. `winipcfg`

   B. `ipconfig /mac`

   C. `ipconfig /all`

   D. `ifconfig`

25. A caller's computer keeps overheating and shutting down. Which of the following is *not* a probable cause?

   A. The client has four hard drives installed.

   B. The CPU fan has stalled.

   C. The chassis cover is removed.

   D. An adapter slot opening is uncovered.

26. A user's machine has lost intranet and Internet access. Which of the following utilities executed on the user's computer is the best to determine if the default gateway is functional?

   A. `nslookup`

   B. `traceroute`

   C. `ping`

   D. `ipconfig`

27. Which of the following is the path to the System Restore utility?

   A. Start ➢ All Programs ➢ Accessories

   B. Start ➢ All Programs

   C. Start ➢ Control Panel

   D. Start ➢ All Programs ➢ Accessories ➢ System Tools

28. What advice would you give to an administrator of a small network that is growing enough to cause the administrator grief as they continue to apply individual permissions to users as new employees come on and needs change in general?

   A. Use Group Policy.

   B. Start placing user accounts in groups, and apply permissions to the groups instead.

   C. Limit permissions to the bare essentials.

   D. Wait until users request permissions.

29. All of the following are recommended laptop troubleshooting techniques *except*:

   A. Remove unneeded peripherals.

   B. Remove the battery.

   C. Remove the AC adapter.

   D. Attach an external monitor.

30. A user with Windows XP Home calls to request assistance setting up a share on their computer. Which of the following is the best response for this user?

   A. Right-click the folder; click Sharing and Security; click Share This Folder.

   B. Folders cannot be shared in XP Home.

   C. Right-click the folder; click Share This Folder.

   D. All folders are shared by default in XP Home and cannot be unshared.

31. While sitting at a `C:\DATA>` prompt, which *two* commands are necessary to change the prompt to `C:\DATA\SUB1>` if the DATA subdirectory currently has no subdirectories?

   A. `CD\SUB1`

   B. `CD SUB1`

   C. `MD C:\SUB1`

   D. `MD SUB1`

32. Which *two* of the following paths take you to Event Viewer?

   A. Start ➢ All Programs ➢ Accessories ➢ System Tools ➢ Event Viewer

   B. Start ➢ Run ➢ `eventvwr.msc`

   C. Control Panel ➢ Administrative Tools ➢ Event Viewer

   D. **Control Panel ➢ Event Viewer**

33. Which of the following is the strongest password?

    A. $ecRet

    B. Secret

    C. SeCrEt

    D. $ecre+

34. Which path takes you to a utility that you can use in conjunction with Terminal Services to create a remote session on another device as if you were local to that machine?

    A. Start ➢ All Programs ➢ Accessories ➢ System Tools

    B. Start ➢ All Programs ➢ Accessories ➢ Communications

    C. Control Panel ➢ Administrative Tools

    D. Start ➢ All Programs

35. Which *two* of the following commands obtain help for the `dir` command?

    A. `dir help`

    B. `help dir`

    C. `dir /?`

    D. `dir /h`

36. Which of the following commands displays a listing of the hidden files and folders in the first-level folder named `data` on drive `E:`?

    A. `dir e:\data /ah`

    B. `dir e:\data /h`

    C. `dir e:\data /ar`

    D. `dir e:\data /x`

37. What is the term that means synchronizing a software battery gauge with the actual battery?

    A. Bsync

    B. Refreshing

    C. Reconciliation

    D. Calibration

38. Which of the following commands clears only the attributes that prevent the file `test.txt` from being deleted at the command line, setting all others?

    A. `attrib test.txt -r +s -h`

    B. `attrib -r +s +h test.txt`

    C. `attrib -r -s -h test.txt`

    D. `attrib test.txt -r -s -h`

39. Which of the following command-line commands allows you to display the contents of a text file without opening it for editing?

    A. `SHOW`

    B. `TYPE`

    C. `PRINT`

    D. `VIEW`

40. Which of the following is a difference between the commands `COPY` and `XCOPY`?

    A. By using the `/Y` switch, you can suppress the prompt to approve the overwriting of existing files with the `XCOPY` command, but not with `COPY`.

    B. `XCOPY` is capable of copying a directory and all of its subdirectories in one command. `COPY` is not.

    C. With the `COPY` command, you are able to specify the source to copy from only, and the destination will have the same name in the current directory. With the `XCOPY` command, you must explicitly specify both source and destination.

    D. The `COPY` command has switches that allow you to copy based on the archive attribute bit. The `XCOPY` command does not.

41. In attempting to use the `CONVERT` command to change the file system, you are not able to perform or confirm the conversion. Which of the following is most likely *not* the issue?

    A. You must reboot to finish the conversion.

    B. You are trying to convert to NTFS, and the volume is already NTFS.

    C. You are running `CONVERT` through Start ➢ Run and using the incorrect syntax.

    D. You executed a syntactically correct command to convert a volume from NTFS to FAT.

42. Which of the following statements about disks, partitions, and logical drives is *not* true?

    A. A drive letter can correspond to either a partition or a logical drive.

    B. One disk can have multiple partitions.

    C. Operating systems based on NT, such as Windows 2000 and XP, can boot from any drive other than `B:`, regardless of its drive letter.

    D. There can be only one extended partition on a disk.

GO ON TO THE NEXT PAGE

43. Which of the following commands is one of the two required at the command line to restart the spooler?

    A. `net stop spooler`
    B. `net spooler /stop`
    C. `net spooler start`
    D. `net restart spooler`

44. What is the term for a partition that has been marked in such a way as to allow it to be made bootable?

    A. Boot-ready
    B. Boot partition
    C. Primary
    D. Active

45. Which of the following gets you to the `C:\level1\level2\level3` directory when the currently logged directory is `C:\level1`?

    A. `cd level2\level3`
    B. `cd level3`
    C. `cd \level2\level3`
    D. `cd \level3`

46. What command would you use to tell if your hard drive needed to be defragmented?

    A. `defrag /a`
    B. `defrag -a`
    C. `defragment -a`
    D. `defragment /v`

47. Which command creates a text file called `test.txt` from the command line and places you into editing mode until you enter the end-of-file character, `^Z`?

    A. `copy test.txt con:`
    B. `copy test.txt con`
    C. `copy con test.txt`
    D. `copy test.txt+con test.txt`

48. Which of the following Windows XP utilities allows you to fix certain disk errors and recover readable information from bad sectors?

    A. FDISK
    B. SCANDISK
    C. CHKDSK
    D. Recovery Console

49. A user calls with a complaint about an inkjet printer that fails to print blue every so often. There are no smudges or smears to speak of, just the occasional loss of blue. Which of the following best explains the cause of the problem?

    A. The blue print cartridge is dirty.
    B. The blue print cartridge is clogged.
    C. The driver has failed.
    D. The interface on the computer or the printer has corroded.

50. Which of the following paths reliably takes you to a utility where you can set services to not start up when XP boots?

    A. Start ➢ Administrative Tools ➢ Services
    B. Start ➢ All Programs ➢ Services
    C. Start ➢ All Programs ➢ Control Panel ➢ Services
    D. Start ➢ Control Panel ➢ Administrative Tools ➢ Services

51. Which *two* of the following paths in Windows XP take you to Windows Explorer?

    A. Right-click the Start button, and then click Explore.
    B. Start ➢ All Programs ➢ Accessories ➢ Windows Explorer.
    C. Start ➢ All Programs ➢ Windows Explorer.
    D. Right-click an unaffiliated area of the Desktop, and then click Explore.

52. In Windows XP, which path accesses Device Manager?

    A. Start ➢ All Programs ➢ Device Manager
    B. Control Panel ➢ Add Hardware ➢ Device Manager
    C. Control Panel ➢ System ➢ Hardware tab ➢ Device Manager
    D. Control Panel ➢ Device Manager

53. What's the easiest way to determine if a device is using DMA channel 2?

    A. Use Device Manager to run through each device in succession, until you find the device using it.
    B. Click View ➢ Devices by Connection in Device Manager.
    C. Click View ➢ Resources by Type in Device Manager.
    D. Open a Command Prompt, and execute the command `net show dma`.

54. Which of the following RAID levels does not employ some form of striping?

    A. 0

    B. 1

    C. 3

    D. 5

55. Which of the following is a session-layer protocol that can be transported using NetBEUI, IPX/SPX, or TCP/IP, the names of which can be converted to IP addresses by WINS for routing over an IP network?

    A. NWLink

    B. AppleTalk

    C. HTTP

    D. NetBIOS

56. All of the following procedures open the Task Manager utility *except*:

    A. Press Ctrl-Alt-Del, and then click the Task Manager button.

    B. Press Ctrl-Alt-Esc.

    C. Press Ctrl-Shift-Esc.

    D. Right-click an unaffiliated portion of the Taskbar, and click Task Manager.

57. A user reports errors on startup related to a specific application that the user needs to continue running when XP starts. Which of the following is the best way to test your theory that a conflict with a recently installed application is to blame?

    A. Use Add or Remove Programs in Control Panel to uninstall the suspected application.

    B. Disable the automatic startup of the suspected application in MSCONFIG.

    C. Use REGEDIT to disable the suspected application.

    D. Use the Recovery Console to test your theory.

58. Where would you most likely find an object named HKEY_LOCAL_MACHINE?

    A. The Registry

    B. My Documents

    C. In the root of the system drive

    D. In `%SystemRoot%\system32`

59. If you want Windows XP to manage virtual memory for you, what should you select?

    A. System Managed Size

    B. No Paging File

    C. Let Windows Choose What's Best for My Computer

    D. Adjust for Best Performance

60. What is the term for a contiguous section of hard drive used to page information in and out of RAM to give the appearance of more RAM than exists?

    A. Expanded memory

    B. Extended memory

    C. Defragmentation

    D. Virtual memory

61. Each time you attempt to make a custom setting to the virtual memory of a computer, click the OK button, and return to check your work, the setting returns to the previous selection. Which of the following is a possible reason for this behavior?

    A. Group Policy prohibits you from making such a change to the virtual memory.

    B. You must click the Set button before clicking the OK button.

    C. You must click the Apply button before clicking the OK button.

    D. Virtual memory is not supported on your computer.

62. In order to use the ASR process, you need each of the following *except*:

    A. The Windows XP distribution disc

    B. A system backup set

    C. The same hard drive the ASR materials were created from

    D. The ASR diskette

GO ON TO THE NEXT PAGE

63. A frazzled user with Windows XP Home Edition calls you lamenting the loss of an important data file that has been deleted. The user has tried in vain to find the file. Which of the following best describes your options for recovery?

    A. Tell the user to use System Restore to roll the system back to a time when the data file was there.

    B. Tell the user to use the ASR process to recover the data file.

    C. Tell the user to use Device Driver Roll Back to return the drive that held the file to its earlier state.

    D. If the file is not in the Recycle Bin, and the user does not have a backup set that includes the file, there may be no way to recover the file.

64. Which of the following battery chemistries is credited with the longest run time in laptops?

    A. LiIon

    B. NiMH

    C. Alkaline

    D. NiCd

65. A user calls to report that their LiIon laptop battery loses its charge twice as fast as it once did. Which of the following represents the best way to handle this situation?

    A. Dispatch a technician with a new laptop.

    B. Replace the user's AC adapter.

    C. Replace the user's battery.

    D. Walk the user through calibrating the battery.

66. You receive a call from a user who has updated a driver. The user has no backup of their system, and now the system boots but fails to make it to the logon screen. Which of the following should you suggest first in order to fix the problem?

    A. Last Known Good Configuration

    B. Safe Mode and System Restore

    C. ASR process

    D. Device Driver Roll Back

67. Which of the following is the best first step to take if you are informed that a service or device failed to start when booting Windows?

    A. Perform a Device Driver Roll Back.

    B. Consult the System category of Event Viewer.

    C. Remove the driver.

    D. Reboot Windows.

68. A computer that boots to an ATA hard drive with only Windows XP installed (no other operating system) fails to boot because of a missing or corrupt file in the root directory of the system partition. Which of the following files could be the problem?

    A. BOOTSECT.DOS

    B. NTBOOTDD.SYS

    C. NTLDR

    D. NTOSKRNL.EXE

69. Which of the following has the best chance of reviving an inaccessible boot drive?

    A. A boot diskette

    B. System Restore

    C. Device Driver Roll Back

    D. Recovery Console

70. During your investigation into why a computer running XP starts up differently, you discover that it has been set for selective startup. Which of the following will return the system to its normal startup behavior?

    A. Click the *Disable All* button on the Startup tab of MSCONFIG.

    B. Select the *Normal Startup* radio button on the General tab of MSCONFIG.

    C. Execute the command net start normal at the Command Prompt.

    D. Enter Startup Options during boot with the F8 key, and choose *Start Windows Normally*.

71. You respond to a service call concerning a computer on which the System File Checker was run. It was intended that the check be done immediately, but it now runs every time the system starts. Which syntax should have been used to run the check one time immediately without needing to restart the system?

- **A.** sfc
- **B.** sfc /scanonce
- **C.** sfc /scannow
- **D.** sfc /scanboot

72. A user calls, stating that their inkjet printer is smudging horizontally and vertically when it prints. Which of the following makes the most sense to try?

- **A.** Use the printer's software utility to clean the print cartridges.
- **B.** Calibrate the printer.
- **C.** Replace the belt for the carriage assembly.
- **D.** Remove the print cartridges, and clean them with a lint-free cloth.

73. If you have a third-party driver that must be installed during the installation of Window XP, which key will you need to press at some point?

- **A.** F2
- **B.** F4
- **C.** F6
- **D.** F8

74. Which of the following has the greatest impact on reducing the amount of time spent on repeat calls and calls for similar symptoms?

- **A.** Test your solution.
- **B.** Be courteous to the customer, and listen actively.
- **C.** Escalate the problem to someone with more expertise.
- **D.** Document the problem and your resolution.

75. No one at your site is able to access network resources. Your IP address scheme dictates that the DHCP server should place everyone on the 172.16.*x.x* network. However, closer inspection shows that each computer you look at has an address on the 169.254.*x.x* network. What is the likely issue here?

- **A.** Everyone is drawing addresses from the wrong DHCP server.
- **B.** The DHCP server is down.
- **C.** TCP/IP has not been installed on any of the machines yet.
- **D.** The default-gateway router is down.

76. You call the network administrator to find out the subnet mask for one of the IP subnets in the enterprise network. They inform you that it is /28. Which of the following is /28 equivalent to?

- **A.** 255.255.255.0
- **B.** 255.255.255.192
- **C.** 255.255.255.240
- **D.** 255.255.255.252

77. Which of the following is a Microsoft protocol that is compatible with a protocol suite created by Novell?

- **A.** IPX
- **B.** NetBEUI
- **C.** NWLink
- **D.** SPX

78. Which of the following is the more robust of two protocols that facilitate the transfer of any file type from one IP host to another?

- **A.** Telnet
- **B.** FTP
- **C.** TFTP
- **D.** HTTP

79. Which *two* of the following technologies provide access rates higher than dial-up but use the same copper pair as dial-up, sometimes with very little conditioning?

    A. DSL

    B. Cable

    C. ISDN

    D. Cellular

80. Your supervisor is soliciting your advice on which authentication technology you think would be best for your computer systems. The supervisor is interested in a technology that requires each user to have something physical as well as to have to remember a personal password. Which of the following should you recommend?

    A. Biometrics

    B. Smart card

    C. Token card

    D. USB token

ontreasonёE

ography soul

Practice Test 2

Answer Key for Practice Test 2

1. D
2. B
3. AB
4. C
5. A
6. D
7. B
8. C
9. D
10. D
11. B
12. A
13. B
14. C
15. A
16. C
17. D
18. C
19. B
20. D

21. A
22. A
23. B
24. C
25. A
26. C
27. D
28. B
29. C
30. A
31. BD
32. BC
33. A
34. B
35. BC
36. A
37. D
38. C
39. B
40. B

41. D
42. C
43. A
44. D
45. A
46. B
47. C
48. C
49. B
50. D
51. AB
52. C
53. C
54. B
55. D
56. B
57. B
58. A
59. A
60. D

61. B
62. C
63. D
64. A
65. C
66. A
67. B
68. C
69. D
70. B
71. C
72. A
73. C
74. D
75. B
76. C
77. C
78. B
79. AC
80. C

235

Answer Explanations for Practice Test 2

1. D. Social engineering is a breach of security that exploits at least one party's trust of credentials that the instigator acquires through dishonest means, often for personal gain or to attack the resources of the target, possibly to degrade the performance of the network. Most often, a social-engineering attack occurs without the attacker coming face-to-face with the target. You'll be able to spot social engineering if you look for the two parts: credentials the attacker acquired in a live social event, and the use of these credentials to fool a gatekeeper between the attacker and the targeted resources. Cracking passwords and sabotage do not exemplify this concept by themselves. Talking a coworker into improving their privileges is called being a good friend.

2. B. This is a problem with the physical backup mechanism, not with the media and not with operator privileges. Backup systems prompt for additional media or automatically switch media until the backup is complete. Therefore, tapes that are too small are not the issue. Damaged tapes generate errors during the backup procedure. In this case, because the write heads need to be cleaned, and the read heads do not, the system believes that the data is writing properly because it is able to synchronize its positioning during the write phase, and the issue is not revealed until the verification phase.

3. AB. Although bubble-jet printers heat the ink to form a bubble, other inkjet printers use different methods to print. Beyond a doubt, the fuser in a laser printer and the print head in a thermal printer use heat to function. Impact printers strike a ribbon in front of the paper to leave an imprint.

4. C. A full waste-toner receptacle is not a common cause of issues with laser printers, although it could cause problems with the cleaning cycle. However, unless the user refills their cartridges with fresh toner, cartridges that hold both fresh and waste toners are engineered to run out of fresh toner before the waste-toner receptacle fills. As a result, the second-best answer is to replace the toner cartridge, which also replaces the waste-toner receptacle. Maintenance kits do not treat toner issues, and there is usually no way to empty the waste-toner receptacle.

5. A. Long before having any display unit opened, make sure the display is really bad. Opening an LCD or CRT monitor's case is a last resort and should be left to a qualified technician because of the dangers lurking within. Flyback transformers are extremely dangerous but exist only on CRT monitors. Related to good customer relations, don't ask a user who has been using an external monitor to try to get by with the built-in monitor unless it is an extremely temporary fix and there is no functional reason why the user has been using an external monitor. In some cases, a user's job requirements necessitate the use of a monitor that exceeds the quality or capabilities of the one built into a laptop, preventing them from being productive with the internal display.

6. D. The `ping` utility was designed to test the availability of a remote IP host. As a byproduct, it also tests a potentially unknown portion of the network between the source and destination of the ping, potentially unknown because IP traffic is capable of traversing any path between any two devices at any given time. Only if there is a single path between the devices can you be sure which part of the network is being tested with the `ping` utility. It tests only intermediate connectivity in addition to destination-host availability. The `traceroute` utility does all of this as well as identifying intermediate devices (routers) in between. The `ipconfig` and `winipcfg` utilities, among others, identify the local device's addressing. The Address Resolution Protocol (ARP) identifies a remote device's MAC address.

7. B. This issue is caused when the local device is set to obtain its IP address automatically and no DHCP server is available from which to acquire an address. APIPA is the term used for this type of auto-configuration from the 169.254.0.0 reserved Class B network. There can be many reasons why the computer is not acquiring an address from a DHCP server. The best clue on the computer comes from the lack of an illuminated LED on the NIC, which can point to the NIC or the device to which it is directly connected, such as a hub or switch. If the NIC appears normal, the problem lies outside the computer. However, a nonfunctional default gateway is not likely the issue unless it doubles as the DHCP server. Regardless, pinging the default gateway is not possible when it does not have an auto-configured address. It constitutes poor design to allow any interface on a router to auto-configure, so it's not likely to be reachable when your computer has one of these addresses. Any existing icon in the notification area (System Tray) will remain there when the computer uses APIPA to configure itself, so that's not a reliable troubleshooting method. Because the problem lies with the local device giving itself an address with a local scope, DNS resolution is not an issue and does not need to be tested. When your computer has one of these addresses, attempting to contact a remote device by name or address is virtually guaranteed to fail.

8. C. The devices with the fastest response time—the hard drives—should be placed on one of the two controllers. There are only two controllers. Devices on the same controller once synchronized with one another and were limited to the performance of the slowest device. Although this is not true with newer devices and controllers, one device in a master/slave pair must wait for the other to finish its use of the channel before it can transfer data on the same channel. The result is that slower devices can cause a faster device to have to wait longer for channel access. Therefore, the slower two devices—the optical drives—should be placed together on the other controller.

9. D. Pre-XP operating systems used the Emergency Repair Disk (ERD). XP uses a process known as Automated System Recovery (ASR). The ASR disk is used in conjunction with the ASR process to access a backup archive for completely restoring the system to the state of the latest backup. As a result, your backup should not be stored on the same physical drive as the one you are archiving. Although the Recovery Console is an incredible utility for a nuts-and-bolts surgical resurrection of a failed system, damaged partitions are best recovered using ASR when available. System Restore requires a working system and is generally best used for rolling back drivers and application settings to a state when the system was stable.

10. D. In a case like this, rule out any option that would affect connectivity with devices on your local subnet and any remote subnet equally. Windows Firewall does not discriminate based on IP subnet. Although not the most likely culprit, a downed DHCP server could cause such an issue. If the local device has an APIPA address, one in the 169.254.0.0 network, then it's not getting an address assigned by the DHCP server and is auto-configuring. If all devices on the local subnet are doing the same thing, and if you're using these APIPA addresses to ping the remote devices, the pings will be successful on the local link. When you need to get the router involved to ping outside your own subnet, a couple of things can go wrong. One possibility is that you will ping a remote device's APIPA address, and your computer will think it is local and try to deliver it directly without the router. Another possibility is that you will ping the remote device's appropriate address through the default router, and your APIPA address will prevent the other device from replying to your echo request through the router. The problem with this scenario is that, as an informed technician, you would not try to ping other APIPA addresses. The huge red flag would stop you before you tried that. Once you saw an APIPA address on your machine and any other local device, you would be on a dead-DHCP hunt, not trying to ping anything. Generally, a misconfigured subnet mask affects local connectivity as well. Your computer places itself on one subnet and places some or all of the local devices on a different subnet. Usually, in the situation described in the question, you will find that the local router (the gateway router) has an incorrect routing table, which could be due to misconfiguration of it or one of its neighbor routers. Because the router is not instrumental in helping you deliver traffic on your local subnet, its incorrect routing table does not affect local delivery.

11. B. You must press F6 when prompted during Windows installation to install SCSI drivers. There is no browse function, so you must know where the drivers are located on the disk you specify. F2 begins the ASR process, and F8 is used during bootup, not setup, to access the Startup Options screen. F12 has no function to speak of.

12. A. Most BIOS routines include a warning threshold for CPU temperature as well as, on occasion, ambient temperature inside the case. They also include a higher cutoff temperature that causes the system to shut down to avoid damage. However, this is not a problem with the BIOS. It's a feature. For the overall health of the system, the BIOS simply maintains vigilance over the CPU, which generates more heat than any other component in a computer. It is most often a failure of the CPU's fan that causes the temperature to rise enough to set off the temperature warning.

13. B. Clumps of dust, dead fans, and blockages of normal airflow are all causes of overheating to the point of a computer shutting itself down for safety. Although some memory modules, especially Rambus modules, call for heat sinks, lack of memory heat sinks is less likely to be the cause of such catastrophic overheating.

14. C. You will find in the majority of cases like this that components that were once working do not cease to work simply because a motherboard was upgraded. Certainly, CPUs and memory modules must be compatible with the new motherboard, but those are not mentioned here. The new motherboard could be defective, but that's not an option either. Therefore, existing cards in any quantity, the power button, and the power supply are likely to be fine. When you change out a motherboard, be absolutely certain that you remove *all* standoffs from the chassis before installing the new motherboard. One errant brass standoff can have disastrous effects if it shorts the underside of the motherboard. Although there are quite a few standards, regarding the location of holes in the motherboard for securing hardware placement, not all positions are used in every motherboard. Again, it takes only one standoff to be left where there is no longer a hole in the motherboard to cause a short. Treat every motherboard installation as a fresh start, and don't try to cut corners. You can destroy quite a few components, otherwise.

15. A. There is no relationship between the number of processors in the system and the amount of RAM that can be accessed. It's a matter of how the operating system is written. You can't access more than 4GB of RAM with the 32-bit version of XP, but with the 64-bit version, you can access up to a whopping 128GB of RAM. Advanced operating systems employ tricks to circumvent the 4GB limitation of the 32-bit address bus width of most modern CPUs. The following table lists the maximum number of processors and the maximum physical RAM for the various modern Windows operating systems.

Windows Operating System	Maximum Processors	Maximum Physical RAM
XP Professional	2	4GB
XP Professional x64 Edition	2	128GB
Server 2003 Standard Edition	4	4GB
Server 2003 Standard x64 Edition	4	32GB
Server 2003 Enterprise Edition	8	64GB
Server 2003 Enterprise x64 Edition	8	1TB
Server 2003 Datacenter Edition	32	128GB
Server 2003 Datacenter x64 Edition	32	1TB
2000 Professional	2	4GB
2000 Server	4	4GB
2000 Advanced Server	8	8GB
2000 Datacenter Server	32	32GB

16. C. Of those listed, only infrared and the CD burner have a chance here without further adjustment. The serial cable must be a null modem cable, not a standard cable. Regardless, infrared is more convenient than burning a CD or using the null modem cable. Bluetooth can be used, with appropriate utilities, to perform this function, but it is more often used as a cord-replacement technology. Windows XP SP2 has the Bluetooth File Transfer Wizard, but both machines must have Bluetooth capability, which is not yet commonly built in to laptops the way infrared is. As this trend continues to change, Bluetooth will likely become the best option here.

17. D. The bottom line is that you can use the 8.3 naming convention in any Microsoft file system. It is required in FAT and exists behind the scenes of long names in FAT32. NTFS does not use it to store files, but that doesn't stop you from naming a file using the convention, which is all the option alluded to. The other options are absolutely distinguishing characteristics. Another major difference is the file-level security available in NTFS that is not available in either version of FAT. The following table details the differences.

File System	Maximum Volume Size	Maximum File Size
FAT	4GB	2GB
FAT32	Format to 32GB; read/write to 2TB	4GB
NTFS	16TB or more	As large as the volume

18. C. No, don't use Safe Mode from now on. Life can't possibly be bad enough for that. Doing so would not satisfy the requirement of getting the system working properly again. To get out of Safe Mode, however, you must fix the driver issue. The most straightforward and noninvasive method for doing that when you know the driver to blame is Device Driver Roll Back, which is accessed through Device Manager. ASR and System Restore are overkill in this situation. ASR rolls *everything* back to the time when the backup was performed with the creation of the ASR disk, and System Restore rolls back all drivers and application settings to the restore point you choose. You cannot be certain that this driver will be the only thing affected on this user's machine when the user runs either of these utilities. Save these big guns for when more needs to be rolled back or for when you are not sure what needs rolling back.

19. B. In the ICMP Settings dialog, accessible on the Advanced page in Windows Firewall, you can allow or disallow each type of ICMP message, including incoming echo requests (pings). Windows XP installs with almost everything disabled for security purposes and leaves the ball in your court to enable what you want. ICMP traffic is disabled by default. The default router plays no part in forwarding traffic to other devices on your local subnet. A standalone firewall does not separate you from others on your subnet. Like routers, firewalls attach to a different subnet on each interface. The DNS angle could be a possibility if you weren't pinging by IP address. DNS converts names to IP addresses and is not called on if you don't use a name and don't request reverse lookup to discover a name based on an IP address. Although a reverse lookup is performed by default with a ping, a failed reverse lookup does not cause a failed ping.

20. D. This is certainly a hot topic, and although you must weigh the intent of the user against the fact that it is against the law to use unauthorized software, in this case you cannot be sure that the law has been broken (yet). Tell the user you need to install the software from the original CD because it is generally regarded as legal to make at least one exact copy of a distribution disc, in order to protect your investment against damage to the original, provided the holder of the copy is the registered owner of the original. This will gracefully allow the user to produce the legal disc or withdraw their request. You must not be party to knowingly installing software from the same distribution disc in more than one location simultaneously, unless the customer's company holds a site license for the software and you can confirm that the company has not reached the maximum number of installed copies. Your role is to refuse to assist in installing such software, educate the user to the fact that such behavior is illegal, and suggest that the illegal copy be destroyed. Make sure the user understands that illegal software could cost the company in fines and lost productivity; upgrades and security updates normally cannot installed on a bootlegged installation. In this case, especially if the user does not appear to be a habitual offender, bringing management or law enforcement into the picture could lead to a strained relationship and indicates questionable confidentiality on your part. Nevertheless, if you feel the law is being broken intentionally and without remorse, you have a civic duty to report the crime, which is not victimless. The market suffers from higher prices for the product, and the integrity of the software can be unfairly brought into question by observers if it fails to function normally.

21. A. Windows XP Professional has no command-line method of creating a bootable diskette. However, XP still maintains the system files required to create a DOS boot disk. You must format the diskette through the GUI. You can access the Format dialog by right-clicking the floppy icon in My Computer and selecting Format from the shortcut menu. Be sure to select the check box beside *Create an MS-DOS startup disk* in order to make the diskette bootable. Creating floppies that cause the system to boot to a particular system disk (hard drive) is a matter of copying the right files to the floppy and editing the BOOT.INI file properly. Control does not remain assigned to the floppy drive the way that it does for a DOS boot disk. There is no such thing as a floppy diskette that boots to the floppy drive's prompt while running the XP operating system; MS-DOS is required for such behavior.

22. A. This is a common result of the Gaussian effect. The shadow mask on the CRT monitor can develop a magnetic field and cause the cathode rays to be bent before striking the dot phosphors, causing them to excite the wrong dots. This results in discoloration, often in the form of a rainbow or oil-slick effect. Degaussing the monitor is the way to reverse this effect. If you're dealing with a CRT, you're already working with an external monitor, and although switching one external monitor out for another is not a bad troubleshooting technique, doing so would not be the appropriate first step here. Because the Gaussian effect follows the monitor and not the computer, you may believe you've solved the issue, but all you've done is condemn an innocent monitor and set yourself up for a repeat call when the new monitor begins exhibiting the same symptoms down the road. Rebooting the system won't have any effect, and power-cycling the monitor will have only a slight effect. Each time the monitor powers on, it performs a less-effective degaussing, which won't boast the longer-lasting result of a controlled degaussing. One note about degaussing: Don't perform more than one degauss in a short period of time. You can damage the monitor.

23. B. Surge protectors are not perfect and should be removed from the wall outlet during electrical storms to protect them and the equipment connected to them. They have varistors that take the brunt of the various inconsistencies found in "dirty" power but do nothing for power loss or brownouts. Their role is to make sure that common power spikes are clipped before they do cumulative damage to sensitive electronic equipment. You should keep an eye on the indicator, if one exists, to tell when the internal protection components are no longer able to do their job. When the protector has run its course, you should replace it immediately. Some UPS units protect equipment in the same way by using the raw power input to constantly charge the battery, which provides the attached equipment with pure power that remains consistent. However, the user does not need the power preservation that a UPS provides. A generator is like a UPS without the power conditioning and provides power only during a power outage. Generators do nothing under normal circumstances to match the capabilities of a surge protector. Power strips are passive outlet multipliers that offer no protection.

24. C. The `winipcfg` utility has not been available since the Windows 9*x* generation. To view similar information, you must abandon the GUI approach and execute the `ipconfig` command at the Command Prompt with the `/all` switch. There is no `/mac` switch for the `ipconfig` command. `ifconfig` is a UNIX command and is not available in Windows.

25. A. To varying degrees, each option alone is capable of raising the temperature within the case. The presence of four hard drives is not capable of increasing the internal temperature to a dangerous level; the other conditions are. If the case will accommodate four hard drives, it should be engineered to cool four hard drives.

26. C. Executing a ping with the default gateway (local router) as the destination is the most logical choice here. Regardless of the number of switches or hubs between the user's computer and the egress router, a ping is a Layer 3 message to which Layer 1 and Layer 2 devices are transparent. Therefore, a ping gets right down to business and involves no other devices in your query. If it is successful, you know the router is healthy. If not, the user's machine, the router, or anything in between, including cabling, may be faulty. A traceroute can yield the same results but is overkill compared to a ping. Traceroutes are designed to identify all Layer 3 devices between the source and destination. In this case, there are none because the user's default gateway is on the same LAN as their computer. `nslookup` is for DNS issues or tests. `ipconfig` only tells you the default gateway address that has been configured on your network interface card, not whether it is responsive.

27. D. The System Restore utility is in the System Tools folder under Accessories and cannot be accessed directly from Control Panel.

28. B. Account groups are an advisable tool for even the smallest of networks that expect growth in the future. Even if the administrator starts out with only one user in the majority of the groups, they will be able to add new users to existing groups later, and all rights and restrictions afforded that group will apply to the new users immediately. Group Policy is much more advanced and possibly not a good fit for a smaller network. Besides, groups should be established before using Group Policy. Limiting permissions or dealing with an onslaught of requests for permissions is not a solution and will spiral out of control in time.

29. C. Although occasionally you will need to swap out the AC adapter during troubleshooting, removing the AC adapter alone is not generally considered a worthwhile troubleshooting step. Doing so requires that the laptop run solely on battery power, which is not recommended. In fact, a common step is to remove the battery because it can adversely affect power delivery to the laptop. Adapters are ordinarily either good or bad, whereas batteries can appear good but actually affect the power and functionality of the laptop. Switch out adapters and remove batteries when troubleshooting. Be aware that batteries can cause problems that do not appear to be related to power. Just as the battery can cause puzzling symptoms, so can many removable peripherals. If you don't need them during troubleshooting, remove them. The external monitor is ideal to diagnose built-in video issues.

30. A. Folders most certainly can be shared in XP Home Edition. XP Home uses a form of file sharing comparable to XP Professional's simple file sharing, which allows you to share folders but not limit access by user accounts. Your only choice once you share a folder is whether users will be able to change the contents of the folder. You share out a folder in XP Home in the same manner that you share it out in XP Professional. The first time you set up sharing on XP Home, you need to run the Network Setup Wizard. After that, you can share any folder by right-clicking it and selecting Sharing and Security to get to the Sharing page of the Properties for the folder.

31. BD. From the question, you can discern that the first-level subdirectory on the `C:` drive named `DATA`, which has no subdirectories of its own, is the currently logged directory. The `MD`, or `MKDIR`, command creates directories. The `CD`, or `CHDIR`, command changes the currently logged directory to the one you specify. The `RD`, or `RMDIR`, command removes directories. With no subdirectories under `DATA` yet, you must create the `SUB1` directory before you can make it the currently logged directory. The `MD SUB1` command creates the `SUB1` directory within the currently logged directory. This is equivalent to each of the following: `MD C:\DATA\SUB1`, `MD \DATA\SUB1`, `MD .\SUB1`, `MD ..\DATA\SUB1`, and so on. The first command in the list uses what is considered an absolute path: one that works from any logged directory because both the drive and the root-based path are specified (the first backslash, which specifies the root directory, is included). The other commands use relative paths that draw on the currently logged directory, the currently logged drive, or both to fill in the details left out. The command `MD C:\SUB1` may look similar, but it uses an absolute path that will not create a subdirectory in the `DATA` directory. It specifies that a first-level directory named `SUB1` be created on the `C:` drive directly in the root, which will be on the same level as the `DATA` directory, not beneath it as the question requires. The `CD SUB1` command, when executed next, draws on the `C:` and `\DATA` parameters of the currently logged directory and causes the prompt (`C:\DATA\SUB1>`) to reflect the newly logged directory, satisfying the requirements of the question. The command `CD\SUB1` uses a relative path that draws on only `C:` because the leading backslash directs the command not to draw on the currently logged directory and instead start at the root and find the `SUB1` directory, which is not at the root—it's under the `DATA` directory. Note that dropping the backslash produces the correct answer and causes the command to draw on the currently logged directory. Using `CD` in place of `MD` in each of the alternative commands listed earlier also works in this case.

32. BC. The Event Viewer can be found in Administrative Tools, which can be found in Control Panel. There is no separate applet in Control Panel for Event Viewer, and Event Viewer is not a System Tools accessory. The MSC file is called `EVENTVWR.MSC` and can be executed from a Command Prompt. Search for `*.msc` on your hard drive to find additional consoles that can be brought up from a prompt.

33. A. The password *$ecRet* contains three elements—lowercase, uppercase, and special characters—making it the strongest of the options. A fourth character type is numeric, which none of the options has. The password *Secret* contains only two elements, as do *SeCrEt* and *$ecre+*. Although *$ecre+* appears highly secure, with its two special characters, the only other character type it possesses is lowercase. Add uppercase and numbers to make it even stronger.

34. B. The utility is Remote Desktop Connection, which uses the same destination TCP port as a Terminal Services client. It resides in the Communications accessories folder.

35. BC. The `HELP` command and the `/?` switch are two ways to obtain command-line assistance with almost any command. There is no `/h` switch for the `DIR` command, and `/h` does not generally produce help for commands.

36. A. When you use the `dir` command without any switches, files and folders with the hidden or system attribute are not displayed. To specify the attributes that files and folders must have to be displayed, you must use the `/a` switch followed immediately by or separated by a colon from one or more attribute letters. The letter for hidden objects is h. Therefore, the correct command is `dir e:\data /ah`. The `/ar` switch displays only read-only objects. The `/x` switch displays short names for non-8.3 filenames as well as the long name for each object. There is no `/h` switch for the `dir` command. If you would like to limit output to files and folders that have both the hidden and system attributes set, for example, the correct switch is `/ahs` or `/a:hs`.

37. D. Although LiIon batteries do not form a chemical memory per se, they do suffer from irreversible life-robbing oxidation. When the battery has a significant charge, this oxidation is exacerbated by heat, such as that generated by the laptop in which the battery is installed or by leaving the battery in the car exposed to ambient heat. Although there is no cure for this effect and the fact that the battery has a finite life expectancy, the effect also has a bearing on how Windows' battery gauge interprets the battery's remaining charge. Calibrating the battery, which really means calibrating Windows' gauge or synchronizing the gauge with the battery, involves allowing the battery to discharge completely once in every 30 charging cycles until the laptop loses power. Doing so keeps the gauge more accurate, and users who watch their gauge vigilantly will not be caught off guard. However, if the battery does not keep an adequate charge, it should be replaced with a new one.

38. C. With respect to the attributes read-only (r), system (s), and hidden (h), setting each one alone or setting any combination of the three prevents a file from being deleted at the command line. You must clear all three in order to delete the file. Because you were not told which attributes were set, you have to play it safe and clear them all, which is easy to do because a minus (−) does not toggle the setting. It clears it or keeps it cleared. Issuing the command `attrib /?` shows that the switches must come before the filename.

39. B. The `TYPE` command displays the contents of a text file on the screen. The `PRINT` command sends a similar file to the printer. The `VIEW` and `SHOW` commands do not exist.

40. B. One of `XCOPY`'s hallmarks is its ability to copy full trees of directory structure, using the `/S` and `/E` switches. Another is its ability to pay attention to the archive attribute bit, using the `/A` and `/M` switches, unlike the way one of the incorrect answers states that `COPY` had this capability. Although it is a difference, the statement is not accurate. Both commands allow implicit destinations.

41. D. The `CONVERT` utility allows a one-way conversion of file systems from FAT to NTFS. Therefore, there's no way to execute a syntactically correct command to convert from NTFS to FAT, making that option impossible. If the `CONVERT` utility cannot gain exclusive control over the volume, it may require a reboot to complete the conversion. If you execute the `CONVERT D: /FS:NTFS` command and `D:` is already an NTFS volume, you receive an error, and the utility ends. Running the utility using Run in the Start menu can work; but entering an incorrect command causes a Command Prompt window to flash open and disappear, perhaps leading you to believe something productive happened when, in fact, nothing did.

42. C. The correct answer is almost true. Since NT came along, the business of booting only from drive `C:` has been relaxed. It's not even a limitation of the drive letter. The drive you boot to can be anything other than `B:`, which is reserved for the second floppy drive. Even when you swap in the BIOS, the system still thinks it is booting from `A:` when it boots from the second floppy. The issue with this answer, then, is that only primary partitions are bootable. A logical drive created on an extended partition is not bootable. So, it's not the *drive letter* part that makes it incorrect. It's the *any drive* part.

43. A. Restarting the spooler from the command line involves first stopping the Spooler service and then starting it. The command to stop it is `net stop spooler`. The command to start it is `net start spooler`. This process may be necessary on occasion if printing fails consistently.

44. D. To be bootable, a partition must be marked active. Only primary partitions can be marked active, but there can be as many as three primary partitions with only one being active at a time. So, neither *active* nor *primary* is synonymous with *bootable*, but you would not mark a partition as active without the intent of making it bootable. Once the partition is marked active, some form of formatting must be performed to transfer the system files to the partition. The *boot* partition, in Microsoft parlance, is the partition that contains the system files that complete the boot process and run Windows for the remainder of the session. Counterintuitively, the bootable partition is called the *system* partition. *Boot-ready* is not a valid term.

45. A. What's needed here is a relative path that gets you from the currently logged folder to another one two levels deeper and beneath the current one. This means you do not have to specify an absolute path that includes the drive letter; but if you do, it must start at the root and include all four subdirectories. None of the options do this. Relative paths do not start with a backslash, which eliminates half of the options. Therefore, the command that works is `cd level2\level3`. The command `cd level3` has a relative path but suggests that the subdirectory `level3` is directly below `level1`, which is not true. The command with the absolute path that works is `cd \level1\level2\level3\level4`. Feel free to add `C:` in front of any of these commands, but it's redundant and is assumed when left off.

46. B. The command `defrag -a` analyzes the currently logged drive and reports on its need for defragmentation. Leaving off the switch performs the defragmentation.

47. C. The `con:` device represents the keyboard for input and the video display for output. It can be used in the `COPY` command to represent input from the keyboard when placed in the source position of the command. Because source comes before destination in commands that copy from one location to another, versions with `con:` last are incorrect. The `con:` device can be specified in the `COPY` command without the colon, making `COPY CON TEST.TXT` the correct answer. The command `COPY TEST.TXT+CON TEST.TXT` appends input from the keyboard to the `test.txt` file and writes the results to the same file.

48. **C.** SCANDISK is not offered with XP, but CHKDSK is, and it offers the features listed in the question by using the /F and /R switches, respectively. FDISK manages partitions, and the Recovery Console gives you access to CHKDSK but does not fix errors and recover data in and of itself.

49. **B.** By far the most likely cause of this problem is a clogged cartridge. Clogged cartridges can cause intermittent failures. A dirty cartridge has a build-up of materials, such as ink, paper, and dust, and causes smudging or streaking. Cleaning will generally solve both problems, but a clogged cartridge may be harder to fix with software or physical cleaning. If the clog is bad enough, replacement of the cartridge may be the only solution. Working drivers don't really fail. If they do, they fail big—not by dropping out a single color intermittently, but by making it easy to believe there *is* life on Mars and that the inhabitants are communicating through your printer. Corroded contacts are rare as well, in all but the harshest of environments. Their failure would likely be complete, or would at least take you back to the Martians again.

50. **D.** The Services utility is found in Administrative Tools, which may be available from various locations, some of them listed in the wrong answers to this question. You can always find Administrative Tools in Control Panel.

51. **AB.** Windows Explorer is basically the GUI environment of Windows. The explorer.exe process runs as long as Windows is running properly. However, in the GUI, Windows Explorer is also a utility similar to My Computer, adding a directory tree to its view. Both utilities are based on explorer.exe. To confirm that, run each one individually, go to the Applications tab, right-click the related application for the utility you're running this time, and click Go To Process. Notice that you are taken directly to the Processes tab, and the explorer.exe process is highlighted. Only the two correct answers launch the explorer.exe process.

52. **C.** The Device Manager button is on the Hardware tab in System Properties, which is labeled System in Control Panel.

53. **C.** There is no such command as net show, and *Devices by Connection* doesn't show you what you need in Device Manager. Between the only two valid answers, shun brute force and let the answer fall in your lap with the *Resources by Type* view in Device Manager.

54. **B.** RAID 0 is a striped array without fault tolerance. It is a way to create a larger volume without using a single larger disk. Just as with a single larger disk, the striped array is an "all for one" situation. If one disk in the array fails, the whole array is lost. This is analogous to the single disk developing an error in only a portion of the disk that makes the entire disk unusable. RAID 3 and RAID 5 are very similar in that they are both fault tolerant, they both stripe data, and they both require a minimum of three disks in the array. They differ in their method of storing parity information. RAID 3 stores all parity information on a single disk. RAID 5 stripes the parity information in with the data across all disks. RAID 1 supports mirroring and duplexing, which is fault tolerance, but there is no striping or parity—just exact copies of the data stored on another disk, possibly connected to another controller.

55. **D.** NetBIOS is an API that specifies device names in a Microsoft environment. It corresponds to the session layer of the OSI model and requires lower-layer protocols to transport it. NetBEUI is a nonroutable transport/network-layer protocol that allows NetBIOS to be networked locally on a LAN. NetBIOS can be routed when converted and transported over the routable IPX/SPX and TCP/IP. NWLink is Microsoft's implementation of IPX/SPX. HTTP is a TCP/IP-only protocol at the application layer. AppleTalk is a suite of protocols similar to IPX/SPX and TCP/IP that work together at the various layers to perform the same type of data communications function.

56. **B.** Pressing Ctrl-Alt-Esc has the same effect as Alt-Esc, which cycles among nonminimized windows on the Desktop, including dialogs that do not appear on the Taskbar. The other three methods bring up Task Manager.

57. **B.** The Startup tab in MSCONFIG is ideal for performing selective startup by disabling the automatic startup of specific applications and then performing a reboot until you have exhausted all options or until you have proven that a specific application is causing a conflict. Uninstalling the application is not recommended, because it may not be the culprit. Reinstalling the application can be time consuming, and you must consider the danger of data loss. REGEDIT should be used only as a last resort: Changes are immediate, and system instability can result with no warning prior to the failed bootup, sometimes necessitating reinstallation of the operating system and causing severe data loss. The Recovery Console is meant for low-level file system recovery operations, not application-conflict testing.

58. A. HKEY_LOCAL_MACHINE is one of five Registry hives, not a folder found on a hard drive. Use REGEDIT to see the contents of this hive.

59. A. In the Virtual Memory dialog, you have three choices: Custom Size, System Managed Size, and No Paging File. System Managed Size creates or keeps the paging file, which is a must for virtual memory to exist, and uses an algorithm to choose the optimal size for the paging file. *Let Windows Choose What's Best for My Computer* and *Adjust for Best Performance* are selections on the Visual Effects tab of the Performance Options dialog and have nothing to do with virtual memory.

60. D. Expanded memory is physical memory that pages contents into RAM when needed. It has nothing to do with the hard drive, though. Extended memory is linear physical memory that extends from around the 1MB mark upward. All systems today technically have extended memory, but modern Windows operating systems no longer use this designation. Defragmentation makes files on a hard drive contiguous but has nothing to do with the contiguous swap file, or paging file, of virtual memory, which is never allowed to become fragmented.

61. B. You must click the Set button in the Virtual Memory dialog before clicking the OK button to close the Virtual Memory dialog. Failing to do so has the same affect as clicking the Cancel button, which ignores your changes even if you click the Set button first. The necessary sequence to save your changes is Set and then OK. If Group Policy were an issue here, you would not be able to think you had made changes to begin with; and all Windows computers that allow you to see the virtual-memory settings support virtual memory. One of the distracters in this question plays on the common misconception that in dialogs with both an Apply button and an OK button, you must first click Apply, which means "save my changes and keep the dialog open," before clicking OK, which means "save my changes and close the dialog." You need to click OK only if you're done making changes. There is no Apply button in the Virtual Memory dialog.

62. C. The ASR process is ideal for situations in which the physical drive is not available, whether due to total loss or just for data transfer. Of course, if the original drive is healthy and available, there is nothing wrong with using the same drive. An ASR recovery requires any destination hard drive; the ASR diskette; a corresponding backup set, which should be as complete as possible; and the original Windows XP distribution disc. You begin the ASR process is begun by pressing the F2 key at the prompted moment after booting with the XP distribution disc, as if you were installing the operating system. ASR sets up a limited Windows installation and then looks for the backup set referenced by the ASR diskette to restore the system to its original state.

63. D. Unfortunately, in this case, if you cannot find the file in the Recycle Bin and the user has not been diligent with their data backups, the file may be all but lost forever. Although there are third-party utilities that can go deeper into the file system as long as that physical location on the disk has not been reused, CompTIA does not mention these in their objectives, and the success of such utilities is never guaranteed. System Restore is useful only for driver and application-settings rollback, not data recovery. The ASR process is not available on XP Home Edition; and in other environments where it is available, if only the ASR disk was created and no data backup was created in conjunction with it, you will wind up with a simplified installation of Windows. A complete backup set is required to return the system to its pre-backup state. As you may already know, drivers have nothing to do with drives; the two words just sound similar. Device Driver Roll Back will have no effect here.

64. A. In order of higher energy density to lower, the technologies are alkaline, LiIon, NiMH, and NiCd. Energy density and capacities, measured in milliamp-hours (mAh), can be misleading. They are fairly proportional to runtime, but only if you match the application to the battery chemistry. When the wrong battery is used, its stats don't mean much. Alkaline batteries can be rated at 2500mAh and higher; but when subjected to high-current drains, these batteries do not last as long as a LiIon battery with less than half the capacity. Therefore, in a hypothetical laptop application, you can expect LiIon to outlast the other technologies.

65. C. In this case, the battery is most definitely the culprit, not the laptop or AC adapter. There would be no value in replacing the laptop or adapter. Calibrating the battery helps when the operating system does not accurately represent the charge left. It can also extend the life of the battery if it's done regularly, starting early in the battery's life. When a LiIon battery begins to exhibit the symptoms shown here, there is little value in starting or continuing calibration with the hope of increasing the performance of the battery. Replacing the battery is the wisest choice and likely the only thing that will help.

66. A. The best way to handle this problem, as well as system lock-ups, auto-restarts, and repeated bluescreen errors, is to have the user hit F8 while booting to access the Startup Options screen. This screen contains a number of choices, including Safe Mode, Safe Mode with Networking, and Last Known Good Configuration (LKGC), among others. Whenever the user logs on, the Registry location that LKGC draws from is updated with the system's current settings. Because the system last made it to this point and the user logged on before the suspect driver was updated, there is an excellent chance that LKGC will be successful in returning the system to a working state. If LKGC does not work, you can have the user boot into Safe Mode and perform a System Restore. You may not want the user to do this first because it will change the LKGC settings, and there may not be a valid restore point set, leaving a clean install with total data loss as one of your only options. The user must be able to log on to Windows normally to perform a Device Driver Roll Back, and the ASR process requires a backup set unless you just want to create a simple installation of Windows. Without a backup set, this won't do much.

67. B. Look in the System category of Event Viewer to discover the service or device that failed. Only then can you formulate the appropriate next step to begin solving the problem. Rebooting will likely give you the same error message. Rebooting is not a suggested fix for such problems. Without finding out which driver has the problem, if the issue even is a driver, you cannot perform a Device Driver Roll Back or remove the driver.

68. C. There are three keys to this question: ATA hard drive, only XP, and root directory. The file NTBOOTDD.SYS doesn't exist if the system partition (the one booted to) is not on a SCSI drive. Although BOOTSECT.DOS exists in the root directory, it is not used unless you have a dual- or multiple-boot scenario with DOS or Windows 9*x* as one or more of the operating systems. Although NTOSKRNL.EXE is a necessary file for a successful boot, it does not reside in the root directory; it can be found in the %SystemRoot% folder (most often \WINDOWS or \WINNT). NTLDR, however, is located in the root directory and is required in all boot situations.

69. D. The best choice of those given is to run the Recovery Console and execute commands such as fixmbr and fixboot to repair the master boot record and the partition boot sector, respectively. A boot diskette is not able to boot up on its own. It points to an actual bootable partition, which is what's missing in this case. System Restore and Device Driver Roll Back both require access to the operating system, which is missing in action here.

70. B. The MSCONFIG utility can be used to selectively enable and disable applications during startup. The Startup tab is used to check or uncheck items, and the General tab is used to return operation to normal. The net start command is used to start services from the Command Prompt. The normal parameter is not valid because it implies that a service by this name exists, which is not the case. On the Startup Options screen, there is a *Start Windows Normally* option in Windows XP (*Boot Normally* in Windows 2000), but booting that way is as if you never pressed F8 to enter the Startup Options screen. The selective startup settings you made in MSCONFIG take effect by booting this way as well.

71. C. The scannow switch of the sfc command causes a scan to be run immediately without the need to restart the system. Apparently, the user or administrator ran the command with the scanboot switch. Although the scanonce switch sounds feasible, it also requires a restart. The only difference is that once a single scan is performed, that's the end of it. Executing the command without a switch is the same as requesting help for the command by executing sfc /?. It does not run a scan.

72. A. Utility-based cartridge cleaning that cleans the cartridges without the need to remove them is ideal to avoid the need for further calibration. Cleaning addresses the problems of smearing and smudging more than the inconsistencies in printing that calibration addresses. Think of calibration as the synchronization between what the printer thinks it is doing and what you observe it doing. Each time you remove the cartridges and put the same ones back in, you run the risk of throwing the printer out of calibration. Cleaning the cartridges this way can require calibration. Use this method if the software-managed cleaning does not work. The fact that smudging occurs horizontally could indicate an issue with the carriage assembly, although this would manifest itself more as printing everything in one place or possibly elongated horizontally. The fact that it also occurs vertically rules out the carriage assembly and points more toward build-up on the cartridges.

73. C. During the installation of Windows XP, you must press the F6 key when prompted to install third-party drivers, most often for SCSI hardware-RAID drivers. When prompted to press the F2 key during installation, you can do so to run the ASR process. The opportunity to press the F8 key doesn't show up until the operating system is installed and you want to bring up the Startup Options screen during bootup. The F4 key doesn't do anything worth mentioning.

74. D. Documenting the resolution is of the utmost importance. Doing so reduces the amount of time for the second or similar calls involving the same problem. Although courteousness doesn't necessarily speed up your visit, it's a highly recommended trait for the customer-facing technician. With regard to proper testing, if you are sure the solution you implement solved the problem, you can be confident that the next service call is a new problem. Proper testing after implementation brings out all but the most hidden weaknesses in your solution. Therefore, plan for repeat visits and similar calls for other users. Have enough confidence in yourself to stick with the problem until it's resolved, even if you have to consult with someone with more expertise while you are working. Don't hand the customer off to anyone else if you can help it, especially if you are the face of your company for that customer.

75. B. Whenever a Microsoft device is set to obtain an IP address automatically, and a DHCP server does not respond to that device's request for an IP address, the device auto-configures itself from the Class B network 169.254.0.0. This is called Automatic Private IP Addressing (APIPA). Routers do not route packets to or from this private network. It would be detrimental if they did. In such a case, auto-configured devices with routers between them would confuse the router, because different interfaces on the same router must be on different IP networks. DHCP servers do not hand out APIPA addresses, so drawing from the wrong DHCP server will not lead to devices having these addresses. However, a downed DHCP server will cause all devices to auto-configure with APIPA addresses. Unless the router acting as the default gateway is also acting as the DHCP server and handing out IP addresses, its failure will limit network access beyond its local interface but not cause the devices on the network to auto-configure. TCP/IP must be installed in order for a device to auto-configure with addresses in the 169.254.0.0 network, so that can't be the problem. For XP devices, TCP/IP is integrated and cannot be uninstalled, only restarted.

76. C. Classless Interdomain Routing (CIDR) notation (/x) is shorthand for subnet masks written in dotted-decimal notation (x.x.x.x). Each binary one in the dotted-decimal form of the subnet mask gets counted. Because ones always come before zeros in a subnet mask, and the two never mix, the number of ones is referred to as a *prefix*. The total count of ones is placed after the slash in CIDR notation. The converse of this rule means that a prefix of /28 corresponds to 255.255.255.240. Each 255 contributes eight binary ones to the count (255 = 11111111), for a subtotal of 24 ones. The 240 (11110000) contributes four more for a total of 28; hence the /28 prefix.

77. C. Novell's protocol suite is called IPX/SPX. IPX and SPX are the primary protocols of this suite. Microsoft's compatible version is known as NWLink. The *NW* evokes *NetWare*, which is Novell's trade name for the company's product line that used to include IPX/SPX. NetBEUI is a Microsoft protocol but is not equivalent to IPX/SPX.

78. B. The File Transfer Protocol (FTP) and the Trivial File Transfer Protocol (TFTP) both transfer files between two IP hosts, but FTP is the more robust of the two. FTP uses TCP for guaranteed delivery, which means applications written as front ends for FTP can be complex and feature-rich. TFTP employs UDP and is limited to best-effort delivery. TFTP is indicated only for situations where the user will verify the results of the transfer, such as downloading or uploading router and switch configurations. Telnet is used for remote configuration. HTTP can be thought of as a sort of file-transfer protocol, but only for certain types of files that fulfill HTTP's primary function of transferring hypertext pages, which are made of text and links to other files.

79. AC. DSL and its older cousin, ISDN BRI, are delivered on a single copper pair. The same pair that POTS is delivered on can be conditioned to carry these higher-rate services. Cable (DOCSIS) is delivered on CATV plant, not a Telco cable pair. Cellular, as its name implies, is a wireless networking technology that rides on the same signals as the cellular phone calls that are so prevalent today.

80. C. In this case, only the key fob meets the requirements set forth. The card is self-contained and does not communicate externally. Therefore, each one must be set up before being deployed, so that it can be synchronized with the authentication server using a key that is shared between the card and server but never transmitted for eavesdroppers to steal. Because the card and server use the same algorithm, they can keep up with one another without further synchronization. With a key fob, the user must enter a PIN into the card in order for the card to produce a pseudorandom string. (Only the user can change the PIN.) The user then inputs the string into the authentication software utility, and it is compared against the rolling set of codes that the authentication server considers currently valid for that key fob. These codes are generated by a one-way algorithm, which means the shared secret cannot be reverse-engineered from any of the valid strings. The server tracks more than one but a very few of these, in case you forget you have requested a string and request another. With each of the other technologies, you need to have only, for example, a fingerprint or retina to scan, a smart card to swipe or insert, or a USB token to plug in. Although it depends on the implementation, there is no need for a separate password—the simple possession of the thing being authenticated is enough. Regardless of how it is implemented, the key fob adds an additional level of security, in case the card falls into the wrong hands.